NEW ENGLAND

Titles in this series include:

- **New England**, with Boston and Cape Cod
- **California**, with Las Vegas and the Grand Canyon
- **New Zealand**, including outdoor activities and national parks
- **Scotland**, including the Highlands and Islands, Royal Deeside and the Whisky Routes
- **Brittany and Normandy**, with scenic routes from the Channel ports
- **Florida**, with a full guide to theme parks
- **Dordogne and Western France**, including Bordeaux, and the Atlantic coast
- **Ireland**, with Eire and Northern Ireland
- **Languedoc and Southwest France**, including Cathar country, the Cevenne, and the Tarn and Gard regions
- **Bavaria and the Austrian Tyrol**, with guides to Salzburg and Munich

For further information about these and other Thomas Cook publications, write to Thomas Cook Publishing, PO Box 227, Thorpe Wood, Peterborough PE3 6PU, United Kingdom

Signpost
Guides

NEW ENGLAND

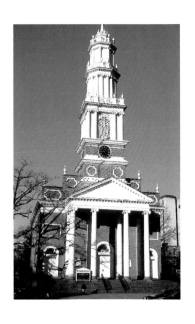

The best of New England's
cities and scenic landscapes,
including Boston and Newport,
Cape Cod, Providence and
New Hampshire

Tom Bross, Patricia Harris,
David Lyon, Stephen H Morgan,
Barbara Radcliffe Rogers
and Stillman D Rogers

Thomas
Cook
Publishing

Published by Thomas Cook Publishing
The Thomas Cook Group Ltd
PO Box 227
Thorpe Wood
Peterborough PE3 6PU
United Kingdom

Telephone: 01733 503571
E-mail: books@thomascook.com
Advertising sales: 01733 503568

ISBN 1 900341 60 3

Publisher: Stephen York
Commissioning Editor: Deborah Parker
Map Editor: Bernard Horton

Series Editor: Christopher Catling
Copy Editor: Posy Gosling
Proofreader: Karen Pieringer
Written and researched by Tom Bross, Patricia Harris, and David Lyon,
Stephen H Morgan, Barbara Radcliffe Rogers and Stillman D Rogers.

About the authors

Tom Bross, a long-time resident of Boston, has been a freelance travel writer/photographer since the mid 1970s. In that capacity, he is a frequent visitor to central Europe–especially Germany–as well as eastern Canada, northern California and the US's six-state New England region. He has contributed Canadian and New England chapters to previous Thomas Cook guidebooks. For this current Signpost volume, he contributed chapters covering Providence, Newport and their respective vicinities in Rhode Island and southwestern Massachusetts, plus all of the chapters focused on cities and regions in Connecticut. Tom would like to thank Evan Smith of the Newport County (RI) Convention & Visitors' Bureau, Jackie LaBella and Diane Moore of the Connecticut River Valley & Shoreline Visitors' Council, and Tom Silvia of the Providence/Warwick Convention & Visitors' Bureau for help given while researching these chapters.

Patricia Harris and David Lyon write about travel, food, gardening and art from their base in Cambridge, Massachusetts. They contributed to the Thomas Cook *Touring Eastern Canada* guide, and they are the authors of *Art of the State: Massachusetts*, as well as several other titles. They are restaurant reviewers for the Boston Sidewalk web site. For this guide, they contributed the chapters covering West of Boston, Massachusetts North, Cape Cod, the Berkshires, Maine's North Woods, New Hampshire and the Southern Maine Coast, Portland, Midcoast Maine, Penobscot Bay and Mount Desert Island.

Stephen H Morgan is a Boston-based travel writer and staff editor at *The Boston Globe*. He edited the Thomas Cook *On the Road Around New England* and *Touring Eastern Canada* guides, and his stories have appeared in a number of US newspapers and magazines. For this guide, Stephen contributed the Boston chapter and Travel Facts section.

Barbara Radcliffe Rogers and Stillman D Rogers belong to a prolific family team of writers and photographers. They specialise in writing about Canada and New England for guidebooks, magazines and their own newspaper column. They are the authors of three books on Vermont, one on New Hampshire and one on Massachusetts. They contributed to the Thomas Cook *Touring Eastern Canada* guide and they write regularly for Yankee Magazine's *Travel Guide to New England*. For this guide they contributed chapters on Pioneer Valley, the Southern Green Mountains, Lake Champlain and the Northern Green Mountains, the Northeast Kingdom, the Upper Connecticut Valley, the New Hampshire Lakes and the White Mountains. They would like to thank Glenn Faria and William DeSousa of Destinations New England for help given during the research for these chapters.

Contents

About Signpost Guides   8
New England at a glance   10
Introduction   12
Travel facts   14
Driver's guide   24
Road signs   29
Getting to New England   30
Setting the scene   32
Three itineraries   40

● **Boston**   42
America's oldest city, home to 25 universities and colleges

● **West of Boston**   56
Battle sites of the American Revolution

● **Massachusetts North Shore**   66
Ocean beaches, dramatic coastal scenery, antique shops and art

● **Southeastern Massachusetts**   76
Visit Plymouth, landfall for the *Mayflower* Pilgrims

● **Cape Cod and its Islands**   84
The windswept dunesand raging surf of New England's summer
playground

● **Pioneer Valley**   96
Living History villages at Deerfield and Old Sturbridge

● **The Berkshires**   104
Gentle hills for roaming on foot or by car

● **Connecticut's Midlands**   114
The cities of Hartford and New Haven, and the University in Yale

● **The Litchfield Hills**   124
Lakes, woods and white-steepled churches

● **The Lower Connecticut Valley**   132
Tidal wetlands and marshes, clear light and limpid skies

● **Connecticut's Southeastern Corner** 140
Picturesque fishing villages dotted along an indented coastline

● **Newport** 150
A base for exploring the islands and villages of Narragansett Bay

● **Providence and Pawtucket** 160
Waterfront city known for its colleges and museums

● **The Southern Green Mountains** 170
Miles of hiking and skiing among green-clad mountains

● **Lake Champlain to the Northern Green Mountains** 180
Historic buildings, steamboats and early Americana

● **The Northeast Kingdom** 190
A remote and uncrowded area where nature reigns

● **The Upper Connecticut Valley** 198
Picture-perfect villages either side of the winding river

● **The New Hampshire Lakes** 208
Sailing, watersports and lakeside resorts

● **White Mountains** 216
Snow-topped peaks and mountain air, waterfalls and streams

● **Maine's North Woods** 230
A true wilderness of untamed woods, lakes, bogs and rivers

● **New Hampshire and the Southern Maine Coast** 236
Family-friendly holiday towns along the Atlantic coast

● **Greater Portland** 246
Bustling cultural capital of New England's north coast

● **Midcoast Maine** 254
Lobstering, clam-digging and scallop-dragging are a way of life

● **Penobscot Bay** 262
Commercial ports, deep-water harbours and spruce-tufted islands

● **Mount Desert Island** 272
Mountains and valleys on the Atlantic Coast's third largest island

Language 282
Index 283
Feedback form 287

Wickford, Rhode Island

About Signpost Guides

Thomas Cook's Signpost Guides are designed to provide you with a comprehensive but flexible reference source to guide you as you tour a country or region by car. This guide divides New England into touring areas – one per chapter. Major cultural centres or cities form chapters in their own right. Each chapter contains enough attractions to provide at least a day's worth of activities – often more.

Symbol key

ⓘ Tourist Information Centre

⮂ Advice on arriving or departing

Ⓟ Parking location

Ⓠ Advice on getting around

⊃ Directions

ⓘ Sights and attractions

Ⓘ Eating

Ⓒ Accommodation

⊖ Shopping

Ⓢ Sport

Ⓐ Entertainment

Star ratings

To make it easier for you to plan your time and decide what to see, every sight and attraction is given a star rating. A three-star rating indicates a major attraction, worth at least half a day of your time. A two-star attraction is worth an hour or so of your time, and a one-star attraction indicates a site that is good, but often of specialist interest. To help you further, individual attractions within towns or theme parks are also graded, so that travellers with limited time can quickly find the most rewarding sights.

Chapter contents

Every chapter has an introduction summing up the main attractions of the area, and a ratings box, which will highlight the area's strengths and weaknesses – some areas may be more attractive to families travelling with children, others to wine-lovers visiting vineyards, and others to people interested in finding castles, churches, nature reserves or good beaches.

Each chapter is then divided into an alphabetical gazetteer, and a suggested tour. You can select whether you just want to visit a particular sight or attraction, choosing from those described in the gazetteer, or whether you want to tour the area comprehensively. If the latter, you can construct your own itinerary, or follow the author's suggested tour, which comes at the end of every area chapter.

The gazetteer

The gazetteer section describes all the major attractions in the area – the villages, towns, historic sites, nature reserves, parks or museums

Practical information

The practical information in the margin or sidebar, will help you locate the services you need as an independent traveller – including the tourist information centre, car parks and public transport facilities. You will also find the opening times of sights, museums, churches and other attractions, as well as useful tips on shopping, market days, cultural events, entertainment, festivals and sports facilities.

that you are most likely to want to see. Maps of the area highlight all the places mentioned in the text. Using this comprehensive overview of the area, you may choose just to visit one or two sights

One way to use the guide is simply to find individual sights that interest you, using the index, overview map or star ratings, and read what our authors have to say about them. This will help you decide whether to visit the sight. If you do, you will find plenty of practical information, such as the street address, the telephone number for enquiries and opening times.

Alternatively, you can choose a hotel, perhaps with the help of the accommodation recommendations contained in this guide. You can then turn to the overall map on page 10 to help you work out which chapters in the book describe those cities and regions that lie closest to your chosen touring base.

Driving tours

The suggested tour is just that – a suggestion, with plenty of optional detours and one or two ideas for making your own discoveries, under the heading *Also worth exploring*. The routes are designed to link the attractions described in the gazetteer section, and to cover outstandingly scenic coastal, mountain and rural landscapes. The total distance is given for each tour, as is the time it will take you to drive the complete route, but bear in mind that this indication is just for the driving time: you will need to add on extra time for visiting attractions along the way.

Many of the routes are circular, so that you can join them at any point. Where the nature of the terrain dictates that the route has to be linear, the route can either be followed out and back, or you can use it as a link route, to get from one area in the book to another.

As you follow the route descriptions, you will find names picked out in bold capital letters – this means that the place is described fully in the gazetteer. Other names picked out in bold indicate additional villages or attractions worth a brief stop along the route.

Accommodation and food

In every chapter you will find lodging and eating recommendations for individual towns, or for the area as a whole. These are designed to cover a range of price brackets and concentrate on more characterful small or individualistic hotels and restaurants. In addition, you will find information in the *Travel Facts* chapter on chain hotels, with an address to which you can write for a guide, map or directory. The price indications used in the guide have the following meanings:

$ budget level
$$ typical/average prices
$$$ de luxe.

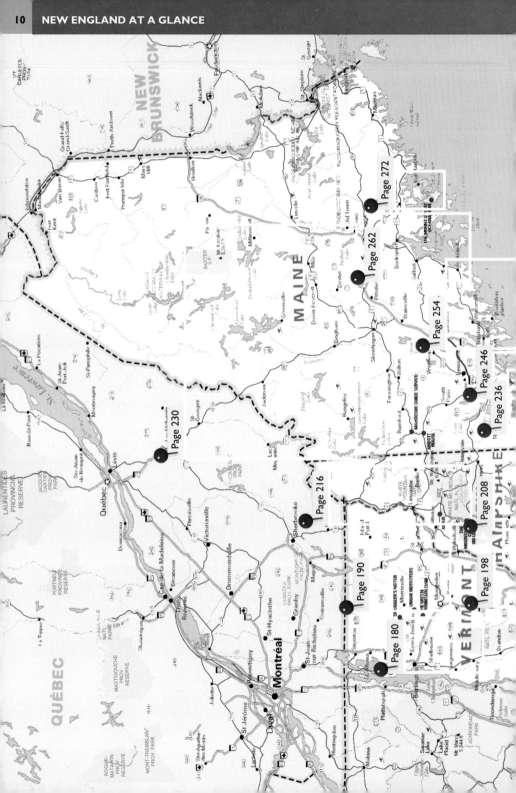

Page 272

Page 262

Page 254

Page 246

Page 236

Page 230

Page 216

Page 208

Page 198

Page 190

Page 180

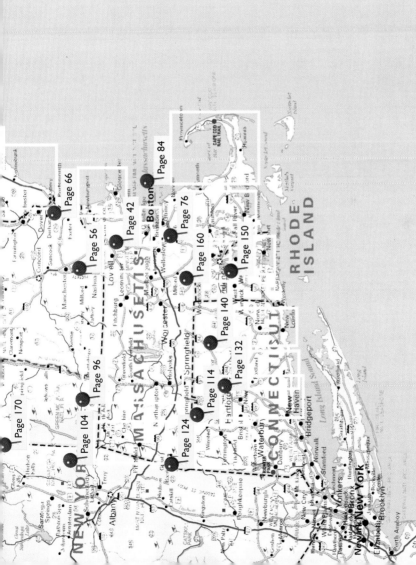

Introduction

Fall colour

The best thing about New England is that every road to nowhere ends up someplace, and apart from the northern reaches of Maine, the trip is usually short. By New World standards New England is a compact region studded with attractions and dense with history. Generations of landscape painters have limned its rocky shores and sandy strands, and some of America's leading poets have been spurred to rhetorical heights by the inland mountain ranges, lakes and woodlands. But the most inspired of all have been the holiday-makers touring the New England landscape in their family Fords, bent on discovering whatever lies around the next bend in the road.

While New England is one of America's more densely populated regions, civilisation always sits in the midst of a natural world. It is a simple matter to park the car and strike out on a hiking trail through a nature preserve, glide through bird-filled marshes in a canoe, or simply stroll a sandy beach picking up shells. All along the New England coast from Cape Cod north, small boats speed to the offshore shoals to observe the great whales – finback, humpback, even the endangered right – that come to New England to feed. More intense natural experiences are also available, from a week of hiking along the mountainous Long Trail in Vermont, ten days of traversing the Allagash Wilderness in a canoe, or single days spent in a sea kayak exploring Nantucket's shores or the small islands between Stonington, Maine and Isle au Haut.

Beauties wrought by human hands abound as well: the skyscrapers of Boston, the artful overpass bridges of the Merritt Parkway, the lovely green ribbon of Boston's Emerald Necklace parks, the sculpted grace of Augustus St-Gaudens' Cornish, New Hampshire, retreat. The engineering feats of the Cape Cod Canal and the long, graceful arc of the Jamestown Bridge between Conanicut and Aquidneck islands actually complement the startling landscapes they conquer.

World-class art museums grace Hartford and Boston, two cities joined by Portland, Maine, and Providence, Rhode Island, as regional centres for theatre, dance and music. New England's long history is recounted in innumerable historic houses, with Portsmouth, New Hampshire, offering perhaps the largest concentration (the wonderful colonial houses of Deerfield, Massachusetts, largely function as decorative arts museums). Domestic history buffs will discover that virtually any town large enough to have a stoplight also has an historic house open to tours when volunteer guides are available. The region's romance with the sea is served at the whaling museums of Nantucket and New Bedford, by the astonishing China Trade collections of Salem's Peabody and Essex Museum, by the delightful

Penobscot Marine Museum in the salty village of Searsport, Maine, and through a complex of wharves and sailing ships at Mystic Seaport in Mystic, Connecticut. So-called 'living history' museums staffed by costumed interpreters enliven the Pilgrim past at Plymouth, Massachusetts, and the rural countryside *circa* 1840 at Sturbridge, Massachusetts.

New England travellers never need fear they will go hungry, as the tastes of the region are every bit a match for the sights. Even the thin soils of eastern Maine spout a kind of gastronomic poetry in their delicate fiddlehead ferns of spring and their tart blueberries of summer. The Maine coast is renowned for its lobster – *Homerus americanus* – which may be consumed cold in a salad with grapefruit in a smart Blue Hill restaurant or simply enjoyed, mallet in hand, at a dockside picnic table on the Pemaquid peninsula. Portland, Boston and Providence can claim some of the finest chefs in North America, and the chic dining scene in all three cities is unequalled. But linen tablecloths and an array of wineglasses are not essential to good eating. One might experience a gourmet epiphany over the local maple syrup in a New Hampshire pancake house, a clam and oyster raw bar on Cape Cod, or from a fine local cheese, fresh sourdough bread and pint of ale in a Vermont brew-pub.

Landing stage at Canterbury, in the New Hampshire lakes region

Travel facts

Accommodation

New England offers accommodation of every style and price level, from five-star hotels and posh inns to budget motels and campsites. Local tourist offices provide lodging lists and telephone numbers, but cannot make bookings.

Children

New England offers many child-friendly attractions. From museums to transport, check for children's rates, often segmented by age, eg, under 3 free, 6–12 years $3, 12–18 years $4.

A few inns are reluctant to host children (and will say so if asked directly), but most driving destinations welcome them and are equipped for children of all ages, from nappies to video games. Most chains allow children under 12, 14, sometimes 18, to stay free in their parents' rooms. Hotels and motels can often arrange for (expensive) baby-sitters; a rollaway child's bed or crib usually comes free or at low cost.

$$$	de luxe
$$	average
$	budget

At chain hotels and motels, even with budget prices, expect a clean, comfortable, relatively spacious room with either one or two double- or queen-sized beds and a private bathroom. Some independent hotels and motels provide a lower standard, but others have good–quality facilities plus charm and character. Motels often line major auto routes and advertise availability with 'vacancy' signs. Most chains have toll-free reservation telephone numbers than can be reached from anywhere in North America.

Bed and breakfasts can be a homier alternative to homogenous hotels, but they are seldom a bargain in New England. In Boston, a B&B might consist of an entire apartment or condominium; in rural areas, it could offer a tidy room with antique furnishings and homespun quilts in a restored 19th-century home. Bath facilities may be private or shared.

Country inns offer charm and personal attention. A small inn might have the look and feel of a B&B, but it will usually offer you more rooms and breakfast choices. Bigger inns typically include a full restaurant with hearthside dining, a wide porch with rocking chairs for relaxing, and high prices to boot.

Camping means a tent or a recreational vehicle (RV) in a rural campsite. Those in state or national parks and forests are the quietest and most primitive, with firewood available but facilities limited to pit toilets and cold showers. Private sites usually offer more facilities but may be crowded with RVs.

Accommodation may be hard to find in major tourist destinations during high season – Memorial Day (end of May) to Labor Day (early Sept). The hardest time to find a room is foliage season (mid-Sept– mid-Oct) in Vermont, New Hampshire and Western Massachusetts; many inns and hotels are fully booked in advance by return clients.

Thomas Cook or any other good travel agent can handle room bookings when purchasing air tickets and local transportation. Advance bookings require a voucher or credit card number to

Thomas Cook Foreign Exchange Bureaux

Thomas Cook Travellers Cheques free you from the hazards of carrying large amounts of cash. Thomas Cook Foreign Exchange Bureaux (listed below) all provide full foreign exchange facilities and will change currency and traveller's cheques (free of commission in the case of Thomas Cook Travellers Cheques). They can also provide emergency assistance in the event of loss or theft of Thomas Cook Travellers Cheques.

Thomas Cook Currency Services
107 Broad Street
Stamford
Connecticut
Tel: (203) 348-5317

Thomas Cook Currency Services
399 Boylston Street
Boston
Massachusetts
Tel: (617) 267-5433

guarantee the booking. Ask for discounts if you're disabled, a senior, a motoring club member or travelling off-season.

Airports

International travellers arrive at Boston's Logan International Airport, New York's John F Kennedy Airport and Newark International Airport in New Jersey. Connecting flights bring travellers into smaller cities such as Providence, Hartford and Portland. All major airports have foreign exchange and banking services, car-hire facilities and public transport to the nearest city. Information booths help travellers with transport, lodging or tourism questions, but cannot make bookings and usually have limited staff hours.

Climate

New England's weather is known more for changeability than for extremes. In general, expect cold and snow from December to March, warm days and cool nights from June to September.

Depending on locale, daytime temperatures in summer are in the 70s or 80s F; July and August usually bring short spells of uncomfortably humid weather with temperatures above 90°F. Winter snows are heaviest in the ski country of Maine, New Hampshire and Vermont. Snowfall is generally light in southern New England, except for occasional big storms; temperatures 20s or 30s F. September and October can be the most pleasant months, with daytime temperatures from the 50s to 70s F, and leaves turning colour dramatically.

Currency

US dollars are the only currency accepted. Bill denominations are $1, $2, $5, $10, $20, $50 and $100. The larger bills have been redesigned to foil counterfeiters but the old bills are still accepted. There are 100 cents to the dollar: coins are the 1-cent penny, 5-cent nickel, 10-cent dime, 25-cent quarter, 50-cent half-dollar and the rare quarter-sized Susan B. Anthony dollar.

Few banks are equipped to exchange foreign currency or travellers' cheques. However, travellers' cheques in US dollars, from well-known issuers, such as Thomas Cook, are acceptable almost everywhere and can be used like cash or changed easily.

Avoid carrying large amounts of cash. The safest forms of money are US dollar travellers' cheques and credit or debit cards. Car-hire companies and hotels and motels require a credit card imprint, even if the reservation has been fully prepaid. Automated teller machines (ATMs) are a ubiquitous source of cash through withdrawals or cash advances authorised by debit or credit card. Check terms and availability with the card issuer before leaving home.

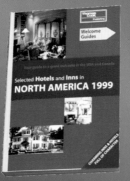

Food

New England is especially known for its fresh seafood, which is served fried (in batter) or broiled (in butter), sometimes baked, and includes locally caught cod and haddock (called 'scrod' or 'schrod'), bluefish, tuna and salmon. Shellfish appearing on menus include clams (fried whole or as 'strips'), steamers (clams steamed in the shell), quahogs (a round-shell clam), mussels, oysters, scallops and shrimp. New England's unique treat is the lobster, which turns bright red after immersion (live) into boiling water. It is served whole (a challenge to eat without making a mess), in parts (tails and claws) or picked out of the shell for salads or 'lobster roll' sandwiches.

Toilets

'Restroom' or 'bathroom' are the common terms; 'toilet' or 'washroom' are acceptable; few people recognise WC.

Most businesses, including bars and restaurants, reserve restrooms for clients. Petrol stations provide keys for customers to access restrooms. Public toilets are not common along city streets, but roadside rest stops often have them. Hotels, museums and other tourist attractions do too, of course.

The classic Maine dish of steamed lobster and fresh corn

Customs regulations

Personal duty-free allowances for visitors entering the USA are 1 US quart (approximately 0.9 litres) spirits or wine, 300 cigarettes or 50 (non-Cuban) cigars and up to $100-worth of gifts. On your return home you will be allowed to take:

• **Australia:** AU$400 in goods (AU$200 under age 18) plus 250 cigarettes or 250g tobacco and 1 litre alcohol.
• **Canada:** C$300 in goods (provided you have been away for over a week) per year; also 50 cigars plus 200 cigarettes and 1kg tobacco (if over 16) and 40oz/1 litre alcohol.
• **New Zealand:** NZ$700 in goods. Anyone over age 17 may also take 200 cigarettes or 250g tobacco or 50 cigars or a combination of tobacco products not exceeding 250g in all plus 4.5 litres beer or wine and 1.125 litres spirits.
• **UK:** allowances for goods bought outside the EU and/or in EU duty-free shops: 200 cigarettes or 50 cigars or 100 cigarillos or 250g tobacco plus 2 litres still table wine plus 1 litre spirits or 2 litres sparkling wine plus 50g/50ml perfume plus 0.5 litre/250ml toilet water.

Drinking

Bottled water is popular, but rarely necessary for health reasons. However, water from streams and ponds in natural areas should be considered contaminated and avoided due to *giardia* or other parasites. Soft drinks (called soda or tonic) and fruit juices are available in

Patron saint festival in Boston

Festivals

Fourth of July
(Independence Day) is
celebrated in every city
and town with cookouts,
concerts and fireworks.
Memorial Day (30 May)
and St Patrick's Day (17
March) are occasions for
parades. See route
chapters for local festivals.

From late August into
October, small towns
throughout New England
hold town or county fairs
– a custom held over from
agrarian times – with
animal husbandry
competitions, games and
thrill rides. The Big E
(Eastern States Exposition)
in West Springfield, Mass.,
is the biggest of these.

stunning variety. American coffee is customarily weak, but cafés and
gourmet coffee shops offer flavourful alternatives. Tea usually means a
cup of hot water with a tea bag.

You must be 21 years old to purchase or to drink alcohol (18 in
Connecticut). State and local laws govern hours at licensed
establishments, which are generally from morning until 2400, 0100 or
0200. Bottled liquor is sold in state-owned stores in New Hampshire,
Maine and Vermont, beer and wine in grocery stores. Elsewhere,
privately-owned liquor (or 'package') stores sell beer, wine and liquor;
some supermarkets sell beer and wine only. Micro-breweries throughout
the region are making interesting local beers these days.

Eating out

American meal portions tend to be large, beginning at breakfast,
which may include thinly sliced bacon and eggs cooked to order with
fried potatoes, toast and endless refills of coffee. Midday lunch
offerings include soups, salads and sandwiches. Evening dinner menus
offer appetisers (starters), salads, soups, pastas, entrées (main courses)
and desserts.

New England is best known for its seafood (*see Food, page 17*), but a
wide variety of cuisine is available, including steak houses, Italian,
Mexican, Chinese, Japanese and Thai. In major cities, the melting-pot of
cuisine includes Brazilian, Cambodian, Caribbean, Greek, Indian,
Middle Eastern, Portuguese, Vietnamese and regional American (such as
Dixie-style ribs and barbecue).

Fast-food joints are popular and cheap (McDonalds, KFC, Arby's Roast
Beef, Burger King, Wendy's, Pizza Hut and Taco Bell). Higher on the
price and quality ladder are chain restaurants such as Friendly's (ice
cream, sandwiches and simple meals), Bertucci's (Italian), Boston Market
(roasted chicken) and International House of Pancakes (IHoP), which
serves all-day breakfast plus safe, unexciting lunch and dinner choices.

Expect to pay $5–8 for breakfast (much more at hotels), $5–12 for
lunch, $15–25 for dinner (plus drinks). Service charges are rarely
added to bills, and tipping is expected – at least 15 per cent of the bill
before taxes and drinks are added in.

Entry formalities

For travellers from British Commonwealth countries, border inspections
are generally routine; have your passport, visa, proof of support and
return ticket in order. Brief crossings into and return from neighbouring
Canada are generally permitted, but they can be time-consuming if
an official targets you for a car search. If you're not carrying illegal
drugs, alcohol, firearms or agricultural products, and if your documents are in order, you should have no difficulty entering the USA
or Canada.

Maps

Good state, regional and city maps are produced by the **American Automobile Association**, known as AAA ('Triple A'), and distributed free at AAA offices, but only to members. Most automobile clubs worldwide have reciprocal agreements with AAA to provide maps and other member services. Be prepared to show a membership card.

The most detailed road maps are produced by **Arrow Map Inc** *50 Scotland Blvd, Bridgewater, MA 02324; tel: (508) 279-1177.* Wire-bound and folding Arrow maps are sold at booksellers, newsstands, souvenir shops and airports. Detailed up-country maps are available from **DeLorme Map Co** *Rte 1, Freeport, ME 04032; tel: (207) 865-4171.*

For back-country travel, US Geological Survey topographic maps show terrain reliably; they can be purchased in Boston at the **Globe Corner Bookstore** (see *Reading,* page 22). For hiking in the White Mountains or along the Appalachian Trail, maps and guidebooks from **The Appalachian Mountain Club** *5 Joy St, Boston, MA 02108; tel: (617) 523-0636,* are indispensable.

Following page
Pemaquid lighthouse, Midcoast Maine

Health

Hospital emergency rooms are the place to go in the event of life-threatening medical problems. If a life is at risk, treatment will be swift and top-notch, with payment problems sorted out later. For mundane problems, doctors' offices or health clinics can provide care.

Non-US national health plans are not accepted by US medical providers, so some form of health insurance coverage is mandatory – at least $1 million of cover is essential.

Bring enough prescription medication to last the entire trip, and carry a copy of the prescription in case of emergency. No inoculations are required, and New England is basically a healthy place to visit. However, when visiting state and national parks or other natural areas, take note of posted warnings about rabies, Lyme disease or other local health risks.

Information

In the USA, each state is responsible for its own tourism promotion. Address requests for information well in advance.

- **Connecticut Office of Tourism** *Department of Economic and Community Development, 505 Hudson St, Hartford, CT 06106; tel: (800) CT-BOUND; www.state.ct.us/tourism*
- **Maine Publicity Bureau** *PO Box 2300, Hallowell, ME 04347-2300; tel: (207) 623-0363;* **Maine Office of Tourism**: *www.visitmaine.com*
- **Massachusetts Office of Travel and Tourism** *100 Cambridge St, 13th Floor, Boston, MA 02202; tel: (800) 447-MASS, ext 300; www.mass-vacation.com*
- **New Hampshire Office of Vacation Travel** *PO Box 586, Concord, NH 03301; tel: (603) 271-2666; www.visitnh.gov*
- **Rhode Island Tourism Division** *1 West Exchange St, Providence, RI 202903; tel: (800) 556-2484/(401) 222-2601; www.visitrhodeisland .com*
- **Vermont Department of Tourism and Marketing** *134 State St, PO Box 1471, Montpelier, VT 0560-1471; tel: (802) 828-3236; www.travel-vermont.com*

Information, brochures, maps and itinerary planning are also available from: **Discover New England** *34 Francis Grove, Wimbledon, London SW19 4DT; tel: (181) 544 1000; fax: (181) 542 6556.* In the USA, the address is *1250 Walterbury Rd, Box 3809, Stowe, VT 05672 02536; tel: (802) 253-2500; fax: (802) 253-9064; www.discovernewengland.com*

Insurance

Experienced travellers carry insurance that covers their belongings, holiday investment (including provision for cancelled or delayed

Public holidays

The following holidays are celebrated nationally: New Year's Day (1 Jan); Martin Luther King Jr Day (third Mon in Jan); Presidents' Day (third Mon in Feb); Memorial Day (last Mon in May); Independence Day (4 July); Labor Day (first Mon in Sept); Columbus Day (second Mon in Oct); Veterans Day (11 Nov); Thanksgiving Day (fourth Thur in Nov); and Christmas (25 Dec).

Post offices and government offices close, as do many businesses and shops. Large department stores stay open and hold huge sales. Convenience stores, supermarkets, liquor stores and petrol stations generally remain open (sometimes with curtailed hours). Nearly everything closes on New Year's Day, Thanksgiving Day and Christmas Day.

Electricity

The USA uses 110v 60hz current. Two- or three-pin electrical plugs are standard. Electrical gadgets from outside North America require plug and power converters. Both are difficult to obtain in the USA. Beware of buying electrical appliances in the USA: few gadgets on the US market can run on 220v 50hz power. Exceptions are battery-operated equipment such as radios, cameras and portable computers – or dual-voltage shavers and hair dryers.

flights and weather problems) and health (including immediate evacuation home in case of medical emergency). Many hospitals refuse treatment without proof of insurance. Thomas Cook and other travel agencies offer comprehensive policies. Medical coverage should be high – at least $1 million.

Museums

Many major museums open seven days a week all year. Others close Mondays, and all close New Year's Day, Christmas and Thanksgiving. Hours are generally 0900 or 1000 to 1700 or 1800, with seasonal variations; some stay open one evening per week. Smaller museums, particularly in less touristy areas, may have limited hours or days of opening and may close in winter.

National parks

The National Park Service administers Acadia National Park in Maine, the Cape Cod National Seashore, historical parks in Boston, Lexington and Concord, Lowell and Salem, Mass., the White Mountains National Forest in New Hampshire and a variety of smaller historical parks, monuments and sites around the region; for details see the appropriate chapters in this book. For general information, contact **National Park Service** *15 State St, Boston, MA 02109; tel: (617) 242-5642; www.nps.gov*

Some sites charge an entry fee. Senior and disabled persons should ask if discounts apply. The Golden Eagle Passport ($50) covers entry to all Park Service properties for one year.

Opening times

Office hours are generally Mon–Fri 0900–1700, although a few tourist offices also keep short Sat hours all year, and weekend hours in summer. Many banks open from 0900 or 1000 to 1500 or 1600; a few stay open Thur to 1900 and Sat 0900–1300. Petrol stations open from early till late; a few stay open 24 hours on major routes. In cities, the big stores and shopping centres open at 0900 or 1000 Mon–Sat and close at 2000 or 2100, with shorter hours Sunday.

Packing

Everything you could ever need is available, so don't worry if you've left anything behind – in fact, most US prices will seem low. Carry all

Shopping in Woodstock

Safety and security

Despite well-publicised incidents of street violence, millions of people travel (and live) in perfect safety each year in the USA. So can you if you follow common-sense precautions.

Never publicly discuss travel plans or money or valuables you are carrying; keep to well-lit areas; do not wear or carry expensive jewellery or flash rolls of banknotes. Use a hidden money-belt for your valuables, travel documents and spare cash. In the unlikely event you are 'mugged', don't resist.

If you do encounter trouble, dial 911 on any telephone for free emergency assistance from police, fire and medical authorities.

Time

New England clocks are set to GMT minus 5 hours, called Eastern Standard Time (EST). From the first Sunday in April until the last Sunday in October, clocks go forward 1 hour to Eastern Daylight Time (EDT).

medicines, glasses and contraceptives with you, and keep duplicate prescriptions to verify your need for a medicine.

Postal services

Every town has at least one post office. Hours vary, although all are open Mon–Fri, morning and afternoon. Major US Postal Service branches are open Saturday, only a select few on Sunday. Stamps may be purchased from machines in some pharmacies and convenience stores. Letters and cards with correct postage may be dropped in blue boxes outside postal branches or on street corners; parcels weighing more than 1lb must be handed to a postal clerk for security reasons. Mail everything going overseas as Air Mail (surface mail takes weeks or even months). All US mail must include the five-digit zip code (also use the four-digit suffix if you know it).

Public transport

Train travel is sparse in the USA. **Amtrak** *tel: (800) 872-7245*, handles passenger service nationwide. The main New England route runs from Boston to New York City, with stops at Providence and points along the Connecticut shore – a five-hour ride. Prices vary according to day and time of travel, but they are always cheaper than air travel, which takes only about one hour from Boston to New York.

Bus (coach) lines serve more destinations, with prices similar to train fares. **Greyhound Bus Lines** *tel: (800) 231-2222*, provides long-distance bus service nationwide between major cities, including Boston. Peter Pan, Bonanza and other local lines carry passengers between cities and towns in New England. The bi-monthly *Thomas Cook Overseas Timetable* and the annual *Thomas Cook North American Rail and Bus Guide* contain timetables and much additional travel information.

Reading

Comprehensive general guides to areas covered in this book as well as maps and more specialised books on New England history, culture and lore may be purchased at **The Globe Corner Bookstore** *500 Boylston St, Boston, and 28 Church St, Cambridge; tel: (617) 523-6658 or (800) 358-6013*, and many other bookshops. Specialised guides you can buy in New England include *In and Out of Boston with (or without) Children*, by Bernice Chessler (Globe Pequot Books) and the *AMC White Mountain Guide* (Appalachian Mountain Club, Boston).

Stores

Large department stores found throughout New England include Macy's and Filene's, plus the Filene's Basement chain of discount

Shopping

Clothing can be a bargain, particularly at discount stores or factory outlets; also cameras and other photo equipment, but do your homework on prices before you go, and shop around. New England prices for alcohol, tobacco and perfume beat most duty-free shops.

New England souvenirs include Vermont maple syrup, live Maine lobsters packed for the flight home, 'Boston Harbor tea', Cape Cod saltwater taffy, hand-made patchwork quilts and the ubiquitous T-shirts.

There is no Valued Added Tax in the USA. Each state imposes its own tax on sales of products, meals and lodgings, ranging from 5 to 10 per cent. Clothing, baby products and grocery items are tax-free in some states.

Sport

Boston is home to several professional sports teams. The Boston Red Sox play baseball at Fenway Park from April to September, the Boston Bruins (hockey) and Boston Celtics (basketball) compete at the Fleet Center from fall into the spring. The New England Patriots (American-style football) are based in Foxborough (a Boston suburb), as are the New England Revolution, a pro team in soccer (football), which has a small following in the USA.

clothing stores. National chains such as Lord & Taylor (clothing), Talbot's (women's fashions), The Gap (jeans), J C Penney (clothing, housewares, furniture, etc) and Sears (clothing, hardware and appliances) are well represented.

For good prices and reasonable quality, follow the locals into discount stores such as Ann & Hope, Ames, Caldor, K-Mart, Marshalls, Wal-Mart and others. In some locales 'factory outlet stores' cluster together as a magnet for shoppers.

Telephones

Dialling instructions are in the local white pages telephone directory. Phone numbers are always seven digits, preceded by a three-digit area code when calling outside the local area. For long-distance calls, precede the area code with a 1.

Pay phones take coins and are located on street corners or inside restaurants, hotels and other public buildings. A local call usually costs $0.35; a computer voice will come on-line to ask for additional coins when needed. Prepaid phone cards are gaining popularity and may be purchased at pharmacies, news-stands and convenience stores. Many hotels and motels add a stiff surcharge to the cost of a call from a room.

In emergencies, dial 911 for police, medical or fire brigade response. Dail 0 for an operator. For local number information, dial 411. For long-distance phone information, dial 1-area code-555-1212. There will be a charge for information calls. Most phone numbers with the 800 or 888 area code are toll-free. Those with the 900 area code charge the caller for information or other services, often at high per-minute rates.

For international dialling, dial 011 -country code-city code (omitting the first 0 if there is one)-local number; eg, to call Great Britain, Inner London, dial: 011-44-171-local number. Some country codes: Australia 61, New Zealand 64, Republic of Ireland 353, South Africa 27, United Kingdom 44.

Travellers with disabilities

State and federal laws, particularly the Americans with Disabilities Act (ADA), require that all businesses, buildings and services used by the public be accessible by handicapped persons, including those using wheelchairs, ie they must have access ramps and toilets designed for wheelchairs. Most cities and towns have ramps built into street crossings, and most city buses have some provision for wheelchair passengers. However, many older facilities do not yet comply with the standards. Special controls for disabled drivers are seldom an option on hired vehicles. For more information, contact: SATH (Society for the Advancement of Travel for the Handicapped), *347 Fifth Ave, Suite 610, New York, NY 10016; tel: (212) 447-7284, or RADAR, 12 City Forum, 250 City Rd, London, EC1V 8AF; tel: (0171) 250 3222.*

Driver's guide

Accidents

In the event of a collision, always stop (penalties for failing to stop can include imprisonment). If either vehicle or any person is injured, immediately report the accident to state police if it occurred on a state or interstate road, or to local police. Everyone involved should exchange numbers of drivers' licences, car registration, insurance coverage information and addresses and telephone numbers for further contact. This same information will generally be provided to the police as well. Collisions with property or personal damage must also be reported to your car-hire company and to the state department of motor vehicles in every state except Connecticut. Although the grace period for reporting to the state varies, doing so within 48 hours ensures legal compliance.

Breakdowns

Should a breakdown occur, pull to the side of the road where you will be visible but out of the way of traffic. Switch on hazard lights and, if it is safe to do so, raise the bonnet and trunk lids. Change a tyre only if you're out of the flow of traffic.

Dial 911 from any telephone to summon emergency medical or police assistance. Report your telephone number, problem, location and any need for medical assistance. Emergency phone boxes are usually placed at frequent intervals along interstate highways. If one is not visible, stay with the vehicle and wait for a patrol car to stop to render assistance.

Car hire

Hiring a vehicle provides you with freedom to travel as you please with a vehicle you can leave behind when you depart. Whether booking a fly-drive package or making independent arrangements, plan well in advance to ensure getting the type and size of vehicle you desire. Unlimited mileage is standard on most auto rental contracts, but not on recreational vehicles (RVs).

Small cars are rarely available and make poor long-distance touring vehicles under US driving conditions. Compact or economy cars are usually the least expensive, with small price increases for intermediate cars. Full-size and luxury vehicles are more expensive to hire and operate. Most US rental cars come with either two or four doors, an automatic transmission and air-conditioning. Intermediate and larger

Caravans and camper vans

Convenient as it may be to drive around in one's lodging, caravans and camper vans can pose some difficulties. Most New England communities require that they be parked in a proper campground before using them as a place to sleep, and some communities prohibit roadside parking, especially after dark. Some urban car-parks lack the overhead clearance to accommodate caravans. Nantucket bans caravans from the island altogether. Very large caravans must follow posted road regulations for trucks (lorries), which generally ban them from high-speed or passing lanes.

Fuel

Petrol (universally called gas or gasoline in New England) is sold by the gallon (3.82 litres) at prices posted in cents and tenths of a cent – usually ranging from 95.9 cents to 145.9 cents, with a great deal of volatility based on season, location, and the political situation in the Middle East. All gasoline sold in New England is unleaded and most also contains various alcohol additives to decrease emissions of sulphur and nitrogen oxides. Diesel fuel is sold at separate pumps. Most fuel pumps are self-service, and many accept credit and bank cards for payment. So-called 'full-service' pumps may charge up to an additional 20 cents per gallon.

vehicles are often equipped with cruise control, which lets the driver take the foot off the accelerator while travelling long distances at constant speeds. Some vehicles may be equipped with four-wheel-drive (4WD), a necessity for traversing some unpaved roads in the north woods or along seashores where permitted.

Most rental companies require that the driver be at least 21 years old (some specify age 25), hold a valid driver's licence and use a credit card to secure the value of the vehicle. Before leaving the hire agency, be certain that you have the car registration and all rental documentation. Also be sure you know how to operate the vehicle (there's nothing more maddening than running low on petrol and being unable to find the fuel tank lid). If possible, ask for a vehicle without obvious rental company identifiers, as thieves often target such cars.

Driving conditions

The worst driving conditions in New England involve snow in the winter, or heavy rains or dense fog at any time of year. Driving with low-beam headlights at all times is a recommended safety precaution. Avoid using high beams in snow, rain or fog to avoid blinding other drivers (or yourself with reflected glare). If visibility is poor, pull over and wait for the storm to pass. The danger of hydroplaning arises during sudden heavy rains, particularly at speeds above 35 mph.

Driving on snow takes skill, and if you are unfamiliar with stopping, turning and negotiating skids on snow, practise in a vacant car-park before venturing out on the road. Apply brakes lightly but repeatedly to stop on snow. Hired cars are generally equipped with all-season tyres, which are not particularly effective at gripping in more than an inch of snow. During winter driving, keep the petrol tank topped up in case you are stuck in a snow bank awaiting help. If you do become stuck in a snowstorm, stay in the vehicle, place a red flag on the antenna or door handle, try to keep warm with blankets, and do not run the engine any more than necessary. Make sure the exhaust pipe is not clogged with snow. Useful winter driving gear includes a blanket, a windscreen ice scraper, a small shovel and a bucket or bag of sand. In most areas of New England, snow is cleared promptly from streets and roads and a mixture of sand and salt is applied to reduce icing.

Barn at Freeman Farm, Old Sturbridge Village

Drinking and driving laws

Driving under the influence of alcohol or other drugs is illegal throughout New England. Intoxication is defined as 0.08 per cent blood alcohol in most states. If a police officer stops you and suspects you may be impaired, you may be asked to take an instant breathalyser test that estimates blood alcohol from alcohol in your breath. You are permitted to refuse the test, but doing so means automatic suspension of your driver's licence.

Police

Police cars signal drivers with flashing blue or blue and red lights and sometimes with a siren. While most police vehicles are marked, some highways are patrolled by unmarked cars. When signalled, pull over to the side and have your driver's licence and vehicle registration ready for inspection. Roll down the window but do not leave the vehicle unless requested. You have the right to ask an officer for identification.

Security

Lock your car. Lock it when you are inside and when you leave it. Do not leave maps, guidebooks or other tourist paraphernalia in clear sight. Try always to park in well-lit areas.

Documents

A valid driver's home country licence should be carried on your person at all times. Vehicle registration and, where applicable, a valid car-hire contract must be in the vehicle when it is under way. Proof of liability insurance must also be supplied in the event of an accident. Minimum driving age in New England is 16.

Information

Many non-North American auto clubs have reciprocal privileges with the American Automobile Association (AAA), including touring books, road maps, discounts at hotels and motels and some roadside assistance. Emergency towing is not always included. For information on services, ask your own club or request Office to Serve You Abroad, American Automobile Association, *1000 AAA Drive, Heathrow, FL 32756-5063; tel: (407) 444-7700.*

Parking

Public car-parks are generally indicated with a blue sign, carrying the letter 'P' and a directional arrow. Rates are posted at the entrance. Urban garages are often expensive but may give discounts to shoppers or theatre-goers who have their timecards stamped with a validation sticker. Coin-operated parking meters are in effect in most areas, with rates ranging from $1 per hour in urban areas to as little as 25 cents per hour in small towns. Parking near a fire hydrant, a red or yellow kerb or in front of a wheelchair access ramp is forbidden. In urban areas, kerbside parking may be banned during morning and evening commuting hours. If you violate parking regulations or let a meter expire, expect to be issued a citation. If you do not pay it, the car-hire company may charge the fine to your credit card along with a substantial penalty.

Road signs

International symbols are used for many road signs in New England; all language signs are in English. Signs may be white, yellow, green, brown or blue. Stop, Yield, Do Not Enter and Wrong Way signs are usually red and white. Warning or direction indicators are generally yellow. Roadwork and temporary detour signs are generally reflective orange. Green indicates highway directions, blue denotes non-driving information (parking, informational radio frequencies). Brown signs are usually reserved to indicate parks, campsites and outdoor activities. Traffic lights are red (stop), green (go) and yellow (caution). Simultaneous red and yellow lights indicate a pedestrian crossing. Unless otherwise posted, it is legal to make a right-hand turn at a red

Tolls

Every New England state has some toll roads, which may include stretches of interstate highway (the Connecticut, Massachusetts, New Hampshire and Maine turnpikes, for example). On short toll roads, drivers are expected to pay cash at the toll booths (a good supply of quarters, also useful for parking meters, comes in handy). On longer toll roads, drivers pick up a toll card when entering the highway and pay a variable rate based on mileage when exiting.

Previous page
Camden Baptist Church, Penobscot Bay

light if there is no traffic and no pedestrian crossing light is lit. Motorists are expected to yield the right of way to pedestrians at all zebra lanes or 'crosswalks', although the law is observed more in the breach than in the practice.

Seat belts

Only New Hampshire, where the state motto is 'Live Free or Die', does not require adults in moving vehicles to use seat belts, and even New Hampshire requires them to be used by persons 12 or younger. Child safety seats are mandatory for age 5 or younger throughout New England.

Speed limits

Official highway speed limits are 65mph in rural areas, 55mph in urban areas. Many New England drivers take these as suggestions rather than law. You are safest when moving with the flow of traffic, neither faster nor significantly slower. Note that most interstate highways also have minimum speed limits. Expect to be overtaken and passed on both sides if you are moving slower than the rest of traffic. This can be disconcerting but is perfectly legal in most states. On secondary roads, speed limits are much lower. When no limit is posted, assume the limit is 30mph in residential areas, 20mph near schools and hospitals.

TYPICAL ROAD SIGNS IN NEW ENGLAND

INSTRUCTIONS

Stop

Give way

Wrong way - often together
with 'No entry' sign

No right turn

No U-turn

One-way
traffic

Two-way left
turn lanes

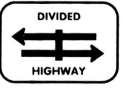

Divided highway
(dual carriageway)
at junction ahead

Speed limit
signs: maximum
and maximum/
minimum limits

WARNINGS

Crossroads

Junction

Curve (bend)

Winding road

Stop ahead

Two-way traffic

Divided highway
(dual carriageway)

Road narrows
on right

Roadworks
ahead

Railway
crossing

No-overtaking
zone

Getting to New England

Mount Washington cog railway

By air

International travellers to New England arrive at Boston's Logan International Airport (BOS), New York's John F Kennedy International Airport (JFK) or Newark International Airport (EWR) in New Jersey. After clearing Customs and Immigration and re-checking baggage, passengers transfer to flights into Providence, Hartford/Springfield, Portland, Burlington or smaller cities. There are car-hire facilities at any airport (always reserve in advance) and public transport of some type (train, bus, limousine, taxi) into the nearest city.

Unless you have a reason to be in New York, arrival and departure are generally easier at Boston. It is much smaller, easier to get in and out of, less expensive and closer to most places in New England. British Airways, Virgin Atlantic, American Airlines and Aer Lingus all offer direct flights into Boston, and any airline can book connecting flights from JFK or Newark. If you do fly into New York, keep in mind that Newark Airport is smaller, less crowded and slightly closer to Manhattan than JFK.

It is always a good idea to book your first night's room in advance, but in Boston and New York it is absolutely essential because rooms can be hard to find.

Consider going without a car if you stay in downtown Boston – after all, public transport into and within Boston is quick and simple, while parking places are scarce and expensive. If you must pick up your hire car on arrival at Logan Airport, arrange parking in advance with your Boston hotel. However, if you stay outside Boston proper, a car is usually a necessity and parking might well be free.

Travellers arriving at New York face a similar choice: a hire car can be a liability in Manhattan but a necessity in the suburbs. If you don't plan to stay in New York, just pick up a hire car and go. You can be well on your way into Connecticut within an hour's driving time from JFK or Newark.

Domestic US air service is extensive and cheaper than within Europe. There are shuttle flights into Boston every hour from New York's LaGuardia Airport and from Washington, DC, plus regularly scheduled flights into Boston, Hartford, Portland, Providence and some smaller New England cities from cities all over the USA and Canada.

By train and bus

Amtrak, the US passenger rail system, offers frequent but limited service into and within New England. The main route is from New

York's Pennsylvania Station to South Station in Boston, with stops along the Connecticut shore and in Providence. New York–Boston is a pleasant ride but extremely slow due to outmoded rail equipment. It takes five hours by train, less than one hour by air.

Another Amtrak route goes north from New Haven to Hartford, Connecticut, and on to Springfield, Massachusetts. A special train on this line, the 'Montrealer', continues into Vermont, then transfers passengers on to buses across the Canadian border to Montreal. There's also the Boston–Chicago service (continuing to California) via Springfield, but trains run infrequently. Most Amtrak passengers headed to New England (from Florida and Washington, DC, and from the West Coast via Chicago) travel through New York.

Bus (coach) lines (Greyhound nationwide; Bonanza, Peter Pan, Plymouth & Brockton and other lines locally) serve many more destinations within New England and in neighbouring regions than rail does. The Boston–New York bus trip, along major highways, is comparable to the train in both duration and price.

By car

The extensive US Interstate Highway system brings car traffic smoothly into and around New England from neighbouring areas. The best of US roads, these are dual carriageway, limited-access highways carrying two, three, four or more lanes of traffic in each direction.

The main routes into New England are I-95 (a north–south route from Florida to Maine) and I-90 (an east–west route from Seattle to Boston). I-95 enters New England from New York City and follows the Connecticut shore to Providence, Boston, Portland and northwards. I-90, which begins (or ends) in Boston, is a toll road where it crosses Massachusetts and upper New York State. Other interstate routes criss cross the region. Driving New York–Boston takes four hours or more, depending on traffic.

Interstates are the quickest, most direct routes but offer little to see. Petrol stations, restaurants and motels generally cluster at exits, off the highway; rest stops between some exits offer parking and often toilet facilities. Rest stops along toll roads (Massachusetts Turnpike and New York State Thruway) offer petrol and food as well.

Sandwich, New Hampshire

Living history at Old Sturbridge Village

Setting the scene

The place

New England is geographically a small segment of the United States. The six northeastern states of Connecticut, Rhode Island, Massachusetts, Vermont, New Hampshire and Maine cover 66,672 square miles, making the region about three-quarters of the area of Great Britain. But New England delivers a great deal of cultural and natural diversity in its compact package.

The New England landscape is extremely varied, its drama deriving from some of the most complex geology in the world. Bits and pieces of three primordial continents adhere to its shoreline and three distinct ranges of ancient mountains, now worn down to their hardest rocks, buckle up along its width. But the most prominent geological features of New England were created by the mile-thick Laurentian ice sheet, which began its retreat about 11,000 years ago. As the glacier's southern edge melted, huge dumps of sand and gravel were left behind to become the islands and sand beaches of the southern New England coast, including Nantucket, Martha's Vineyard and Cape Cod. The coast of northern New England, on the other hand, pre-dates the glaciers by hundreds of millions of years, representing the continental face shattered by separation from northern Europe aeons ago. Maine's rocky coast bears a striking resemblance to the Hebrides and to Scandinavia for good reason, as they once fitted together like puzzle pieces.

But even the Maine coast was altered by the great ice sheet, which etched the entire New England landscape in a north–south pattern, scraping the mountain ranges to their backbones of quartzite and granite. As a result, the river valleys of New England follow the same north–south track as the glaciers, and the mountains, while perhaps lacking the soaring heights of the limestone Alps and Rockies, rise with startling rapidity.

The largest of New England's rivers is the Connecticut, an ancient split in the planetary crust extending from northern New England to Long Island Sound. At various periods a lake bed, a swampland or a river, the Connecticut Valley was home during the Jurassic period to many species of dinosaurs, whose tracks lie preserved in the ancient sediments. New England's other major rivers are younger by far, and are all found in the north, where they drain the flanks of the White Mountains and Maine's less-known Longfellow Range. Thousands of smaller streams and rivers flow off New England's central highlands to the sea, providing the water power for mill works in virtually every hamlet. While few of those mills continue to grind corn or to power spinning machinery, almost every village in interior New England has a mill dam and a mill building, more often than not occupied by a dealer in antiques.

Farming is still a way of life in the Lake Champlain valley and the fertile floodplains of the Housatonic and Connecticut rivers. But most of New England is cursed with stony glacial soils – evident in stone walls throughout the region – and agriculture declined in New England as soon as other alternatives became available. The opening of fertile land in Ohio in the 1830s came on the heels of several disastrous crop years, and many New England farms were abandoned and allowed to return to forest by 1845. Farming today is typically limited to speciality crops such as herbs and flowers in eastern Massachusetts, cigar-wrapper tobacco in the Connecticut River Valley and 'wild' blueberries on the Maine coast north of Bar Harbor. Dairy farming, while always threatened, maintains a strong presence in Vermont, given a boost by the popularity of Ben & Jerry's ice-cream and the elevation of the Holstein cow to pop cultural icon.

The past

Apparently New England has always attracted hardy souls. Native peoples were scattered through the region, mostly on now-submerged coastline, even before the glaciers retreated. By 1600 at least nine distinct tribal divisions of the Algonquian linguistic group inhabited the region, living mostly along the coast and riverbanks where they augmented hunting and gathering with agriculture. Slash-and-burn farming was based on the triad of maize, beans and squash that first took hold in the Mexican highlands and spread to New England around AD 900. Contrary to many early anthropological character-isations, these 'Indians' lived in relatively stable communities. Shell middens at the mouth of the Damariscotta River in Maine, for example, indicate more than 2000 years of continuous inhabitation at that oyster-rich site. The shells were so extensive that they were mined commercially for agricultural limestone from 1650 into the beginning of the 20th century.

Portuguese, Spanish and perhaps Irish fishermen knew New England waters well in the century immediately prior to the 'official' discovery of the New World. But colonisation of New England began with the conjunction of two significant historical circumstances. The pre-colonial population of the region crested in the 1590s at around 90,000 souls, but crashed to fewer than 30,000 by 1619 as a result of successive plagues of European diseases. Many of the most desirable settlement sites were abandoned and burned just before the English sailed over the horizon looking for homesteads. At the same time, English political tensions swelled the ranks of religious separatists and dissenters ready to flee a repressive regime to build a New Jerusalem in the wilderness. As a result, the first substantive towns in New England

– Plymouth, Salem and Boston of the Massachusetts Bay Colony – were settled by unusually well-educated ideologues. The tall spires of white Congregational churches found on virtually every New England town green have been one of their most enduring legacies. Another has been their dedication to education, of which Harvard College was the first fruit.

Intellect, however, does not necessarily imply tolerance. The Massachusetts Bay Colony expelled anyone who disagreed with Puritan orthodoxy, leading Roger Williams (a Baptist at the time) and Anne Hutchinson (a Quaker) to found Rhode Island. Quakers also settled throughout southern New England, and in the 17th century they constituted a majority in much of Rhode Island and on the islands of Martha's Vineyard and Nantucket. The austere Quaker architecture of Nantucket remains one of the island's hallmarks. Connecticut and western Massachusetts became Puritan strongholds, as their richest river bottomlands were settled by land-hungry immigrants who pressed westwards from Boston and Salem.

Northern New England remained largely unsettled until the 1760s, despite the planting of a few coastal trading posts in the mid 17th century. The deep forested interior was inhabited, if at all, by Native Americans and French trappers. The French had laid claim to much of New England well before the English arrived, and continuing French claims put a damper on settlement of the interior.

Settlement of the coastal region continued apace, however, and once-cordial relations between the English and the Native tribes deteriorated. Finally, in 1675 the Wampanoag chieftain Metacom (called King Philip by the English) united many of the coastal tribes in a scorched-earth war intended to drive the English off the continent. The fighting lasted for nearly two years, and historians argue that Philip might have succeeded with a few good breaks. He and his troops truly savaged the English villages, killing one colonist in ten and putting their buildings and crops to the torch. But the Natives fared even worse. Entire communities were destroyed; their survivors either fled to Canada or were sold into slavery in the Caribbean. Connecticut's few surviving Wampanoags and Mohegans have exacted a form of 20th-century revenge through federally sanctioned gambling casinos. Once King Philip's War ended in 1676, the colonists enjoyed only the briefest period of peace. By the 1690s, they were drawn into a frontier echo of the European wars between the French and English, doing battle repeatedly with French colonists and their Native allies in what North Americans call the French and Indian Wars.

In an almost Nietzchean fashion ('what does not kill me makes me stronger'), the French and Indian Wars forged great strengths in the New England colonies. By the time France withdrew from North America in 1763, the colonies had two generations of battle-hardened militia men who would make up the corps of American troops in the

The Battle of Lexington is re-enacted at dawn on 19 April every year

Revolution. Barred from expansion into the interior, New England had grown rich from the sea, exploiting its cod fisheries and perfecting the 'triangle trade' of African slaves, Caribbean molasses and New England rum. When the wars did end, a cash-strapped Crown paid off many of its soldiers with land grants to the interior of New England, salting the region with independent spirits who knew how to use a gun.

Given New England's dependence on seaborne trade, it is little wonder that New Englanders bridled at the imposition of British trading rules and cargo taxes to pay for the colonial wars. Boston, in particular, was a hotbed of rebellion, and hostilities began following the 1770 'Boston Massacre' in which a squad of British soldiers fired on a hostile crowd pelting them with snowballs, killing five civilians and wounding several others. In 1773, patriots dressed as Indians tossed a valuable shipment of British tea into the harbour as a protest against the Stamp Tax, and in 1775 armed troops finally clashed in Lexington and Concord, Massachusetts, considered the first battles of the Revolution. Throughout the war, the British Navy ravaged the New England coast, which is why most coastal towns have no pre-1780 buildings. Field warfare was limited to the Boston area and to New England's western flank, where the Bennington Monument marks the successful American defence of the Lake Champlain valley.

The Revolution dragged on into the 1780s, but New England swiftly rebuilt its merchant navy after Independence. Shut out of British ports (indeed, out of much of Europe), New England traders led the way in opening Japan, China and Korea to world trade. During this same

The elegant brick architecture of the Georgian-era Athenaeum in Portsmouth

period, Massachusetts whalers from Nantucket and (after 1820) from New Bedford dominated the worldwide whaling industry until the discovery of petroleum in the 1850s. Salem, Massachusetts, led world trade in the 1790s, but all up and down New England's northern coast, the tall timber of the newly inhabited interior was sent downriver to be transformed into sailing vessels. Much of the wealth still visible in northern New England's shore towns dates from the period 1790–1890, when every port town bristled with shipyards and most of America's overseas trade sailed on vessels under the command of New England captains. The heritage of those years has been surprisingly well preserved in the whaling museums of New Bedford and Nantucket, the art and history museums of Salem, and the maritime museums of Salem and Searsport, Maine.

A young America grew rich on trade, and New England grew richest in the years leading up to the American Civil War. New England merchants visiting Britain observed early textile machinery with great interest. They returned home with sufficiently accurate drawings to place New England in the thick of the Industrial Revolution by the 1830s. As the region's farmers migrated westwards to better land, the population that stayed behind flocked to the new mill towns as the first generations of industrial workers. New England was transformed from a rural to an industrial economy in the space of a single generation – a transformation visible today in the sites of Old Sturbridge Village and the Lowell National Historical Park.

Architecture

That sudden 19th-century wealth found architectural expression first in the Federal style, which harked back to Greek and Roman neo-classical models as styles appropriate to the ideals of a fledgling democracy. The Massachusetts State House, the quintessential Federal-style building designed in 1795 by Charles Bulfinch, so seized the

American imagination that it was imitated in the US Capitol and subsequently in half the state capitols across the country. Domestic architecture, especially after 1830, favoured a style known in the US as 'Greek Revival' – a grandiose boxiness with a blend of Greek capitals on massive columned façades. Only in the second generation of wealth, as Americans began to travel in Europe, did the 'Italianate' style begin to compete, with its square turrets and long hip roofs. A growing cosmopolitanism also found expression at the end of the 19th century in several forms of Romanesque Revival architecture, notably the work of Boston-based H H Richardson and his followers. Richardson's Trinity Church in Boston is considered the high-water mark of the movement.

Ironically, the turn of the 20th century sent Americans in general and New Englanders in particular into a frenzy of rediscovering their English colonial roots. The architectural spawn of this social phenomenon was an eclectic style called 'Colonial Revival', notable chiefly for grafting large columned porches on to vaguely Georgian houses, then painting them stark white with either black or green wooden shutters. A mid-century version of this architectural nostalgia is reflected in the proliferation of Cape Cod 'saltbox' houses throughout New England – modern versions of the 1½-storey 18th-century homes of Cape Cod, America's first indigenous domestic architecture.

Seeing the sights

Even today travellers crisscrossing New England are driving on roads that parallel the old railroad beds. Although some hardy coach travellers came looking for 'sublime' Nature in the New England mountains early in the 19th century, it took the railroad to open up the region to pleasure travel. Initially the rail lines followed the major north–south river valleys. When the Grand Trunk Railroad cut across the mountains in the 1850s, rail travel opened up the coast of Maine to the wealthy denizens of Montreal and gave Bostonians access to the wilderness lakes and woods of northern New England. By 1870, a traveller could board a train in Boston and ride all the way to the summit of Mount Washington without changing cars.

Many spots in New England developed an early cachet. Families who acquired great industrial fortunes at the end of the 19th century created a new social set that shuttled from mammoth 'cottage' to mammoth 'cottage' in Newport, the Berkshires of western Massachusetts, and Mount Desert Island on the Maine coast. Today the surviving cottages are often tourist attractions in themselves, and a few, such as Wheatleigh in the Berkshires, have become luxury resorts. During the same period, sometimes called the 'Gilded Age', hunting and fishing became the vogue for some of America's richest men, leading to the development of the 'sporting camp' where robber barons would retreat to smoke cigars, drink brandy and kill trout. Many such camps survive, albeit with less well-heeled clientele, in the north woods of Maine and New Hampshire. The workingman's equivalent, the modest private cabins often called 'camps', are found along the shores of the more accessible lakes throughout New England.

Resort hotels flourished both in the mountainous areas of New Hampshire and Vermont and at coastal beaches from Connecticut to Maine. While the structures have largely disappeared (with a few delightful exceptions such as the Balsams and the Mount Washington Hotel, both in New Hampshire), the resort ambience lingers on from Watch Hill, Rhode Island, to Old Orchard Beach, Maine. The ultimate democratisation of tourism in New England began with the automobile. Auto touring spawned the roadside diner (still visible throughout New England) and classic motel architecture. Route 1 in coastal Maine has particularly well-preserved examples of 'motor hotels' ranging from homespun individual cabins to streamline structures that echo the tail fins of the first automobiles that stopped at them.

Pleasure travel in New England has not changed dramatically from that golden age of auto touring other than the rise of the B&B and the 'country inn' in the last 20 years. In-town hotels are so unusual outside major urban centres that they are often advertised as 'classic' or 'heritage' properties. Virtually every hamlet large enough to appear on a map has at least one house where the family take in guests for the night and serve them breakfast before they hit the road in the morning. Ironically, such facilities began as a low-cost alternative to motels, but now often cost 10–20 per cent more. If you plan to make extensive use of B&Bs and country inns, be prepared for gregarious hosts – a liability or an asset, depending on personal style.

The seasons

New England's busiest travel season begins unofficially on Memorial Day weekend (usually the weekend that includes the last Sunday in May) and concludes with Labor Day weekend (the weekend that includes the first Monday of September). In practice, the 'high season' is July and August, when the ocean and inland waters are warm enough for swimming and the weather is shirtsleeve balmy.

The second season for travel in New England is autumn, especially during the fall foliage period. The foliage season is unpredictable from year to year, but generally peaks in northern New England during the third week of September and in southern New England during the second week of October. The original forests encountered by Puritan settlers have long since been cleared, but the forests that have grown up since farms were abandoned in the 19th century contain a much higher percentage of deciduous trees than the primeval forest.

Moreover, they are composed of a greater percentage of maple trees than hardwood forests anywhere else on the planet. And several strains of maples found only in New England produce greater quantities of red pigments in the fall than maples elsewhere. Although spring travel in New England is slight, the region enjoys a reverse of the fall foliage displays as spring blooms begin in southern New England in March and spread to northern New England by early June.

Most overseas travellers tend to overlook New England's winter season, when the cities of Boston, Hartford and Providence become lively centres of performing arts and the north country is transformed into some of the world's finest ski terrain. US alpine skiing began in Vermont, and while both Vermont and Maine boast some dramatic, state-of-the-art ski facilities, the northern states also have many delightful small ski areas such as Mount Snow, the first 'modern' ski resort. Its developer, Walter Schoenknecht, once petitioned (unsuccessfully) to explode a nuclear bomb underground to create more vertical drop for his ski mountain. Diversification has become the ski country watchword, exemplified by Stowe, Vermont. A pioneer in alpine skiing, Stowe launched cross-country skiing in America and has emerged in the 1990s as the snowshoeing capital of New England. But Sugarloaf/USA in Maine has gone one better than Stowe, with a world-class golf course that blurs all seasonal lines.

Three itineraries

These three itineraries capture different aspects of the New England experience. Because so many travellers enter New England through Boston, all routes circle from the Hub.

Rocky coast and high peaks

This itinerary takes advantage of the proximity of New England's wildest coastline and its most rugged mountains. While the route can be appreciated through the windscreen, it is more rewarding for travellers who enjoy outdoor activities.

From Boston, drive north on Rte 1 to Salem, following the route in 'Massachusetts North Shore' (*see page 66*). Continue north on Rte 1 to the route suggested in 'New Hampshire and Southern Maine Coast' (*see page 236*) to take in the sandy beaches *en route* to 'Portland' (*see page 246*) on Casco Bay. The 'rocky coast of Maine' begins here heading north on Rte 1 with detours down the rocky peninsulas of 'Midcoast Maine' (*see page 254*) into the ocean-overlook highlands of 'Penobscot Bay.' From Blue Hill, follow Rte 172 to Ellsworth, then Rte 3 to 'Mount Desert Island' (*see page 272*) to experience the jaw-dropping scenery of Acadia National Park. To move quickly to the high country, backtrack on Rte 3 through Belfast. Follow Rte 3 west 45 miles to the Maine Turnpike (I-495) and drive south 32 miles to exit 11 on to Rte 202 west. In 3 miles, turn right on to Rte 302 west through the Sebago Lakes region to Conway, New Hampshire, in the 'White Mountains' (*see page 216*). At Conway, the Kancamagus Highway (Rte 112) cuts through the heart of the White Mountain National Forest, concluding in Lincoln at I-93, which leads due south to Boston.

The grand foliage circuit

Many 'scenic roads' become so gridlocked during the foliage season that traffic obscures the leaves. This itinerary skips famous leaf-peeper routes in favour of small towns and forested northern interiors where the foliage is equally fine and the traffic is lighter.

From Boston, drive west on Rte 2 through Lexington and Concord ('West of Boston', *see page 56*), continuing 42 miles west to the junction with Rte 202 (exit 19). Drive north on Rte 202 through the arts colony region of Jaffrey and Peterborough, New Hampshire. Seven miles north of Peterborough, follow the left fork on to Rte 123, which winds 34 leafy miles west through tiny villages to Alstead. At Alstead, turn on to Rte 12A to connect with Rte 12 in South Charlestown. Rte

12 and Rte 12A continue north through the area described in 'Upper Connecticut Valley' (*see page 198*) until they connect with I-89 in West Lebanon. Follow I-89 west to cross into Vermont and take the first exit for Rte 4 west to follow the Quechee River stream bed through stunning little Woodstock and on to Killington, one of the more striking skiing centres in the 'Green Mountains' (*see page 170*). At Sherburne Pass, turn right on to Rte 100 north to follow the eastern ridges of the Green Mountains through Warren and Waitsfield, the ski village of Stowe, and on to Newport (Vermont) at the south tip of Lake Memphremagog in the 'Northeast Kingdom' (*see page 190*). East of town, connect with I-91 south for a strikingly scenic drive to St Johnsbury, Vermont, where I-93 crosses the Connecticut River and descends through Franconia Notch in the 'White Mountains' (*see page 216*) to return to Boston.

New England roots

This itinerary encompasses some of the early settlements and boom towns while visiting the region's three great living history museums. The swiftest of the three routes, it is a good choice for travellers with limited time.

Tour the Freedom Trail in 'Boston' (*see page 48*) before driving west on Rte 2 through Cambridge, Lexington and Concord, detailed in 'West of Boston' (*see page 56*). Backtrack on Rte 2 to I-95 south to Rte 3 in Quincy, following Rte 3 south to Plymouth to visit Plimoth Plantation, detailed in 'Southeastern Massachusetts' (*see page 76*). Continue south to exit 5, following the Myles Standish State Forest road to I-195 to New Bedford and Fall River. Turn south on Rte 24 to Rte 114 into Newport, Rhode Island, the yachting capital of New England ('Newport', *see page 150*). Continue west on Rte 138 to Rte 1 south along the Rhode Island coast into 'Connecticut's southeastern corner' (*see page 140*) to visit the sail-era museum of Mystic Seaport. Eight miles west in New London, follow Rte 32 north to I-395 north through eastern Connecticut over the border into Massachusetts. At exit 6, drive 12 miles west on Rte 20 to visit Old Sturbridge Village, detailed in 'Pioneer Valley' (*see page 96*). The Massachusetts Turnpike,

Boston

Ratings

Arts and culture	●●●●●
History	●●●●●
Museums	●●●●●
Children	●●●●○
Shopping	●●●●○
Food and drink	●●●○○
Beaches	●○○○○
Scenery	●○○○○

Boston is 'The Hub' – a name bestowed in 1858 by Oliver Wendell Holmes, who wrote that Bostonians considered their city 'the Hub of the Universe'. Learning and culture rank high in this Athens of America, where the first school was built in 1636 and 25-odd colleges and universities thrive today. The oldest US city, founded in 1630, Boston was once a Brahmin town – 'the home of the bean and the cod, where the Lowells speak only to Cabots, and the Cabots speak only to God'. There's still a Yankee establishment, but it's matched by an Irish one, and ethnic diversity is on the rise. The compact size of Boston's centre surprises visitors, who find they can get nearly everywhere on foot.

Getting there and getting around

ⓘ Greater Boston Convention and Visitors Bureau (GBCVB) 2 Copley Pl, Suite 105; tel: (617) 536-4100 or (800) 888-5515; www.bostonusa.com, operates visitor information centres on Boston Common and in the Prudential Center. Along the Freedom Trail is the **National Park Service Visitor Center** 15 State St; tel: (617) 242-5642; www.nps.gov

Arriving and departing

Logan International Airport is in East Boston, directly across the harbour from downtown, 20–30 minutes by public transport. A free shuttle connects the international terminal (E) to domestic terminals (A–D) and the airport subway station. By car, downtown is 3 miles away via toll tunnel. Free shuttle to car-hire location. Taxis and hotel shuttles available; for suburban express buses, *tel: (617) 23-LOGAN*.

Amtrak *(tel: (617) 482-3660 or (800) 872-7245)* has train services from South Station, at the corner of Summer St at Atlantic Ave. Also at South Station is the Bus Terminal serving Greyhound *(tel: (617)*

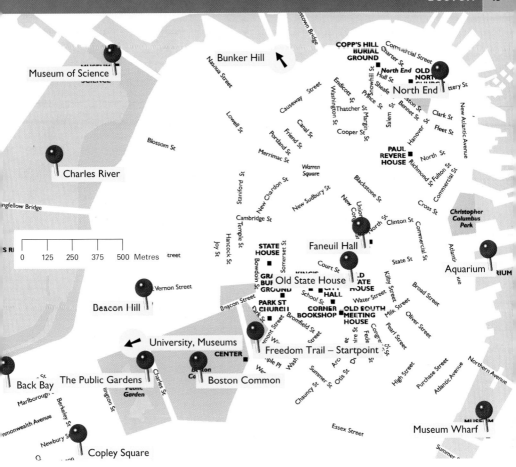

Museum of Science

Bunker Hill

COPP'S HILL
BURIAL
GROUND

North End OLD
NORTH

North End

Charles River

Blossom St

PAUL
REVERE
HOUSE

Warren
Square

ngfellow Bridge

Cambridge St

Christopher
Columbus
Park

S RI

| | | | | |
|0|125|250|375|500 Metres|

STATE
HOUSE

Faneuil Hall

Vernon Street

GRA
BUF Old State House ATE
GROUND HOUSE
HALL

Aquarium RIUM

Beacon Hill

PARK ST
CHURCH

CORNER OLD SOUTH
BOOKSHOP MEETING
HOUSE

University, Museums

CENTER

Freedom Trail – Startpoint

Back Bay The Public Gardens
Public
Garden

Boston Common

Marlborough

Museum Wharf

nmonwealth Avenue

Newbury S

Essex Street

Copley Square

P Public parking is
limited and pricey
downtown; metered street
parking is especially scarce.
If you absolutely must bring
a car, leave it in hotel
parking or a multi-storey
public car-park and see the
city by foot and public
transport.

526-1808 or (800) 231-2222) and other intercity coach services. The
Massachusetts Bay Transportation Authority (the 'T') operates
Commuter Rail service to suburbs and nearby cities from North
Station, Causeway St, and Back Bay Station, *tel: (617) 722-3200 or
(800) 392-6100.*

Getting around
Boston is America's most walkable city and among the worst to drive
in because of traffic congestion and a confusing street pattern. Most
major tourist attractions are within a compact, walkable area
downtown or a short distance from public transport.

Massachusetts Bay Transportation Authority (*see above*) operates
buses, streetcars and subways in Boston and nearby suburbs. Subway
tokens are sold at all T stations; buses and streetcars take tokens
or exact change. Information, schedules and multi-day passes (Boston
Passport) are available at Downtown Crossing station and Bostix booths.

Sights

🚇 New England Aquarium $$ *Central Wharf (T: Aquarium); tel: (617) 973-5200. Open daily 0900–1800, Wed and Thur till 2000 (July through Labour Day), Mon, Wed and Fri 0900–1700, Thur 0900–2000, weekends 0900–1800 (rest of year).*

State House *Beacon St (T: Park St); tel: (617) 727-3676. Tours weekdays 1000–1600.*

Museum of Afro-American History *46 Joy St (T: Park St); tel: (617) 742-5415. Open Mon–Fri 1000–1600.*

Aquarium***

On the waterfront near **Faneuil Hall**, the New England Aquarium is Boston's biggest attraction for children of all ages. The main feature is a four-storey glass ocean tank, encircled by a winding walkway, from which you can watch sea life swimming in and out of a coral reef. There's an open-air penguin rookery, a sea lion show and exhibits of exotic ocean life. Avoid school vacation weeks and rainy weekends, when the din of squealing children peaks. From adjacent Long Wharf, tour boats depart for Boston harbour cruises – the best way to see the waterfront, which otherwise offers little public access.

Back Bay*

Originally a foul-smelling mudflat, Back Bay was filled in during the late 1800s and laid with a grid of parallel streets, an oddity in Boston. Alphabetically named (from Arlington to Hereford), those streets are now lined with smart town houses, many occupied by schools, consulates and condominiums, making it an interesting place to wander from the shops and restaurants along Newbury St. Also here is Boston's prettiest promenade: tree-lined Commonwealth Ave, which shows its finest colours in May with cherry, apple and magnolia blossoms.

Beacon Hill***

Early Boston was a tiny peninsula on which stood three prominent hills. Two were cut down and used as landfill, but atop the tallest early colonists erected a signal beacon. On that site today is the gold-domed 1797 **State House***, the seat of the Massachusetts Legislature, an architectural treasure designed by Charles Bulfinch. Bordered by **Boston Common** and antiques-shop-lined Charles St, Beacon Hill is one of the oldest parts of the city, a European-looking warren of narrow streets and brick town houses.

Rambling through it is the **Black Heritage Trail***, a 1.6-mile walking tour that includes several stops on the Underground Railroad, which shepherded runaway slaves from the US South to Canada. Pick up a map at the Boston Common Visitor Center or the **Museum of Afro-American History***. The trail starts at **The Robert Gould Shaw and 54th Regiment Memorial***, on Boston Common opposite the State House, depicting the first black regiment of the US Civil War.

Boston Common** and Public Garden**

America's first public park, 50-acre Boston Common was laid out in 1634 as a common pasture area for colonists' cows. They also used it for public hangings of criminals, including those whom today we might call victims of religious persecution. On the other side of Charles St is the Public Garden, the first US botanical garden (1837), where swan boat rides have soothed summer afternoons since 1877.

Left
Brick town houses in the Beacon Hill District

Bunker Hill Monument
Monument Sq, Charlestown (T: Community College); tel: (617) 242-5641.

Bunker Hill Pavilion $
55 Constitution Rd, Charlestown; tel: (617) 241-7575.

John Hancock Tower Observatory $ *200 Clarendon St, Copley Sq (T: Copley); tel: (617) 572-6429. Open daily 0900–2200, Sun 1200–2200.*

Bunker Hill*

After the opening shots of the American Revolution at Lexington and Concord on 19 April, 1775, British forces tried to lift a rebel siege of Boston. The misnamed Battle of Bunker Hill (it actually took place on Breed's Hill) on 17 June, 1775 was a victory for Britain, though a costly one, and British troops evacuated Boston for good the following March. Marking the battleground is a 221-ft obelisk, the **Bunker Hill Monument*** in Charlestown. **Bunker Hill Pavilion**** at nearby Charlestown Navy Yard has a multimedia show about the battle, in which the American commander told his Minutemen, 'Don't fire until you see the whites of their eyes!'

Charles River**

The Esplanade, a greenbelt along the Boston side of the Charles River Basin, is where Bostonians go to stroll, sunbathe, rollerblade, bicycle and 'hang out' on Sunday afternoons. The Hatch Shell hosts summer concert series. A pathway for pedestrians and cyclists continues for several miles along the Boston shore and across the bridges to Cambridge, where the best views of sailboats and Boston's skyline can be had.

Copley Square**

One of Boston's main plazas, Copley Square is where shoppers rest their feet, office workers munch sandwiches at noon and skateboarders test their skills. Two architectural treasures face each other across the square: the 1877 **Trinity Church****, the brownstone Romanesque Revival masterpiece of architect Henry Hobson Richardson, and the 1895 **Boston Public Library****, worth a peek inside for its marble main staircase and quiet central courtyard. At one corner of the square is **John Hancock Tower**, whose 60th-storey **observatory**** gives city views to the north and west; at another is an entrance to the Copley Place mall. The other two corners lead to shopping along Boylston and Newbury Sts.

Emerald Necklace*

Between 1884 and 1896 Frederick Law Olmsted designed a system of nine parks as an 'Emerald Necklace' around the city; they still form a greenbelt for walking or cycling through Boston. The system begins downtown with **Boston Common** and the adjacent **Public Garden** and continues down Commonwealth Ave out to 527-acre Franklin Park, which has a small zoo, mostly of

Arnold Arboretum
main entrance 125 Arborway, Jamaica Plain (T: Forest Hills); tel: (617) 524-1718. Open dawn to dusk.

Faneuil Hall
Faneuil Hall Marketplace (T: Haymarket, State St or Government Center); tel: (617) 242-5675.

Above
Faneuil Hall

Left
Charles River promenade

local interest. The greatest draw for visitors is **Arnold Arboretum**✶✶, whose 265 acres include gardens with 7000 varieties of trees, shrubs and flowers, all labelled: a gardener's delight. The quiet paths and rolling hills are perfect for a relaxing stroll.

Faneuil Hall✶✶
At Faneuil Hall, firebrands such as Samuel Adams once aired ideas that led to the American Revolution, earning this historic 1742 meetinghouse-atop-a-marketplace its title as the 'Cradle of Liberty'. Today it is still a meeting house, hosting public debates, lectures and political rallies. It is also a stop on the **Freedom Trail**, and Park Service rangers explain its history every half-hour. Beside it is popular Faneuil Hall Marketplace.

Fenway Park✶
A true Boston landmark and one of the last old baseball stadia in the US, Fenway Park, outside Kenmore Sq in the Fenway neighbourhood, is home to the Boston Red Sox, who play professional baseball here from April to October. The team plans to tear it down soon to build a new facility, but fans consider its ground hallowed. The best way to see it is during a game.

The Isabella Stewart Gardner Museum

Museum of Fine Arts $$ 465 Huntington Ave (T: Museum); tel: (617) 267-9300. Open daily from 1000

Isabella Stewart Gardner Museum $$ 280 The Fenway; tel: (617) 566-1401. Open Tue–Sun 1100–1700.

Institute of Contemporary Art $ 955 Boylston St (T: Hynes/ICA); tel: (617) 266-5152. Open Wed–Sun 1200–1700, Thur 1700–2100 free.

Park St Church 1 Park St (T: Park St); tel: (617) 523-3383. **Granary Burying Ground** Tremont St. Gate open 0900–1700, winter 0900–1500.

Fine arts museums✦✦✦

Boston has a trio of top-notch art museums. For paintings, prints, sculpture and other artworks from a wide range of periods, there's the **Museum of Fine Arts**✦✦✦. Of special note is its Asiatic art. A short walk from the MFA is the unique **Isabella Stewart Gardner Museum**✦✦✦, showing works by Rembrandt, Botticelli and Titian, along with tapestries and Graeco-Roman statuary – the eclectic collection of a 19th-century socialite inside a re-created 15th-century Venetian palazzo. Its rooms overlook an ornate courtyard of trees, flowering plants and artworks. Located in a former **Back Bay** police station is the smaller **Institute of Contemporary Art**✦✦, with changing exhibitions of photography, painting, sculpture and performance art.

Freedom Trail✦✦✦

The 2.5-mile Freedom Trail, marked with a red line along the sidewalk, leads visitors to 16 sites in the heart of downtown Boston, covering 350 years of history. The trail begins at Boston Common Visitor Center, where you can pick up a map. Halfway along is the National Park Service office, with a better map, public toilets and rangers who know the history.

From Boston Common and the State House, the trail leads on to **Park St Church**✦✦ (*limited tours July and Aug*), where abolitionist William Lloyd Garrison first spoke out against slavery (1829) and the hymn *America* was first sung (1831). A few steps away on Tremont St,

King's Chapel 58
Tremont St; tel: (617)
227-2155. Open Mon, Fri,
Sat 0930–1600, Tue, Wed
0930–1100 in summer;
limited hours other seasons.

**Old South Meeting
House** $ Washington and
Milk Sts; tel: (617) 482-
6439. Open Apr–Oct 0930-
1700, Nov–Mar 1000-1600.

**John F Kennedy Library
and Museum** $$
Columbia Point, Dorchester
(T: JFK/UMass); tel: (617)
929-4523. Open 0900–
1700.

**John F Kennedy
Birthplace National
Historic Site** $
83 Beals St, Brookline (T:
Coolridge Corner);
tel: (617) 566-7937 tours
Wed–Sun 1000–1630.

Museum of Science $$
1 Science Park (T: Science
Park); tel: (617) 723-2500.
Sat–Thur 0900–1700 (early
Sept–4 July), 0900–1900
(rest of year), Fri 0900–
2100 (all year).

Computer Museum $$
300 Congress St, Museum
Wharf (T: South Station);
tel: (617) 427-6758.
Closed Mon.

Children's Museum $$
300 Congress St, Museum
Wharf (T: South Station);
tel: (617) 426-8855.
Closed Mon except summer
and school vacations.

**Boston Tea Party Ship
and Museum** $$ Congress
St Bridge at Museum Wharf
(T: South Station); tel: (617)
338-1773. Closed Dec–Mar.

the 17th-century **Granary Burying Ground**✦✦ holds the graves of revolutionary leaders John Hancock and Samuel Adams and Patriot Paul Revere. The 1754 **King's Chapel**✦✦ was Boston's first Anglican church (in 1785 it became Unitarian); beside it is **Boston's oldest burial ground**✦✦, where Puritan Governor John Winthrop is buried. Around the corner on School St is the site of Boston's first Public School and the 1862 Old City Hall. The Old Corner Bookstore, School and Washington Sts, was a gathering place for early 1800s writers who made Boston the 'Athens of America'.

Next, the 1729 Georgian-style **Old South Meeting House**✦✦, Washington and Milk Sts, is a colonial church where the Boston Tea Party was launched. The **Old State House** and **Faneuil Hall** lead on to the Blackstone Block, the only part of Boston that approximates to the look of the 1700s. The trail continues into the **North End**, with **Paul Revere House, Old North Church** and **Copp's Hill Burial Ground**, then to Charlestown for **Old Ironsides** and **Bunker Hill**.

John F Kennedy Library and Museum✦✦✦

The 35th US president started in politics by running for a seat in Congress representing parts of Boston, Cambridge and Charlestown. His grandfather, John F 'Honey Fitz' Fitzgerald, was one of Boston's early Irish mayors. And the story of his brief presidency is told here at the John F Kennedy Library and Museum, Columbia Point, south of the city centre on a dramatic point of land with a sweeping view of Boston harbour and Dorchester Bay. Just outside Boston, but not near the museum, is the modest Brookline home where he was born, now administered by the National Park Service as the **John F Kennedy Birthplace National Historic Site**✦✦.

Museum of Science✦✦

Another site with kids in mind is the Museum of Science, which reveals the secrets of everything from anthropology to space exploration, with many hands-on exhibits. Separate admissions get you into the Charles Hayden Planetarium show and the giant-screen 70mm films shown in the Mugar Omni Theater. The complex was built on a dam at the mouth of the **Charles River**.

Museum Wharf✦✦✦

Three museums near the waterfront serve different interests, but all appeal to children. The world's only **Computer Museum**✦ has vintage computers and hands-on exhibits, but its centre-piece is a giant walk-through computer that explains how all the parts function. Next door, the **Children's Museum**✦ is completely designed to entertain and educate kids, and includes a playspace for the littlest ones. The **Boston Tea Party Ship and Museum**✦✦ features *Beaver II*, a replica of one of the ships from which rebellious colonists dumped crates of tea to protest British taxes.

Paul Revere House
$ 19 North Sq; tel:
(617) 523-2338. Closed
Mon in winter.

**Old State House
Museum** $ 206
Washington St (T: State St);
tel: (617) 720-3292. Open
0900-1700 (Apr–Oct),
0930-1600 (Nov– Mar).

Old North Church
193 Salem St;
tel (617) 523-6676. Open
0900–1700.

**Prudential Skywalk
Observation Deck** $
Prudential Tower, 800
Boylston St; tel: (617) 859-
0648. Open daily 1000–
2200.

North End✢✢

Boston's Italian neighbourhood is a maze of narrow streets lined with restaurants, cafés and apartment houses. Zigzagging through it, a portion of the **Freedom Trail** leads to some of the city's best-known sites, including *circa*-1680 **Paul Revere House✢✢**, Boston's only remaining 17th-century house. It was home to silversmith Paul Revere, famed for his midnight ride of 18 April, 1775 to warn Patriot leaders at Lexington and Concord of British troop movements. On nearby Hanover St is a landmark statue of Revere on horseback, and a small park leads to the 1723 **Old North Church✢✢** (Christ Church), from whose steeple two lanterns were hung as a signal ('one if by land, two if by sea') on the night of Revere's ride. Uphill from the church, between tenements, is **Copp's Hill Burial Ground✢✢**, where Cotton Mather and other Puritans were laid to rest in the 1600s (*open daily*).

Old State House✢✢

Surrounded now by tall buildings, the 1713 Old State House was the seat of British government between 1713 and 1776 (its eastern end still bears the royal lion and unicorn) and later of the Massachusetts legislature. Inside is a museum of colonial and maritime memorabilia. Outside is a circle of cobblestones marking the site of the 1770 Boston Massacre, in which British sentries fired on a mob protesting against taxes and killed five colonists (who now lie in the nearby Granary Burying Ground).

Prudential Center✢✢

Boston's first tall building and possibly its ugliest landmark, the Prudential Center has a 50th-storey **Skywalk Observation Deck✢✢** that offers views denied to Hancock Tower visitors, particularly to the south. The Greater Boston Convention and Visitors Bureau (GBCVB) staffs an information booth in the lobby level, amid mall shops and

The Boston Tea Party

In the 1760s, Britain tried to defray the costs of defeating France in the Seven Years' War with new taxes on colonists in North America. Some were repealed after boycotts, but an import duty on tea stood. In 1773 Parliament agreed to let the East India Company dispose of its tea surplus here and to refund the duty in order to break the boycott.

When the *Dartmouth, Eleanor* and *Beaver* arrived in Boston harbour, patriot leaders were determined to stop their cargo of tea from unloading. After a rally at Old South Meeting House on 16 December, 1773, 50 to 100 men dressed up as Mohawk Indians and boarded the three ships at Griffin's Wharf. They tore open the 342 chests of tea and dumped them into the harbour. Similar acts followed in other ports, and Parliament punished the colonies harshly, setting the stage for revolution.

The original site is now on dry land, but a replica ship *Beaver II* and a small waterfront museum recount the history.

Paul Revere House, the sole surviving 17th-century house in Boston

USS Constitution Museum $
Building 22, Charlestown
Navy Yard, Charlestown;
tel: (617) 426-1812.
The ship 'Old Ironsides' tours
0930 to sunset.

restaurants. On Boylston St in front of the 'Pru', **Boston Duck Tours** *(tel: (617) 723-3825)* and several trolley tour companies sell tickets and board passengers.

USS Constitution (Old Ironsides)***

Permanently docked at Pier 1 in Charlestown is the 52-gun frigate USS *Constitution*, the world's oldest commissioned warship (still part of the US Navy), whose solid oak hull caused British cannonballs to bounce off during the War of 1812 with England, earning it the nickname 'Old Ironsides'. The ship's history is told in the nearby USS Constitution Museum.

Entertainment

The Calendar section in Thursday's *Boston Globe*, Scene in Friday's *Boston Herald* and the weekly *Boston Phoenix* have listings of what's happening.

The theatre district around Tremont and Boylston Sts hosts mostly blockbuster shows at the cavernous Wang Center, the classy Colonial, the more intimate Wilbur and Emerson Majestic and the tiny Charles Playhouse. There's a thriving small-theatre scene, and classic and contemporary drama are performed at the Lyric Stage, *140 Clarendon St*, and Huntington Theater Company, *264 Huntington Ave*. Half-price same-day tickets are sold, cash only, at Bostix booths at Faneuil Hall and Copley Sq; no phone.

Musical offerings include the Boston Symphony Orchestra, directed by Seiji Ozawa, at the venerable 2600-seat Symphony Hall, *301 Massachusetts Ave; tel: (617) 266-1492* (information) or *266-1200* (tickets), from early Oct to mid-Apr. The Boston Pops, a smaller group of BSO musicians, plays in summer at Symphony Hall and gives free

Below
Charles River waterfront

Boston's main shopping district is **Downtown Crossing**, a crowded pedestrian mall centred on Washington and Winter Sts, where the big department stores (Filene's and Macy's) and many smaller shops are located. Bargain shoppers enjoy the frenzy in Filene's basement, especially on the 'automatic markdown' tables.

Back Bay's **Newbury St** is a people-watcher's paradise amid galleries, cafés and boutiques, ranging from posh to funky. Paralleling it is a mile-long indoor concourse with moderate to pricey shops and restaurants. The 70-shop Prudential Center mall connects via walkway to 100-shop Copley Place.

Faneuil Hall Marketplace, packed with tourists and local people day and night, is a group of three renovated 1825 market buildings, supplemented by newer structures, that house 125 shops, restaurants, food stalls and pubs.

concerts at the Hatch Shell on the Esplanade in early July. There's also the Boston Ballet at the Wang Center, Boston Lyric Opera at Emerson Majestic Theater, and the Handel & Haydn Society, the oldest continuing US arts organisation, at Jordan Hall and other venues.

Boston also has a lively rock, jazz and folk scene at clubs in Kenmore Sq, Allston and elsewhere. Don't overlook Boston's public lecture series, especially the renowned Ford Hall Forum, plus poetry and prose readings. See local media for listings.

The Boston Marathon draws runners from around the world on Patriots Day (19 April or the closest Monday), a celebration of the Revolutionary War battles of Lexington and Concord; fans turn the Back Bay into a giant party. The weekend-long Boston Harborfest culminates in fireworks at the giant Fourth of July Concert (attendance: 500,000 or more) by the Boston Pops on the Charles River Esplanade.

Accommodation and food

As Boston is a popular tourist, convention, business and academic city, hotels are always heavily booked. Moderate rooms are scarce, budget rooms almost non-existent.

Top of the scale are the venerable, old-fashioned **Ritz-Carlton $$$** *15 Arlington St; tel: (617) 536-5700*, and its modern, posh competitor, the **Four Seasons $$$** *200 Boylston St; tel: (617) 338-4400*, both facing the Public Garden. **Omni Parker House $$$** *60 School St; tel: (617) 227-8600*, is right on the Freedom Trail and steeped in Boston history.

The **Fairmont Copley Plaza $$$** *138 St James Ave; tel: (617) 267-5300*, commands a grand view of Copley Sq. Close to shopping is the compact 143-room **Copley Square Hotel $$** *47 Huntington Ave; tel: (617) 536-900*. **Shawmut Inn $$** *280 Friend St; tel: (617) 720-5544*, with kitchenettes, is on the upper floors of a commercial building near North Station. Just out of Boston on a streetcar line are several small guesthouses, such as the 25-room Victorian-style **Beacon Inn $** *1087 Beacon St, Brookline; tel (617) 566-0088*.

The GBCVB offers lodging information by mail and on its website, but cannot make bookings. Instead, try **A Bed & Breakfast Agency**, *47 Commercial Wharf; tel: (617) 720-3540 or (800) 248-9262*, for rooms in local homes, including waterfront lofts, and **Citywide Reservation Service**, *36 Huntington Ave; tel: (617) 267-7424 or (800) 468-3593*.

At the table, Boston is still best known for fresh, simply prepared seafood. There's also no shortage of traditional Irish, Italian and Yankee fare, such as pot roast, baked beans and Indian pudding. But these are now complemented by a whole world of ethnic cuisine, plus trendy restaurants offering nouveau variations on American and other

'Ben Franklin' greets Boston shoppers

dishes. Browse through Hanover St in the North End and take your pick of Italian eateries; do the same on Beach St in Chinatown for Chinese.

Biba $$ *272 Boylston St; tel: (617) 426-7878,* is informal and trendy, with an eclectic, creative cuisine. **Durgin-Park** $$ *340 Faneuil Hall Marketplace; tel: (617) 227-2038,* is a taste of old Boston, with hearty New England fare. **Faneuil Hall Marketplace** $–$$$ has restaurants and food stalls offering everything from pizza and hot dogs to Greek and Chinese to white-linen dining.

Legal Sea Foods $$ *35 Columbus Ave; tel: (617) 426-4444,* and at Copley Place, Prudential Center, Kendall Sq in Cambridge, Chestnut Hill and Logan Airport, is a casual, crowded, noisy local chain. **Olives** $$$ *10 City Sq, Charlestown; tel: (617) 242-1999,* has diners queuing up outdoors for its elegant dishes. **Vinny Testa's Bar Ristorante** $$ *867 Boylston St (opposite the Pru); tel: (617) 262-6699,* is good for gargantuan Italian portions.

Suggested tour

Total distance: 2.5 miles for the **Freedom Trail**, plus diversions for special interests

Time: All day if you enter all the **Freedom Trail** sites. Casually walking it to catch the city's flavour takes a couple of hours.

Route: Park your car in the garage under **Boston Common ❶** (entrance on Charles St) and forget about it; one-way streets and difficult parking render it too frustrating to use for sightseeing. Cross the Common and pick up a map at the GBCVB visitor centre (near Park and Tremont Sts) to begin the **Freedom Trail ❷**.

Alternatively, you could cross Charles St into the **Public Garden ❸**, then stroll down Newbury St for shopping. Off Newbury St one block left are **Copley Square ❹** and the **Prudential Center ❺**; to the right are **Back Bay ❻** streets heading towards the **Charles River** Esplanade

❼. From there, veer right again to wander into **Beacon Hill** ❽ and back to **Boston Common** ❶. Carry a map and you can't get lost – it's a small area.

From Park St Station on **Boston Common** ❶, you could also take a Green Line train to **Copley Square** ❹, the **Prudential Center** ❺ or out to Huntington Ave to the Museum of Fine Arts; or take a Red Line subway train to South Station for **Museum Wharf** ❾ or JFK/UMass for the **JFK Library** ❿.

Freedom Trail ❷ directions are easy: Just follow the red line along the sidewalk. Or make your own tour by wandering on and off the Trail. The red line leads up to the State House on **Beacon Hill** ❽ (where it intersects the **Black Heritage Trail** ⓫), then doubles back to Tremont St and down School St to Washington St. Here, you are only a few minutes from Downtown Crossing shops or the city's financial district. **Faneuil Hall Marketplace** ⓬ is a convenient stop for lunch and more shopping, and you also have the choice of diverting to the New England **Aquarium** ⓭, then farther along the waterfront to Museum Wharf. Staying instead on the **Freedom Trail** ❷ leads you through the **North End** ⓮'s intriguing lanes, then it's a hike over the Charlestown Bridge to the **USS *Constitution*** ⓯ site and up to **Bunker Hill Monument** ⓰. The easiest way back downtown is by taxi.

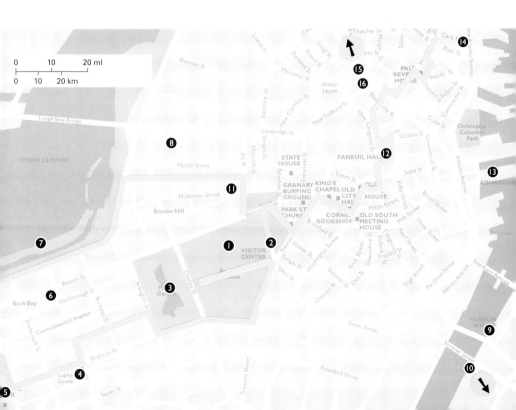

HAWTHORNE

West of Boston

Ratings

Arts and culture	●●●●●
History	●●●●●
Food and drink	●●●●○
Museums	●●●●○
Shopping	●●●○○
Children	●●○○○
Nature/ scenery	●●○○○
Beaches	●○○○○

One could say that America came of age in the communities just west of the circumscribed confines of Boston, where revolutionary thought and action neither began nor ended with America's War of Independence. Anchored by Harvard University, Cambridge is a leader in American intellectual thought and popular culture trends. The first shots of the American Revolution rang out in the more bucolic towns of Lexington and Concord, and, half a century later, Concord's authors launched a revolution of their own in 19th-century American letters. Battle sites alternate with authors' homes as attractions. On the banks of the Merrimack River, Lowell sprang up as the birthplace of the American version of the Industrial Revolution. An impressive historical park preserves and interprets both the mechanical ingenuity of the era as well as American industrial labour history.

CAMBRIDGE✦✦✦

ⓘ Cambridge Office for Tourism *18 Brattle St; tel: (617) 441-2884.*

Harvard Information Center Holyoke *1350 Massachusetts Ave; tel: (617) 495-1573. Harvard Yard tours (free) offered Sept–May Mon–Fri 1000 and 1400, Sat 1400, June–Aug Mon–Sat 1000, 1115, 1400 and 1515, Sun 1330 and 1500.*

Harvard University and the city of Cambridge are forever locked in symbiotic embrace, and only the historical record makes clear which was the chicken and which the egg. The oldest (1631) part of the city is **Harvard Square✦✦✦**, just outside the college walls, where street layouts have barely changed since the 1660s but where the passing scene changes almost daily in anticipation of the next fad in dress style, music or pose. The square's most enduring charm is one of the world's densest concentrations of bookstores. A bustling café scene and a veritable frenzy of street performers give the square a lively air throughout the year.

'Other American colleges have campuses' wrote poet David McCord, 'but Harvard has always had and always will have her Yard of grass and trees and youth and old familiar ghosts.' Surrounded by brick walls, the inner sanctum of **Harvard Yard✦** is haunted by many spirits,

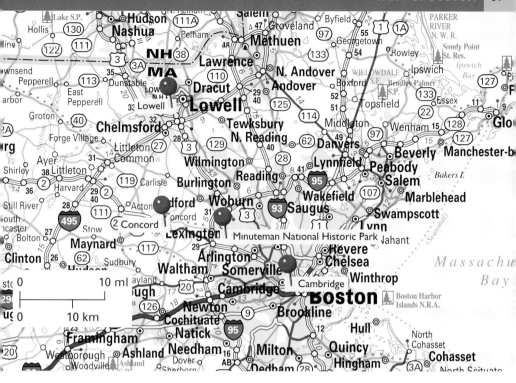

Harvard University Art Museums $
Fogg Art Museum and Werner Otto Hall
32 Quincy St; tel (617) 495-9400. Open Mon–Sat 1000–1700, Sun 1300–1700.

Sackler Museum
485 Broadway;
tel: (617) 495-9400. Open (see above)

Harvard Museums of Cultural and Natural History $ *24–26 Oxford St; tel: (617) 495-3045. Open Mon–Sat 1000–1700, Sun 1300–1700.*

Longfellow House $
105 Brattle St;
tel: (617) 876-4491.
Closed for restoration until autumn 1999; call for hours.

including the young cleric John Harvard, who left half his money and all his books to the fledgling college when he died in 1638, two years after it was founded. Student-led tours hit the highlights, pointing out splendid buildings whose creators read like an honour roll of America's leading architects.

The extraordinary collections of the Harvard Art Museums are spread out in three buildings behind Harvard Yard. The **Fogg Art Museum***, built around a central courtyard adapted from a 16th-century Italian church, is a veritable survey course of Western European art. **Werner Otto Hall*** specialises in Germanic art, with an exquisite Expressionism collection. The **Sackler Museum*** houses classical, Asian, Islamic and later Indian art. The nearby **Harvard Museums of Cultural and Natural History*** hold the typical examples of minerals, stuffed animals and anthropological objects, as well as a unique collection of stunningly beautiful blown-glass botanical specimens, famous as the 'Glass Flowers'.

Brattle St north of Harvard Sq is called Tory Row, after the fine houses built by rich merchants who fled during the American Revolution. The **Longfellow House*** was confiscated and served as headquarters for General George Washington during the siege of Boston. Later it was the home of poet Henry Wadsworth Longfellow and his family, and the house depicts their comfortable mid-19th-century lifestyle.

P Parking in or near Harvard Sq is very limited. Metered spaces on the streets cost only 50c per hour. Rates at more expensive car-parks on Eliot and Church Sts vary with hour and day.

American Repertory Theatre 64 Brattle St; tel: (617) 547-8300. One of America's leading avant-garde theatres.

Head of the Charles Regatta tel: (617) 864-8414. Largest rowing event in the world is held during the height of the mid-Oct foliage season.

Club Passim 47 Palmer St; tel: (617) 492-7679. Legendary singer-songwriter venue has launched careers of the likes of Joan Baez and Patty Larkin.

House of Blues 96 Winthrop St; tel: (617) 491-2583. Leading electric blues artists perform in this funky space where the chain began. Reserve early for Sun gospel brunch.

Regatta Bar Charles Hotel, 1 Bennett St; tel: (617) 876-7777. Top local, national and international jazz artists.

Accommodation and food in Cambridge

A Friendly Inn at Harvard Square $–$$ *1673 Cambridge St, Cambridge; tel: (617) 547-7851.* Overseas visitors favour this casual B&B about a five-minute walk from Harvard Sq.

Casablanca $$–$$$ *40 Brattle St; tel: (617) 876-0999.* The bar with Bogart murals on the walls is a favourite hangout of local celebrities and the dining-room serves delicious bistro food with a North African flavour.

Charles Hotel in Harvard Square $$–$$$ *1 Bennett St, Cambridge; tel: (800) 882-1818 or (617) 864-1200.* Modern hotel in the heart of Harvard Sq offering many packages. The swanky Rialto ($$$) restaurant is among the best in Boston area.

Isaac Harding House $$–$$$ *288 Harvard St, Cambridge; tel: (617) 876-2888.* Historic home about a ten-minute walk from Harvard Square with large, elegant rooms.

John Harvard's Brewhouse $$ *33 Dunster St; tel: (617) 868-3585.* Pub food and ales rise above the average at this friendly spot near the site of the first brewery in Cambridge.

Toscanini $ *1310 Massachusetts Ave; tel: (617) 354-9350.* There are many who happily make a meal of the home-made ice-creams with flavours such as burnt caramel, saffron and green tea.

Up Stairs at the Pudding $$$ *10 Holyoke St; tel: (617) 864-1933.* Formal dining-room is a favourite with Harvard academics. Á la carte Sun brunch and lunch (on a hidden deck during summer) are good deals on gourmet fare.

The statue of three lies

The university's favourite photo opportunity, the statue of John Harvard in Harvard Yard above is widely known as the 'statue of three lies'. It is inscribed, 'John Harvard, Founder, 1638'. The college was founded in 1636 while Harvard was still in England. The young minister was the college's benefactor, not its founder. And since no likeness of the man survived, Daniel Chester French modelled the sculpture's features on a popular student of the class of 1882.

Harvard University's 17th-century elegance

CONCORD❖❖

ℹ Concord Chamber of Commerce
21 Lexington Rd;
tel: (978) 369-3120.

🏛 Emerson House $
28 Cambridge Turnpike,
tel: (978) 369-2236. Open
mid Apr–Oct Thur–Sat
1000–1630,
Sun 1400–1630.

Orchard House $
399 Lexington Rd;
tel: (978) 369-4118.
Open Apr–Oct Mon–Sat
1000–1630, Sun
1300–1630.

This Boston dormitory community was the scene of an extraordinary blossoming of American letters in the mid 19th-century, when writers seized on Ralph Waldo Emerson's philosophy and created a self-consciously national literature. The **Emerson House**❖, where the 'sage of Concord' lived between 1835 and 1882 has been maintained largely as he left it, complete with books, personal belongings and furniture. The **Orchard House**❖, which Louisa May Alcott described in loving detail in *Little Women*, captures the Alcott family experience of rich emotions amid modest circumstances. Displays in the attached barn give the general outlines of Concord's literary blossoming. Many Concord literati rest in peace on 'Author's Ridge' in **Sleepy Hollow Cemetery**❖, including Ralph Waldo Emerson, Henry David Thoreau, Nathaniel Hawthorne and Louisa May Alcott. Pilgrims to this low-key cemetery frequently leave tokens of their admiration. Thoreau's beloved **Walden Pond**❖❖ is a popular place for swimming, boating and fishing. A model of Thoreau's cabin in the car-park reminds visitors of the writer's somewhat loftier concerns about the place. Rangers can provide directions to the site of the original cabin, still marked by the crumbled chimney hearth.

Right
Antique trolleys carry visitors round Lowell National Historic Park

Below right
Inside Boott Cotton Mills

Sleepy Hollow Cemetery
Bedford St (Rte 62); no tel. Open daily dawn–dusk.

Walden Pond $
Rte 126; tel: (978) 369-3254. Open daily dawn–dusk.

Accommodation and food in Concord

Concord Inn $$–$$$ *48 Monument Sq, Concord; tel: (978) 369-9200.* Original section of inn dates from early 1700s; additions from each century since. Dining room ($$) features traditional New England fare.

Guida's Coast Cuisine $$ *84 Thoreau St; tel: (978) 371-1333.* Portuguese-style seafood is the house speciality of Azores-born chef.

LOWELL✦✦✦

Greater Merrimack Valley Convention & Visitors Bureau
22 Shattuck St; tel: (800) 443-3332 or (978) 459-6150.

P On-street parking is limited in Lowell; follow signs to free Dutton St lot behind the National Historic Park's Visitor Center.

Native son Jack Kerouac once described Lowell as 'the textile factories built in brick, primly towered, solid, all ranged along the river and the canals, and all night the industries hum and shuttle'. By 1950, when he wrote this nostalgic sketch, Lowell's textile industry was on its deathbed. But the mills were revolutionary in the 1830s, when they brought all the processes of textile manufacture under a single roof and transformed an agricultural economy into an industrial one. Using the structures and canals of the mill city, **Lowell National Historic Park✦✦✦** conveys the entrepreneurial excitement of the era while also paying due respect to the workers. Park rangers offer informative free tours on foot or bicycle. Canal tours by boat ($)

During summer, a free electric trolley, modelled on a 1901 streetcar, connects several sites within Lowell National Historic Park.

Lowell National Historic Park
Visitor Center
67 Kirk St; tel: (978) 970-5000. Open daily 0830–1700.

Boott Cotton Mills $
John St; tel: (978) 970-5000. Open daily 0930–1700.

Mogan Cultural Center
Boardinghouse Park; tel: (978) 970-5000. Free admission. Open July–Aug daily 1200–1700, Sept–June Sat–Sun 1300–1700.

American Textile Museum $ 491 Dutton St; tel: (978) 441-0400. Open Tue–Fri 0900–1600, Sat–Sun 1000–1600.

New England Quilt Museum $
18 Shattuck St; tel: (978) 452-4207. Open Tue–Sat 1000–1600, May–Nov also open Sun 1200–1600.

provide another perspective on the layout of the industrial city. **Boott Cotton Mills***** is one of the best surviving examples of early mill architecture in Lowell. Although fewer than a dozen of the 88 first-floor power looms are operated for visitors, the din is deafening, even through the ear plugs supplied to visitors. The mill owners initially hired the daughters of New England farmers as their labour force. As a trade-off for the demands of the job, the young women gained a social freedom unusual in their day. Even after working 13 to 14 hours a day Monday to Friday and 8 hours on Saturday, they attended lectures, created pottery (now much sought by collectors) and even organised the first labour strikes in the US. Their story, as well as that of later immigrant workers, is the focus of the **Mogan Cultural Center**** adjacent to Boott Mills.

Two additional Lowell museums augment the picture presented by the national historic park. **The American Textile Museum**** traces cloth-making in America from hand-spinning and weaving to computer-controlled looms. The collections include more than 1000 pre-industrial tools (over 300 spinning wheels alone on display), together with more than 300 industrial machines and samples of old fabrics, bed covers and clothing. The **New England Quilt Museum**** has a select permanent collection of historic and contemporary quilts and mounts several temporary exhibitions each year. Its galleries are among the best to see new quilt design, and the museum shop is an excellent resource for books and other quilt-related items.

Lowell Celebrates Kerouac
Tel: (978) 458-1721. Early Oct event celebrates native son, poet and novelist Jack Kerouac, with music, poetry readings and tours of his haunts.

Lowell Folk Festival
Tel: (978) 970-5000. With a large and diverse ethnic population, Lowell is a fitting place for the largest free folk festival in the US, held in late July.

Accommodation and food in Lowell

Courtyard by Marriott $$ *37 Industrial Ave E; tel: (800) 321-2211 or (978) 458-7575.* Although a short drive from the historic district, this 120-room motel is a good base for exploring the city.

Doubletree Hotel $$–$$$ *50 Warren St; tel: (978) 452-1200.* The lobby of this 259-room hotel looks out on Pawtucket Canal in the middle of Lowell National Historic Park.

Four Sisters Owl Diner $ *244 Appleton St; tel: (978) 453-8321.* Open only for breakfast and lunch, this diner used to serve mill workers and offers 'one of the best breakfasts in the Northeast'.

La Boniche $$–$$$ *143 Merrimack St; tel: (978) 458-9473.* Bistro fare in a stately beaux arts-style building is Lowell's best fine-dining choice.

Old Worthen House $ *141 Worthen St; tel: (978) 459-0300.* The pub grub is unremarkable, but half the patrons come to look for the table where Jack Kerouac carved his name.

Southeast Asian Restaurant $–$$ *343 Market St; tel: (978) 452-3182.* Large Cambodian and Vietnamese populations have brought a cosmopolitan quality to Lowell's dining scene. The weekday lunch buffet is a good deal.

MINUTEMAN NATIONAL HISTORIC PARK✦✦✦

Lexington Chamber of Commerce Visitor Centre
1875 Massachusetts Ave; tel: (781) 862-1450.

Minute Man Bikeway, a 10.5-mile paved trail on a former rail bed follows the route of the British retreat to Boston after the Battle of North Bridge in Concord.

This park commemorates the events of 19 April, 1775, when British troops making a show of force in Lexington and Concord were met by such intense armed resistance that they were driven to retreat. Most of the park follows Rte 2A along that retreat path, called 'Battle Road'. The **Battle Road Visitor Center**✦✦ presents an excellent video encapsulating the events that are widely credited as the first volleys of the American Revolution. A diorama traces the first 4 miles of the

British retreat along Battle Road. **Lexington Green**✦✦, site of the dawn skirmish, is surrounded by white-spired churches and the yellow clapboard Buckman Tavern, where militiamen assembled overnight, only to be routed by the British forces. **North Bridge**✦✦✦ in Concord was the next major battle site, and disciplined colonials turned the tables and sent the Redcoats packing. Both sides are memorialised here, with

Battle Road Visitors Center *Rte 2A, Lexington; tel: (781) 862-7753. Free admission. Open mid April–Oct daily 0900–1700.*

North Bridge Visitor Center *Minute Man National Historic Park 174 Liberty St, Concord; tel: (978) 369-6993. Free admission. Open daily 0900–1730.*

Museum of Our National Heritage *33 Marrett Rd (Rte 2A), Lexington; tel: (781) 861-6559. Free admission. Open Mon–Sat 1000–1700, Sun 1200–1700.*

Patriots Day *tel: (781) 862-7753. Each year on or near 19 April, costumed re-enactors play out the battles of Lexington Green and North Bridge.*

the Minute Man Statue by Daniel Chester French and a plaque on the opposite side of the bridge remembering British soldiers who died far from home. Costumed re-enactments of both battles are held each April, just as spring flowers begin to emerge and the trees leaf out.

Although separate from the national historic park, the **Museum of Our National Heritage**✦✦ in Lexington displays the original 'Lexington Alarm', a call to arms penned on 19 April, 1775, that successfully rallied the other American colonies to revolution. Most of the museum is dedicated to an often fascinating exploration of 20th-century American popular culture.

Right
His Majesty's troops prepare to re-enact the battle of Old North Bridge

Concord's Wayside Inn, former home of the Alcott family and Nathaniel Hawthorne

Suggested tour

Total distance: 38 miles; 40 miles with detours

Time: 2 hours' driving. Allow 2–3 days.

Links: Connects via city streets to Boston (see pages 42–55).

Route: Much of this route follows urban streets with frequent stoplights. Begin at Harvard Sq and follow Massachusetts Ave (Rte 2A) north and west for 4 miles into the shopping centre of **Arlington** ❶, a pleasant residential community with many inexpensive restaurants. Continue west on Rte 2A another 5 miles to the outskirts of **Lexington** ❷ and **The Museum of Our National Heritage** ❸. Leaving the museum, turn left on to Massachusetts Ave and drive 1.5 miles to Lexington Green. Continue on Massachusetts Ave towards **Concord** ❹, rejoining Rte 2A as Marrett Rd in 1.5 miles. In 2.5 miles, veer right on to Lexington Rd, following it past several historic sites for less than 2 miles to **CONCORD** ❹ centre and the **Emerson House** ❺. In the village centre, Bedford Rd leads northeast half a mile to **Sleepy Hollow Cemetery** ❻; Monument St leads half a mile north to the **North Bridge battle site** ❼. Walden St leads south from the centre of Concord 2 miles to **Walden Pond** ❽ and the associated state recreation area.

Great Meadows National Wildlife Refuge *Weir Hill Rd, Sudbury; tel: (978) 443-4661.*

From **Walden Pond** ❽, drive east on Rte 2 for 2 miles to I-95 and Rte 128. Follow them north for three exits (2 miles) to Rte 3, the Middlesex Turnpike. This old Lowell–Cambridge highway parallels a former shipping canal and cuts through beautiful farmland, a seeming anomaly so close to urban centres. In 11 miles, the Lowell Connector splits to the right. Follow it, taking exit 5N ('Thorndike St') into **LOWELL** ❾. Follow signs leading to 'Lowell National and State Park Visitor Parking' at the Dutton St lot.

Also worth exploring

The best inland bird-watching in New England is found in the **Great Meadows National Wildlife Refuge***, a wetlands preserve set aside to provide habitat to migrating birds. Tens of thousands of waterfowl stop during annual migrations, and resident birds include many raptors, herons and sandpipers. A check-list of 231 species identified here is available from the visitor centre. The refuge consists of two units, one south of Concord along the Sudbury River, the other north of Concord centre on the Concord River. Diked impoundments in the Concord unit abound with American lotus.

Massachusetts North Shore

Ratings

History	●●●●●
Nature/ scenery	●●●●●
Arts and culture	●●●●○
Beaches	●●●○○
Museums	●●●○○
Children	●●○○○
Food and drink	●●○○○
Shopping	●●○○○

The shore towns north of Boston concentrate New England's chief appeals: an overlay of history, long ocean beaches, dramatic coastal scenery and even a local food speciality. Founded as religious refugee colonies, these communities once dominated the world's cod fisheries and trade with the Far East before settling into a genteel old age. Today, yachts and pleasure craft far outnumber fishing boats, and the glories of the China Trade are more evident in antiques shops and museums than on the wharves. Landscape painters are more common than overseas traders, and art galleries overshadow chandlers.

Although highways link the North Shore to Boston, smaller roads are less congested, more direct and more interesting. Moreover, the compact area allows for more time on foot and less behind the wheel.

GLOUCESTER**

ⓘ Cape Ann Chamber of Commerce Information Center
33 Commercial St; tel: (800) 321-0133 or (978) 283-1601; Website: cape-ann. com/cacc offers regional information for Gloucester, Rockport and Essex.

Gloucester Visitors Welcoming Centre
Stage Fort Park, Hough Ave; tel: (978)281-8865.

Gloucester fishermen have gone to sea since 1623 and maritime painters have made the port their base for more than 150 years. The interplay of arts and fishing is epitomised at the **Cape Ann Historical Museum**, where exhibitions trace the fishing and boatbuilding heritage (Gloucester shipwrights invented the three-masted schooner). But the museum's glories are its magnificent paintings by native son Fitz Hugh Lane, America's

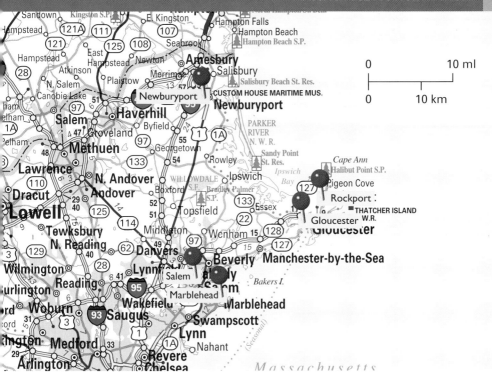

premier maritime painter. Lane built his granite house and studio on a stone outcrop with a commanding view of the harbour, now the centrepiece of **Fitz Hugh Lane Park** on Rogers St. The house is closed to visitors but a striking statue of Lane at work reclines outside.

Rocky Neck Art colony, arguably the oldest working artists' colony in the US, sits directly across the harbour on a knob of land with a nearly 360-degree view of sky and water. Today's artists are less indigent than those of years past, but the Neck retains a bohemian, imaginative quality, and painters working on their decks or along narrow streets encourage curious visitors.

Gloucester's dramatic seascape also attracted millionaires. Inspired by his European journeys, inventor John Hays Hammond Jr built **Hammond Castle Museum**, a medieval-style castle, to house the collection of early Roman, medieval and Renaissance artefacts that constituted his vision of more romantic days. **Beauport**, also known as the Sleeper-McCann House, is another fantasy house, where a theme from literature or history defines the décor in each of the 26 rooms open to tour.

Because Gloucester lies just 15 miles from important whale feeding grounds, it is one of New England's best places for **whale watching** cruises. Most operators guarantee rare sightings of humpbacks and finbacks, and occasionally of northern right whales.

Cape Ann Historical Museum $ 27 Pleasant St; tel: (978) 283-0455. Open Tue–Sat 1000–1700. Closed Feb.

Hammond Castle Museum $ 80 Hesperus Ave; tel: (978) 283-7673. Open June–Oct 1000–1700.

Beauport (Sleeper-McCann House) $ 75 Eastern Pt Blvd; tel: (978) 283-0800. Open mid-May –mid Oct Mon–Fri 1000–1600.

McT's Lobster House and Tavern $$ 25 Rogers St; tel: (978) 282-0950. Amid the fish docks, McT's excels at simple preparations of exceedingly fresh catch.

Ocean View House $–$$ 171 Atlantic Rd, tel: (978) 283-6200. Eight buildings on landscaped grounds looking out on ocean.

Saint Peter's Festa tel: (978) 283-1601. Four-day festival in late June honours patron saint of fishermen.

Schooner Festival tel: (978) 283-1601. Large and small schooners compete in three-day early Sept regatta.

Clam confusion

New England has mussels, but its cockles are scallops, and most restaurants serve only the hinge muscle of tiny ('bay') and large ('ocean') scallops. Two types of clam are harvested in New England: the soft-shelled clam, also known as the 'steamer clam', and the quahog (an Indian name). Small quahogs called 'cherrystones' are often eaten raw. Medium-sized quahogs called 'littlenecks' are generally fried. Large quahogs are usually baked and filled with a cracker stuffing.

MARBLEHEAD❖❖

ℹ Chamber of Commerce Information Booth
At the intersection of Pleasant and Spring Sts; tel: (781) 631-2868.

🏛 Abbot Hall
Washington Sq; no tel. Open Mon–Sat 0900–1700, Sun 1100–1800. Free.

Marblehead Historical Society $ 170 Washington St; tel: (781) 631-1768. Open Mon–Sat 1000–1600.

Colonel Jeremiah Lee Mansion $ 161 Washington St; tel: (781) 631-1069. Open mid May–mid Oct Mon–Sat 1000–1600, Sun 1300–1600.

King Hooper Mansion 8 Hooper St; tel: (781) 631-2608. Open Tue–Sat 1000–1700. Free.

🪁 Marblehead Kite Company
1 Pleasant St; tel: (781) 631-7166 sells simple trapezoids, box kites and fighting kites for flying at beaches and Fort Sewall Park.

Marblehead is the best preserved of the early North Shore communities. Some 250 structures predating the American Revolution dot the historic district of Waldron Ct and Essex, Elm, Pond and Norman Sts.

Abbot Hall❖ on Washington Sq houses town government and many community treasures, including the massive painting *The Spirit of '76*, an American patriotic icon. Far more interesting are the naïve artworks of John Orne Johnson Frost at the nearby **Marblehead Historical Society❖❖**. Frost's art depicts the hard life of a fisherman and captures Marblehead's past with rough charm.

The **Colonel Jeremiah Lee Mansion❖❖** counters Frost's workingman's vision with trader's wealth in a Georgian-style mansion built in 1768. Lee's widow entertained new president George Washington in 1789, perhaps to show off the hand-painted wallpaper and grand public rooms.

Once a town of overseas traders, Marblehead now has more artists than sea captains. The Marblehead Arts Association makes its headquarters in the **King Hooper Mansion❖**, a handsome 1745 manse filled with members' works for sale.

British soldiers built the simple earth embankment of **Fort Sewall❖** in 1742 to protect Marblehead harbour from French marauders, only to find colonists aiming the cannons on British ships during the Revolution. The surrounding park off Front St has excellent views of sailing regattas in this yachting capital.

Accommodation and food in Marblehead

King's Rook $$ *12 State St; tel: (781) 631-9838*. Locals favour this café and wine bar in a 1747 building for light lunches and romantic dinners.

Oceanwatch $$ *8 Fort Sewall Ln, Marblehead; tel: (781) 639-8660*. Three guest rooms in a Victorian-era home share a superb harbour view with adjacent Fort Sewall.

Truffles $–$$ *114 Washington St; tel: (781) 639-1104*. Casual café and deli sells take-away sandwiches and elegant ready-to-cook meals for self-catering.

Previous page
Fisherman's memorial, Gloucester harbour

Above left
Marblehead Cove

Right
Sailing schooner off the coast of New England's yachting capital

NEWBURYPORT✦✦✦

Newburyport Chamber of Commerce 29 State St; tel: (978) 462-6680.

Custom House Maritime Museum $ 25 Water St; tel: (978) 462-8681. Open Mon–Sat 1000–1600 (closed Nov–May Wed afternoon), Sun 1300–1600.

Parker River Wildlife Refuge $ Plum Island Turnpike; tel: (978) 465-5753. Open daily sunrise–sunset. Some beaches close Apr–July to protect nesting habitat of endangered piping plovers.

The three-storey mansions in the **High St✦**, crowned with hip roofs and cupolas, attest to the wealth of Newburyport's 18th-century ship owners. Elegant cornices, doorways and windows carved by ships' carpenters place this district among the nation's finest examples of Federal architecture.

An 1811 fire destroyed the commercial sector, so downtown Newburyport was rebuilt in red brick that came as ballast in ships from Asia. Newburyport shifted to European trade in the 19th century, and those ships registered cargo at the granite temple of commerce now converted to the **Custom House Maritime Museum✦**, where exhibitions evoke the town's overseas trade days. Merrimac, Water and State Sts have developed as a district of boutiques and antiques shops. At the foot of the commercial district, **Waterfront Park✦** is the site of summer concerts and fireworks and celebrations during the Christmas shopping season.

Newburyport is the gateway to **Plum Island✦**, dominated by **Parker River National Wildlife Refuge✦✦✦**. The 4662 acres of sand beach and dunes, bogs and tidal marshes support more than 800 species of birds, plants and animals. Plum Island ranks among North America's top ten bird-watching sanctuaries.

Yankee Homecoming
tel: (978) 462-6680. Nine-day event begins last Sat in July and includes parade, concerts, fireworks, crafts, food and races.

Accommodation and food in Newburyport

Clark Currier Inn $$ *45 Green St; tel: (978) 465-8363.* Four antiques-filled guest rooms retain the period architectural detail of a shipwright-built 1803 'square house'.

Glenn's Restaurant $$ *44 Merrimac St; tel: (978) 465-3811.* Contemporary bistro favours fresh fish and has a lively bar scene.

Ten Center Street $$ *10 Center St; tel: (978) 462-6652.* Locals favour the ground-floor pub in this 1790 building for its cosy atmosphere and casual menu. The upstairs dining-room is more formal.

The Windsor House $$ *38 Federal St; tel: (888) TRELAWNY or (978) 462-3778.* A fine 18th-century brick Federal Mansion with four guest rooms.

ROCKPORT**

Rockport Chamber of Commerce
Upper Main St; tel: (978) 546-6575.

Rockport Art Association
12 Main St; tel: (978) 546-6604. Open Mon–Sat 1000–1700, Sun 1200–1700.

Halibut Point State Park $ Rte 127 & Gott Ave; tel: (978) 546-2997. Open Apr–Oct dawn–2000.

Picturesque Rockport is an artists' town and every painter seems to have made at least one canvas of the dusky red 1½-storey fishing shack at the end of Bradley Wharf, **Motif No 1***. The densest concentration of galleries, boutiques, eateries and souvenir shops is found on **Bearskin Neck***, a rocky peninsula that forms the north side of Rockport harbour. Best of the galleries is the **Rockport Art Association***, housed in a mid-1700s tavern and barn.

Located at the tip of the granite peninsula of Cape Ann, Rockport once supplied stone for major buildings up and down the Atlantic seaboard. **Halibut Point State Park***, a 54-acre reserve at the northern tip of the cape, has picnic areas and walking trails through woodlands and along the ocean. The most interesting trail explores a quarry last excavated in 1929. The stunning view over the water-filled quarry to Ipswich Bay is best at sunset, which unfortunately occurs after the park closes in July and August.

Accommodation and food in Rockport

In 1856, more than 200 hatchet-wielding women destroyed every container of alcohol in Rockport. The town remains officially 'dry', but many establishments allow patrons to bring their own beer or wine.

Bearskin Neck Motor Lodge $–$$ *74 South Rd; tel: (978) 546-6677.* Modest eight-room motel occupying prime spot near shops and restaurants with fine ocean views.

Harbor Grille $$ *8 Old Harbor Rd, tel: (978) 546-3030.* Ideal spot on Bearskin Neck seawall to consume a bucket of peel-and-eat shrimps followed by seafood stew or lobster roll on a baguette.

Left
Bearskin Neck, Rockport

Inn on Cove Hill $–$$ *37 Mt Pleasant St; tel: (978) 546-2701.* Financed in 1791 with pirates' gold, the inn is close to Front Beach and Bearskin Neck.

Yankee Clipper Inn $$$ *96 Granite St; tel: (978) 546-3407.* Elegant compound on high coastal overlook between downtown Rockport and Halibut Point features 26 radically different rooms in four buildings.

SALEM✦✦✦✦

🛈 Salem National Historic Site
Visitors Center
193 Derby St; tel: (978) 740-1660. Open daily 0900–1700. Guided tours $.

🛈 Peabody Essex Museum $$
East India Sq, Plummer Hall (Essex Institute collections) at 132 Essex St and East India Hall (Peabody collections) at 162 Essex St; tel: (978) 745-9500. Open Mon–Sat 1000–1700, Sun 1200–1700 (Nov–late May closed on Mon).

House of Seven Gables $$ *54 Turner St; tel: (978) 744-0991. Open July–Oct daily 0930–1800, Nov–June daily 1000–1630.*

◉ Haunted Happenings
tel: (800) 777-6848. Salem celebrates Halloween throughout October with candlelight tours, haunted houses, psychic fairs and other events.

Salem remains notorious for executing 20 'witches' in the 1690s, but is prouder of its 1790–1830 status as the 'Venice of America'. Guided tours by rangers of the **Salem National Historic Site✦✦✦** bring to life the era when the riches of the Orient spilled on to Salem's wharves.

The **Peabody Essex Museum✦✦✦** also vividly captures life at sea and at home. Overseas adventurers brought back curios that formed the basis of the Peabody's 100,000-object collection, including the world's most extensive holdings in Asian export art. The Essex Institute branch counters the Peabody's global view with portraits of Salem's prominent citizens and galleries brimming with Salem's fine 17th- and 18th-century cabinetry. Three house museums on the grounds reflect Salem's expanding domestic wealth between 1684 and 1805.

A few blocks northeast of the Peabody Essex Museum, the 9-acre **Salem Common✦** rivals any in New England with its central bandstand, 19th-century cast-iron fence and leafy arcade. The houses at 74, 82 and 92 Washington St E are associated with Samuel McIntire, Salem's self-taught master architect of the early 19th century. Architecture buffs may also wish to stroll **Chestnut St✦**, lined with merchants' and sea captains' Federal mansions designed or inspired by McIntire. The street begins three blocks west of Old Town Hall.

In a less grand harbour neighbourhood stands the **House of Seven Gables✦**, inspiration for Nathaniel Hawthorne's second novel. The

Above
The Salem Witch Museum

Far right
The House of Seven Gables

ⓘ Salem Witch Museum $
Washington Sq; tel: (978) 744-1692. Open July–Aug daily 1000–1900, Sept–June daily 1000–1700.

Witch Dungeon Museum $ *16 Lynde St; tel: (978) 741-3570. Apr–Nov daily 1000–1700.*

grounds include striking seaside gardens and the modest home where the author was born.

The witch trials may have been Salem's most shameful period, but they are still a lucrative tourist draw. The **Salem Witch Museum⁕** features histrionic narration in darkness punctuated by suddenly lit dioramas. The **Witch Dungeon Museum⁕** dramatises transcripts from the trial of Sarah Good and has a re-created dungeon in the basement. The tasteful and reflective **Salem Witch Trial Memorial⁕** was erected in 1992 on New Liberty St next to the old cemetery.

Accommodation and food in Salem

Derby Fish & Lobster $–$$ *215 Derby St; tel: (978) 745-2064.* The fresh fish at this casual spot is equally good whether ordered at the counter or through table service.

Grapevine Restaurant $$ *26 Congress St; tel: (978) 745-9335.* This stylish trattoria with broad wine list specialises in seafood.

Inn at Seven Winter Street $$ *7 Winter St; tel: (978) 745-9520.* Several guest rooms have fireplaces or decks in this 1870s Empire-style B&B decorated with period furnishings.

Lyceum Bar & Grill $$ *43 Church St; tel: (978) 745-7665.* The restaurant side is formal, the bar more casual, but dark wood and white linens dominate both. Both rooms give stylish updates to classic dishes.

The Hawthorne Hotel $$ *On the Common, Salem; tel: (800) SAY-STAY or (978) 744-4080.* Built in 1925, this red-brick member of Historic Hotels of America is well situated for touring and completely renovated its 89 guest rooms in 1998.

Suggested tour

Total distance: 65 miles with detour

Time: 2 hours' driving. Allow 1½ days. Those with limited time should focus on Salem and Newburyport.

Links: From Newburyport at the end of this route, join the New Hampshire and Southern Maine Coast route *(see page 236)* or return via I-95 Rte 1 to Boston *(see page 42).*

Route: From Boston's Callahan Tunnel follow Rte 1A north 6 miles through the honky-tonk beach community of Revere Beach and on to Lynnway, taking the right fork in Swampscott for 6 miles on to Rte 129, which provides fleeting glimpses of an ever-rockier shore as the geology shifts from river-mouth to limestone cliffs en route to **MARBLEHEAD ❶**. Pleasant St at Washington Sq becomes Rte 114 west, a residential district until it enters **Salem ❷** in 4 miles.

The coastline becomes more rugged between Salem and Cape Ann, a peninsula of solid granite jutting 15 miles out to sea. Follow Rte 1A north 2 miles through Beverly to the intersection with Rte 127 east, the scenic cliffside road to **Gloucester ❸**. In 10 miles turn right on to Hesperus Ave for a 2-mile ocean drive past vigorous surf and craggy cliffs topped with millionaires' mansions. Hesperus Ave rejoins Route 127 just before entering **GLOUCESTER ❸** at Stage Fort Park. Rte 127 circles Cape Ann, going 4 miles through wooded countryside to

Crane Properties $$
290 Argilla Rd, Ipswich;
tel: (978) 356-4351.
Open late May–mid Oct.
House tours Wed–Thur
1000–1600. **Boat tour**
($$$) to offshore islands of
Crane Wildlife Refuge also
available.

Woodman's of
Essex $
Main St, Essex;
tel: (978) 768-6451.
The family claims to have
invented the fried clam *circa*
1915 at this outstanding 'in-
the-rough' seafood
restaurant.

Rte 133 in Essex is
lined with antiques
shops for more than a mile.
Most dealers feature small
20th-century collectibles.

Rockport ❹. Route 127A is the alternative, slightly longer route that skirts the eastern coast of the peninsula for steady views of crashing waves. At Rockport, Rte 127 continues for 7 scenic anticlockwise miles through the summer villages of Lanesboro and Annisquam to return to Gloucester.

In Gloucester, veer right on to Rte 133. The landscape switches abruptly from granite cliffs to tidal marshes and barrier beaches for the rest of the route. Continue 4 miles to **Essex⁎ ❺**, a town dedicated to fried clams and antiques shops.

Detour: Three miles past Essex on the right is a turn on to Northgate Rd, which connects to Argilla Rd. Two miles off Rte 133 are the **Crane Properties⁎⁎ ❻**, a turn-of-the-century, 2000-acre estate donated by Chicago industrialist Richard T Crane to the Trustees of Reservations. The Stuart-style mansion and formal plantings of Castle Hill serve as the backdrop to informal picnics and many weddings, but the 5 miles of sandy **Crane Beach⁎⁎ ❼** are the chief summer draw. Surrounding marshes and dunes comprise a famous bird habitat.

Route 1A continues 1 mile into Ipswich village. The 11 miles to **Newburyport ❽** pass through farmland, much of it planted in cutting flowers, and protected wetlands.

Southeastern Massachusetts

Ratings

History	●●●●●
Nature/scenery	●●●●●
Museums	●●●●○
Arts and culture	●●●●○
Beaches	●●●○○
Children	●●○○○
Food and drink	●●○○○
Shopping	●●○○○

In the pantheon of American legend and lore, the Pilgrims are right up there with George Washington, Ben Franklin, Abe Lincoln, Mickey Mouse and baseball slugger Babe Ruth. A fervent group of religious dissidents, they crossed the Atlantic aboard the crowded *Mayflower*, eventually landing on the Massachusetts coast in December 1620, at what they nostalgically called Plymouth – England's first permanent New World settlement north of Virginia, which makes that town a prime destination for patriotic visitors.

By meandering elsewhere on a swing past Cape Cod, you'll come upon grey-shingled coastal villages, plus a pair of working-class burgs: New Bedford, awash in whaling history, and Fall River, with worn-out textile mills for possibly your first impression. Don't let those distract you from Battleship Cove, another source of star-spangled patriotism.

FALL RIVER***

❶ Fall River Tourism Office
1 Government Center; tel: (508) 324-2620; www.fallrivertourism.com

ⓗ Heritage State Park *200 Davol St West; tel: (508) 675-5759.*

Carousel $ *tel: (508) 324-4300. Open June daily 1000–1600, summer 1000–2000; rest of year Sat–Sun 1200–1600.*

This blue-collar city attained prominence as a thriving centre of cotton textile manufacturing from 1811 until the Great Depression of the 1930s. Now some of the huge mills have been converted to factory-outlet shopping warehouses. Fall River remains best known for the unsolved hatchet murder allegedly perpetrated by Lizzie Borden on her father Andrew Jackson Borden and her stepmother Abby in 1892.

Riverfront **Heritage State Park*** is a multiple attraction, having textile-mill historical exhibits as well as providing visitor information. It's alongside a pavilion featuring a 1920s **Carousel***. Dwarfing all else is **Battleship Cove***, where the USS *Massachusetts* can be boarded for on-deck touring (as well as cafeteria-style luncheon meals in the ward room). Also at permanent anchor and open to the public are the USS

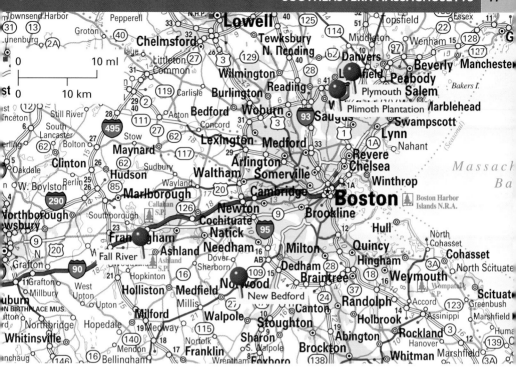

Battleship Cove $
Take Exit 5 off I-195 or Exit 7 off Rte 24 southbound; tel (800) 533-3194 or (508) 678-1100. Open daily 0900–1700.

Marine Museum $
70 Water St; tel: (508) 674-3533. Open Mon–Fri 0900–1700, Sat 1200–1700, Sun & holidays 1300–1700.

Fall River Historical Society $ *451 Rock St; tel: (508) 679-1071. Open Tue–Fri 0900–1630, Sat–Sun 1300–1700 (closed Jan–Mar).*

Joseph P. Kennedy destroyer and USS *Lionfish* submarine, plus the *Hiddensee*, a Russian missile corvette acquired by reunified Germany's Baltic fleet. Two PT torpedo boats (small attack boats used in World War II) stand high and dry in an adjacent shed.

For more nautical stuff, stroll from that armada to Fall River's **Marine Museum❖❖❖**, showcasing an array of *Titanic* memorabilia, including Mrs John Jacob Astor's life-jacket, numerous documents and other artefacts and an intricately detailed 28-ft model of the doomed White Star liner, made for a 1953 Hollywood melodrama.

Uptown, in a 19th-century mill owner's mansion, the **Fall River Historical Society❖** concentrates on period furnishings, decorative arts and, inevitably, details of the notorious Borden case.

Accommodation and food in Fall River

Off the I-195 motorway on the east side of town, the 133-room **Hampton Inn $** *53 Old Bedford Rd, Westport; tel: (800) 426-7866 or (508) 675-8500*, features an indoor pool and complimentary continental breakfast.

The Abbey Grill $$ *100 Rock St; tel: (508) 675-9305*, in a former 1865 church in Fall River's Historic Highlands ('the Hill') neighbourhood, is the dining room of the International Institute of Culinary Arts, so you can look forward to fine, creative cooking.

Downtown's **Eagle $$** *35 N Main St; tel: (508) 677-3788*, is Fall River's oldest restaurant, opened in 1929; a reliable pasta–seafood–steak kind of place.

The pleasantly casual **Waterstreet Café $** *36 Water St; tel: (508) 672-8748*, is conveniently situated on the fringe of the riverfront park.

Right on the park's shoreline, the **Regatta $$** *392 Davol St; tel: (508) 679-4115*, has a huge bar, menu selections suiting everyone's taste and an umbrella-shaded deck for broadside views of Battleship Row's war vessels.

Considering Fall River's strong Portuguese, Azorean and Cape Verdean ethnicity, you're in luck if you'd like to sample some tasty Portuguese cooking. Choose **Estoril $$** *1577 Pleasant St; tel: (508) 677-1200*, or **Sagres $$** *181 Columbia St; tel: (508) 675-7018*.

NEW BEDFORD**

New Bedford District Information Center
33 William St; tel: (800) 508-5353 or (508) 996-6201. Sponsors free walking tours of the Whaling National Historical Park.

New Bedford Whaling Museum $
18 Johnny Cake Hill; tel: (508) 997-0046. Open Mon–Sat 0900–1700, Sun 1300–1700; Sun 1100–1700 (July–Aug).

Seamen's Bethel
15 Johnny Cake Hill; tel: (508) 992-3295. Open mid May–mid Oct Mon–Sat 1000–1600, Sun 1300–1600; rest of year Mon–Fri 1100–1300, Sat 1100–1600, Sun 1300–1600.

Rotch-Jones-Duff House & Garden Museum $
396 County St; tel: (508) 997-1401. Open Tue–Sun 1000–1600.

Founded in 1652 by Baptists and Quakers from the Plymouth Colony, named after Britain's Duke of Bedford, and surpassing Nantucket as the world's leading whaling centre by 1830, New Bedford was home port to 329 whale-hunting ships at the height of prosperity in 1857 – when whalebone was a desirable commodity, used for products including corset stays, umbrella handles and knitting needles; lamps fuelled by whale oil illuminated entire cities. *Moby Dick*, Herman Melville's allegorical masterpiece, immortalised the city and that heady era. It's long gone, but present-day New Bedford still harbours one of the largest commercial fishing and scalloping fleets in the eastern US.

The New Bedford Whaling Museum*** is reason enough to come this way. Devoted to local maritime history, its centre-piece is a walk-on, half-scale model of the *Lagoda*, a square-rigged whaling bark. Here, too, are a 98-ft mural depicting a round-the-world whaling voyage, a humpback whale's skeleton, galleries displaying scrimshaw (etchings on whalebone), ship models, figureheads, whaling implements, photographs, folk art and paintings. A 22-minute film captures the adventure of an actual whaling chase.

In Moby Dick, Melville set an evocative scene in the grey clapboard **Seamen's Bethel****, an 1832 chapel with a preacher's pulpit shaped like the bowsprit of a whaleboat. Marble cenotaphs memorialise crewmen lost at sea.

A 22-room Greek Revival mansion is the focal point of the **Rotch-Jones-Duff House & Garden Museum***. Built by a Quaker merchant, it reflects the lifestyles of three privileged families who resided here between 1834 and 1981.

Accommodation and food in New Bedford

Two homey inns are welcoming alternatives to the area's chain hotels: **Cynthia & Steven's Bed & Breakfast $** *36 Seventh St; tel: (508) 997-6433*, and **Orchard Street Manor $** *139 Orchard St; tel: (508) 984-3475*.

Davy's Locker $$ *1489 E Rodney French Blvd; tel: (508) 992-7359*. Overlooking Clark's Cove, primarily a seafood restaurant but also serving steaks, chicken and ribs.

Freestone's City Grill $–$$ *41 William St; tel: (508) 993-7477*. The historic district's standout, in a rock-solid recycled 19th-century bank building with fireplace and mahogany woodwork; casual atmosphere for fish chowder, grilled seafood, char-grilled hamburgers and serious salads.

Left
The Battleship USS *Massachusetts*, now a World War II naval memorial, anchored in the Fall River

PLIMOTH PLANTATION***

Plimoth Plantation $$$ *Rte 3A; tel: (508) 746-1622. Open Apr–Nov daily 0900–1700.*

A re-created 1627 village where interpreters attired in Pilgrim garb cook, harvest, tend farm animals, make candles and clapboards, play games and speak to visitors in authentic Elizabethan dialect. Just outside the stockade settlement, a Wampanoag campsite demonstrates Native American folkways at the time of the Pilgrims' arrival. Stay in Plymouth (just 3 miles away) if you are visiting Plimoth Plantation.

PLYMOUTH***

Plymouth Visitors Information Center *130 Water St; tel: (800) 872-1620 or (508) 747-7525.*

Pilgrim Hall Museum $ *75 Court St; tel: (508) 746-1620. Open Feb–Dec daily 0930–1630.*

Sites recalling *circa*-1620 Pilgrim endurance are close together in this handsome old town. In Plymouth centre, **Pilgrim Hall Museum**** houses pertinent portraits, furniture, maps and humble clothing and personal effects. A remarkable number of artefact-filled historic dwellings can be visited – among them the 1749 **Spooner House****, owned by generations of Spooners for 200 years.

Down on harbourside Water St, a Grecian portico shelters **Plymouth Rock**, supposedly the stepping-stone where the newcomers clambered ashore after their 66 days at sea.

That suspicious boulder is outmatched by the *Mayflower II***, a faithful replica of the original three-masted bark. Sailing from

The Pilgrims

Early in the 17th century, a group of religious dissidents – many from the northern English village of Scrooby – rebelled under the strict rules and rituals imposed by the Church of England. Led by William Brewster and William Bradford, these Separatists were systematically hunted down and arrested for their defiant beliefs. A sizeable number of families sailed from England to Leyden in the Netherlands; once there, however, they became concerned about losing their English way of life. So some of them decided to emigrate to colonial America, where they believed they could have religious freedom while remaining English.

On 16 September, 1620, 102 passengers and a crew of 26 began the long and difficult journey across the frigid Atlantic. They sailed aboard the *Mayflower*, a small-capacity merchant vessel. It measured merely 104ft long, 25ft wide and, because of a late start, encountered the season's stormiest weather. The passengers spent much of their time below deck in cramped quarters while the ship bucked winds and downpours.

The Pilgrims had planned to sail for Virginia, but raging gales blew them north. They finally stepped ashore at what is now Provincetown on Cape Cod on 21 November, then at Plymouth on 16 December. Scurvy and the extremely harsh weather claimed the lives of about half the Pilgrims during the first gruelling winter on land.

With the help of Native American inhabitants, the new arrivals learned how to grow vegetables, fish and hunt. Pilgrims and tribespeople joined together for a harvest festival in 1621, which Americans now celebrate as Thanksgiving Day on the fourth Thursday in November.

Plimoth Plantation

ⓘ Spooner House $
27 North St; tel: (508)
746-0012. Open July–Aug
Thur–Sat 1000–1600; June,
Sept–mid Oct Thur–Sat
1000–1530.

Mayflower II $
State Pier off Water St;
tel: (508) 746-1622.
Open July–Aug daily
0900–1900; Apr–June &
Sept–Nov daily 0900–1700.
Available: combination $$$
Plimoth Plantation/
Mayflower II admittance.

**Cranberry World
Visitors' Center**
225 Water St; tel: (508)
747-2350. Open May–Nov
daily 0930–1700.

Plymouth, England, in 1954, it followed the original vessel's transatlantic course. On-board narrators provide vivid insights into the Pilgrims' seagoing hardships while making their long 17th-century journey to the New World.

Switching to modern times, the Ocean Spray cooperative's **Cranberry World Visitors' Center*** details the growing and harvesting of the area's cash crop.

Accommodation and food in Plymouth

Two properties, each with a restaurant and swimming-pool, are recommendable. The **John Carver Inn $–$$** 25 Summer St; tel: (800) 274-1620 or (508) 746-7100, is downtown. Overlooking the waterfront is the **Governor Bradford Motor Inn $** 98 Water St; tel: (800) 332-1620 or (508) 246-6200.

For seafood dining, choose from among three harbour-view eateries: **Isaac's $$** 114 Water St; tel: (508) 830-0001; **Weathervane $$** 6 Town Wharf; tel: (508) 746-4195; and **Wood's Seafood Market & Restaurant $** Town Pier; tel: (508) 746-0261.

Many of the buildings in New Bedford feature in Herman Melville's novel *Moby Dick*

Suggested tour

Total distance: 97 miles

Time: You'll need enough time for adequate, non-rushed sightseeing – especially in Fall River, New Bedford and Plymouth. So allow at least 2 full days.

Links: Driving west beyond Fall River, you can join the Providence/ Pawtucket Route *(see page 160)*. From the Plymouth vicinity, you connect with the Cape Cod, Mass., Route *(see page 84)* or the Boston, Route *(see page 42)*. A summer-season ferry-boat service from New Bedford links that city with Martha's Vineyard *(see page 89)*.

Route: Leaving Fall River, take the time for a scenic drive by forsaking the I-195 motorway at Exit 10. Head south 10 miles on Rte 88, leading to the high sand dunes of 2-mile-long **Horseneck Beach State Reservation** ❶. Then follow signs for a north-by-east loop via salt marshes and boat harbours. Tiny communities to seek out within the Westport and South Dartmouth townships are **Pandanarum Village** ❷, **Russell Mills Village** ❸, **Central Village** ❹ and **Westport** ❺, all dating from US colonial times.

At North Dartmouth, take Rte 6 to head 1 mile into **NEW BEDFORD** ❻; follow Kempton St to reach downtown's historic waterfront area. Back on Rte 6, cross the Acushnet River bridge to arrive in **Fairhaven** ❼, where Rte 6 coincides with Huttleston St, named after Standard Oil tycoon Henry Huttleston Rogers, a native son and civic benefactor. His generosity becomes evident in Centre St's 1894 **Town Hall** ❽, resembling a Flemish Castle. Standing directly across the street is the equally flamboyant 1893 **Millicent Public Library** ❾, an Italian Renaissance show-piece inside and out. Continue west on Centre St to Old Fort Rd, where you'll reach **Fort Phoenix** ❿, bristling with six Revolutionary War cannons; here US militiamen repulsed British invaders on 7 September 1778. High ground affords panoramic views of Buzzards Bay and New Bedford's harbour.

East from Fairhaven, Rte 6 curves alongside jagged coastline. After 3 miles, you'll be in **Mattapoisett** ⓫, where most of New Bedford's

Fairhaven Visitors Center *27 Center St, Fairhaven; tel: (508) 979-4805.*

Cape Cod Region Chamber of Commerce *70 N Main St, Buzzards Bay; tel: (508) 759-6000,* provides information about the Outer Cape's Marion/Onset/Wareham area.

whaling ships were built between 1752 and 1878 – barks, brigs, sloops, schooners, launched at six shipyards. Herman Melville's 1841 sea duty on the *Acushnet* inspired the *Moby Dick* saga. Early 19th-century shingle-sided houses line Water St. Next comes **Marion ⑫**, the most affluent village on Buzzards Bay's western shore, with a sizeable millionaire population and, at Sippican Harbor, the 1872 Beverly Yacht Club, America's second-oldest after its counterpart in New York City.

Passing cranberry bogs, continue another 6 miles to Wareham. Consider a short detour to **Onset ⑬**, a placid Victorian hamlet overlooking Onset Bay and the public beach at **Fort Independence ⑭**. Departing Wareham, drive through Buzzards Bay village, then follow Rte 6 alongside the Cape Cod Canal in order to reach Rte 3. (This entails careful sign-reading, and you'll encounter two daredevil roundabouts at cross-bridge approaches to Cape Cod. Stay calm.) Shortly after turning on to Rte 3, take Exit 2 for scenic Rte 3A to head north past cranberry bogs while enjoying ocean views. Turn on to Rte 3 – but soon thereafter veer on to Rte 3A for a drive alongside Cape Cod Bay. At Manomet Point, adjoining **White Horse Beach ⑮** and **Priscilla Beach ⑯** form a sandy crescent. They're 1 mile south of **Plimoth Plantation ⑰** which, in turn, is 3 miles south of **PLYMOUTH ⑱**.

Cape Cod and its Islands

Ratings

Beaches	●●●●●
Nature/ scenery	●●●●●
Children	●●●●○
Food and drink	●●●○○
Museums	●●●○○
Shopping	●●●○○
Arts and culture	●●○○○
History	●●○○○

On a map, Cape Cod resembles a strongman's flexed arm, with Falmouth on the triceps, Chatham at the elbow and Provincetown the clenched fist. Many New Englanders equate Cape Cod with summer, as it has been the holiday spot of choice for nearly a century. The finest recreational beaches in the Northeast attract literally millions of visitors to a region with a winter population in tens of thousands. Yet much of the Cape remains seemingly deserted, a landscape of windswept dunes and relentless surf, or of tranquil farmland dotted with windmills and saltbox houses. Depending on the town, Cape Cod can spell days of indolence in the sun or non-stop partying, dining and shopping.

CAPE COD BAY✢✢

⊕ Sandwich Glass Museum $ *129 Main St; tel: (508) 888-0251. Open Apr–Oct daily 0900–1700, Nov, Dec, Feb, Mar Wed–Sun 0930–1600.*

Thornton Burgess Museum $ *4 Water St; tel: (508) 888-6870. Open Mon–Sat 1000–1600, Sun 1300–1600.*

The placid communities of Cape Cod Bay are strung along the old King's Highway, Rte 6A. They are preserves of 18th- and early 19th-century houses (many converted to B&Bs), village greens and antiques dealers. Closest to Boston, **Sandwich**✢✢ features three museums. The **Sandwich Glass Museum**✢ chronicles the local pressed glass industry that flourished 1828–88. The charming **Thornton Burgess Museum**✢ features a collection of the author's children's books and original illustrations. **Heritage Plantation of Sandwich**✢✢ has spectacular rhododendron gardens and several buildings exhibiting Indian artefacts, Colonial furniture and weapons, and vintage automobiles. Along with sea captains' homes, **Dennis**✢✢ boasts the **Cape Cod Playhouse**✢✢, last of the summer stock venues. On the same grounds, the **Cape Museum of Fine Arts**✢ displays work by local artists.

0   10 ml
0   10 km

Massachusetts Bay

Cape Cod Bay

Cape Cod National Seashore

Outer Cape

Nantucket Sound

Nantucket Island

Martha's Vineyard

Cape Cod Bay

Cent Hyannis

East Falmouth

Falmouth

Rhode Island Sound

Heritage Plantation of Sandwich $$ *Grove and Pine Sts; tel: (508) 888-3300. Open mid May–Oct daily 1000–1700.*

Cape Museum of Fine Arts $ *Main St, Rte 6A, Dennis; tel: (508) 385-4477. Open Tue–Sat 1000–1700, Sun 1300–1700.*

Cape Cod Museum of Natural History $ *Rte 6A; tel: (508) 896-3867. Open Mon–Sat 0930–1630, Sun 1230–1630.*

Cape Cod Playhouse *Main St, Dennis; tel: (508) 385-3911.*

Almost at the geographic centre of Cape Cod, **Brewster**❖❖ capitalises on its sedate landscape. The activities at the **Cape Cod Museum of Natural History**❖❖ target younger children, but the 82-acre site also contains three self-guided nature trails. The 2000 acres of **Nickerson State Park**❖❖❖ are dotted with glacial kettle ponds and tracked with trails. Directly across Rte 6A from Nickerson is **Linnell Landing Beach**❖❖, with excellent wheelchair access.

Accommodation and food on Cape Cod Bay

Nickerson State Park *3488 Main St, Rte 6A; tel: (508) 896-3491.* Camping reservations: *(508) 896-4615.* Nickerson's 420 tent and recreational vehicle (RV) pitches ($) are the Cape's most popular.

Ocean Edge Resort and Golf Club $$–$$$ *2907 Main St, Brewster; tel: (800) 343-6074 or (508) 896-9000.* Lodging choices include rooms in a massive stone hotel or self-catering condo units on this property with a private beach and the Cape's best golf course.

Wingscorton Farm Inn $$–$$$ *11 Wing Blvd, E Sandwich; tel: (508) 888-0534.* An unusual opportunity to stay in the 1758 farmhouse of this working 13-acre farm.

Chillingsworth $$$ *2449 Main St, Brewster; tel: (508) 896-3640.* This classic French restaurant is a top Cape dining destination.

CAPE COD NATIONAL SEASHORE❖❖❖

Cape Cod National Seashore Salt Pond Visitor Center *Rte 6, Eastham; tel: (508) 255-3421. Open mid March–Dec dawn–dusk.*

Provincelands Visitor Center *Rte 6, Provincetown; tel: (508) 487-1256. Open late May–early Sept dawn to dusk.*

The best way to explore the marsh near Nauset Beach is by canoe or kayak, either of which can be rented from **Goose Hummock Shop** $$$ *15 Rte 6A, Orleans; tel: (508) 255-0455.*

The National Seashore encompasses almost 45,000 acres of fragile dunes, fertile marshes, woodlands and deserts, cranberry bogs, cedar forest and long sandy beaches along a 40-mile stretch between **Chatham** and **Provincetown**. Ranger-led programmes explore these varied ecosystems. Little explanation is required to enjoy the beaches, which include **Coast Guard Beach**❖❖, with excellent surfing; **Nauset Light Beach**❖❖, with good surfing and surf-casting; **Head of the Meadow Beach**❖❖❖, with great views of Provincetown and Truro dunelands; **Race Point Beach**❖❖❖, with spectacular dunes and some of the Cape's finest swimming; and **Herring Cove Beach**❖❖, which has the calmest waters and faces west into the sunset. Lifeguards are posted late June–early Sept. Watch for heavy surf and rip tides.

CHATHAM✦✦✦

ⓘ Chatham Chamber of Commerce Info Booth 533 Main St; tel: (800) 715-5567 and (508) 945-5199.

ⓜ Old Atwood House Museum $ 347 Stage Harbor Rd; tel: (508) 947-2493. Open mid June–Sept Tue–Fri 1300–1600.

South Monomoy Island tours $$$ are operated by the **Massachusetts Audubon Society** tel: (508) 349-2615 and the **Cape Cod Museum of Natural History** tel: (508) 896-3867.

◐ Band Nights tel: (508) 945-5199. Fri evening band concerts held in Kate Gould Park during July and Aug are best enjoyed with chocolate-covered cranberries from Chatham Candies on Main St.

Chatham is a close-knit community where its shell fishermen harvest some of the world's finest clams, oysters and mussels and the whole town turns out for civic band concerts. Art galleries and boutiques dominate the village. The **Old Atwood House Museum**✦ details local history and display provocative murals by Alice Stallknect depicting Christ as a modern fisherman. **Sheltered Oyster Pond Beach**✦✦, just a block from Main St, is superb for small children. The long strand of **Chatham Light Beach**✦✦ is reached from the lighthouse car-park. Naturalist organisations operate tours of **South Monomoy Island**✦✦✦, a barrier island bird sanctuary.

Accommodation and food in Chatham

Above right
Chatham Band Night

Chatham Wayside Inn $$ 512 Main St; tel: (800) 391-5734 or (508) 945-5550. In the village centre, an 1860 inn with restored rooms lies at the heart of a recent expansion.

Impudent Oyster $$ *15 Chatham Bars Ave; tel: (508) 945-3545.* A good place for fresh fish and cold draft beer.

Port Fortune Inn $$ *201 Main St; tel: (800) 850-0792 or (508) 945-0792.* This recently renovated B&B near Chatham Light features 14 rooms.

Sea in the Rough $–$$ *Rte 28; tel: (508) 945-1700.* Casual spot to sample Chatham shellfish.

FALMOUTH

Falmouth Chamber of Commerce *20 Academy Ln; tel: (800) 526-8532 or (508) 548-8500.* Provides an excellent brochure, *A Walk Through Falmouth History.*

Woods Hole Oceanographic Institute Exhibit Center *$ 15 Market St, Woods Hole; tel: (508) 457-2000.* Open Apr–Oct Tue–Sat 1000–1630, Sun 1200–1630.

National Marine Fisheries Service Aquarium *Albatross St, Woods Hole; tel: (508) 548-7684.* Open mid June–mid Sept daily 1000–1600 (closed Sat–Sun during remainder of year). Free

Handsome **Falmouth**❖❖, with its fine old village centre and green, is usually bypassed in the rush to get to Woods Hole, but has fine architecture, a striking yacht harbour and good swimming beaches.

The picturesque village of **Woods Hole**❖❖ is an enclave of oceanographic research. The **Woods Hole Oceanographic Institute Exhibit Center**❖❖ focuses on underwater research. The **National Marine Fisheries Service Aquarium**❖❖ eschews high tech in favour of educational exhibits of commercially important local fish.

Accommodation and food in Falmouth

Palmer House Inn $$–$$$ *81 Palmer Ave; tel: (800) 472-2632 or (508) 548-1230.* Full-blown Victorian frills in the village centre. There is a separate suite on the grounds that is ideal for romantic getaways.

Park Beach Ocean Front Motel $–$$ *241 Grand Ave S; tel: (800) 341-5700 or (508) 548-1010.* Two-storey motel sits across the street from Falmouth Heights beach.

Regatta of Falmouth-by-the-Sea $$–$$$ *217 Clinton Ave; tel: (508) 548-5400.* Spectacular gourmet dining at yacht harbour.

HYANNIS❖

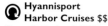
Hyannisport Harbor Cruises $$ *Ocean St Dock; tel: (508) 778-2600* makes a narrated hour-long tour past the Kennedy family compound.

All Cape highways converge in Hyannis, the sprawling commercial centre of the Cape haunted by memories of President Kennedy. The exhibits at the modest **John F Kennedy Hyannis Museum**❖❖ include many of the most memorable photographs of the president and his family, taken at the nearby Kennedy compound.

Accommodation in Hyannis

DeCota Family Inn $–$$ *Rte 132, Hyannis; tel: (508) 362-3957.* With a lakefront beach, this 24-room motel is excellent for families.

John F Kennedy Hyannis Museum $
397 Main St; tel: (508) 790-3077. Open mid Apr–mid Oct Mon–Sat 1000–1600, Sun 1300–1600. Call for off-season hours.

Right
Nob light stands between Falmouth and Woods Hole

MARTHA'S VINEYARD***

Martha's Vineyard Chamber of Commerce *Beach Rd, Vineyard Haven; tel: (508) 693-0085.*

Martha's Vineyard & Nantucket Steamship Authority *tel: (508) 477-8600. Provides the only year-round and only auto crossings (reservation essential) to Martha's Vineyard. Operates all year between Woods Hole and Vineyard Haven and adds summer service to Oak Bluffs.*

Martha's Vineyard Preservation Trust *$ 99 Main St, Edgartown; tel: (508) 627-8619. Tours of three historic properties offered daily in summer, Mon–Sat during spring and autumn; call for hours.*

Of the two large islands off Cape Cod, 100-square-mile Martha's Vineyard offers more for day-trippers who often don't get beyond the tourist shops and ice-cream parlours of **Vineyard Haven***. Oak **Bluffs*** is the home of Martha's Vineyard Camp Meeting Association, with more than 300 gingerbread cottages. The downtown carousel is one of America's oldest. The majestic whaling captains' homes in **Edgartown***, with their signature white clapboards and black shutters, lend historic charm to the Vineyard town with the most amenities and best beach access. **Martha's Vineyard Preservation Society** offers a tour of two houses and the 1843 Old Whaling Church. Three-mile **Katama Beach*** has good surfing and many shore birds. A ferry at the foot of Dock St makes a 2-minute crossing to **Chappaquiddick Island***, where the Cape Pogue Wildlife Refuge has 2 miles of stunning beach. **Menemsha*** is the Vineyard's last working fishing village. The Aquinnah Wampanoag tribe owns the **Gay Head cliffs*** at the southwestern end of the island. The brightly-coloured cliffs, sacred to the tribe, capture 100 million years of geological history in layers of sand, gravel and clay.

Accommodation and food on Martha's Vineyard

Colonial Inn $$–$$$ *38 N Water St, Edgartown; tel: (508) 627-4711.* One of Edgartown's larger properties, central to the shopping district and waterfront.

Striped Bass and Bluefish Derby *tel: (508) 693-0728.* Martha's Vineyard is known for sport fishing; this competition takes place mid-Sept–mid-Oct.

Yellow Line Public Bus Service $ *tel: (508) 693-1589* connects the villages of Edgartown, Oak Bluffs and Vineyard Haven. **Martha's Vineyard Bus Tour $$$** *tel: (508) 693-1589 offers a 2½-hour tour of the Island, including a stop at Gay Head cliffs.* **Martha's Bike Rentals $$$** *4 Lagoon Point Rd,* **Vineyard Haven;** *tel: (508) 693; tel: (508) 693; tel: (508) 693; tel: (508) 693-6593 is next to the steamship docks.*

Larsen's Fish Market $–$$ *Menemsha Harbor; tel: (508) 645-2680.* Fish market cooks steamers, lobsters and mussels to order and always has a supply of chowder and crab cakes.

Lothrop Merry House $$–$$$ *Owen Park, Vineyard Haven; tel: (508) 693-1646.* Seven-room historic B&B has tiny private beach and boats for guest use.

Nancy's $–$$ *Oak Bluffs Harbor; tel: (508) 693-0006.* Excellent fish and chips, lobster rolls and stuffed quahogs (round-shell clams) to eat at picnic tables overlooking harbour.

Seafood Shanty $$ *31 Dock St, Edgartown; tel: (508) 627-8622.* Spacious room looks out on harbour; specialises in local shellfish.

Tuscany Inn $$–$$$ *22 N Water St, Edgartown; tel: (508) 627-5999.* Italianate Victorian home brings a touch of Mediterranean to Martha's Vineyard. Seats in the five-table dining-room ($$$) are in great demand.

Webb's Camping Area $ *Barnes Rd, Oak Bluffs; tel: (508) 693-0233.* Wooded camping 3 miles from either Vineyard Haven or Oak Bluffs.

Wesley Hotel $$ *70 Lake Ave, Oak Bluffs; tel: (508) 693-6611.* Victorian resort hotel overlooking harbour also has modern rooms in a new annexe.

Right
This horse-shoe crab is for studying by naturalists, not for eating

NANTUCKET ISLAND✦✦✦

ⓘ **Nantucket Chamber of Commerce** *48 Main St; tel: (508) 228-1700.*

Ⓑ **Nantucket Regional Transit Authority** $ *tel: (508) 228-7025* operates a bus service between villages and a seasonal beach shuttle. At Steamship Wharf, **Nantucket Bike Shop** *tel: (508) 228-1999* and **Young's Bicycle Shop** *tel: (508) 228-1151* rent bicycles and mopeds. **Great Point Natural History Tours** $$$ *tel: (508) 228-6799* traverse the dunes and barrier beach at the northeast tip of the island in four-wheel-drive vehicles.

ⓜ **Nantucket Whaling Museum** $ *Broad and South Beach Sts; tel: (508) 228-1894. Open late May–mid Oct daily 1000–1700, (daily 1100–1500 remainder of Oct), Nov–late May Sat–Sun 1100–1500.*

First Congregational Church $ *62 Centre St; no tel. Tower open mid June–mid Oct Mon–Sat 1000–1600, also July–Aug Wed 1800–2000.*

ⓐ **Daffodil Festival** *tel: (508) 228-1700.* Celebrates the bloom of more than three million daffodils in late Apri

Thirty miles out to sea, the island of Nantucket stands aloof from the Cape's hubbub. Quaker whalers made Nantucket's fortunes, and their Spartan mien still influences local style. The island is small enough to negotiate on a bicycle, yet dense enough with natural and historic sites to be endlessly beguiling.

The **Nantucket Whaling Museum**✦✦✦, kingpin site of the Nantucket Historical Society, illuminates the enterprise and adventure that made Nantucket rich. The landscape and layout of the island are best appreciated from the belfry look-out of the **First Congregational Church**✦✦. Tiny houses with roses climbing their walls and roofs dominate the former fishing village of **Sconset**✦✦, now an up market preserve on the east end of the island.

Accommodation and food on Nantucket Island

Camping is prohibited on Nantucket and caravans are not permitted on the island.

Café at Le Languedoc $–$$ *24 Broad St; tel: (508) 228-2552.* Cheery basement café is the bargain sibling of one of Nantucket's best French restaurants.

Jared Coffin House $$–$$$ *29 Broad St; tel: (800) 248-2405 or (508) 228-2400.* This brick mansion is a social centre of island life; 60 rooms are spread among six buildings. The restaurant's ($$$) Wed and Sun seafood buffets attract many islanders.

Quaker House Inn $$ *5 Chestnut St; tel: (508) 228-9156.* Small rooms are simply but comfortably furnished. The chef gives Nantucket shellfish their imaginative due at **Kendrick's**, the street-level restaurant ($$$).

Ship's Inn $$–$$$ *13 Fair St; tel: (508) 228-0040.* There are ten guest rooms in this 1831 whaling captain's home as well as a gourmet restaurant ($$$) where the chef creates a new lobster dish each year.

Straight Wharf Fish Store $ *Harbor Sq; tel: (508) 228-1095.* Outstanding take-away items include lobster rolls, seafood gumbo and swordfish sandwiches.

The Wauwinet $$–$$$ *120 Wauwinet Rd; tel: (800) 426-8718 or (508) 228-0145.* Posh resort next to Great Point Nature Preserve houses the island's leading gourmet restaurant ($$$).

NANTUCKET SOUND*

Roadside development has run amok on Rte 28 between Hyannis and Chatham, but good bargain motels are found here, and striking sandy beaches usually lie less than a mile south of the highway.

Accommodation on Nantucket Sound

Campers Haven $ *184 Old Wharf Rd, Dennisport; tel: (508) 398-2811.* This 265-pitch campground has a private beach on Nantucket Sound.

Town and Country Motor Lodge $ *452 Main St, Rte 28, W Yarmouth; tel: (800) 992-2340* or *(508) 771-0212.* This complex about 5 miles from the beach has 150 rooms, 3 pools, sauna, whirlpool and putting green.

Pilgrims at Provincetown

Popular history forgets that the *Mayflower* Pilgrims didn't make their first landfall on Plymouth Rock, but on the sandy shores of Provincetown. After raiding the grain stores of the Nauset tribe in nearby Wellfleet, they sailed on to settle Plymouth – but not before signing the Mayflower Compact, which would become the first building block of American self-governance. That first landing is commemorated by Provincetown's 255-ft Pilgrim Monument, the tallest granite structure in the US.

OUTER CAPE**

Art's Dune Tours $$ *Standish and Commercial Sts, Provincetown; tel: (508) 487-1950,* in operation since 1946, are the best way to tour the environmentally sensitive dune habitat. Book early for the sunset tour.

Dolphin Fleet of Provincetown $$$ *tel: (508) 349-1900* operate whale-watching boats staffed by naturalists.

The most dynamic landscapes of the forearm of Cape Cod belong to the **Cape Cod National Seashore***, but the towns of Wellfleet and Provincetown pulse with human activity. **Provincetown**** conjoins an art colony, a Portuguese fishing village and a gay and lesbian resort. **Provincetown Art Association*** has an outstanding collection of work by some of America's leading artists – including Edward Hopper and Robert Motherwell – who chose to paint the interstice of sea, land and sky on the outer Cape. Naturalist excursions include **guided dune tours** and **whale-watching cruises**. Wellfleet Bay Wildlife Sanctuary, with nearly every natural habitat found on Cape Cod is a magnet for bird-watchers. Wellfleet Drive-In, one of the regions last outdoor movie theatres, turns its car-park to good use by day when it serves as the venue for a huge flea market.

Provincetown Art Association $ *460 Commercial St; tel: (508) 487-1750. Open June–mid Sept daily 1200–1700 and 2000–2200, Nov–Apr Sat–Sun 1200–1600.*

Wellfleet Drive-In and Flea Market *Rte 6A; tel: (508) 349-2520. Cape Cod's largest flea market is held mid-Apr–Sept on Sat–Sun, also on Wed–Thur during July–Aug.*

Accommodation and food on the Outer Cape

Beaconlight Guesthouse $$–$$$ *12 Winthrop St, Provincetown; tel: (800) 696-9603 or (508) 487-9603.* Transplanted Brits create a country house feel in this 15-room inn that welcomes couples of all sexual orientations.

Dancing Lobster Cafe/Trattoria $$–$$$ *463 Commercial St, Provincetown; tel: (508) 487-0900.* One of the best places to eat fish in Provincetown.

Surfside Inn $–$$ *543 Commercial St, Provincetown; tel: (508) 487-1726.* Large motor inn outside town centre boasts private beach.

The Moors $–$$ *Bradford St Ext, Provincetown; tel: (508) 487-0840.* Portuguese seafood restaurant recalls Provincetown's fishing heritage.

Right
Artists are everywhere in Provincetown

❶ Cape Cod Chamber of Commerce and Visitor Bureau *jct Rtes 6 and 132, Hyannis; tel: (888) 332-2732 or (508) 362-3225* offers information for the entire Cape.

❷ Two bottleneck bridges cross Cape Cod Canal: **Bourne Bridge (Rte 28)** on the west and **Sagamore Bridge** (Rte 6) on the east.

❸ Aficionados cite semi-professional **Cape Cod Baseball League** as the purest surviving example of the all-American game. Schedule is posted in the *Cape Cod Times*. Free admission.

Suggested tour

Total distance: 192 miles; ferry detours add 66 miles

Duration: 8 hours' driving in July–Aug, 5 hours' rest of year. Allow 5–6 days. Those with limited time should follow Rte 6 and focus on Cape Cod National Seashore.

Links: Connects via Rte 3 or Rte 6 to Southeastern Massachusetts Route (*see page 76*).

Route: Begin at Bourne Bridge at the west end of Cape Cod Canal, heading south 4 miles on Rte 28. Veer right on to Rte 28A to follow shoreline road past beaches and quiet villages for 5 miles before returning to Rte 28, 3 miles north of **FALMOUTH ❶**. At Falmouth, follow Woods Hole Rd 4.5 miles to Woods Hole.

Detour: Take the ferry to **MARTHA'S VINEYARD ❷**.

Backtrack from Woods Hole to Falmouth and follow Rte 28 east for 10 miles and turn left on Great Neck Rd N to **Mashpee*❸**, a village set aside in 1660 as a Wampanoag reservation. Turn left on Rte 130 to visit the **Mashpee Wampanoag Indian Museum*❹**. Follow Rte 130 south 2 miles to rejoin Rte 28, which passes through several wealthy villages in the 10 miles into **HYANNIS ❺**.

Detour: Take the ferry to **NANTUCKET ISLAND ❻**.

The 23 miles of Rte 28 east of Hyannis *en route* to **CHATHAM ❼** usually suffer the Cape's worst traffic. Periodic breaks for oceanfront scenery along **NANTUCKET SOUND ❽** can be made by turning south on any large street. At Chatham, Rte 28 doglegs north, following the Nauset Marsh 10 miles to Orleans, where Rte 6 is the only road extending the length of the **OUTER CAPE ❾**, passing all of the entry points to the **CAPE COD NATIONAL SEASHORE ❿** in a 34-mile stretch to **Provincetown ⓫**.

From Provincetown, backtrack 34 miles to the Orleans traffic roundabout and take Rte 6A for 5 miles to Brewster, another 6 miles to Dennis and another 18 miles to **Sandwich ⓬**, watching for art potters, art galleries and antiques dealers along the way. Just over a mile west of Sandwich, Rte 6A joins Rte 6 at the Sagamore roundabout. A 5-mile drive west along the Cape Cod Canal returns to the starting point. Alternatively, Rte 3 from the roundabout crosses the Sagamore Bridge and continues north to Plymouth .

North Scituate
ompatuck
Scituate
123 Greenbush
inippi Marshfield Hills
3 Humarock
139 Ocean Bluff
Marshfield Brant Rock
Pembroke Green Harbor
3A
antville JOHN ALDEN HOUSE
53 Duxbury
S. Duxbury
27 MYLES STANDISH MON.
106 Kingston
Plymouth
80 3 PILGRIM MEM. S.P. (PLYMOUTH ROCK)
Plympton PLIMOTH PLANTATION
er 44 White Horse Beach
oro Carver Manomet Beach
58 MYLES 3A
STANDISH
Garver S.P. Vallersville
South Middleboro 3
28 White
areham Island
Wareham Shores
25 6 Sagamore Beach
Onset SUSSET BEACH ST. RES.
Buzzards Bay Sagamore
Monument 6A Sandwich
E. Marion Beach Bourne East Sandwich
195 Marion 6A
Pocasset Barnstable
Mattapoisett Forestdale 14
ven N. Falmouth 149 Wakeby
nix St. Res. Mashpee 28
28A 3 4 Centerville
151 Cotuit Osterville
Buzzards
West Falmouth East Falmouth
Bay Popponesset
Seasonal) Sippewisset Teaticket Beach
Falmouth 1 South Cape Beach
Woods Hole S.P.
MARINE FISHERIES SERVICE
AQUARIUM
shon I.
OLD SCHOOLHOUSE
MUS. 2 Vineyard Haven
Oak Bluffs
Joseph Sylvia
hawena I. S.B.
North Tisbury MANUEL
CORRELLUS Ferry
West Tisbury S.F. Edgartown
nemsha VINEYARD Chappaquiddick I.
MUS.
Chilmark Katama
Nashaquitsa Martha's
Vineyard

Cape Cod
Bay

PROVINCE LANDS VIS. CTR.
RACE POINT LIGHTHOUSE 11 Provincetown
PILGRIM MON. North Truro
Long Pt. HIGHLAND LIGHTHOUSE
Truro
South Truro 6
Wellfleet
South Wellfleet
MARCONI STATION SITE
Cape Cod
North Eastham 10 NAUSET BEACH LIGHTHOUSE
Eastham SALT POND VIS. CTR.
Orleans 13
East Brewster 6A East Orleans
Brewster 9
S.P. South Orleans
East Dennis 137
Dennis 28 East Harwich
134
South RAILROAD MUS.
Yarmouth 10 Dennis 39 7 Chatham
6 Harwich CHATHAM LIGHTHOUSE
S. Yarmouth Dennis Port
5
Hyannis West Yarmouth
Monomoy I.
8
Monomy Pt.

Nantucket Sound

NANTUCKET Great Pt.
N.W.R.

Wauwinet
Quidnet
Polpis
WHALING MUS. Sankaty Head
Tuckernuck I. Nantucket
Madaket 6 Siasconset
Muskeget Surfside
Channel Muskeget I.
Nantucket Island

0   10 ml
R.

0   10 km

Pioneer Valley

Ratings

Arts and culture	●●●●
History	●●●●
Museums	●●●●
Food and drink	●●●
Children	●●
Nature/ scenery	●●
Shopping	●●
Beaches and watersports	●

By the time it reaches Massachusetts, the Connecticut River is wide and imposing, carving a flat floodplain hemmed by rolling hills on either side. Farms have flourished here since tiny Deerfield was a colonial outpost in the early 1700s, and homes from that era still grace village greens.

For travellers, the highlights of the centre of Massachusetts are two quite different historical villages, of different eras, different styles and with different artefacts and interpretation. Serious collectors should visit Historic Deerfield, which unlike Old Sturbridge Village, is not a museum village showing how people lived. Deerfield focuses on the artefacts, and a fine collection it has. Families and those who like to learn how people lived in other times and places shouldn't miss Old Sturbridge Village. Most visitors try to see both.

DEERFIELD^{❖❖❖}

ⓘ Pioneer Valley Tourist Information Center Rte 5/10, South Deerfield; tel: (413) 665-7333.

Deerfield's several museum houses are seen by tours, scheduled so you cannot see them all in a day. Make straight away for the Visitors Center opposite the Deerfield Inn to sign up. All tours are limited, so early arrivals get the day's best choices.

Ask first for the **Hinsdale and Anna Williams House❖❖**, home of a prosperous merchant in the early 1800s, and **Stebbins House❖❖**, an earlier home with fine examples of decorative arts. For an interesting look at the mid-1700 village, when revolutionary plotting was afoot, visit **Barnard Tavern❖❖**, and its upstairs assembly room. Some of the finest needlework examples are in **Allen House❖**, a bit of a hodge-podge, but well worth asking for; it is often the only way to see the extraordinary **Textile Museum❖❖❖** with its collections of early

Historic Deerfield
$$ Rte 5; tel: (413) 774-5581. Open daily 0930–1630, tours 1000–1600. All houses shown only on guided tours. Special advance arrangements for private tours (up to four people) focusing on special interests, such as needlework.

Memorial Hall Museum
$ Memorial St; tel: (413) 774-3768. Open May–Oct daily 0930–1630. Admission free with Historic Deerfield unlimited tour ticket.

costumes and bed coverings. Those and the **Silver and Metalware Collection**✧✧ are grouped into one tour.

However discouraging this may be, the two largest assemblages are open on a regular schedule without tours. Deerfield's 'don't miss' attraction is the local historical society's **Memorial Hall Museum**✧✧✧, which traces Deerfield's history from its most famous event, when in 1704 the entire town was destroyed in an Indian raid and its inhabitants taken prisoner to Canada. You can see excellent examples of the famous Deerfield embroidery, quilts and everything from kitchen utensils to portraits and ladies' fans, at your own pace.

The entire village, including private homes, is a National Historic District, worth strolling through even if the buildings are closed. Few places offer such outstanding domestic architecture of late Colonial and Federal periods.

Accommodation and food in Deerfield

Deerfield Inn $$–$$$ *Old Deerfield; tel: (413) 774-5587 or (800) 333-4667.* Fine old inn, restored and furnished in antiques, with outstanding dining-room $$–$$$; *open daily 1800–2100.*

The Terrace Café $ *Deerfield Inn; tel: (413) 774-5587. Open daily 0930–1630, lunch 1200–1400.* Cafeteria with hearty stews, sandwiches, snacks.

NORTHAMPTON✧✧

Smith College Art Museum Elm St; tel: (413) 585-2760. Open Sept–June Tue–Sat 1200–1700, Sun 1400–1600, hours may vary; July–Aug Tue–Sun 1200–1600.

Words and Pictures Museum $ 140 Main St; tel: (413) 586-8545. Open Tue–Sun 1200–1700, longer hours Thur and Sat.

Lyman Plant House
College Lane, tel: (413) 585-2740. Open daily 0900–1600. Free

A college town with the attendant cultural and social life, Northampton is known for its restaurants and hip shops. The **Smith College Art Museum**✧✧✧, one of the nation's most important college art collections, is strong in Connecticut Valley and American artists, plus French Impressionists, Greek vases, Dutch landscapes and sculpture by Rodin. The **Words and Pictures Museum**✧✧ features sequential art, which means comic books and graphic novels, although they make the case that this art form began with cave paintings.

Smith College's **Lyman Plant House**✧✧ is a glass-house world of growing things, with 3500 species indigenous to places from the Amazon to Zanzibar. Fourteen solaria sit amid gardens and an arboretum.

Accommodation and food in Northampton

The Knoll $ *230 North Main St; tel: (413) 584-8164.* Small B&B. **Hotel Northampton** $$ *36 King St; tel: (413) 584-3100.* Well-kept downtown hotel with inn flavour and the **Wiggins Tavern** $$.

SHELBURNE FALLS❖❖

ℹ **Tourist Information Center** 75 Bridge St; tel: (413) 625-2544.

🍴 **McCusker's Market** State St; tel: (413) 625-9411. Deli counter with fresh salads and other picnic makings.

☾ **1797 House $** Upper St; tel: (413) 625-2975. B&B in historic home.

The river that divides Shelburne Falls in half also gives it two of its attractions. In the riverbed below the falls, at the foot of Deerfield St, are dozens of glacial pot-holes in the ledges, formed millions of years ago by the swirling and falling waters of melting glaciers. As large as 40ft in diameter, the pot-holes are the town's swimming 'beach' in the summer.

Above the falls is the unusual **Bridge of Flowers**❖❖ a colourful linear garden atop the arches of a redundant trolley bridge. To see the trolley car that once travelled it, drive up the hill to the **Shelburne Falls Trolley Museum**❖ (tel: (413) 625-9443 or 625-6707), where the car, unused since 1927, is under restoration.

SPRINGFIELD✦✦

ⓘ Greater Springfield CVB *1500 Main St; tel: (413) 787-1548.*

ⓠ Tinkerbell Riverboat Cruises $ *West Columbus Ave; tel: (413) 746-6679. Summer only, from Riverfront Park.*

ⓖ The Quadrangle Museums $ *222 State St; tel: (413) 739-3871. Open Wed–Sun 1200–1600.*

Basketball Hall of Fame $$ *1150 West Columbus Ave; tel: (413) 781-6500. Open May–Aug daily 0900–1800, Sept–June 0900–1700.*

ⓡ The Fort Restaurant $–$$ *8 Fort St; tel: (413) 734-7475. Open daily lunch and dinner; a local tradition for hearty German/American fare.*

ⓒ Springfield is filled with chain hotels; it's much better to stay and eat in Northampton (which is very close).

Remarkably for a small city, Springfield has an entire complex of museums known as **The Quadrangle✦✦✦** (or 'The Quad'). The buildings themselves are interesting, ranging from Italianate to art deco, and together they create one of New England's finest art ensembles. At the **George Walter Vincent Smith Art Museum✦✦✦** are Asian collections including Japanese armour, netsuke, carved jade, silk embroidery and cloisonné. The facing **Museum of Fine Arts✦✦✦** represents American painters from John Singleton Copley to Winslow Homer and Georgia O'Keefe, as well as French Impressionists.

Springfield Science Museum✦✦ *(tel: (413) 263-6800)* is perfectly designed for children, spotlighting the region's many palaeontological finds with a life-sized replica of *Tyrannosaurus rex* and a dinosaur footprint large enough to climb into. The fourth museum in 'The Quad' is the **Connecticut Valley Historical Museum✦✦**, with the work of itinerant painters and fine New England-made furniture shown in period rooms.

A virtual outdoor museum of Victorian architecture includes more than 400 elegant 1870–1910 homes in the **McKnight District✦✦** *(tel: (413) 736-8583)*, east of the Quadrangle.

The **Basketball Hall of Fame✦✦** has films on the sport, memorabilia and high-tech displays, fun even for those who don't give a hoot about hoops.

Right
Freeman Farm, Old Sturbridge Village

STURBRIDGE***

Old Sturbridge Village $$$ *tel: (508) 347-3362. Open Apr–Nov daily 0900–1700; mid Feb–Mar daily 1000–1600; Jan–Feb Sat–Sun 1000–1600.*

Old Sturbridge Village*** is New England's finest restoration, re-creating an entire mid-19th-century village of homes, workshops, mills and barns brought from all over the region. Costumed interpreters farm, cook, weave and work just as people would have in a small 1840s village. In a tidy circle facing the village green are church, general store, tavern, bank, the **Tinsmith's Shop**** and several houses, including the handsome **Salem Towne House*****, the most formal, with painted murals, fine furnishings and an excellent period ornamental garden.

Reached by a walk through the woods or by oxcart ride, is the **Freeman Farm*****, with working gardens, barns, animals and fields, as well as a **Cooper's Shop****. Something interesting is always happening here, from cheese-making to the birth of a lamb. Near by is the **Blacksmith Shop**** and **Bixby House****, home of the village blacksmith.

Water-powered mills from the early 1800s grind grain, card wool, and saw boards, and you can see their great wheels at work. Throughout the village are demonstrations of home industries, perhaps dyeing wool with plant colours or pressing apples into cider. Several homes have gardens, but the showpiece is the large, well-designed **Herb Garden*****, with period plant varieties. Special displays show other facets of 19th-century life, and the Museum Shop is filled with reproductions, books and crafts.

Accommodation and food in Sturbridge

Oliver Wight House and **Old Sturbridge Village Lodge $–$$** *Rte 20; tel: (508) 347-3327.* Original stencilled walls and Federal furnishings or modern motel-style rooms.

Commonwealth Cottage $–$$ *11 Summit Ave; tel: (508) 347-7708.* Hilltop cottage B&B with afternoon tea.

The Publick House $$ *Rte 131; tel: (508) 347-3313 or (800) PUBLICK.* Fine old inn with excellent traditional foods. Open 0730–2200.

Tap Room $ *The Tavern, Old Sturbridge Village; no phone. Open daily 1130–1500.* Buffet of pot pies, beans, cornbread and Indian pudding.

Suggested tour

Brimfield Flea Market $ *tel: (413) 245-9329. Held one weekend each in May, July and Sept.*

Total distance: 155 miles; 183 miles with detour

Time: 4 hours' driving. Allow 2 days for the main route, 3 days with detours. Those with limited time should concentrate on Sturbridge or Deerfield.

The Dickinson Homestead $ 280 Main St, Amherst; tel: (413) 542-8161. Tours Apr–Nov Wed–Sat 1300–1600, and other times. Reservations are advised.

Hadley Farm Museum 147 Russell St (Rte 9), Hadley; tel: (413) 584-8279. Open mid May–mid Oct Tue–Sat 1000–1630, Sun 1330–1630.

Allen House Inn $–$$ 599 Main St, Amherst; tel: (413) 253-5000. Victorian B&B near downtown Amherst.

Salem Cross Inn $$ Rte 9, West Brookfield; tel: (508) 867-2345. Country restaurant serving traditional New England dishes.

Links: I-91 leads north to Brattleboro, joining the Upper Connecticut Valley Route and south to join the Lower Connecticut Route. I-90 connects Springfield and Boston.

Route: From I-91 north of **SPRINGFIELD** ❶ take I-91 and I-90 to Palmer (Exit 8), then follow Rte 32 to **Ware** ❷.

Detour: Instead of leaving the highway, continue on I-90 to **STURBRIDGE** ❸, then follow Rte 20 to Brimfield and Rte 19 north through Warren to West Brookfield, going west on Rte 9, past **Rock House Reservation**✦✦ ❹, where trails lead to a huge overhanging rock uncovered by glaciers. The cave-like area beneath it was used by Native Americans as a winter hunting camp, and their implements have been found there. Trails lead to other exposed rocks and around a small pond. Continue to Ware, where you rejoin the main route.

From Ware, follow Rte 9 past the huge **Quabbin Reservoir Park**✦✦ ❺, with scenic picnic sites overlooking the water, through **Amherst**✦ ❻. This attractive college town was home to poet Emily Dickinson, whose house, **The Dickinson Homestead**✦ ❼, is open to tour. Continue on Rte 9 to Hadley, where you will pass the **Hadley Farm Museum**✦✦ ❽ a three-storey 1782 barn packed full of old-time implements, vehicles and treasures of rural life in the past. Highlights are a Concord Coach and a peddler's wagon, as well as a dugout canoe.

From Hadley, follow the winding Rte 47 along the river to Sunderland, crossing the river to South Deerfield. From there, Rte 5 leads north to **DEERFIELD** ❾. Continue north on Rte 5 to Rte 2A, which leads east to Rte 2 and back over the river on the French King Bridge and to Rte 63. Follow this north to the **Northfield Mountain Recreation and Environmental Center**✦✦ ❿. Here you can walk the nature trail to an abandoned stone quarry, climb to panoramic river views or take a tour (reservations *tel: (800) 859-2960*) to the top of the mountain to learn how water is pumped from the river to the mountaintop at off-peak times, then used to generate electricity for high-usage hours. The Visitors Center's animated displays tell the story, too, along with the history of the river valley.

Beside the river is a large picnic area and a dock where the open-air riverboat *Quinnetukut II*✦✦ ⓫ meets passengers for a 12-mile cruise on this scenic part of the Connecticut River. The banks are densely wooded here, giving way to ledges, then to bird-filled grassy marshes downstream. Eagles are often spotted over the water.

Just beyond, Rte 63 becomes the main street of **Northfield**✦ ⓬, lined with Colonial-era homes. At the northern end of town, side streets are filled with fine Victorian homes, one of which houses the AYH Hostel, a programme which had its American origins in Northfield, in 1934.

From Northfield, cross the Connecticut on Rte 10 and follow Rte 5 south to Greenfield. From there, take Rte 2 west, the Mohawk Trail, past **Old Greenfield Village**✦✦✦ ⓭, a museum of entire workshops and

Northfield Mountain Recreation and Environmental Center and *Quinnetukut II $$*
Rte 63, Northfield; tel: (413) 659-3714.

Old Greenfield Village *$ Rte 2, Greenfield; tel: (413) 774-7138. Open mid May–mid Oct Wed–Mon 1000–1600.*

American Youth Hostel *$ Pine and Highland Sts; tel: (413) 498-3505. Open summer only.*

Barton Cove Campground *$ Rte 2, Gill; tel: (413) 863-9300.* Tent pitches in a grove of tall pines on the riverbank.

stores, housed in 14 buildings, including a general store, an original pharmacy, blacksmith shop, tinshop, butcher, soda fountain, doctor's office, barber shop and more. No costumed guides or videos, just the real things, arranged just as they were.

Just off the Mohawk Trail, **SHELBURNE FALLS** ⓮ is at the intersection of Rte 112, which leads south to Rte 9, where a left turn (southeast) takes you into **NORTHAMPTON** ⓯. From there, I-91 leads back to Springfield.

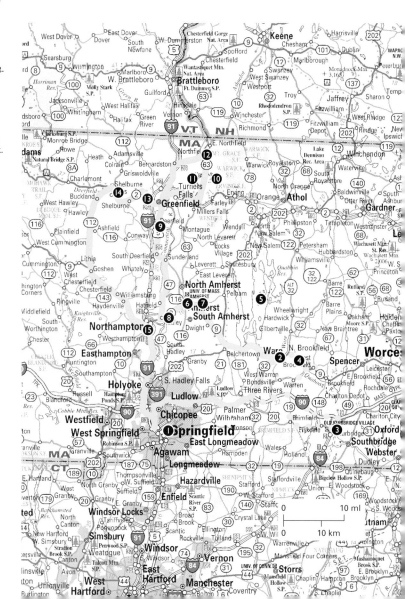

The Berkshires

Ratings

Arts and culture	●●●●●
Nature/ scenery	●●●●○
Food and drink	●●●○○
Shopping	●●●○○
History	●●○○○
Museums	●●○○○
Beaches	●○○○○
Children	●○○○○

The tame and rounded mounds of the Berkshire Hills in western Massachusetts are the best places in New England to spend summer days hiking a mountain or perusing art galleries while enjoying orchestral and chamber music, modern dance or theatre by starlight. Wealthy rusticators from New York and Boston transformed the sleepy farms and hill towns of the region at the end of the 19th century by building lavish summer homes and turning the Berkshires into a chic scene for high society in the late summer and early autumn. Vestiges of this booming age of conspicuous consumption persist in private estates (many now refitted as museums or inns) and in the modern social flutter associated with the most prestigious of the performing arts groups, particularly the theatres and the Boston Symphony Orchestra.

GREAT BARRINGTON✦

Monument Mountain *Rte 7 S, 3 miles south of Stockbridge; tel: (413) 298-3239.*

Aston Magna Festival *St James Church, Rte 7; tel: (413) 528-3595. Baroque and classical chamber music are performed on period instruments July–early Aug.*

Great Barrington's counter-cultural ambience so evident in its craft galleries and New-Age emporia scarcely hints at a progressive past when the town was the first in the world to enjoy electric streetlights and electric lights in its homes. (Local inventor William Stanley pioneered the use of alternating current for streetlights, then sold the rights to the General Electric Company.) In-town shops will pique the interest of antiques hunters, but the greater concentration of dealers is found in the houses and barns along Rte 7 south of town.

Perhaps the most accessible mountain peak in the area is 1735-ft **Monument Mountain**✦✦, where the summit gives a sweeping overview of hills and valleys. Two trails, each taking 45 minutes, diverge from the roadside trailhead. The 0.75-mile Hickey Trail is steeper, while the 1.25-mile Monument Trail is more gradual.

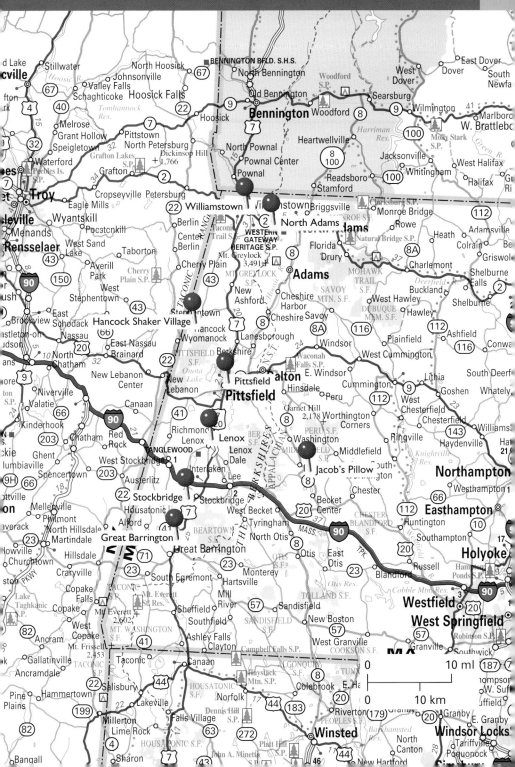

The spare simplicity of the Shaker lifestyle

Accommodation and food in Great Barrington

The moderately priced **DI** on *Main St*; *tel: (413) 528-3150* is well located for walking to shopping and dining.

Castle Street Café $$ 10 Castle St; *tel: (413) 528-5244*. The menu of this stylish café features produce from the area's organic and speciality farmers.

HANCOCK SHAKER VILLAGE❖❖❖

Hancock Shaker Village $$$ *Rtes 20 and 41; tel: (413) 443-0188. Open late May–Oct daily 0930–1700, Apr–May and Nov daily 1000–1500.*

Country Inn at Jiminy Peak $$–$$$ *Brodie Mountain Rd, Hancock; tel: (413) 738 5500. Ski-style self-catering lodgings at the foot of ski mountain.*

Among the most enduring Shaker settlements, the 'City of Peace' was inhabited between 1790 and 1959 by the celibate communal sect. Twenty buildings, most from the 19th century, illustrate their ways. For example, although Shaker brothers and sisters did not dwell together, they ranked as equals. Thus, the five-storey 1830 Brick Dwelling is built in two separate but identical sections. Pegs for hanging clothes, tools, chairs and brooms speak of the Shaker penchant for order and cleanliness. 'There is no dirt in heaven' an eldress declared.

The striking 1826 **Round Stone Barn**❖❖ was built to speed the care of 50 cattle, yet its practical design is also aesthetically appealing, almost as a prayer in stone. Hancock's architecture strongly influenced non-Shaker builders throughout New England, just as the spare and elegant Shaker furniture and baskets had a lasting impact on domestic design. Hancock has the largest collection of Shaker furniture and artefacts in an original site.

Jacob's Pillow****

**Jacob's Pillow
Dance Festival**
*George Carter Rd off Rte 8;
tel: (413) 243-0745.
Performances late June–late
Aug Tue–Sun.*

At the end of a twisty mountain road in Becket stands America's summer Mecca of modern dance, Jacob's Pillow. For more than six decades, Pillow programming has promoted ground-breaking choreography and the integration of folk dance, modern ballet and ethnic dance into the modern repertoire. Works in progress appear on a small stage in the woods. The Ted Shawn Theatre, with its back opening to the mountain nightscape, was the first stage built specifically for dance in the US.

Lenox****

**Lenox Chamber of
Commerce** *75 Main
St; tel: (800) 255-3669 or
(413) 637-3646.*

The Mount $
*Plunkett St and Rte 7;
tel: (413) 637-1800. Open
late May–Oct daily
0900–1500, last tour at
1400.*

Hoadley Gallery *21
Church St; tel: (413)
637-2814* distinguishes
itself from other crafts
galleries with a superb
selection of ceramic art.

Ute Stebich Gallery *69
Church St; tel: (413) 637-
3566* features international
folk art and cutting-edge
contemporary art.

**Shakespeare &
Company** *in the
grounds of The Mount; tel:
(413) 637-3353.
Performances mid May–Oct.*

Tanglewood *Rte 183,
West St; tel: (413) 637-
5165.* Concerts late
June–early Sept.

Right
The Daniel Chester French
Studio in Lenox

In the decades before income tax, Lenox flourished as a seasonal playground of the rich, many of whom built estates (which they called 'cottages') here between 1890 and 1910. The Berkshires social season, which revolves around music, theatre and dance, is still centred in Lenox. Although small, the town boasts more boutiques, restaurants and up-market lodgings than any nearby community.

Several 'cottages' are open as museums, of which the most interesting is **The Mount**, completed in 1902 for novelist Edith Wharton who wrote extensively about architecture and design. She practised what she preached by designing and decorating this estate, basing the building on a Lincolnshire manor in England, then adding French and Italian accents. Her interior decoration eschewed the Victorian overstuffed vogue of her day in favour of more classical spareness.

The Mount's woodsy grounds are the summer stage for **Shakespeare & Company**. Sitting on the lawn with a picnic supper (and lots of insect repellent) while watching a scene unfold has created many devoted Shakespeare fans.

Another summer estate turned to artistic purposes is **Tanglewood***, the summer home of the Boston Symphony Orchestra. In addition to the BSO, concerts feature chamber music, jazz and contemporary artists. The priciest tickets are for seats in 'the Shed', a roofed open auditorium built in 1938 that seats 5000. Less expensive 'lawn' tickets are more fun and concert-goers have raised the Tanglewood picnic to an artform of its own.

Edith Wharton's splendid mansion, The Mount, in Lenox

Accommodation and food in Lenox

Café Lucia $$–$$$ *80 Church St; tel: (413) 637-2640.* The tables on the covered wooden deck of this northern Italian trattoria are in great demand.

Church Street Café $$–$$$ *65 Church St; tel: (413) 637-2745.* A comfortable, casual spot to enjoy fresh-market meals, including light pastas and bright salads.

The Gables Inn $$–$$$ *103 Walker St; tel: (413) 637-3416.* This Queen Anne-style 'cottage', once owned by Edith Wharton's mother-in-law, has 19 guest rooms decorated with period antiques and fine art.

The Village Inn $$–$$$ *16 Church St; tel: (413) 637-0020 or (800) 253-0917.* There are 32 guest rooms in this 1771 inn in the heart of the downtown shopping and dining district.

NORTH ADAMS*

Western Gateway Heritage State Park *Rte 8; tel: (413) 663-6312. Open daily 1000–1700. Free admission.*

Massachusetts Museum of Contemporary Art $ *87 Marshall St; tel: (413) 664-4481. Limited schedule. Call for hours.*

Mount Greylock Reservation Headquarters *Rockwell Rd, Lanesboro; tel: (413) 499-4262. Open mid May–mid Oct daily 0900–1700. Free.*

Bascom Lodge $ *Mount Greylock summit; tel: (413) 443-0011.* This rustic lodge built by Depression-era work crews has co-ed dormitory bunkrooms and four private rooms.

Abandoned by industry, gritty North Adams has turned its strategic location and empty buildings into an incubator for education, computing and the arts. A smattering of bookstores, galleries and coffee bars hints of approaching prosperity.

Western Gateway Heritage State Park* relates North Adams' role as a 19th-century boom town, thanks to the construction of the Hoosac Tunnel to link the Berkshires by train to Boston on the east and New York on the west. Under construction for more than a decade, the **Massachusetts Museum of Contemporary Art**✧✧ began opening exhibits in 1999. Housed in a cavernous factory building, the museum specialises in art of a scale too immense for other institutions.

North Adams is also a gateway to the 12,500-acre **Mount Greylock State Reservation**✧✧ via Notch Rd. The 3491-ft mountain is laced with more than 45 miles of marked trails. Some short loops near the summit can be traversed in an hour or less. Rare alpine flora are found on higher elevations and the reservation provides a nesting habitat for more than 100 bird species.

Hoosac Tunnel

Steep grades kept trains out of the Berkshires until the 1870s, when the Boston & Albany Railroad decided to dig its 4.75-mile Hoosac Tunnel. At a staggering cost of $14 million, the tunnel was the longest bore in the world when it opened in 1875. Workers dug from both ends, meeting in a final dynamite blast. The engineering was so precise that the two sides lined up with an error of less than 1in in 25,000ft.

PITTSFIELD*

Berkshire Visitors Bureau *Berkshire Common Plaza Level; tel: (413) 443-9186* provides information on the entire Berkshires region.

Festival Americana *tel: (413) 499-3861.* Pittsfield celebrates Independence Day (4 July) with one of the largest parades in the US.

All major Berkshire roads converge at Pittsfield, the commercial heart of the region. Hints of wealthier days survive in the **Berkshire Athenæum***, *Wendell Avenue, tel:(413) 499–9480; open daily except Sun,* where local donors contributed 19th-century American art and furniture. The natural science collections give a good picture of Berkshire flora and fauna. The Herman Melville Memorial Room displays some of the author's books and papers as well as his writing desk. Melville's home from 1850 to 1863 is the 1780s farmhouse, **Arrowhead**✧✧ *780 Holmes Rd, tel: (413) 442–1793; open daily in the summer, Fri–Mon rest of year.* Few of the author's personal belongings are here (bankruptcy claimed everything, including the house), but his study window looks out on Mount Greylock, a great white hump of landscape in winter – mountain as *Moby Dick*.

STOCKBRIDGE✧✧✧

Norman Rockwell Museum $$ Rte 183; tel: (413) 298-4100. Open May–Oct daily 1000–1700, Nov–Apr Mon–Fri 1100–1600.

Chesterwood $$ Williamsville Rd; tel: (413) 298-3579. Open May–Oct daily 1000–1700.

Naumkeag $$ Prospect Hill Rd; tel: (413) 298-3239. Open late May–mid Oct daily 1000–1700.

Berkshire Theater Festival Main St; tel: (413) 298-5536. One of the oldest summer theatres in the nation, BTF performs in a Gilded Age playhouse.

Main Street at Christmas tel: (413) 298-5200. This holiday event re-creates Norman Rockwell's well-known painting *Stockbridge Main Street at Christmas.*

Founded in 1734 as a Puritan mission to the Indians, Stockbridge today bears little trace of either. Like Lenox, it contains many vast 'cottages', but unlike its neighbour, it still feels like a rustic village endeavouring to live up to its Norman Rockwell image. The **Norman Rockwell Museum**✧✧ chronicles the illustrator's prolific career, which held a small-town mirror up to American popular culture. Stockbridge was also the summer home of sculptor Daniel Chester French, best known for his *Seated Lincoln* in Washington, DC's Lincoln Memorial. Tours of his estate, **Chesterwood**✧, feature both the sculptor's house and his studio, filled with drawings, plaster casts and bronze models. **Naumkeag**✧, residence of Joseph Choate, who served as ambassador to England from 1899 to 1905, is a posh example of how the rich and famous summered in the Berkshires. Original furnishings and Chinese decorative arts fill the 26-room 1886 mansion. No visit to Stockbridge is complete without a stint in a rocking chair on the porch of the **Red Lion Inn**✧, the town's *de facto* social centre.

Accommodation and food in Stockbridge

Red Lion Inn $$–$$$ *30 Main St; tel: (413) 298-5545.* One of the few American inns in continuous use since the 18th century, the Red Lion's rooms have an updated country style. The semi-formal dining room (**$$$**) serves such traditional American cuisine that Norman Rockwell ate here once a week.

The Inn at Stockbridge $$–$$$ *Rte 7; tel: (413) 298-3337.* This 1906 country inn a mile from town has seven guest rooms in the original house and four suites in a new cottage.

Theresa's Stockbridge Café $$ *Main St; tel: (413) 298-5465.* If there's such a thing as a counter-cultural institution, this hippie café with a good choice of vegetarian meals is it.

WILLIAMSTOWN✦✦✦

ⓘ Sterling and Francine Clark Art Institute *225 South St; tel: (413) 458-2303. Free admission. Open Sept–June, Tue–Sun 1000–1700, July and Aug daily 1000–1700.*

Williams College Museum of Art *Main St; tel: (413) 597-2429. Free admission. Open Tue–Sat 1000–1700, Sun 1300–1700.*

◉ Williamstown Theater Festival *Adams Memorial Theater, 1000 Main St; tel: (413) 597-2429. June–Aug season includes classics, premieres and cabaret.*

The artistry of **Williamstown Theatre Festival**✦✦ is good reason to visit this pleasant college town in the summer. The **Sterling and Francine Clark Art Institute**✦✦✦ makes a stopover essential in any season. The Clarks inherited a large industrial fortune and amassed impressive collections of works by Pierre Auguste Renoir, Claude Monet, J M W Turner and Winslow Homer. Blessed with the presence of the Clark, the **Williams College Museum of Art**✦ instead emphasises modern, contemporary and non-Western art. One American masterpiece is Edward Hopper's *Morning in a City.*

Accommodation and food in Williamstown

Field Farm Guest House $–$$ *554 Sloan Rd; tel: (413) 458-3135.* This 1948 modern-design masterpiece offers a distinct change from the usual Victorian B&B. The grounds include 4 miles of hiking trails flanked by wild flowers and some rare ferns.

Northside Motel $–$$ *45 North St; tel: (413) 458-8107.* This 30-room motel is conveniently located in the downtown district.

Wild Amber Grill $$ *101 North St; tel: (413) 458-4000.* This contemporary American restaurant is also the scene of cabaret by the performers at Williamstown Theater Festival.

Suggested tour

Total distance: 87 miles; 110 miles with detours

Time: 3–4 hours' driving. Allow 3 days.

Links: Connects via Rte 7 at Williamstown or via Rte 100 at North Adams with Southern Green Mountains Route, via Rte 2 at North Adams to northern end of Pioneer Valley Route, via Massachusetts Turnpike at Lee to southern end of Pioneer Valley Route, or via Rte 7 south from Sheffield to Litchfield Hills Route.

Route: The ideal route for touring the Berkshires begins on Rte 2 in **NORTH ADAMS ❶** by entering town from the east through the aptly-named **Hairpin Turn**✦ ❷ on Rte 2, the scenic mountain road known as the **Mohawk Trail** ❸.

Left
The Stockbridge home of the Berkshire Theater Festival

Egremont Inn $$
Old Sheffield Rd, South Egremont; tel: (800) 859-1780 or (413) 528-2111. Classic *circa*-1820 country inn with original architecture and modern comforts.

La Bruschetta $$$ *I Harris St, West Stockbridge; tel: (413) 232-7141.* One of the most popular and stylish restaurants in the Berkshires makes great use of local produce, cheeses and meats.

Berkshire Center for Contemporary Glass *6 Harris St, West Stockbridge; tel: (413) 232-4666* has a good selection of work by the artist–owners and other artists and allows visitors to watch pieces being made in the hot and cold glass working studios.

Detour: One mile west of North Adams centre is Notch Rd, a 5-mile drive to the summit of Mount Greylock.

Rte 2 continues past meadows and gentle uplands west for 5 miles to **WILLIAMSTOWN** ❹, where it meets Rte 7 descending from Bennington, Vt. Rte 7 follows the broad north–south valley of the Housatonic River between the Hoosac and Taconic ranges of the Berkshires. In Lanesboro, 18 miles south, is a turn-off for Rockwell Rd, the more-travelled 12-mile dirt ascent of Mount Greylock. Rte 7 continues 6 miles south to **PITTSFIELD** ❺. In the centre of town, Rte 20 leads west for 5 miles to **HANCOCK SHAKER VILLAGE** ❻. Some of New England's most fertile farmland lies in the river plain south of Hancock along Rte 41. **West Stockbridge**⁺ ❼, something of an outpost for craftspeople, lies 8 miles south. Rte 41 returns to the Housatonic's banks at **GREAT BARRINGTON** ❽ in 18 miles. **South Egremont**⁺ ❾, a handsome village with several good antiques shops and a fine inn, lies 3 miles further south on Rte 41. South of Egremont, Rte 41 trails the eastern edge of a mountain range, hence the highway is known as Under Mountain Rd. In 4 miles, a left turn on to Berkshire School Rd leads 3.5 miles into the centre of **Sheffield**⁺ ❿, distinguished by having the largest number of antiques dealers in the Berkshires. Most of them ply their trade along Rte 7, which leads north 7 miles back to Great Barrington, then another 6 miles north past **Monument Mountain** ⓫ to bucolic **LENOX** ⓬. Most travellers connect to the Massachusetts Turnpike from Lenox by driving 4 miles east on Rte 20 to **Lee**⁺ ⓭, which has a dusty, old-fashioned downtown and a huge cluster of factory outlet shopping on the edge of town.

Detour: Rte 8 joins Rte 20 in Lee to go east for 15 miles to George Carter Rd, which winds 3 miles north to **JACOB'S PILLOW** ⓮.

Also worth exploring

Bash Bish Falls⁺⁺

Fine riverside walking trails and dramatic, picturesque falls make Bash Bish worth the woodsy drive through thickets of mountain laurel and along old fields where deer often graze. From South Egremont village, follow Rte 41 south half a mile. Turn right on to Mt Washington Rd, which doglegs left in 3 miles and continues 2 miles south into Mt Washington village. In 1.7 miles, a right turn leads to Bash Bish Falls on a narrow, steep road alternating between pavement and dirt for 3 miles to a car-park with a steep trail. In another half-mile (over the New York line) a second trailhead offers easier walking access to the falls along a woodland trail that follows the river upstream for a mile. The 80-ft waterfall divides around a huge basalt boulder. According to legend, an Indian maiden dived over the falls to escape lecherous white trappers and was never seen again.

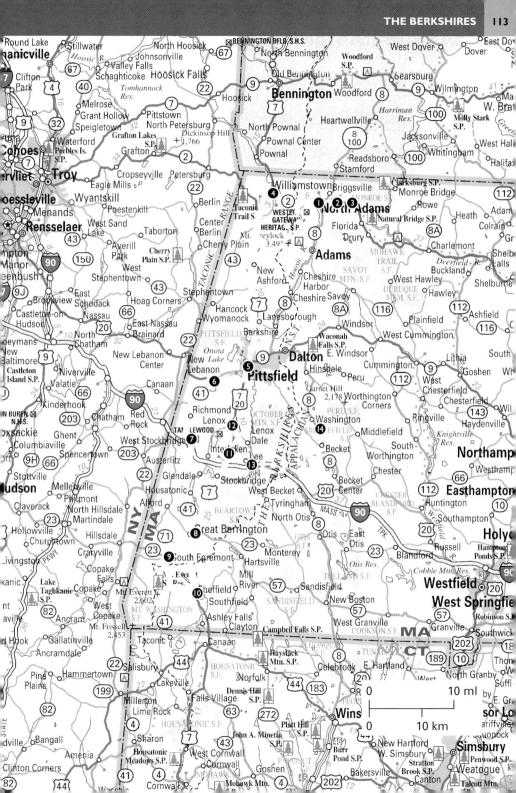

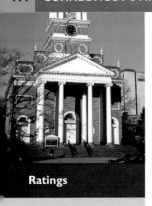

Connecticut's Midlands

Ratings

Arts and culture	●●●●●
History	●●●●○
Museums	●●●●○
Children	●●○○○
Food and drink	●●○○○
Nature/ scenery	●●○○○
Beaches	●○○○○
Shopping	●○○○○

Two of Connecticut's most noteworthy cities, just about equal in population, have distinctive, contrasting identities. State capital Hartford is the headquarters base for several nationally recognised insurance companies. Directly south from there – less than an hour's drive via an interstate motorway – New Haven takes particular pride in Yale, an elite university in the US's so-called Ivy League. However, both places have more to offer than big business and higher education. Hartford has an outstanding art museum, plus the houses where authors Mark Twain and Harriet Beecher Stowe lived. In New Haven, treat yourself to such cultural perks as Yale's Center for British Art and its Peabody Museum of Natural History. Communities of varying size comprise a high-density sprawl between Hartford and New Haven. Some merit a stopover; we've pointed them out in this chapter.

Hartford sights

ℹ Greater Hartford Tourism District
234 Murphy St, Hartford;
tel: (800) 793-4480 or
(860) 244-8181;
www.travelfile.com/get/ghtd

Ⓗ Hartford, 102 miles from Boston, rises amid a bridge-crossing tangle of highways and interstate motorways at the pivotal, busy juncture of north–south I-91 and east–west I-84.

Bushnell Park and Carousel✷✷
Hartford's premier open space, amounting to 37 acres lies, in the heart of the city. At its centre the **Corning Fountain** honours the region's original Native American inhabitants. On the greenery's east, Trinity St side is a tall brownstone **Soldiers & Sailors Memorial Arch**. The park's **Carousel** is a 1914 merry-go-round with 48 hand-carved horses, spinning to the tunes of a 1925 Wurlitzer band organ – in a pavilion emblazoned with folk art and more than 800 light bulbs.

Center Church✷✷
Dating from 1807, and modelled after London's St-Martin-in-the-Fields, the interior is embellished by stained-glass windows, including six by Louis Comfort Tiffany. Outside is the **Ancient Burying Ground**, where Hartford's 17th-century founders are interred.

Mark Twain's House

**Bushnell Park
Carousel** $ *Park at
Jewell St; tel: (860) 249-
2201. Phone for opening
times at various times of
year.*

Center Church *675
Main St; tel: (860) 249-
5631. Open Wed & Fri
1100–1400.*

**Connecticut State
Capitol** *210 Capitol Ave;
tel: (860) 240-0222. Daily,
hourly: guided tours. Free*

**Elizabeth Park Rose
Gardens** *Prospect Ave; tel:
(860) 722-6514. Open
dawn–dusk. Free*

**Harriet Beecher Stowe
House** $ *Farmington Ave at
Forest St; tel: (860) 525-
9317. Open Sat 0900–
1600, Sun 1200–1600. Also
Mon 0930–1600 (June–mid
Oct & Dec).*

Previous page
Hartford's State Capitol

Connecticut State Capitol♦♦♦

Hartford's hilltop showpiece, opened in 1879, bristles with Gothic spires and classical and Second Empire-style adornments, topped by a dome sheathed in gold leaf. Medallions and bas-reliefs are carved on the white marble façades. Interior features include bullet-riddled Civil War battle flags and a statue of Connecticut patriot Nathan Hale.

Elizabeth Park Rose Gardens♦♦♦

The nation's first municipal park devoted to roses (14,000 bushes, 900 varieties) also includes greenhouses, perennials, a rock garden and pathways on its 1000-acre expanse.

Harriet Beecher Stowe House♦♦♦

In what had been Hartford's semi-rural Nook Farm enclave a century ago: the 'cottage' where the celebrated author of *Uncle Tom's Cabin* lived from 1873 to 1896. It includes her writing table, period furnishings and personal memorabilia.

Mark Twain House♦♦♦

Close to the Stowe abode, the turreted 'steamboat Gothic' Victorian manse – with multicoloured brickwork exterior and Tiffany-designed interiors – was the writer's home for 17 years beginning in 1874. Where Samuel Langhorne Clemens (aka Mark Twain) wrote seven of his best-known books, including *Tom Sawyer, The Adventures of Huckleberry Finn, The Prince and the Pauper* and *A Connecticut Yankee in King Arthur's Court*.

Museum of Connecticut History♦♦

Displays include the colony's 1662 royal charter, Connecticut-made

Mark Twain House
$ 351 Farmington Ave; tel: (860) 493-6411. Open Mon–Sat 0930–1700, Sun 1100–1700 (June–mid Oct & Dec). Mon–Sat 0930–1700, Sun 1200–1700 (mid Oct–May).

Museum of Connecticut History
231 Capitol Ave; tel: (860) 566-3056. Open Mon–Fri 0930–1600.

Old State House 800 Main St; tel. (860) 522-6766. Open Mon–Fri 1000–1600, Sat 1100–1600.

Travelers Tower Observatory 1 Tower Sq; tel: (860) 277-4208. Open Mon–Fri 1000–1500.

Wadsworth Atheneum $$ 600 Main St; tel: (860) 278-2670. Open Tue–Sun 1100–1700 (1st Thur each month 1100–2200).

clocks and Colt firearms, governors' portraits and the desk upon which Abraham Lincoln signed the 1863 slave-freeing Emancipation Proclamation.

Old State House*
A 1796 brick-and-brownstone Federal-style classic, the Old State House was Boston architect Charles Bulfinch's first public building – and the nation's first state capitol, site of the drafting of colonial America's first written constitution, the Fundamental Orders (in 1639).

Travelers Tower Observatory*
There are sweeping views of the city and surroundings from the 527-ft altitude atop the headquarters skyscraper of Hartford's pioneer insurance company.

Wadsworth Atheneum*
America's oldest continuously functioning public art museum (founded in 1842) is especially strong on Hudson River School landscapes, Flemish/Dutch and Impressionist paintings and Early American furniture.

Accommodation and food in Hartford

Exodus to Suburbia has sucked considerable life out of downtown. Nevertheless, a few bright spots do exist.

Goodwin Hotel $$–$$$ 1 Haynes St; tel: (800) 922-5006 or (860) 246-7500. An 1881 Queen Anne beauty, built as a town house for zillionaire J P Morgan. Fine cuisine downstairs in his namesake restaurant, **Pierpont's $$**.

Max Downtown $$$ 185 Asylum St; tel: (860) 522-2530, is downtown's classiest eatery.

No Fish Today $$ 80 Pratt St; tel: (860) 244-2100, in an historic brick building, is recommended for its Italian specialities and – despite the name – seafood. If you're a meat eater, choose **Chuck's Steak House $$** 1 Civic Center Plaza; tel: (860) 241-9100. **Hartford Brewery LTD $** 35 Pearl St; tel: (860) 246-BEER, beckons with roast chicken, pot roast and three dozen choices of ales, stouts and porters.

Suggested walk

Total distance: Walking a bit more than 1 mile, 2 miles at most, is all it takes to 'do' central Hartford thoroughly. The Harriet Beecher Stowe and Mark Twain Houses are approximately 1 mile from downtown.

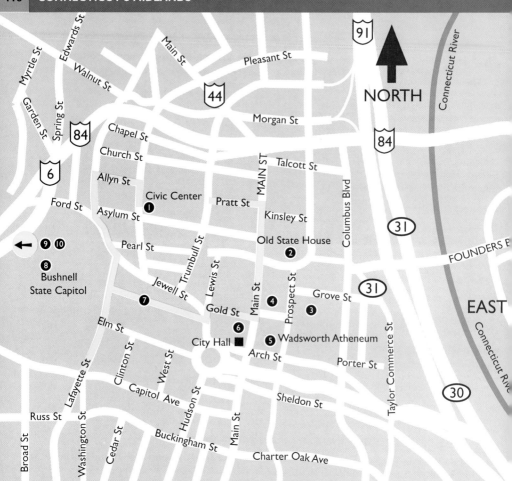

Time: Allow half a day, more for getting to the Stowe and Twain houses by foot, auto or public transportation. The Wadsworth Atheneum deserves a minimum of 2 hours of your time.

Starting at the concrete-behemoth **Hartford Civic Center ❶**, walk eastward via Pratt St to Main St. The **OLD STATE HOUSE ❷** stands where Main St meets Asylum and Pearl Sts. Behind the Old State House – between Market St and Columbus Blvd – **Constitution Plaza ❸**, overlooking the Connecticut River, is a 1960s urban-renewal expanse encompassing office buildings and mall-type shops.

Continuing south on Main St brings you to the **TRAVELERS TOWER ❹**, then the **WADSWORTH ATHENEUM ❺**. From that castellated edifice, take Gold St past **CENTER CHURCH ❻** to the eastern perimeter of **BUSHNELL PARK ❼**. Crossing Trinity St midway in the

Greater New Haven Convention & Visitors Bureau; 59 Elm St; tel: (800) 322-STAY or (203) 777-8550; www.newhavencvb.org

Yale Visitor Information Center 149 Elm St; tel: (203) 432-2300.

New Haven, 101 miles west of Providence, is reachable via two interstate motorways: east–west I-95 and north–south I-91.

Beinecke Rare Book & Manuscript Library 121 Wall St; tel: (203) 432-2977. Open Mon–Fri 0830–1700, Sat 1000–1700. Free

New Haven Green Bordered by Church, Elm, College & Chapel Sts; split by Trinity St.

Peabody Museum of Natural History $ 170 Whitney Ave; tel: (203) 432-5050. Open Mon–Sat 1000–1700, Sat–Sun 1200–1700.

Yale Center for British Art 1080 Chapel St; tel: (203) 432-2800. Open Tue–Sat 1000–1700, Sun 1200–1700. Free

Yale University Art Gallery 1111 Chapel St; tel: (203) 432-0600. Open Sept–July Tue–Sat 1000–1700, Sun 1300–1800. Free

park, you're sure to see Connecticut's hilltop **STATE CAPITOL** ❽. After meandering in an easterly direction on park walkways, return to the Civic Center by turning right on to Allyn St.

To reach the **HARRIET BEECHER STOWE** ❾ and **MARK TWAIN HOUSES** ❿, go west on Asylum St, leading to Farmington Ave.

New Haven sights

Beinecke Rare Book & Manuscript Library*
A sunken sculpture garden graces this Yale institution, with collections including an original Gutenberg Bible, Charles Dickens manuscripts and rare Audubon *Birds of America* prints.

New Haven Green**
Textbook example of a New England town common, laid out in 1638, site of three churches regarded as outstanding exemplars of Federal, Georgian and English Gothic design. On this 16-acre open space is the Philip Sherman Bennett Fountain (1907) and a Memorial to New Haven Soldiers of World War (1928).

Peabody Museum of Natural History**
Built in 1866 as part of Yale, this museum ranks among the world's best, with global 'finds' by generations of university archaeologists. In the Great Hall is a 67-ft brontosaurus skeleton and enormous *The Age of Reptiles* mural.

Yale Center for British Art***
The Yale Center houses the largest and broadest-ranging collection of British art to be found outside the UK: a bequest from philanthropist and Yale alumnus Paul Mellon, housed in the last building to be designed by big-name US architect Lewis Kahn.

Yale University Art Gallery***
America's oldest academic art museum, founded in 1832, with paintings, sculptures, artefacts and decorative arts from ancient Egypt through the Italian Renaissance and French and American Impressionist periods.

Accommodation and food in New Haven

New Haven is small but Yale is big, exerting a favourable influence on the lodging and dining scene.

Louis' Lunch $ *263 Crown St; tel: (203) 562-5507*, claims to be the birthplace (in 1895) of the original American hamburger sandwich.

Pepe's Pizzeria $ *157 Wooster St; tel: (203) 865-5762*, takes credit for baking the first US pizzas, in 1925.

Omni New Haven $$ *155 Temple St; tel: (800) THE-OMNI or (203) 772-6664*. Conveniently near the green and the campus.

Scoozi Trattoria & Wine Bar $$ *1104 Chapel St; tel: (203) 776-8268*. A trendy pasta place.

The Colony $$ *1157 Chapel St; tel: (800) 458-8810 or (203) 776-1234*. Another good close-to-everything choice.

Three Chimneys Inn $$ *1201 Chapel St; tel: (203) 789-1201*. Be pampered in a centrally located Victorian mansion reborn as a ten-room bed & breakfast.

Union League Café $$ *1032 Chapel St; tel: (203) 562-4299*. Casual French bistro ambience.

Suggested walk

Total distance: Figure on about 2 miles of walking if you concentrate on the compact downtown district and adjacent Yale University area. Add another 2 miles if you decide to extend your touring to the neighbourhood around Wooster Square.

Time: Despite those short in-town distances, treat yourself to a full day's sightseeing, thereby allowing time for sufficient looking-around. But doing justice to any of Yale's compelling museums necessitates an extra 2–3 hours, at the very least, for each of them.

Route: Begin by walking east across the **NEW HAVEN GREEN ❶**, split by north–south Temple St. On the green, note its trio of early 19th-century churches: **United ❷** (Federal), **Center ❸** (Georgian), **Trinity ❹** (Gothic Revival). Crossing Church St, you'll see New Haven's 1862 clock-towered **City Hall ❺**, a polychrome limestone and sandstone High Victorian whopper. Go south down Church St to Chapel St; here at the scruffy edge of downtown, turn left; cross a bridge spanning railroad tracks to reach elegant **Wooster Square ❻** and its Christopher Columbus monument. Wooster St here on this east side of town defines New Haven's Italian–American neighbourhood.

Back downtown, walk west across the green; cross College St to reach the **Yale campus ❼**. Pass through Phelps Gate to reach the Old Campus quadrangle, where the university's oldest building, **Connecticut Hall ❽**, dates from 1750. The brick dormitory is where Nathan Hale, Noah Webster and US president-to-be William Howard Taft resided as undergraduates. Cross High St to a latter-day campus courtyard, dominated by 221-ft **Harkness Tower ❾**.

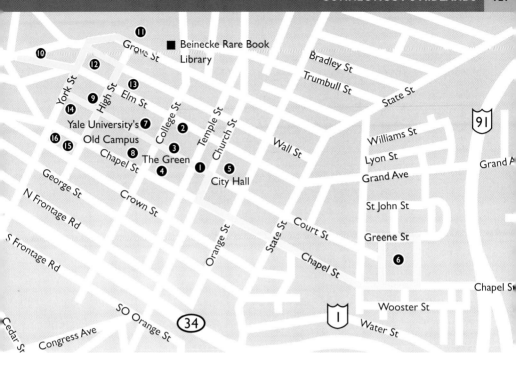

Turn right on to York St to reach Broadway, locale of the **Yale Co-op** ⑩, a modernistic students' store designed by Finnish architect Eero Saarinen. Or, for a small variation, back on York St, head north to Grove St, thereby reaching **Grove Street Cemetery** ⑪, burial place of such Connecticut luminaries as lexicologist Noah Webster and inventors Eli Whitney, Charles Goodyear and Samuel F B Morse.

From Broadway, turn on to Wall St, then right on to High St to pass Yale's **Sterling Memorial Library** ⑫ and the **Cross Campus Library** ⑬. Former Yalie Maya Lin, creator of Washington, DC's Vietnam Veterans Memorial, designed the fountain sculpture on the latter building's plaza. Continuing south along High St gets you to Chapel St, where Yale's **University Art Gallery** ⑭, **Center for British Art** ⑮ and **Repertory Theater** ⑯ are prestigious landmarks.

Suggested driving tour

Total distance: 36–40 miles; 80–85 miles with detours

Time: 1–1.5 hours' driving. But allow half a day for an easygoing drive on the main route. If you have limited time, focus your sightseeing on downtown Hartford and New Haven, allowing at least half a day in each city centre. Allow a full day if you choose detours.

ⓘ Wethersfield Historical Society 200 Main St, Wethersfield; tel: (860) 529-7656.

Farmington Valley Visitors Association PO Box 1015, Simsbury; tel: (800) 493-5266 or (860) 651-6950.

ⓜ Webb-Deane-Stevens Museum $ 211 Main St; tel: (860) 529-0612. Open May–Oct Tue–Sun 1000–1700 Nov–Apr Fri–Sun 1000–1700.

Sleeping Giant State Park 200 Mt Carmel Ave (off Rte 10), Hamden; tel: (203) 789-7498. So-named because the crest resembles a gigantic reclining head atop 1500 acres of terrain for picnicking and hiking on a 33-mile trail network.

Eli Whitney Museum $ 915 Whitney Ave; tel: (203) 777-1833. Open Wed–Fri & Sun, 1200–1700, Sat 1000–1500.

Hill-Stead Museum $ 35 Mountain Rd, Farmington; tel: (860) 677-9064. Open May–Oct Tue–Sun 1000–1700 Nov–Apr Tue–Sun 1100–1600.

International Skating Center of Connecticut 1375 Hopmeadow St, Simsbury; tel: (860) 651-5400. Open daily 0600–2400; phone ahead for schedules. Public skating times (rentals available): Wed & Fri 0815–2215, Sat 1300–1500, 1800–2000, 2115–2215, Sun 1300–1500, 1800–2000.

Links: Heading north from Hartford, connect on to the Pioneer Valley Route (*see page 96*) at Springfield, Mass. By driving 15 miles south from Hartford, via I-91 and Rte 9, to Middletown, you can link with the Lower Connecticut Valley Route (*see page 132*).

Route: Head south from central Hartford on the featureless I-91 motorway. After 3 miles, exit on to much more scenic Rte 99, which brings you to charming little **Wethersfield ❶**, where Main and Broad Sts are lined with houses spanning the 17th, 18th and 19th centuries. Three of them comprise the **Webb-Deane-Stevens Museum**✦✦ **❷**, showcasing the lifestyles of a wealthy merchant, diplomat and tradesman. From there, drive west on Rte 175, then 5 miles south via Rte 5 (the Berlin Turnpike) to Berlin. Switch on to westbound Rtes 71 and 364 through Southington and Plantsville to reach Rte 10 in the midst of mid-Connecticut tobacco-growing country. Take Rte 10 due south past **Sleeping Giant State Park**✦ **❸** to Hamden and its **Eli Whitney Museum**✦ **❹**, devoted to the Hamden-born inventor of the agriculturally revolutionary cotton gin. Then on into suburban sprawl outside **NEW HAVEN ❺**, overall a 23-mile drive. Follow signs leading into the downtown district.

Detour: From metro Hartford, drive 9 miles west on Rte 4 to Farmington, home of preppy Miss Porter's School (where the future Jackie Kennedy studied) and **Hill-Stead Museum**✦✦✦ **❻**, an industrialist's turn-of-the-century mansion designed by his architect daughter, showcasing their impressive collection of French and American Impressionist paintings (Degas, Manet, Monet, Cassatt, Whistler) along with antique furnishings, Chinese porcelains and Japanese woodblock prints, with a sunken garden on the 152-acre site. Via Rte 10, continue 7 miles through the lush, fertile (and affluent) Farmington River Valley to Avon. At the Rte 185 juncture, turn east if you'd like to indulge in some 'nature time' in **Penwood/Talcott Mountain State Parks ❼**, extensive side-by-side green spaces with hiking trails, picnic shelters, lakes and scenic overlooks – especially from the Heublein Tower atop 1000-ft Talcott Mountain. Otherwise go another 5 miles on Rte 10 from Avon to Simsbury, giving you an opportunity to visit that town's **International Skating Center of Connecticut**✦ **❽**, home ice of US, World and Olympic ice-skating medalists – where you can watch Olympic figure-skaters' workouts and performances. Return southbound to Hartford on Rte 189.

Also worth exploring

Take the I-84 motorway (the Yankee Expressway) from Hartford to New Britain, an 11-mile drive, worthwhile because of that small city's **Museum of American Art**✦✦, in a 19th-century mansion. The collection contains over 4500 paintings, graphics and sculptures

ⓘ Central Connecticut Tourism District
1 Grove St (Suite 310), New Britain; tel: (860) 229-1665; www.centralct.org.

ⓘ Museum of American Art $ 56
Lexington St, New Britain; tel: (860) 229-0257. Open Tue–Fri 1300–1700, Sat 1000–1700, Sun 1200–1700. Free admission Sat 1000–1200.

American Clock & Watch Museum $ 100
Maple St, Bristol; tel: (860) 583-6070. Open Nov–Apr daily 1000–1700.

spanning national art history from 1740 to present times – including the pre-Revolutionary period, Impressionism, the Hudson River and Ash Can Schools, plus Thomas Hart Benton's 1930s *The Arts of Life in America* murals. Then head west an additional 7 miles on Rte 372 through Plainville to Bristol, where the **American Clock & Watch Museum**❖❖, pays homage to timepieces made in Bristol and vicinity, filled with more than 3000 ticking, striking and chiming instruments, from stately grandfather and church-steeple clocks to the earliest Mickey Mouse watches, initially produced in nearby Waterbury.

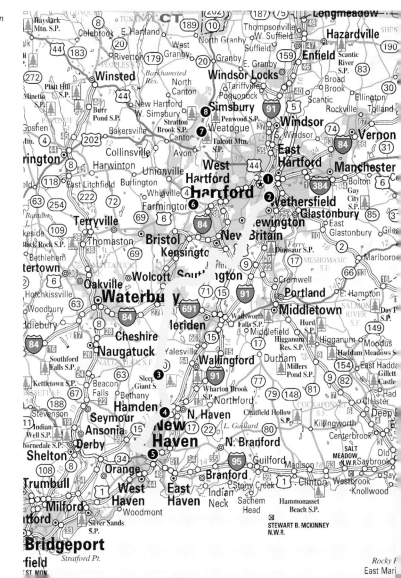

The Litchfield Hills

Ratings

Nature/scenery	●●●●●
Food and drink	●●●○○
History	●●●○○
Museums	●●●○○
Arts and culture	●○○○○
Children	●○○○○
Shopping	●○○○○
Beaches	●○○○○

It doesn't get better than this, at least not in inland New England. The state's northwestern corner offers travellers with a zest for wandering a mix of hilly topography, pastoral farmlands, wayward side-roads, covered bridges, state parks and woodsy nature sanctuaries, clear-water lakes and prototype Connecticut Yankee villages with white-steepled churches and grassy commons. Old-timers might grumble that their upstate region has become more than a little bit gentrified over recent years. True enough: increasing numbers of celebrities – often escapees from high-profile glamour cities – are pleased to count themselves as full- or part-time residents. Among them are actresses Meryl Streep and Mia Farrow, fashion gurus Bill Blass and Oscar de la Renta, novelist Philip Roth, TV newsman Tom Brokaw and elder statesman Henry Kissinger. But their affluence and visibility are understated, even hidden away in here-and-there enclaves of Litchfield-country valleys and hills.

KENT❖❖❖

🛈 For overall coverage: **Litchfield Hills Travel Council** PO Box 968, Litchfield, tel: (860) 567-4506; fax: (860) 567-5214; www.litchfieldhills.com Locally: **Kent Chamber of Commerce** PO Box 124, Kent; tel: (860) 927-1463.

🏛 **Kent Falls State Park** $ Rte 7; tel: (860) 927-3238. Open Apr–Dec daily 0800–dusk.

Iron-ore mines and blast furnaces in the bucolic Litchfield Hills? Indeed, pig-iron production was the region's economic engine for a century and a half beginning in 1750, and Kent was the centre of it all. Now that all evidence of industrial toil has faded into past history, this tweedy, up-market town has emerged as an arts community. You'll come upon galleries and studios (crafts shops, too) on Station Sq and the inevitable Main St – plus an ice-cream parlour and a cluster of gift and clothing boutiques.

If that's too mercantile for you, head 5 miles north to **Kent Falls State Park**❖❖❖, where wooden stairs lead to the top of the cascade's 200-ft plunge over white limestone. Also, Kent is merely 2 miles from **Macedonia Brook State Park**❖❖❖ where hikers reaching the summit of Cobble Mountain enjoy vistas of New York state's Catskill and Taconic ranges.

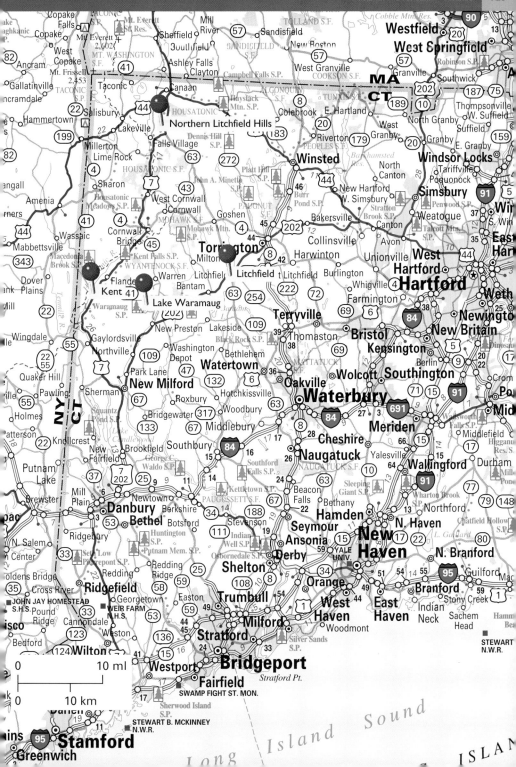

Macedonia Brook State Park
Macedonia Brook Rd (off Rte 341); tel: (860) 927-3238. Free

Sloane-Stanley Museum & Kent Furnace $ *Rte 7; tel: (860) 927-3849. Open mid May–late Oct Wed–Sun 1000–1600.*

Going 4 miles in the opposite direction gets you to **Bull's Bridge** (1842). Spanning the Housatonic River, it's one of only two Connecticut covered bridges still open to auto traffic. View the river and its gorges from rocky ledges, ideal for an impromptu picnic spread. And if old-time ironworks perk your curiosity, tour the **Sloane-Stanley Museum & Kent Furnace**. The house and studio of 20th-century landscape painter Eric Sloane is on the site of a furnace that belched tool-making fire between 1826 and 1892.

Accommodation and food in Kent

Bull's Bridge $ *333 Kent Rd; tel: (860) 927-1617.* Basic but satisfying meat-and-potatoes fare, plus a salad bar and fireplace.

Constitution Oak Farm $$ *36 Beardsley Rd; tel: (860) 354-6495.* An ex-dairy farm where the house dates from the late 18th century.

Fife 'n Drum Restaurant & Inn $$ *59 N Main St; tel: (860) 927-3509.* Centre-of-town convenience; sizeable wine list in the barnwood restaurant.

Stroble's Bakery $ *14 N Main St; tel: (860) 927-4073.* For heavenly buttered baguettes and apricot tarts.

The Villager $ *28 N Main St; tel: (860) 927-3945.* A favourite for all-American burgers and milkshakes as well as heavy-duty breakfasts.

Below
Bull's Bridge

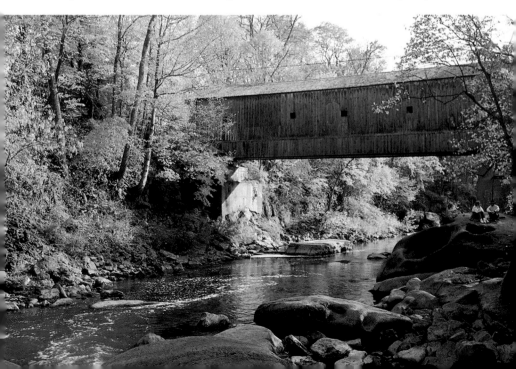

LAKE WARAMAUG✥✥✥

Lake Waramaug State Park *off Rte 45 from New Preston; tel: (860) 868-2592. Free*

Hopkins Vineyard *Hopkins Rd, New Preston; tel: (860) 868-7954. Call ahead for different hours at different times of year; guided winery tours. Free*

Institute for American Indian Studies $ *36 Curtis Rd, Washington; tel: (860) 868-0518. Open Mon–Sat 1000–1700, Sun 1200–1700; closed Mon–Tue (Jan–Mar).*

The Silo *44 Upland Rd, New Milford; tel: (860) 355-0300.*

Its shores comprising one of the Litchfield Hills' many state parks, this 680-acre body of water is popular for swimming, boating and camping (88 sites in woods and open fields). Verdant hills surrounding the lake give it a Swiss-Austrian aura. As an extra treat, several idyllic villages are close by: notably New Preston, Woodville, Marble Dale, Washington/Washington Depot and New Milford. So is **Hopkins Vineyard**✥ for the pleasure of wine-tasting in an old red barn. For all manner of trendy cookware, drive to **The Silo**✥ on New Milford's northerly outskirts, run by New York Pops conductor Skitch Henderson and his cookbook-collaborator wife.

Washington's **Institute for American Indian Studies**✥ covers 10,000 years of Native American life, highlighted by a replica 17th-century Algonquian village, garden and rock shelter.

Accommodation and food in the Lake Waramaug vicinity

Boulders Inn $$$ *East Shore Rd, New Preston; tel: (800) 552-6853 or (860) 868-0541.* Classy, casual lodgings in an 1875 Victorian mansion; fine restaurant with lake and Pinnacle Mountain views.

Hopkins Inn $$ *22 Hopkins Rd, New Preston; tel: (860) 868-7295.* A Federal-style country inn and Swiss-Austrian restaurant, across the road from the vineyard and overlooking Lake Waramaug.

Lakeview Inn $$ *North Shore Rd, New Preston; tel: (800) 525-3466 or (860) 868-0563.* A sprawling country inn since 1880; 'New American' cuisine, with a deck for alfresco dining.

Le Bon Coin $$$ *Rte 202, New Preston; tel: (860) 868-7763.* Out here in the country, big-city standards for a French *haute-cuisine* dining experience.

Mayflower Inn $$$ *118 Woodbury Rd, Washington; tel: (860) 868-9466.* The *crème de la crème* of posh New England country inns, on a 28-acre spread including woods, duck ponds and hillside gardens, plus a health spa and a stellar gourmet restaurant.

The Pantry $ *Washington Depot; tel: (860) 868-0258.* A restaurant, deli, bakery and health-food store in the village centre; handy for choosing picnic supplies.

LITCHFIELD✥✥✥

Towns described as having 'quintessential New England' charm possess several requisite components: at least one pointy white church spire, central common, a row or two of small local-colour shops,

ⓘ Northwest Connecticut Chamber of Commerce *333 Kennedy Dr, Torrington; tel: (860) 482-6586.*

ⓣ Litchfield Congregational Church *On the Green, East St/South St intersection. Open Mon–Fri 0900–1700, Sun services 1030, but 0930 summertime.*

Tapping Reeve House $ *South St; tel: (860) 567-4501. Open Tue–Sat 1100–1700, Sun 1300–1700 (mid May–mid Oct).*

Historical Society Museum $ *On the Green, East St/South St intersection; tel: (860) 567-4501. Open Tue–Sat 1100–1700, Sun 1300–1700 (Apr–mid Nov).*

Haight Vineyard *29 Chestnut Hill Rd (off Rte 118); tel: (800) 577-9463 or (860) 567-4045. Open Mon–Sat 1030–1700, Sun 1200–1700. Hourly winery tours.*

White Memorial Foundation & Conservation Center *Rte 202; tel: (860) 567-0857. Open daily, dawn–dusk.*

ⓐ Warner Theater *$–$$ 68 Main St, Torrington; tel: (860) 489-7180.*

streets lined with old trees and impeccably cared-for Early American houses and scenic surroundings. A courthouse, historical society and respectable library would clinch the title.

Litchfield qualifies on all counts. What's more, it's the birthplace of Revolutionary War hero Ethan Allen and Harriet Beecher Stowe, whose abolitionist (ie anti-slavery) best-seller, *Uncle Tom's Cabin*, came out in 1852. Her father, an equally outspoken abolitionist, was minister of the much-photographed **Congregational Church**✦✦ from 1810 to 1826. Add to that pedigree the **Tapping Reeve House**✦✦, the nation's first independent law school, established in 1784, with an honour roll of graduates starring Vice Presidents Aaron Burr and John C Calhoun along with 6 cabinet ministers, 26 senators, 3 Supreme Court justices and 16 state governors.

A browse through the Litchfield **Historical Society Museum**✦ acquaints newcomers with the area's early years. For Chardonnay/Riesling/Merlot wine-tasting, reaching **Haight Vineyard**✦ entails a short drive into hill country east of town. Drive westward to Connecticut's biggest nature sanctuary: 4000-acre **White Memorial Foundation & Conservation Center**✦✦, pine-forested and boggy terrain bordering **Bantam Lake** and **Bantam River** for camping, swimming, bird-watching, bicycling and hiking (35-mile trail network). A 1.2-mile boardwalk encircling **Little Pond** puts you in close touch with a virginal wetland environment.

With just enough of a commercial core and the obvious past significance of its Naugatuck River millworks, **Torrington** is more of a small city than a large town. Its standout landmark is the **Warner Theater**✦, exemplifying over-the-top art deco design, now a venue for stage shows and Nutmeg Ballet performances.

Accommodation and food in Litchfield and Torrington

Stone House Café and Gallery $$$ *637 Bantam Rd, Litchfield; tel: (860) 567-3326.* As the name and address imply, a stone house overlooking the Bantam River and featuring an art gallery. Extra-good cuisine and wine list.

Tollgate Hill Inn $$ *Rte 202 and Tollgate Rd, Litchfield; tel: (800) 445-3903 or (860) 567-4545.* Two 18th-century buildings amid a grove of white birch trees; hearty food in the original tavern.

West Side Grill $$ *West St, Litchfield; tel: (860) 567-3885.* Great for celebrity-watching and internationally inspired food, plus home-made peasant bread.

Yankee Pedlar Inn $ *93 Main St, Torrington; tel: (800) 777-1891 or (860) 489-9226.* A spruced-up 1891 oldie with 60 rooms and in-town convenience; pub-style downstairs restaurant.

Northern Litchfield Hills✦✦✦

Lime Rock Park $$
Rte 112, Lakeville; tel:
(860) 435-0896. Open
Apr–Nov.

Audubon Center $ Rte
4, Sharon; tel: (860) 364-
0520. Open year-round
Mon–Sat 0900–1700, Sun
1300–1700.

Battell Chapel 12 Village
Green, Norfolk; tel: (860)
542-5721.

Hitchcock Museum
Riverton Rd, Riverton; tel:
(860) 738-4950. Open
Wed–Sat 1100–1600, Sun
1200–1600 (Apr–Dec).

**Norfolk Chamber
Music Festival $$**
Tel: (860) 542-3000.
June–Aug.

Speckled with glacial lakes and ponds, the landscape a mix of rolling highlands and small-acreage farm fields, the Litchfield Hills' least-populous upper half could be mistaken for the far reaches of New Hampshire or Vermont. Just about every town and village is near a state forest or park.

Amid the prevailing tranquillity, the eight-turn course at **Lime Rock Park**✦ is a hotbed of pro/am auto racing. **West Cornwall** shares noteworthiness with Kent for having the other of Connecticut's two covered bridges still accessible to vehicular traffic. Sharon's **Audubon Center**✦ is a wildlife sanctuary with herb and wildflower gardens. High-altitude **Norfolk**, with a perfect village green, hosts a major **Chamber Music Festival**✦✦; the Congregational Church's **Battell Chapel**✦✦ features art nouveau stained-glass windows crafted by Louis Comfort Tiffany. **Riverton**, where the **Hitchcock Museum**✦ (in the *circa*-1829 Old Union Church) displays locally made hand-stencilled chairs, nestles amidst pine and hemlock forests.

Accommodation and food in the northern Litchfield Hills

Brookside Bistro $$ *Rte 128, West Cornwall; tel: (860) 672-6601*. French bistro fare, indoors or on the deck alongside Mill Brook.

Collins Diner $ *Rte 144, Canaan; tel: (860) 824-7040*. One of five classic US diners listed on the National Register of Historic Places.

Mountain View Inn $$ *67 Litchfield Rd, Norfolk; tel: (860) 542-6991*. An 1875 Victorian dowager in a well-nigh perfect New England village; Sat–Sun fireside dinners.

Old Riverton Inn $–$$ *Rte 20, Riverton; tel: (860) 379-8678*. Countrified seclusion beside the Farmington River in an inn dating from 1796, with a cosy colonial dining-room.

White Hart Inn $$ *Village Green, Salisbury; tel: (860) 435-0030*. Landmark village-centre inn; seafood specialities in the restaurant.

Suggested tour

Total distance: 120 miles; 130–135 miles with detour

Time: You're in hill country with curving roads, plus scenery and villages worthy of *en-route* stopovers, so allow a full day.

Link: Starting on the region's eastern flank connects you with the Connecticut Midlands Route (*see page 114*).

ⓘ Housatonic Valley Tourism District *30 Main St, Danbury; tel: (800) 841-4488 or (203) 743-0546; www.housatonic.org*

Ridgefield Chamber of Commerce *9 Bailey Ave, Ridgefield; tel: (203) 438-5992.*

Ⓐ Charles Ives Center for the Arts *$$ Mill Plain Rd, Danbury; tel: (203) 837-9226.*

ⓘ Aldrich Museum of Contemporary Art *$ 258 Main St, Ridgefield; tel: (203) 438-4519. Open Thur–Sun 1300–1700.*

Weir Farm *735 Nod Hill Rd, Ridgefield/Wilton; tel: (203) 834-1896. Call for studio tours at designated times.*

Route: Begin by heading west from metro Hartford on Rte 44; 3 miles beyond New Hartford, turn on to Rte 181, passing Pleasant Valley for an 8-mile drive through **Peoples State Forest ❶** alongside the **Barkhamsted Reservoir ❷** (a secondary road through the pine groves gets you to Riverton, if desired). Reach Rte 20 for a southbound swing to Winsted, followed by a 16-mile, Rte 44 drive to Norfolk in the Berkshire foothills – temptingly close to **Haystack Mountain State Park ❸** and **Campbell Falls ❹** with its multiple cascades – and tiny Canaan.

Continue on Rte 44 to Salisbury and Lakeville. If you're energetic, hike to the summit of 2361-ft **Bear Mountain ❺** for panoramic vistas of Connecticut, Massachusetts and New York.

Once past Falls Village and Lime Rock, swing over to Rte 7 to reach West Cornwall's historic **covered bridge ❻** after 4 miles and a further 10 miles through **Housatonic Meadows State Park ❼** to Kent and *that* town's **covered bridge ❽**. The super-scenic West Cornwall–Kent segment features lofty cliffs flanking the Housatonic River, with maple and oak trees at water's edge. Upon arrival in West Cornwall, consider a 7-mile westbound sidetrack to Sharon, with its **Audubon Center ❾** and cluster of stone and brick Early American houses.

Detour: From Kent, take Rte 341, then Rte 45 for a 2-mile loop around LAKE WARAMAUG ❿. Veer south for some short distance meandering through **New Preston ⓫**, **Marble Dale ⓬**, **Washington Depot ⓭** and **Washington ⓮** – the latter a enchantingly quaint hilltop hamlet overlooking the **Shepaug River Valley ⓯**, habitat for bald eagles.

Via Rte 202 going past **Bantam Lake ⓰**, reach Litchfield after 10 miles, plus another 6 miles to Torrington. From that mini-city, take Hwy 8 for a quick northbound jaunt to Winsted, which gets you back on to east–west Rte 44.

Also worth exploring

Upstate Litchfield hill country's predominant river continues its southward course to form the **Housatonic Valley** in a more urbanised patch of Connecticut. But you'll discover plenty of open spaces, cute communities and definitely an artistic heritage. Focus your touring on two close-together cities. Danbury is the birthplace of composer Charles Ives, hence the **Charles Ives Center for the Arts**✦✦ on a college campus, an outdoor summer-concert venue where the stage perches on an island in a pond.

Smaller Ridgefield beckons with the world-class **Aldrich Museum of Contemporary Art**✦✦, complete with the sculpture garden – also 50-acre **Weir Farm**✦✦✦, a National Historic Park where painter J Alden Weir became a founder of American Impressionism.

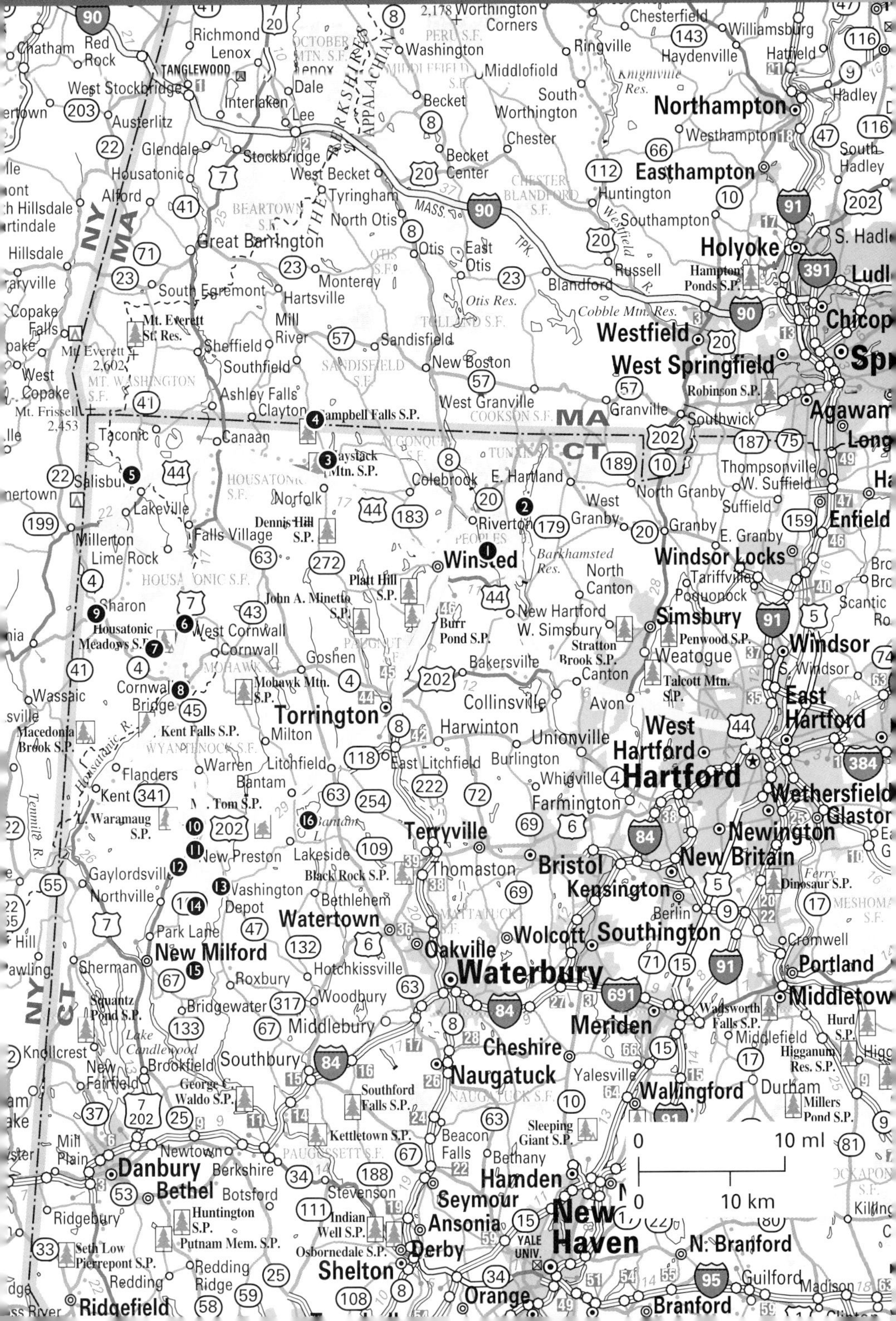
Chatham
Red Rock
Richmond
Lenox
TANGLEWOOD
West Stockbridge
Interlaken
Dale
Lee
Austerlitz
Glendale
Stockbridge
Housatonic
Alford
Great Barrington
South Egremont
Hillsdale
Copake Falls
Mt. Everett 2,602
Mt. Everett St. Res.
MT. WASHINGTON S.F.
West Copake
Mt. Frissell 2,453
Sheffield
Southfield
Ashley Falls
Clayton
Mill River
Hartsville
Monterey
BEARTOWN S.F.
OCTOBER MTN. S.F.
Washington
Worthington Corners
2,178
PERU S.F.
Middlefield
Becket
Becket Center
West Becket
Tyringham
North Otis
Otis
East Otis
Otis Res.
TOLLAND S.F.
Sandisfield
SANDISFIELD S.F.
New Boston
West Granville
COOKSON S.F.
Chester
South Worthington
Ringville
Chesterfield
Williamsburg
Haydenville
Hatfield
Northampton
Westhampton
Hadley
South Hadley
Easthampton
Huntington
CHESTER-BLANDFORD S.F.
Southampton
Holyoke
Hampton Ponds S.P.
Russell
Blandford
Cobble Mtn. Res.
Westfield
West Springfield
Robinson S.P.
Granville
Southwick
Agawam
Chicopee
MASS. TPK.
THE BERKSHIRE APPALACHIAN
NY MA
MA CT
NY CT
Taconic
Canaan
Campbell Falls S.P.
Haystack Mtn. S.P.
Salisbury
Lakeville
Millerton
Lime Rock
Falls Village
HOUSATONIC S.F.
Norfolk
Dennis Hill S.P.
Colebrook
E. Hartland
Riverton
West Granby
North Granby
Granby
E. Granby
Thompsonville
W. Suffield
Suffield
Enfield
Windsor Locks
Tariffville
Poquonock
Winsted
Barkhamsted Res.
North Canton
New Hartford
W. Simsbury
Simsbury
Penwood S.P.
Weatogue
Stratton Brook S.P.
Talcott Mtn. S.P.
Windsor
S. Windsor
East Hartford
Sharon
Housatonic Meadows S.P.
West Cornwall
Cornwall
Cornwall Bridge
Platt Hill S.P.
John A. Minetto S.P.
Burr Pond S.P.
Goshen
Mohawk Mtn. S.P.
Torrington
Bakersville
Canton
Avon
Collinsville
Wassaic
Macedonia Brook S.P.
Kent Falls S.P.
Milton
Harwinton
Unionville
West Hartford
Hartford
Kent
Flanders
Warren
Litchfield
Bantam
East Litchfield
Burlington
Whigville
Farmington
Wethersfield
Glastonbury
L. Waramaug S.P.
Mt. Tom S.P.
New Preston
Lakeside
Terryville
Thomaston
Bristol
Newington
New Britain
Dinosaur S.P.
Gaylordsville
Northville
Washington Depot
Black Rock S.P.
Bethlehem
Watertown
Kensington
Berlin
Southington
Cromwell
Portland
Park Lane
New Milford
Sherman
Roxbury
Hotchkissville
Oakville
Wolcott
Waterbury
Meriden
Middletown
Squantz Pond S.P.
Bridgewater
Woodbury
Middlebury
Cheshire
Wadsworth Falls S.P.
Middlefield
Hurd S.P.
Knollcrest
New Fairfield
Lake Candlewood
Brookfield
Southbury
Naugatuck
Yalesville
Wallingford
Durham
Higganum Res. S.P.
Millers Pond S.P.
George C. Waldo S.P.
Southford Falls S.P.
Kettletown S.P.
Beacon Falls
Sleeping Giant S.P.
Bethany
Mill Plain
Newtown
Danbury
Bethel
Berkshire
Botsford
Hamden
Stevenson
Seymour
Ansonia
Ridgebury
Huntington S.P.
Putnam Mem. S.P.
Indian Well S.P.
Osbornedale S.P.
Derby
New Haven
YALE UNIV.
N. Branford
Seth Low Pierrepont S.P.
Redding
Redding Ridge
Ridgefield
Shelton
Orange
Guilford
Madison
Branford
0 10 ml
0 10 km

Ratings

Arts and culture	●●●●●
Beaches	●●●●●
Nature/ scenery	●●●●○
Children	●●●○○
Food and drink	●●○○○
History	●●○○○
Museums	●●○○○
Shopping	●○○○○

The Lower Connecticut Valley

After curving for 410 miles from the Quebec–New Hampshire border, Connecticut's namesake river spills into Long Island Sound. Shipbuilding, fishing and furniture-making were important regional occupations when America was a British colony and then a young republic.

But this part of the state never underwent heavy-industry development – evident in the estuary's pristine salt marshes, a tidal wetland protected to impressive extent by the US Nature Conservancy. Unlike other major northeastern US rivers, there's no commercial port city at the Connecticut's mouth. That's because the delta's shifting sand bars impede deep-draft shipping – another plus for the area's ecology. Enthralled by the reflective 'painters' light' and contrasting colours of river, sky, marshes, salt meadows and foliage, prominent American Impressionists (notably Childe Hassam, Willard Metcalf and William Chadwick) made Old Lyme famous as an art colony during the first two decades of the 20th century.

CHESTER***

Town Office Building 65 Main St, Chester; tel (860) 526-0013; www.chesterct.com. For advance information about Lower Valley places and attractions, contact **Connecticut Valley & Shoreline Visitors Council** 393 Main St, Middletown; tel: (800) 486-3346 or (860) 347-0028; www.cttourism.org

Like many New England towns, this one got rich as an 18th-century mercantile trading centre, switched to mundane industrial production during the following century (when workers turned out knitting needles by the umpteen thousands), subsequently declined and ultimately revived to the present-day extent of spruced-up riverside charm. Also as usual, local history includes a titbit of Yankee ingenuity: Chester's Samuel Silliman invented the inkwell here in 1857. For

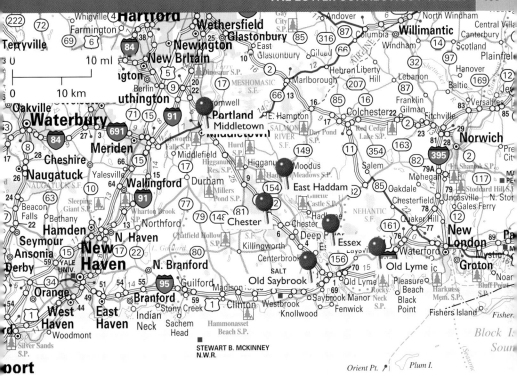

Chester–Hadlyme Ferry $ Carrying eight to nine vehicles per crossing, *Selden III* service operates *Apr–Nov, Mon–Fri 0700–1845; Sat–Sun 1030–1700.*

Connecticut Valley Artisans Cooperative 4 Water St, tel: (860) 526-5575.

Nilsson Spring Street Studio 1 Spring St; tel: (860) 526-2077.

Cockaponsett State Forest tel: (860) 345-8521. Via Rte 148 from Chester/Deep River; car-park off Cedar Lake Rd. Free

orientation, pick up a free pamphlet at the Town Office Building; it maps out self-guided walking tours ranging from 1.7 to 3.6 miles through Chester's immediate surroundings. For a quirky way of getting here westbound by car, drive on to the **Chester–Hadlyme Ferry**, a cross-river service in continuous operation since 1769.

Chester has become an artsy-craftsy community – apparent in a cluster of galleries and craft shops, the most prominent being **Connecticut Valley Artisans Cooperative** and **Nilsson Spring Street Studio**.

Nature lovers should delve into **Cockaponset State Forest**, at 15,652 acres the state's second-biggest. Alongside **Deep River**, Chester's neighbouring hamlet, 300-acre **Canfield-Meadow Woods Nature Preserve**, features 13 trails wending through a wooded realm of ridges and valleys.

Accommodation and food in Chester

Fiddlers $$ *4 Water St; tel: (860) 526-3210.* Specialises in fresh seafood.

Mad Hatter Bakery & Café $ *16 Main St; tel: (860) 526-2156.* A funky hangout for light lunch or early supper; delectable hearth-baked breads.

Canfield-Meadow Woods Nature Preserve *tel: (860) 526-6020.* Off Rte 154 in Deep River

Late August's Chester Agricultural & Mechanical Society Fair *Rte 154; tel: (860) 526-5947* has been a folksy event since 1877. One of the town's recycled knitting-needle factories is now the **Goodspeed-at-Chester/Norma Terris Theater** (*tel: (860) 873-8668*), a try out venue for new musicals produced by **East Haddam**'s Goodspeed Opera House company, staged in summer and autumn. A Yankee-doodling **Ancient Fife & Drum Muster and Parade**, biggest in the US, rattles Deep River's Main St windows during July's third Saturday; *tel: (860) 526-5947.*

Restaurant du Village $$$ *59 Main St; tel: (860) 526-5301.* Chester's *haute-cuisine* eatery, with French-Alsatian accentuation.

The Inn at Chester $$ *318 Main St; tel: (800) 949-STAY or (860) 526-9541.* A modernised 42-room country inn, colonial décor and 'Post and Beam' dining-room.

EAST HADDAM❖❖

Goodspeed Opera House $$$ *Rte 82, East Haddam; tel: (860) 873-8668. Apr–Dec season, Wed–Sun performances. Definitely purchase tickets well in advance.*

A single eye-catching landmark is reason enough for a stopover. It's a six-storey Victorian 'wedding-cake' built in 1876 by shipping/banking tycoon William H Goodspeed that's become the appropriately named **Goodspeed Opera House❖❖❖**, renowned for world-premiering such bound-for-Broadway musical successes as *Man of La Mancha* (1966) and *Annie* (1977). Another attraction is 2.7 miles downriver, on the outskirts of Hadlyme: a state park atop a promontory leading to **Gillette Castle❖❖**, a craggy fieldstone edifice with melodramatic

Gillette Castle $ *67 River Rd, Hadlyme; tel: (860) 526-3226. Plan at least an hour for an absorbing tour. Open May–mid Oct daily 1000–1700; mid Oct–mid Dec 1000–1600.*

Devil's Hopyard State Park *Rte 82 from East Haddam; tel: (860) 873-8566.*

Rhineland inspiration, completed in 1919 for actor William Gillette, long-time portrayer of Sherlock Holmes. With river views from on high, the park is delightful for picnicking. So is **Devil's Hopyard State Park**✤ and its 60-ft Chapman's Falls, reached via a scenic 6-mile drive east from East Haddam. The park's hiking trails total 15 miles.

Accommodation and food in East Haddam

Predating the adjacent opera house by 23 years, the comparable gingerbread-Victorian **Gelston House $$** *8 Main St; tel: (860) 873-1411*, is recommend for lodging and River Grill cooking.

For a bed-and-breakfast alternative, **Bishopsgate Inn $$** *7 Norwich Rd; tel: (860) 873-1677*, dates from the early 19th-century shipbuilding boom.

Wolf's Den Campground $ *Rte 82; tel: (860) 873-9681*, has 205 pitches, plus swimming and tennis facilities.

ESSEX✤✤✤

Essex Steam Train & Riverboat Ride *$$ Board at 1 Railroad Ave near Exit 3 off Rte 9 on the west end of Essex; tel: (800) ESSEX TRAIN or (860) 767 0103. Phone for seasonal schedules. The* **North Cove Express** *dinner train runs May–Dec.*

Connecticut River Museum $ *67 Main St; tel: (860) 767-8269. Open Tue–Sun 1000–1700.*

In 1995, the residents became more self-satisfied than ever. That's when their community topped a publication's list of 100 entries – in the 5000–15,000 population range – as the Best Small Town in America. Essex qualifies in many respects, appreciated by strolling the tree-shaded streets, poking into a modest amount of cute shops, admiring the Georgian and Federal domestic architecture and exploring the riverfront with its North and South Coves, piers, boatyards, town dock and not-too-snobbish Essex Yacht Club.

Main St dead-ends at Steamboat Landing, site of the **Connecticut River Museum**✤✤, occupying an 1878 warehouse converted into a repository of riverine and maritime history. Displays include a model of colonial America's first custom-built warship, the *Oliver Cromwell*, launched in 1775, a full-scale replica of the world's first seaworthy submarine, Connecticut-built *Turtle* (1776).

Essex Station is the embarkation point for the **Essex Steam Train & Riverboat Ride**✤✤✤, beginning with a 90-minute rail trip aboard 1920s coaches. At Deep River Landing, passengers can optionally transfer on to the triple-deck *Becky Thatcher* for an hour-long cruise past **Chester** to **East Haddam** and return.

In neighbouring Ivoryton, the **Ivoryton Playhouse**✤✤ (*103 Main St*), originally a factory recreation hall, is the summer-stock home of the River Rep Players, who present half a dozen productions, June–Sept. This is small-town straw-hat stuff with a big reputation. Over the decades, such stars as Katherine Hepburn, Marlon Brando, Tallulah Bankhead and Gloria Swanson have been on stage here.

Accommodation and food in Essex

The Griswold Inn $$ *36 Main St, Essex; tel: (860) 767-1776.* Essex wouldn't be Essex without the 'Gris', reputedly Connecticut's first three-storey structure. Along with guest rooms and suites, appealing atmospherics include Currier & Ives steamboat prints in the Covered Bridge dining-room. More nautical illustrations embellish the timber-beamed tavern, a local watering hole with musical entertainment. A humongous Hunt Breakfast is served every Sunday, 1100–1430.

Copper Beech Inn $$ *46 Main St, Ivoryton; tel: (860) 767-0330,* was constructed for one of the village's 19th-century ivory merchants; named for the copper beech tree standing in the front. A more intimate, secluded alternative to the 'Gris' for lodging and meals.

MIDDLETOWN✧

⊕ General Mansfield House $ *151 Main St; tel: (860) 346-07467. Phone for times of Sun–Mon guided tours.*

⊕ America's Cup $$ *80 Harbor Dr; tel: (860) 347-9999.* Lunch and dinner served in what used to be the riverside Middletown Yacht Club, built in 1915.

◈ Wesleyan Center for the Arts *High St; tel: (860) 685-2000. Galleries open during school year Tue–Fri 1200–1400, Sat–Sun 1400–1700; summer Tue–Sat 1200–1600. For the Center's theatre and concert tickets, call the box office: (860) 685-3355.*

Make the Lower Valley's only *bona fide* city a pitstop for petrol, supplies, whatever. Students attending Wesleyan University exert a generally well-behaved influence, so there's no lack of budget stores and eateries, including three all-American diners right downtown. Wesleyan's **Center for the Arts✧** comprises three performance halls plus two avant-garde galleries: Davis Art Center (prints and photographs) and the Zilkha Gallery (contemporary paintings and sculpture). The *circa*-1810 **General Mansfield House✧** is big on US Civil War history and 18th- to 19th-century decorative arts. Crave fresh air and exercise? Hike up the **Mattabesett Blue Trail**, reaching rocky ledges for panoramas of Middletown and the river.

Right
The Florence Grizwold Museum in Old Lyme

Right
Old Lyme's Congregational
Church

OLD LYME/OLD SAYBROOK**

Old Saybrook Chamber of Commerce *103 Main St, Old Saybrook; tel: (860) 388-3266; fax: (860) 388-9433.*

James Pharmacy *2 Pennywise Lane; tel: (860) 388-2566.*

Florence Griswold Museum $ *96 Lyme St; tel: (860) 434-5542. Open June–Nov Tue–Sat 1000–1700, Dec–May Wed–Sun 1300–1700.*

Divided by the river but connected by the interstate motorway's Baldwin Bridge, these are the closest towns to the Connecticut River's delta. Hustle and bustle? A commercial centre? You'll find neither in staid Old Lyme. Owners of its stately homes tend toward an anti-development attitude, willing to drive to bland strip malls on the outer fringe or to stores over in busier Old Saybrook. That said, Old Lyme's repute as an 'American Barbizon' is undeniable, thanks to a sea captain's daughter who turned her inherited 1817 mansion into a boarding house for turn-of-century American Impressionists – today's **Florence Griswold Museum**, bedecked with their paintings, also self-portrait caricatures on the dining-room mantle.

Map-read your way to Smith Neck Rd, off Rte 156, to reach Old Lyme's **Bird Observation Platform**, vantage point for nesting

Thimble Islands Cruise $ *Stony Creek dock; tel: (203) 481-3345. Mid May–mid Oct. Phone ahead for weekday and weekend timetable.*

Sundial Gardens $ *Brault Hill Road, Higganum; tel: (860) 345-4290. Open June–mid Oct Sat–Sun 1000–1700.*

ospreys in their Great Island habitat. Extending across a causeway south from downtown Old Saybrook, Rte 154 loops around **Fenwick***, an enclave of exclusive summer houses, site of the lighthouse depicted on Connecticut licence plates. In town, don't bypass the genuinely old-time **James Pharmacy****, complete with an 1896 soda fountain. Yale University began its stellar existence as the Collegiate School, located in Old Saybrook from 1707 to 1716, when it moved to New Haven.

Accommodation and food in Old Lyme/Old Saybrook

Bee & Thistle Inn $$ *100 Lyme St, Old Lyme; tel: (800) 622-4946 or (860) 434-1667,* is in the historic district – as is **The Old Lyme Inn $$** *85 Lyme St, Old Lyme; tel: (800) 434-5352 or (860) 434-2600.*

Dock & Dine $$ *Saybrook Point; tel: (860) 388-4665.* A casual seafood restaurant where picture windows and an outdoor deck overlook the confluence of the Connecticut River and Long Island Sound.

Old Saybrook Inn & Spa $$$ *2 Bridge St, Old Saybrook; tel: (800) 243-0212 or (860) 395-2000.* Modernistic design, fitness facilities, a grillroom restaurant and a gorgeous waterfront setting.

Suggested tour

Total distance: 68–70 miles; 98–100 miles with detour

Time: 3 hours' leisurely driving. Figure on a full morning or afternoon at that pace, full day or a bit more with detour.

Links: At **Old Lyme**, connect with the Connecticut's Southeastern–Corner Route (*see page 140*). By driving east from Middletown, you can join the Connecticut Midlands Route (*see page 114*). The detour terminus at Stony Creek connects on to the Connecticut's Midlands Route by way of Branford on New Haven's eastern outskirts.

Route: Heading west from **OLD LYME ❶**, cross the I-95/Baldwin Bridge to reach Rte 154 in **OLD SAYBROOK ❷** for a scenic riverside-marshland drive north to **ESSEX ❸** and **CHESTER ❹**. Cross the river aboard the Chester–Hadlyme Ferry if you'd like to visit **Gillette Castle ❺** on the east bank. Otherwise, continue on Rte 154 to Tylerville; cross the river's Swing Bridge (a 1913 iron-girder contraption, 'swingable' for passage of tall-masted boats) for arrival in East Haddam. If you wish, sidetrack via Rte 82 to **Devil's Hopyard State Park ❻**. Otherwise, backtrack across the bridge; continue north on Rte 154 to Higganum, locale of 18th-century-style **Sundial Gardens*** ❼ with topiaries and herb gardens. West of that village, connect on to Rte 9 for a swift drive into **MIDDLETOWN ❽**. Complete the loop by

ⓗ Hammonasett State Beach Park $
Rte 1, Madison; tel: (203) 245-2785. Open year-round 0800–sunset.

Henry Whitfield State Museum $ *248 Old Whitfield St, Guilford, tel: (203) 453-2457. Open Feb–mid Dec Wed–Sun 1000–1630). The house museum is well supplied with visitor information for Guilford and vicinity.*

returning southbound to the coast. Two idyllic country byways, with miles of stone fences, are Rte 79 through Rockland to Madison and Rte 81 through Killington to Clinton.

Detour: Begin it at **Old Saybrook ❷**; drive close to shoreline and marshy wetlands via Rte 1 (the old Boston Post Rd) through Westbrook to above-mentioned Madison and Clinton. Midway between those pleasant towns, **Hammonasett Beach State Park** ❾ features Connecticut's longest beachfront (2 miles), nature trails and 550 campsites.

Continue to very photogenic **Guilford ❿**, wrapped around an extra-large town green and locale of the **Henry Whitfield Museum** ⓫, eminent as New England's oldest stone house, built in 1639. Pink granite shipped from a local quarry to New York City went into the construction of Grand Central Station and the pedestal of the Statue of Liberty.

From Guilford, steer on to Rte 146 for a super-scenic 10-mile jaunt with close-ups of coves and salt marshes, reaching tiny Stony Creek – 'port of call' for cruises through the scattered, rocky, partially residential **Thimble Islands** ⓬, purported pirates' hideaways in past history.

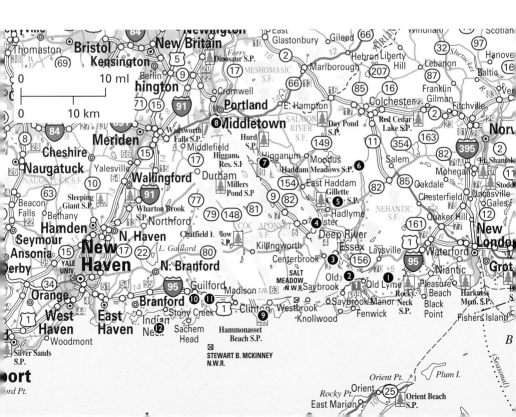

Connecticut's Southeastern Corner

Ratings

Children	●●●●
History	●●●●
Art and culture	●●
Beaches	●●
Food and drink	●●
Museums	●●
Nature/ scenery	●●
Entertainment	●

Connecticut's contrasts are especially apparent in the state's southeastern corner. Compare, for instance, the picturesque fishing-boat villages of Noank and Stonington Borough with citified New London and Norwich. In between, depending upon where you choose to travel, are spectacular stretches of indented coastline and some of the prettiest forested hills in all of New England – in the midst of which the world's largest casino complex attracts daredevil gamblers by the many thousands every day. The further reward of opting for a close-to-shore drive, with Long Island Sound in view, is Mystic Seaport, the nation's biggest, best and best-known maritime museum.

Because point-to-point distances are scant throughout this region, you're never far from adjacent Rhode Island's southwestern-most edge of land, where the Watch Hill resort community and Misquamicut State Beach are summertime favourites.

Groton❖

❶ Southeastern Connecticut Tourism District *470 Bank St, PO Box 89, New London; tel: (800) TO ENJOY or (860) 444-2206; www.mysticmore.com.* Visitor enquiry services covering New London/Groton along with the state's entire southeast region.

Don't be put off by first impressions of Groton's outward junkiness. Westbound trucks and autos, after negotiating a tangle of motorway interchanges, rumble towards the Gold Star Memorial Bridge – an arched span high above the Thames River. With that milieu, drivers encounter consistently heavy traffic, billboards galore, a shopping 'plaza' and random motels.

But a short diversion, north alongside the river, is worthwhile for anyone interested in undersea strategy and technology. Explore the tight innards of the USS *Nautilus*❖❖❖, the world's first nuclear-powered submarine (launched in 1954) and the first (in 1958) to cross beneath the North Pole's ice cap. That main attraction is augmented by the **Submarine Force Museum**❖❖, displaying scale models, periscopes, torpedoes, sonar gear, signal flags, mini-subs and much else connected with what Navy veterans call the 'silent service'.

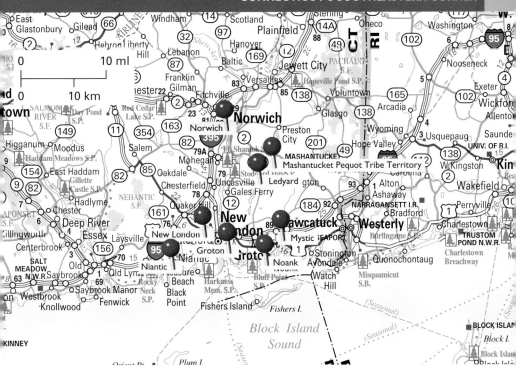

USS Nautilus & Submarine Force Museum *Navy Submarine Base, 1 Crystal Rd (off Rte 12); tel: (800) 343-0079. Open mid Apr–mid Oct Wed–Mon 0900–1700, Tue 1300–1700; mid Oct–mid Apr Wed–Mon 0900–1600.*

Fort Griswold Battlefield State Park✢ *(Monument St and Pratt Ave; tel: (860) 449 6877; open daily)* harks back to earlier warfare, commemorating a bloody American defeat or a British victory (depending upon your allegiance) in 1781, when 800 Redcoats commanded by traitor General Benedict Arnold attacked the fort. Gun emplacements remain intact and the 17-acre site is a peaceful picnic spot. For coastal vistas from an observatory platform at 134-ft altitude, climb the spiral staircase inside the granite monument tower.

LEDYARD✢

Foxwoods information *tel: (800) PLAY-BIG; www.foxwoods.com.* Exit 92 off the I-95 motorway for a Rte 2 drive to the complex. From just about any direction in southern New England, roadside signs point the way. Free

For some miraculous reason, this drowsy little place hasn't been swallowed up by the colossal neighbour dominating the Mashantucket Pequot Tribal Nation's 5000-acre chunk of territory, namely: **Foxwoods Resort & Casino**✢✢, whose turquoise and teal buildings rise Oz-like out of cornfields and cow pastures in hilly farm country. What began in 1986 as a bingo parlour is now a mighty complex comprising three vast gambling halls (buzzing and jingling around the clock) where get-rich-quick hopefuls play all conceivable games of chance. Plus a Vegas-type nightclub starring showbiz entertainers, Cinetropolis movie theatre, high-tech past-times for the kids, loads of eateries and shops as well as three different-size hotels.

Mashantucket Pequot Museum & Research Center $$ *110 Pequot Trail; tel: (800) 411-9671. Open daily 1000–1900.*

Along with this the **Mashantucket Pequot Museum & Research Center*** provides insights into the Pequot tribe's Native American culture and 10,000-year history.

Accommodation and food at Foxwoods

For copious amenities despite the high-wattage glitz: **Foxwoods Resort Hotel** $$ or the 800-room **Grand Pequot Tower** $$–$$$. For something more countrified: **Two Trees Inn** $$ *Tel: (800) FOXWOOD.* Reserve well in advance in any season.

Restaurants include **Cedars Steak House** $$ combining a grill room and seafood raw bar, **Al Dente** $$ for Italian meals and **Han Garden** $–$$ for its Chinese atmosphere. **Branches** $$ is a fireside in Two Trees Inn.

MYSTIC✦✦✦

Mystic Chamber of Commerce *16 Cottrell St, Mystic; tel: (860) 572-9578.*

Mystic Seaport $$$ *75 Germanville Ave (Rte 27); tel: (860) 572-5315. Open daily year-round. Call for times, variable depending upon time of year.*

Mystic Marinelife Aquarium $$ *55 Coogan Blvd (Exit 90 off I-95); tel: (860) 572-5955. Open daily 0900–1900 summertime, 0900–1700 otherwise.*

Argia Schooner $$$ *73 Steamboat Wharf; tel: (860) 536-0416. Half-day cruises depart daily 1000 and 1400, sunset cruises 1800 (May–Oct).*

Re-creating a 19th-century New England seaport village and keeping it from a becoming a trite Disneyfied theme park is no small accomplishment. **Mystic Seaport**✦✦✦ succeeds (as Connecticut's foremost tourism attraction) because of its authenticity, craftspeople and interpreters, interactive demonstrations, informational facilities and – above all – fully rigged vessels that really went to sea in years gone by. Tied to the shipyard docks, they include the 1841 *Charles W. Morgan* (the last surviving wooden whaling ship), an 1882 square-rigger and a Gloucester fishing schooner. The 1907 *Sabino*, one of the last coal-fired steamers afloat, takes passengers on Mystic River excursions.

Another crowd-pleaser is **Mystic Marinelife Aquarium**✦✦, populated by more than 3500 aquatic creatures including sharks, stingrays, seals, sea lions, a penguin colony, Beluga whales and bottle-nose dolphins.

In Mystic's town centre, where the oddest (and traffic-delaying) landmark is a 1922 bascule drawbridge, the gaff-rigged schooner *Argia** goes cruising on Fishers Island Sound.

Accommodation and food in Mystic

For overnight stays in Mystic centre, three hostelries are recommendable. Lauren Bacall and Humphrey Bogart honeymooned in the **Inn at Mystic** $$ *PO Box 216, Mystic; tel: (800) 237-2415 or (860) 536-9604.* On-site: the praiseworthy **Flood Tide Restaurant** $$. The **Steamboat Inn** $$ *73 Steamboat Wharf, Mystic; tel: (860) 536-8300,* stands alongside the drawbridge. A grouping of four 19th-century buildings comprises the **Whalers' Inn**, *20 E Main St, Mystic; tel: (800) 243-2588 or (860) 536-1506.*

Downtown Mystic's sidewalks are taken over by a juried **Outdoor Arts & Crafts Festival**⁺ during the first weekend of August, 1000–dusk.

Italian/Continental/American choices and a waterfront terrace highlight **Bravo Bravo** *$$ 20 E Main St; tel: (860) 536-3228.* Dine overlooking the drawbridge and river at **S & P Oyster Co** *$ 1 Holmes St; tel: (860) 536-2674.* Right next to Mystic Seaport, **Seamen's Inne** *105 Germanville Ave; tel: (860) 536-9649,* is a seafood restaurant and pub.

NEW LONDON✧

ℹ Refer to Groton in this chapter for **Southeastern Connecticut Tourism District**.

ⓘ Ye Antientist Burial Ground
Between Hempsted and Huntington Sts downtown.

Shaw Mansion $ *11 Blinman St; tel: (860) 443-1209. Open May–Oct Wed–Fri 1300–1600, Sat 1000–1600.*

Robert Mills US Custom House Museum *Free 150 Bank St; tel: (860) 447-2501. Limited hours, so phone ahead.*

Monte Cristo Cottage $ *325 Pequot Ave; tel: (860) 443-0051. Open Tue–Sat 1000–1700, Sun 1300–1700 (late May–early Sept).*

Lyman Allyn Art Museum $ *625 Williams St; tel: (860) 443-443-0051. Open Tue–Sat 1000–1700, Sun 1300–1700.*

US Coast Guard Academy *Mohegan Ave (off Rte 32); tel: (860) 444-8270. Free. Visitors' pavilion open May–Oct Mon–Fri 0900–1700, Sat–Sun 1000–1700. Museum open May–Oct Mon–Fri 0900–1630 (Thur 0900–2000) Sat 1000–1700, Sun 1200–1700. When in port, the Eagle can be boarded Mon–Fri 1300–sunset, Sat–Sun sunrise–sunset.*

Nothing's fancy or overtly touristy here. Mid-size New London has deep-water harbour facilities near the mouth of the Thames River (which rhymes with James on this side of the Atlantic). That location made quite a few folks wealthy during the whale hunting era, which began locally in 1784 and peaked by mid-19th century.

A free walking-tour map acquaints you with what's historically interesting about compact inner New London. It covers places with such evocative names as the **Captain's Walk**✧✧ and **Whale Oil Row**✧✧, the latter lined with stately 1830s Greek Revival houses. Also on the route are: **Ye Antientist Burial Grounds**✧, with headstones dating from Puritan settlement in the mid 1600s, the 1756 **Shaw Mansion**✧, Connecticut's Naval Office during the Revolutionary War; and 1833's **Robert Mills US Custom House Museum**✧, America's oldest functioning custom house.

Nobel and Pulitzer Prize-winning playwright Eugene O'Neill spent his boyhood years in New London's **Monte Cristo Cottage**✧✧, named for his actor father's signature stage role and the setting of two O'Neill plays: *Long Day's Journey Into Night* and *Ah! Wilderness*.

The **Lyman Allyn Art Museum**✧✧ is strong on colonial furniture, paintings, silver, china and glassware. If you're here with children, treat them to the museum's collection of dolls, dollhouses and antique toys.

The **US Coast Guard Academy**✧✧, upriver from downtown, is New London's link with its seagoing past. The academy's campus, on high ground overlooking the river, is pleasantly walkable. For orientation and background see a multimedia presentation in the visitors' pavilion and historical displays in Waesche Hall's Coast Guard Museum. The cadet's tall-masted training ship, the barque *Eagle*, captured from the Germans and brought here after World War II, is occasionally away on tour. If not, it's open to the public.

Accommodation and food in New London

Lighthouse Inn $–$$ *6 Guthrie Pl; tel: (800) 678-8946 or (860) 443-8411.* Waterfront lodgings in a pink stucco 1902 mansion with elegant **Mansion Restaurant** $$–$$$.

The Queen Anne Inn $ *265 Williams St; tel: (800) 347-8818 or (860) 447-2600.* As the name implies, a Victorian 'painted lady' bed & breakfast.

Lorelei $ *158 State St; tel: (860) 442-3375.* A fun place with tin ceilings and a convivial bar.

Timothy's $$ *181 Bank St; tel: (860) 437-0526.* Downtown's continental cuisine touch of class.

NIANTIC⁕

ℹ️ Rocky Neck State Park $ *Rte 156; tel: (860) 739-5471. Open daily 0800–sunset.*

Children's Museum of Southeastern Connecticut $ *409 Main St; tel: (860) 691-1111. Open Tue–Sat 0930–1630 (Fri 0930–2000) Sun 1200–1700. Otherwise 0930–1630.*

Millstone Information & Science Center Free *278 Main St; tel: (860) 691-4670. Open in summer Mon–Tue 0900–1600, Wed–Fri 0900–1900, Sat–Sun 1200–1700; Sept–June Mon–Fri 0900–1600.*

Driving southwest from New London brings you to a string of specks on the map – Jordan Village, Graniteville, Crescent Beach – where a general store, petrol pumps and perhaps a clam shack are the primary sources of income and social activity. Another such speck is Niantic, better known because of desirably plump Niantic Bay scallops. The village is 4 miles from **Rocky Neck State Park⁕⁕**, with a crescent-shaped beach, promontories, boardwalk, woodland hiking trails, picnic grounds and a stone pavilion constructed by WPA (Works Progress Administration) labourers during the 1930s Depression. Edged by salt marshes, Bride's Brook flows through the park.

If you're touring with youngsters, take them to the interactive **Children's Museum of Southeastern Connecticut⁕**. Walk from there to Northeast Utilities' **Millstone Information & Science Center⁕** to learn about the workings of a nuclear power station.

Accommodation and food in Niantic and vicinity

Inn at Harbor Hill Marina $$ *60 Grand St, Niantic; tel: (860) 739-0331.* Eight water-view rooms in an 1870s building; continental breakfast included.

The Shack $–$$ *Flanders Rd (Rte 161); tel: (860) 739-8898.* Three miles inland from Niantic, in Flanders Village, part of another speck on the map: East Lyme. Down-home cooking, all-you-can-eat fish fry daily. Serving Niantic Bay scallops.

NOANK⁕⁕⁕

This coast-of-Maine lookalike, clustered atop a rocky outcrop and complete with lobster traps stacked on weatherbeaten piers, merits a sidetrack while you're driving in either direction between Groton/New London and Mystic. At an easygoing pace, you can see all that's in the nationally registered historic district – mainly fine old houses, a general store, grocery store and a couple of art galleries – in less than an hour.

Accommodation and food in Noank

The Palmer Inn $$ *25 Church St; tel: (860) 572-9000.* Epitomises a Yankee bed & breakfast, in this case built by a shipwright in 1907.

Abbott's Lobster in the Rough $$ *117 Pearl St; tel: (860) 572-9128.* A setting at ocean's edge for New England shore dinners (clam chowder, boiled lobster, 'steamer' clams, corn on the cob).

NORWICH❖

Norwich Tourism Office 69 Main St, Norwich; tel: (860) 886-4683.

Leffingwell House $ 348 Washington St; tel: (860) 889-9440. Open mid May–mid Oct Tue–Sun 1300–1600.

Slater Memorial Museum $ 108 Crescent St; tel: (860) 887-2505. Open June–Sept Tue–Fri 0900–1600, Sat–Sun 1300–1600; July–Aug Tue–Sun 1300–1600.

Not flashy but historic, Norwich was founded in 1635 by three dozen English settlers who knew a favourable locale when they saw one. It's situated at the confluence of three rivers which form the Thames – an ideal location for water-powered mills. The tourism office provides three walking-tour maps for 5.2 miles of independent sightseeing. They cover three episodes of local history – Norwichtown is the colonial-era district, with a houses in every Early American style. Among the oldest is Norwichtown's *circa*-1675 **Leffingwell House❖**, built by an original settler, then used as a meeting place for Revolutionary War patriots.

On the campus of Norwich Academy, **Slater Memorial Museum❖** is an attention-getter because of its major, rather weird collection of plaster casts of Greek, Roman and Renaissance sculptures, among them *Winged Victory*, *Venus de Milo* and Michelangelo's *Pietà*.

Accommodation and food in Norwich

Norwich Inn & Spa $$ *607 W Thames St (Rte 32); tel: (800) 275-4772 or (860) 886-2401.* Luxurious turn-of-the-century country inn with up-to-date resort amenities.

Americus on the Wharf $$ *American Wharf; tel: (860) 887-8555.* The wharf symbolises downtown Norwich's Thames riverside revitalisation; the restaurant's décor is appropriately nautical.

Below
Stonington Borough's shoreline

Right
Stonington Borough's Cannon Square commemorates Yankee victories over the British during the American Revolution

STONINGTON BOROUGH❖❖❖

Old Lighthouse Museum $ 7 Water St; tel: (860) 535-1440. Open May–Oct daily 1100–1700.

Although Stonington is just another 'gasoline alley' burg on the Boston Post Rd, its Stonington Borough appendage vies with Noank as Connecticut's most charming shoreline community. Squeezed on to a narrow spit of land, the village is home port for Connecticut's only remaining commercial fishing fleet. Maritime miscellany crams the 1823 **Old Lighthouse Museum**❖❖.

Accommodation and food in Stonington

Randall's Ordinary $$ *Rte 2, North Stonington; tel: (860) 599-4540.* Rooms in a colonial homestead and a converted 1819 dairy barn; costumed waiters and waitresses serve hearth-cooked meals.

Boom $$ *194 Water St, Stonington Borough; tel: (860) 535-1381.* What you'd expect in a fishing-boat village: fresh-caught seafood.

Mystic Seaport

Suggested tour

Total distance: 45–50 miles, 57–62 miles with detours

Time: Maximum 2 hours' driving; add half a day for detours. Allow at least half a day for Mystic Seaport.

Links: Join the Newport/Narragansett Bay Route (*see page 150*) at Stonington or Westerly. Connect onto the Lower Connecticut Valley Route (*see page 132*) at Niantic/Rocky Neck State Park.

Route: From New London, go north on Rte 32 through Uncasville to reach **NORWICH/NORWICHTOWN** ❶, a 12-mile drive. For a same-distance southbound return to **GROTON** ❷ on the opposite side of the Thames River, cross over to Rte 12.

Heading east from Rocky Neck State Park for **NIANTIC** ❸, follow rural Rte 156 to Waterford; from there via Rte 1 into New London for connection onto I-95 across the Gold Star Memorial Bridge to reach **GROTON** ❷. Rte 12 gets you south into town, north to the US Submarine Base. Beyond Groton, take Rte 1 to the Rte 215 juncture in order to swoop down and through Noank, continuing past Beebe Cove to **MYSTIC** ❹. Resume driving on Rte 1. At Rte 1A in Stonington, signs sidetrack you a bit south to **STONINGTON BOROUGH** ❺. Rte 1 continues 4.5 miles to the Connecticut/Rhode Island state line at the Pawcatuck River.

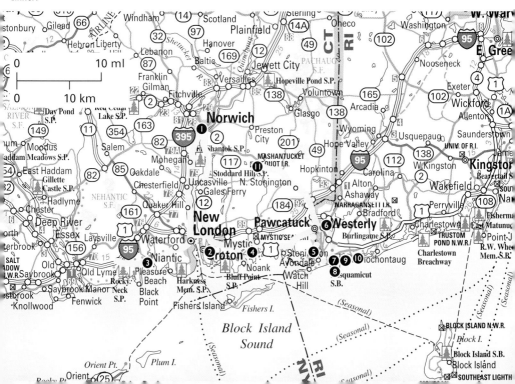

**ⓘ Westerly-
Pawcatuck
Chamber of
Commerce** 55 Beach St,
Westerly; tel: (401) 596-
7761.

ⓘ A stopover in
Westerly is
worthwhile, if only to
stroll through Victorian
Wilcox Park, behind the
brick-and-granite public
library, Granite St.

Flying Horse Carousel
$ Bay St. Open Mon–Fri
1300–2100, Sun & holidays
1100–2100.

**Misquamicut State
Beach** $ Auto entrance on
Atlantic Ave, off Rte 1A
(Shore Rd).

**ⓘ Olympia Tea
Room** $ Bay St; tel:
(401) 348-8211. For
breakfast, lunch and
dinner.

Detour: Immediately upon arriving in Rhode Island, you're in
Westerly ❻. Turn on to Rte 1A for a 5-mile drive past Avondale to the
peninsular **Watch Hill**⁕ ❼, which began attracting urban vacationers
who turned it into a mini-Newport during the Gilded Age (late 19th
century). It's still a popular warm-weather destination, thanks to
breezy air, nearby beaches and plenty of lodgings in inexpensive-to-
moderate price categories. Grown-ups and kids enjoy the 19th-century
Flying Horse Carousel⁕ ❽, with each steed sculpted out of a single
block of wood. Watch Hill's **Olympia Tea Room**⁕⁕ ❾ has been in
business non-stop since 1916. Splendid sand-and-dunes **Misquamicut
State Beach**⁕ ❿ is 3 miles away.

Once you're at the Connecticut/Rhode Island state line, Rte 2
northbound takes you (12 miles) to **Foxwoods** ⓫ (see **Ledyard**).

Also worth exploring

Uncasville, midway between New London and Norwich, would be
unassuming were it not for adjacent **Mohegan Sun**⁕, the second of
Connecticut's gambling palaces – this one on Mohegan Tribal Nation
land. If you haven't gone bankrupt at Foxwoods, try your luck at this
less overwhelming place, with nightclub, 24-hour restaurants and
shops in addition to the essential table games and slot machines.

Newport

Ratings

Arts and Culture	●●●●●
Beaches	●●●●●
History	●●●●●
Museums	●●●●○
Children	●●○○○
Food and drink	●●○○○
Nature/ scenery	●●○○○
Shopping	●●○○○

For several primary reasons, Newport heads the list of Rhode Island's most popular visitor destinations. First of all: the palatial Gilded Age 'summer cottages' on and near Bellevue Ave. To those exemplars of conspicuous consumption, add intriguing aspects of US colonial and Revolutionary War history, complete with public buildings and clapboard houses dating from the era. Furthermore, this small peninsular city still exudes the yachting aura of its America's Cup heyday. Make Newport your base for bridge-connected drives to Conanicut Island and – along Narragansett Bay's western shore – charming towns and terrific beaches. East Bay scenery and villages are compelling, too. As a bonus extra, Newport is a port of embarkation for auto-ferry crossings to Block Island, ideal bicycling and nature-walking terrain.

Sights

Hammersmith Farm $$ *Ocean Ave; tel: (401) 846-7346. Open Apr–mid Nov daily 1000–1700; also Mar & late Nov Sat–Sun; 1000–1900 summertime.*

International Tennis Hall of Fame $ *194 Bellevue Ave; tel: (401) 849-3990. Open daily 1000–1700.*

Hammersmith Farm✦✦✦
This is the sprawling bayfront estate of the Auchincloss family, which included Jacqueline Bouvier. The interiors are loaded with intimate memorabilia, the gardens were designed by Frederick Law Olmsted, creator of Manhattan's Central Park and Boston's 'Emerald Necklace' park system. Jacqueline and Massachusetts senator John F Kennedy had their outdoor wedding reception here in September 1953, having been married in town at **St Mary's Church**, Rhode Island's oldest Roman Catholic parish.

International Tennis Hall of Fame✦✦✦
Originally Newport's shingle-sided casino (not a gambling joint, but a country club in its previous existence). From 1881 to 1914 it was the

Van Zandt Ave

Washington Street

Second Street

Warner Street

Broadway

HUNTER
HOUSE
The
Po

Thames Street

Wanton-Lyman-
Hazard House

WAN
HAZA

Battery
Park

Gateway Visitors Center
CENTER

Museum of Newport History

OLD
HOUS

ONY

Touro Synagogue

Goat
Island

NEWPORT

Trinity Church

Congregational Ch.

TRINITY

Mill St

Newport Art Museum/Old Stone Mill/Redwood Library and Athenæum

CHURCH

Memorial

OLD STONE MIL
DWOOD LIBRA

International Tennis Hall of Fame

Spring Street

Bellevue Ave

TERNATIONA
TENNIS
HALL OF FAME

Fort Adams State Park

FORT ADAMS
STATE PARK

Wellington Ave

Narragansett Ave

THE ELMS

Halidon Ave

Harrison Ave

Carroll Ave

ter Street

CHATEAU-
R-MER

Chateau-Sur-Mer

BREA

HAMMERSMITH
Hammersmith Farm

Harrison Ave

Ruggles Ave

Coggeshall Ave

Bellevue Ave

ROSECLIF

Ridge Road

BEECHWO

Castle Hill Lighthouse

CASTLE HILL
LIGHTHOUSE

Marble House

ARBLE
OUSE

Harrison Ave

BELCOURT
CASTLE

Ocean Ave

Brenton Road

Ocean Ave

BRENTON POINT
Brenton Point State Park

0   1 km

The Mansions $$
For days, times and individual or combination admittance prices at the six maintained by the **Preservation Society of Newport County** *tel: (401) 847-1000.* Regarding the other two, call ahead for days, hours, costs.
Beechwood *580 Bellevue Ave; tel: (401) 846-3772.*
Belcourt Castle *657 Bellevue Ave; tel: (401) 846-0669.*

Museum of Newport History $ *Brick Market at 120 Thames St; tel: (401) 841-8770. Open Mon & Wed–Sat 1000–1700, Sun 1300–1700.*

Naval War College Museum *Coasters Island, 686 Cushing Rd (US Naval base); tel: (401) 841-4052. Open Mon–Fri 1000–1600; plus Sat–Sun 1200–1600 (June–Sept).*

Newport Art Museum $ *76 Bellevue Ave; tel: (401) 848-8200. Phone ahead for seasonal hours. Free.*

site of the US National Lawn Tennis Championships which became the US Open. The Hall of Fame is the sport's Valhalla; a museum covers the history of tennis, and the original 13 courts are America's only competition grass courts available for public play.

The Mansions✦✦✦

Collectively, the city's paramount attraction consists of eight open-to-the-public 'summer cottages'. Six are maintained by the Newport Preservation Society:

The Breakers, *Oche Point Ave*, emulating a 16th-century Italian palazzo, was built for railroad tycoon Cornelius Vanderbilt in 1895. **Chateau-sur-Mer**, *Bellevue Ave*, a shipping magnate's abode dating from 1852, exemplifies full-blown mid-Victorian architecture. A 1901 extravaganza resembling a French château, **The Elms**, *Bellevue Ave*, was the summer residence of a Pennsylvania coal-mining magnate. An 1839 Gothic Revival spread, **Kingscote**, *Bellevue Ave*, was built for the George Noble Jones family of Savannah, in Georgia. Inspired by the Grand and Petit Trianons at Versailles, William K Vanderbilt's 1892 **Marble House**, *Bellevue Ave*, cost a then-outrageous $9 million. Terracotta **Rosecliff**, *Bellevue Ave* (1902), with its 22 bedrooms, a heart-shaped staircase and Newport's biggest private ballroom, was modelled after Versailles' Grand Trianon by Stanford White, the era's most sought-after architect.

Two additional mansions can be visited: **Beechwood** belonged to William Backhouse Astor and his wife, the *grande dame* of 1890s Newport society. Sixty-room **Belcourt Castle**, another little Vanderbilt getaway, sports the first-ever indirect lighting, installed by Thomas Edison in 1894.

Museum of Newport History✦✦

Here can be found overviews of colourful local history and accomplishments through artefacts, displays, dioramas, paintings, photographs, decorative arts, cinema and interactive computers and videos. The 1762 Brick Market building, an attraction in its own right, was designed by Peter Harrison, architect of the Redwood Library.

Naval War College Museum✦

As the name implies, this museum covers global maritime warfare, with emphasis on US Navy exploits on Narragansett Bay. Collections include ship models and World War II battle-at-sea photos. Also displayed is the first American torpedo, Newport-made in 1869.

Newport Art Museum✦

The main building is the main attraction: the former Grisold mansion of 1864, a stick-style Victorian house designed by celebrity architect Richard Morris Hunt. The art collection leans heavily toward 19th- and 20th-century Americana, including paintings by Winslow Homer and Fitz Hugh Lane.

The Redwood Library, America's oldest

Newport Congregational Church *Corner Spring & Pelham Sts; tel: (401) 849-2238. Open to visitors summertime Tue & Thur 1000–1200.*

Old Colony House *Washington Sq; tel: (401) 846-2980. Open summertime Mon–Sat 1000–1600, Sun 1200–1600. Free.*

Old Stone Mill *Off Bellevue Ave between Mill & Pelham Sts.*

Redwood Library & Athenaeum *50 Bellevue Ave; tel: (401) 847-0292. Open Mon–Sat 0930–1730. Free.*

Newport Congregational Church✧✧

Even if you're a heathen, look inside to admire the breathtaking interior, all of it – floor-to-ceiling, including opalescent windows – the masterwork of American art nouveau maestro John La Farge.

Old Colony House✧✧✧

A 'hallowed hall' of American patriotism, where General Washington and French Comte de Rochambeau planned the war-winning Battle of Yorktown – also where the legislature denounced its allegiance to King George III on 4 May, 1776, making Rhode Island the first colony to declare independence. Plus one of Rhode Island's two original Gilbert Stuart portraits of George Washington. The other hangs in the Rhode Island State House (*see page 164*).

Old Stone Mill✧

Flimsy legend has it that Norse Vikings erected this oddity – made of clamshell mortar and stones – long before Columbus crossed the Atlantic. Less carried-away theorists place what was probably a farmer's grain silo and windmill closer to 1660.

Redwood Library and Athenaeum✧✧

No, this oldest US library (1747) isn't constructed of redwood; it's named for founder Abraham Redwood. Peek inside the reading room to imagine frequent patrons Edith Wharton and Henry James scribbling on their manuscripts. The portrait gallery includes six by Gilbert Stuart, and a full-length statue of George Washington stands out front. Turn toward the building's left side to see a portion of the chain formerly extended across the Hudson at West Point, New York, thwarting upriver passage of the British enemy's warships.

Touro Synagogue
85 Touro St; tel: (401)
847-4794. Open Sun–Fri
1000–1600. Fri religious
services 1800 winter, 1900
summer; Sat services 0900.

**Trinity Episcopal
Church** Queen Anne Sq;
tel: (401) 846-0660. Open
Mon–Fri 1000–1300; Sun
services 0800, 1030.

**Wanton-Lyman-
Hazard House** $ 17
Broadway; tel: (401) 846-
0813. Open Thur–Sat
1000–1600, Sun
1300–1600 summertime.

Touro Synagogue*
Dedicated in 1763 for stature as North America's first Jewish house of worship. Another of Peter Harrison's architectural commissions, this one is a Georgian-style beauty.

Trinity Episcopal Church**
Patterned after those designed in Britain by Christopher Wren and in use since 1726. Elizabeth II and the Archbishop of Canterbury attended services during America's 1976 bicentennial. Watch for pew No 81, where George Washington sat, also No 66, where the Vanderbilts prayed (for eternal wealth?).

Wanton-Lyman-Hazard House*
Newport's oldest restored dwelling, dating from 1675, exemplifies American-style Jacobean architecture, with fine furnishings and an 18th-century herb garden. Site of the inflammatory Stamp Act Riot of 1765, a pivotal event leading to American independence.

Spring Street antiques

Entertainment

Refer to listings in the *Newport Daily News* and the free *Newport This Week* tabloid. Get what's-going-on updates by dialling the 24-hour *Newport Activity Line; tel: (401) 848-2000.*

Sundry nightspots along Thames St pack 'em in for jazz, rock, rhythm 'n blues, even karaoke sing-alongs. The town's cheeriest Irish pubs are **O'Brien's**, *501 Thames St; tel: (401) 849-2633*, and **Sabina Doyle's**, *359 Thames St; tel: (401) 849-4466*. **The Daisy**, *Bannister's Wharf; tel: (401) 849-2900*, thumps to disco music.

Annually during the third week in August, Newport's **Jazz Festival** is famously big, showcasing fusion and modern jazz at **Fort Adams State Park;** *tel: (401) 847-3700.* Same location, phone number for early August's **Folk Music Festival.**

Two boat piers have become buzzing retail bazaars: **Bannister's Wharf** and **Bowen's Wharf.** Nearby **Brick Market Place** encompasses gift/souvenir shops, galleries and clothing boutiques. You'll find more such establishments along

Newport County Convention & Visitors Bureau 23 America's Cup Ave, Newport; tel: (800) 976-5122 or (401) 849-8048; www.GoNewport.com

Same location for the **Gateway Visitors Center**, where facilities include direct-access accommodation bookings.

South County Tourism Council 4808 Tower Hill Rd, Wakefield; tel: (800) 548-4662 or (401) 789-4422; www.southcountyri.com

Newport is 75 miles from Boston, 25 miles from Providence. To reach the city, choose scenic routes on either side of Narragansett Bay; both entail toll-bridge crossings. In town, be prepared for crowded traffic conditions during summer high season.

P Anticipating midsummer jam-ups, savvy drivers opt for the 24-hour garage alongside downtown's Gateway Visitors Center.

Downtown Newport is squeezed between Washington Sq on the north, Memorial Blvd on the south. From there, the longest and swankiest section of Bellevue Ave's 'mansion row' runs due south. Bellevue Ave, in turn, leads to a sensational Ocean Drive loop around the tip of Aquidneck Island. City-wide service is provided by **Rhode Island Public Transit Authority** (RIPTA) buses; tel: (401) 781-9400.

Thames St, and a Bellevue Ave shopping mall is situated where 'Mansion Row' begins. **Spring St** exudes small-scale mercantile charm with shops devoted to such items as antiques, pottery, quilts and ship models. **The Coop**, 99 Spring St; tel: (401) 848-2442, is a crafts cooperative. Antiques and fine-art dealers occupy an 1894 heavyweight, the **Armory**, 365 Lower Thames St; tel: (401) 848-6313.

Accommodation and food

Because Newport is a small city (population around 30,000) on a point of land, you can count on overnighting close to or right on some part of its waterfront. Lodgings run the gamut from slick hotels to bed & breakfasts tucked away on neighbourhood side streets. In addition to the free decision-making facility at the Visitors Center, there's no charge for bookings arranged by **Taylor-Made Reservations** tel: (800) 848-8848 or (401)848-0300.

Newport Harbor Hotel & Marina $$–$$$ 49 America's Cup Ave; tel: (800) 955-2558 or (401) 847-9000 and **Newport Bay Club & Hotel** $$$ 337 Thames St; tel: (401) 849-8600, both overlook the yacht harbour. **Hotel Viking** $$ 1 Bellevue Ave; tel: (800) 556-7126 or (401) 847-3300, is a 1920s landmark with **Vanderbilt Restaurant**. A 19th-century mill building has become an all-suite hotel, **Mill Street Inn** $$-$$$ 75 Mill St; tel: (800) 392-1316 or (401) 849-9500.

Two bed & breakfast standouts are the **Francis Malbone House** $$ 392 Thames St; tel: (401) 846-0392, and **Admiral Benbow Inn** $$ 93 Pelham St; tel: (800) 343-2863 or (401) 848-8000, a mid-1800s sea captain's house.

Historic New England atmosphere and a tourism-reliant economy results in an eclectic range of local cuisine.

Splurge at Newport's priciest and New England's oldest restaurant (cooking since 1687): **White Horse Tavern** $$$ Marlborough/Farewell Sts; tel: (401) 849-3600. Beef Wellington and Châteaubriand are specialities, as is high-calorie triple chocolate silk pie.

Also in the haute-cuisine echelon: French **Restaurant Bouchard** $$$ 505 Lower Thames St; tel: (401) 846-0123.

Antique-filled, waterfront **Elizabeth's Café** $$ 404 Lower Thames St; tel: (401) 846-6862, is well known for its Welsh–English adaptation of prodigious bouillabaisse seafood stew.

Additional eateries feature harbourside ambience and seafood menus. **Christie's** $$ Christie's Landing; tel: (401) 847-5400. Also **The Black Pearl** $$ Bannister's Wharf; tel: (401) 846-5264.

Eat heartily but cost-effectively at **Brick Alley Pub & Restaurant $–$$** *140 Thames St; tel: (401) 849-6334,* as well as **Muriel's $–$$** *58 Spring St; tel: (401) 849-7780,* and the **Music Hall Café $–$$** *250 Thames St; tel: (401) 848-2330,* specialising in Tex-Mex food.

At **La Forge Restaurant & Casino $$** *186 Bellevue Ave; tel: (401) 847-0418,* dine in the pub or on the covered porch overlooking the Tennis Hall of Fame's Horseshow Piazza grass court.

Suggested tour

Total distance: 10–12 miles

Time: Whole day for full enjoyment, mixed with walking and driving or partially by public transport.

Starting at the **Gateway Visitors Center ❶** on America's Cup Ave, do a harbourfront walk, poking into the shopping and boat-dock wharves. At the America's Cup Ave/Lower Thames St juncture, backtrack westward to stroll along shop- and restaurant-filled Thames St, bringing you to Queen Anne Sq and its landmark, **TRINITY CHURCH ❷**. Continue to Washington Sq, site of **OLD COLONY HOUSE ❸** and (nearby on Broadway) **WANTON-LYMAN-HAZARD HOUSE ❹**. From the square, head up Touro St in Newport's **Historic Hill ❺** neighbourhood, thereby reaching **TOURO SYNAGOGUE ❻**, then onward towards a right turn at Bellevue Ave, reaching the **REDWOOD LIBRARY ❼**, **Art Museum ❽** and, centred on a park, the

Marble House, on Bellevue Avenue, built for William Vanderbilt in 1892

Hunter House $ 54
Washington St; tel:
(401) 847-7516. Open Daily
1000–1700.

OLD STONE MILL ⑨. Meander amid side-streets in this vicinity, graced with rows of Early American houses.

Bellevue Ave's swanky segment begins where that thoroughfare meets Memorial Blvd. First comes the **INTERNATIONAL TENNIS HALL OF FAME ⑩**, then the fabled 'summer cottages'. At Webster St, deviate a block from Bellevue Ave to see Cornelius Vanderbilt's **THE BREAKERS ⑪** on Ochre Point Ave. Also consider an oceanside deviation: the **Cliff Walk ⑫**, extending 3.5 miles from **Easton's Beach ⑬** southward to **Land's End ⑭**.

Bellevue Ave ends at Ocean Ave, whereupon you'll undoubtedly require transportation for the very scenic 7-mile Ocean Ave–Ridge Rd–Wellington Ave loop around the tip of Aquidneck Island – via **Brenton Point State Park ⑮**, **Castle Hill Lighthouse ⑯**, **HAMMERSMITH FARM ⑰** and **Fort Adams State Park ⑱**. Wellington Ave meets Lower Thames St, so you've arrived back in downtown Newport.

Additional walking tour: The Point

This compact, walkable neighbourhood rivals Historic Hill for its abundance of 18th- and early 19th-century domestic architecture. Begin at the **Gateway Visitors Center ❶**; turn left on to Long Wharf St, left again on to Washington St, where **Battery Park ⑲** overlooks the bay and 1748 **Hunter House**✶✶ ⑳ contains an important collection of colonial pewter and authentic Chippendale, Queen Anne and Hepplewhite furniture. Walk as far as Van Zandt St; return through The Point by way of Second St.

Also worth exploring

East Bay
Choosing Rte 138, drive 11 miles north through commercialised Middletown, then Portsmouth (see Providence/Pawtucket, page 169); cross the Sakonnet River bridge linking Aquidneck Island with **Tiverton**, where **Weetamoo Woods** has nature-hiking trails. Tiverton's Lawton Rd ends at **Fort Barton**, a Revolutionary War redoubt, now a park with river and bay panoramics. Head south via Rte 77, passing miles of stone fences and Nannaquaket Pond to **Tiverton Four Corners**, then along Pachet Brook Reservoir to arrive at **Little Compton**, an unspoiled hamlet clustered around a village green, church and cemetery. Tiverton–Little Compton distance: 11 miles. Three miles south beyond Little Compton, Rte 77 ends at Sakonnet Harbor. At Little Compton's **Sakonnet Vineyards**, wines have such jaunty names as Eye of the Storm, America's Cup Red and Spinnaker White: 162 West Main Rd (off Rte 77); tel: (401) 635-8486.

ℹ Block Island Tourism Council
Water St, Block Island; tel: (800) 383-2474 or (401) 466-5200; www.blockisle.com.

Island Navigation Company *PO Box 482, New London; tel: (401) 783-4613 (in RI) or (860) 442-7891 (in CT).*

West Bay

From Newport, cross the 2-mile Newport Bridge (toll) to **Conanicut Island**, 9 miles long, 1 mile wide. **Jamestown** is the sole community, with appealing restaurants on Narragansett Ave and a resort hotel: **The Bay Voyage $$–$$$** *150 Conanicus Ave, Jamestown; tel: (401) 423-2100.* A north–south loop around the island via East Shore Rd and North Shore Rd features the **Conanicut Sanctuary** wildlife habitat, the 1789 **Jamestown Windmill** standing in pastureland, clifftop **Fort Wetherill State Park** and a beach at **Mackerel Cove**. The 1856 **Beaver Tail Lighthouse** flashes signals from the island's southern tip.

Drive west across the Jamestown Bridge to reach Rhode Island's mainland; detour 3 miles north on Rte 1A to **Wickford**, where elm-shaded Main St leads to a boat harbour and has parallel rows of 18th-century clapboard dwellings and the oldest Episcopal church (1707) north of Virginia. Then backtrack via Rte 1A to **Narragansett Pier**, with elegant summer homes along Ocean Rd and a mile-long beach favoured by surfers. From there, drive 2 miles west to lively little **Wakefield**, then 5 miles on Rte 1 to Matunuck Beach Rd, your access to **Matunuck**, home of the May–October **Theater by the Sea**, in a converted barn at *364 Card's Point Rd; tel: (401) 782-8587*, and **Trustom Pond National Wildlife Refuge**, where a sand barrier shelters Rhode Island's only undeveloped salt pond. Here on the state's marshy south coast, **Block Island Sound** washes 20-plus miles of sheltered beaches.

Block Island

This 11-square-mile offshore haven has a year-round population of 850 or so; stoplights, parking meters and house numbers don't exist, and 25 per cent of the island is environmentally protected by the US Nature Conservancy. Car ferries operated by **Island Navigation Company** reach this 'Bermuda of the North' from Newport during summertime – year-round from Point Judith, RI, 12 miles away (also from New London, CT). **Old Harbor**, the arrival point, is a quaint village with Victorian-period hotels and laid-back eateries facing Block Island Sound.

Touring beyond Old Harbor by car or bicycle opens on to grassy moors, bayberry shrubs, blackberry patches, rose bushes, salt marshes and fresh-water ponds. Springtime brings countless daffodils into full bloom. Migratory birds travelling the 'Atlantic Flyway' make stopovers *en route* to South America. Four hundred miles of three-century-old stone fences criss-cross the terrain; sublime **Crescent Beach**, near Old Harbor, is 4.5 miles long. The south-coastal **Mohegan Bluffs** – resembling West Ireland's Cliffs of Moher – tower above rocky coves. From the overlook, a wooden stairway clambers down to a pocket beach. Atop the headland is brick **Southeast Lighthouse**. Ask at the Tourism Council for a Nature Conservancy trail map, detailing five walking pathways, exceeding 20 miles overall.

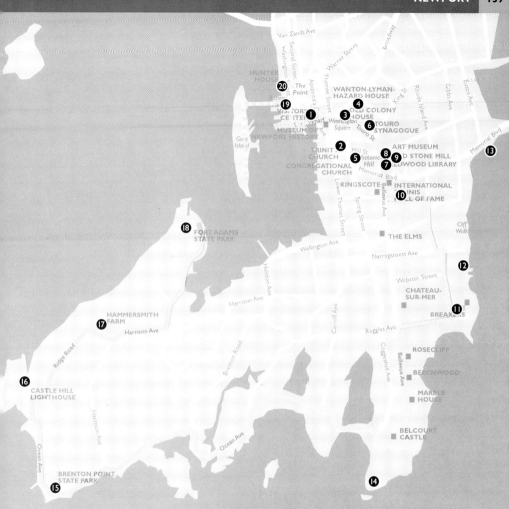

Providence and Pawtucket

Ratings

Architecture	●●●●●
Food and drink	●●●●●
Art	●●●
Museums	●●○○○
Shopping	●●○○○
Beaches	●○○○○
Children	●○○○○
Shopping	●○○○○

You won't find any such thing as a large city in America's smallest state. No matter, for Providence's abundant attractions and mini-metropolitan diversity are out of proportion to its modest size. Its stature is augmented by the prestige and energising influence of the excellent university and school of design. Furthermore, 'Little Rhody's' capital is a top-notch restaurant town, partly because the design school has a culinary curriculum and Johnson & Wales University educates future chefs.

Geographically, Providence qualifies as a waterfront city: the Seekonk River flows into the Providence River which, in turn, empties into delightful Narragansett Bay. But urban shorelines have mostly been industrialised for nearly 200 years – accounting for Pawtucket's inclusion in this chapter.

Getting there and getting around

ℹ️ **Providence Warwick Convention & Visitors Bureau** (PWCVB) *I W Exchange St, Providence; tel: (800) 233-1636 or (401) 274-1636; www.providencecvb.com.* The CVB's **Visitor Information Center** is located in Waterplace Park's pavilion; *tel: (401) 751-1177.*

Arriving and departing
Providence is 45 miles south of Boston via the I-95 motorway, so figure on about an hour's drive. You can also get here quickly from Boston via **Amtrak's Northeast Corridor** rail service (*tel: (800) 872-7245*). For air travel (from, for instance, Boston and Cape Cod), suburban Warwick's **T F Green Airport** is 8 miles from downtown Providence (*tel: (401) 737-8222*).

Getting around
After exiting off I-95, avoid misery by steering clear of inner downtown's tangle of narrow, one-way streets. Thanks to Providence's compact dimensions, it's easier to see the sights on foot and by using public transport. Kennedy Plaza is where **Rhode Island Public Transit**

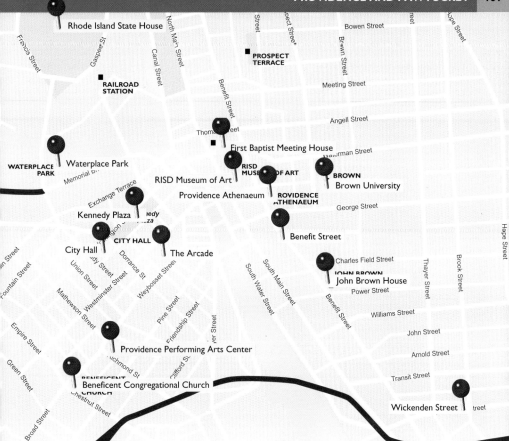

For a long-term stay downtown, you're best advised to use downtown's Convention Center garage; entrances on West Exchange St. Other big-capacity garages are on Eddy St downtown and alongside the Amtrak station on Gaspee St.

Authority (RIPTA) buses fan out for service throughout the metro area, also to Newport (*tel: (401) 781-9400*) for schedule and fare information. The third Thursday of each month year-round is Gallery Night, made convenient by the **ArTrolley**, free shuttle transport between galleries, museums, antiques shops and arts and performance events. *Service operates non-stop 1700–2100; tel: (401) 751-1177.*

Sights

The Arcade❖❖❖❖
Completed in 1828, this quaint little skylit enclosure qualifies as America's first indoor market-place, the forerunner of a zillion look-alike shopping malls from coast to coast. A National Historic Landmark, the Greek Revival structure features massive Ionic columns, the original cast-iron railings and three tiers of speciality shops and inexpensive eateries.

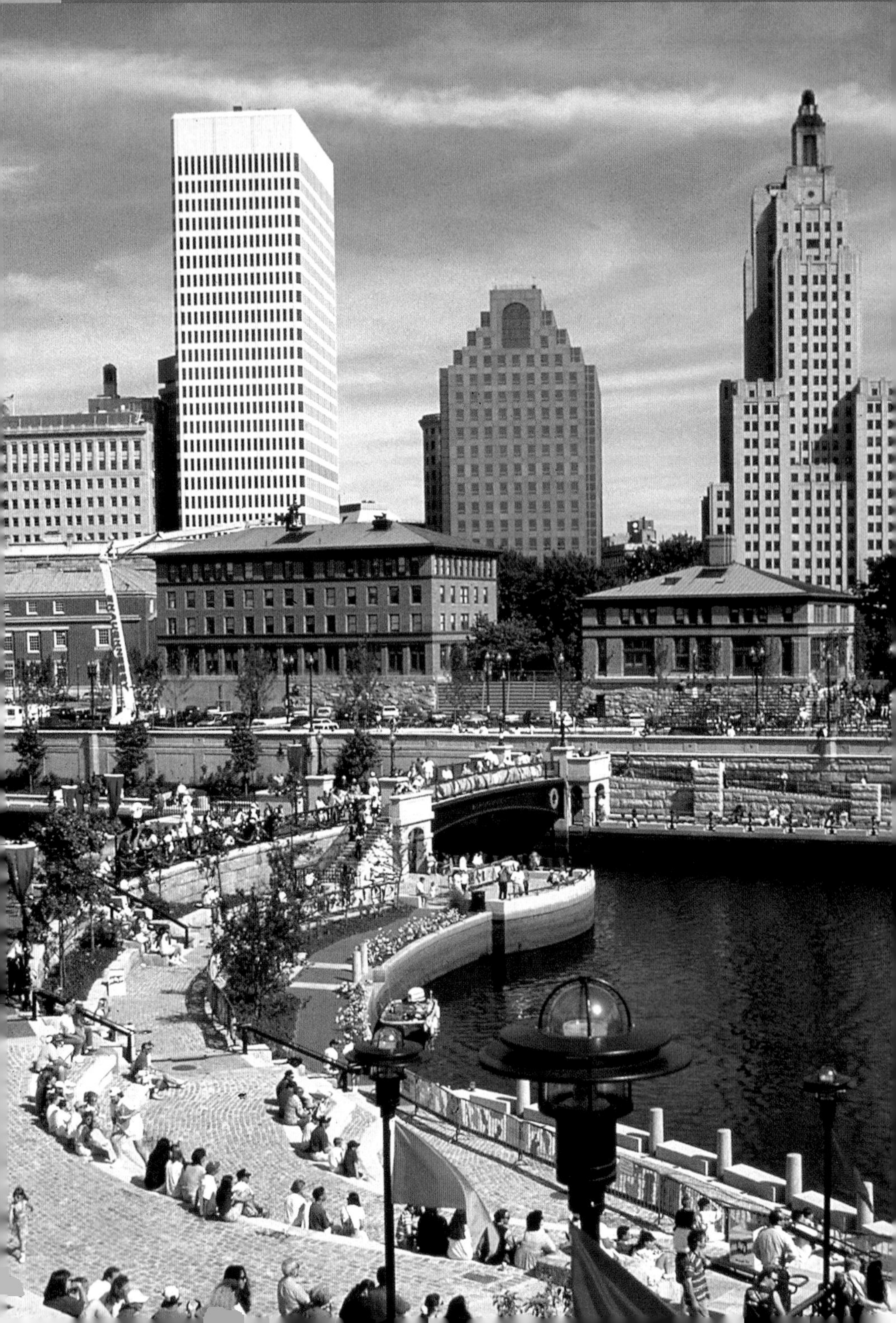

Benefit St On the East Side alongside College Hill. The street's most historic portion extends from Howland St south to James St.

First Baptist Meeting House 75 N Main St; tel: (401) 454-3418. Open Mon–Fri 0930–1530; guided tour following Sun 1100 worship service.

John Brown House $ 52 Power St; tel: (401) 331-8575. Tours Tue–Sat 1000–1630, Sun 1200–1630.

Johnson & Wales Culinary Archives & Museum $ 315 Harborside Blvd; tel: (401) 598-2805. Open Mon–Fri 0900–1600, Sat 1000–1500.

Providence Athenaeum 251 Benefit St; tel: (401) 421-6970. Open Mon–Fri 0830–1730, Sat 0930–1730. Free

Benefit St****

East Side Providence's brick-paved 'Mile of History' – illuminated by antique gas lamps after nightfall – encompasses the US's most impressive concentration of clapboard Colonial bungalows and mansions, plus textbook examples of New England Federal and flamboyant Victorian styles, along with colonnaded rowhouses from the Civil War period. Parallel and criss crossing streets on higher ground – notably Prospect, Hope, Williams, Congdon, Charlesfield and Porter – exude comparable grace and charm. The fact that Benefit St was 'slum central' back in the 1950s makes it all the more remarkable today.

First Baptist Meeting House**

Members of America's Baptist congregation regard this Benefit St gem, topped by a 185-ft steeple, as their 'Mother Church'. An outstanding example of Georgian architecture and design, the interior features a Waterford crystal chandelier dating from 1782.

John Brown House**

The aggressive ship-owner merchants who made bundles of money during early America's China Trade spared no expense in building and furnishing lavish dwellings for themselves and their usually large families. Such is the three-storey pride of Power St, epitomising grand Georgian-style domestic architecture, fine craftsmanship and belongings befitting a refined late-18th-century lifestyle. The mansion is a veritable museum of porcelain, glassware, pewter, silver and paintings.

Johnson & Wales Culinary Archives & Museum**

Known as the 'Smithsonian Institution of the food-service industry', this unique museum contains more than 300,000 items related to culinary arts and hospitality – including a gallery of chefs through the ages, cooking tools from as far back as the third millennium BC, 1000-year-old utensils, a bread ring from Pompeii(!), stoves from the past two centuries, silverware from famous hotels and restaurants, vintage menus, White House dinner invitations and much else connected with eating and drinking through the ages.

Providence Athenaeum**

Benefit St's literary haven, a granite edifice built in 1828 to resemble a Greek Doric-style temple, is one of the country's oldest libraries and cultural centres. Creaky floorboards and cast-iron spiral stairs lead to shelves crammed with old and current books. Watch for announcements of exhibitions of volumes and folios from the Athenaeum's rare-book archives. Gossip item: secluded in the recessed alcoves, Edgar Allan Poe and local socialite Sarah Helen Whitman conducted what was then regarded as a steamy courtship.

ℹ **Rhode Island State House** Enter at 82 Smith St; tel (401) 277-2357. Free tours Mon-Fri 0830-1630.

RISD Museum of Arts $ 224 Benefit; tel: (401) 454-6500. Tues-Wed, Fri-Sat 1030-1700, Thur1200-2000, Sun 1300-1600 (mid Sept to late June), Wed-Sat 1200-1700 summertime.

Waterplace Park North edge of downtown; midway between I-95 exit and Benefit St; downhill from Rhode Island State House, and a short walk from the Amtrack station.

Rhode Island State House✦✦✦

Manhattan-based McKim, Mead and White – high society's pet architectural firm early this century – designed the gigantic state capitol, employing tons of white Georgia marble and a reported 15 million bricks. Visible from points near and far, this 1891–1904 hilltop whopper is crowned by one of the world's biggest self-supporting domes. Depending upon who's claiming what, the 250-ft-high dome ranks second, third or fourth after the one atop St Peter's Basilica in the Vatican City. Displayed inside are regimental battle flags, cannons fired during Civil War combat and Rhode Island's original charter, on parchment and granted by Charles II in 1663. Another attention-getter is Rhode Island-born Gilbert Stuart's portrait of George Washington. From that full-length painting comes the head-and-shoulders engraving on US one-dollar bills.

RISD Museum of Art✦✦

RISD: that's student shorthand for the Rhode Island School of Design. The museum's permanent collections total some 75,000 works of art, ranging from French Impressionist paintings by Cezanne and Manet to a 9-ft Buddha; from a Kyoto temple to ancient Greek bronzes and Roman mosaics. There's also an unsurpassable assemblage of 18th-century American furniture and decorative art in the adjoining Pendleton House wing.

Waterplace Park✦✦✦

Four acres of ambitious urban redevelopment on what had been the city centre's decrepit backside: completed in 1994, this handsome open space features a stone-stepped amphitheatre overlooking a fountain-splashed pond, a Riverwalk and curved pedestrian bridges connecting the park with downtown's financial and theatre district. The amphitheatre has become a popular venue for open-air concerts and theatrical performances. A Venetian-type gondolier wearing a straw boater takes passengers on 45-minute rides, and on certain occasions a local artist lights up the evening with a spectacle called Water Fire.

Entertainment

Providence packs a steady barrage of serious art and culture – both highbrow and main-stream, with much going on in the far-out realm of jazz, folk, blues, country and rock – into its relatively small size. For decision-making, consult the daily 'What's Happening' section of the *Providence Journal* and listings in two hip, alternative tabloids, the *Phoenix* and the *Nice Paper*.

A nationally acclaimed award-winner, the **Trinity Repertory Company** *201 Washington St; tel: (401) 351-4242*, produces classic and

Roger Williams

London-born Roger Williams arrived in Boston in 1631, became Anglican minister of the church in nearby Salem – and promptly fell foul of the no-nonsense Puritan bluenoses who headed the Massachusetts Bay Colony. Not willing to tolerate his radically 'new and dangerous opinions' on religious freedom, they banished him to England in 1636. Instead, the renegade preacher ventured south. Finding a natural spring in what's now a downtown park, Williams drank the water, thankful for 'God's providence'. Purchasing a tract of uninhabited land from the Narragansett Indians, he established a plantation settlement dedicated to – of course – religious freedom. The smallest US state is still officially named the State of Rhode Island and Providence Plantation.

contemporary works. The extra-large stage at the **Providence Performing Arts Center** *220 Weybosset St; tel: (401) 421-2787,* accommodates road-show versions of the blockbuster Broadway musicals. **Veterans Memorial Auditorium** *69 Brownell St; tel: (401) 831-3123,* schedules ballet, opera and Rhode Island Philharmonic concerts.

Groundwerx Dance Theater *95 Empire St; tel: (401) 454-4564,* concentrates on offbeat, cutting-edge choreography. **Brown University's Stuart Theater** *on campus; tel: (401) 863-2838,* is a venue for visiting performers and student productions as is **Rhode Island College's Roberts Auditorium** *600 Mt Pleasant Ave; (401) 4560 8060.* **AS220** *115 Empire St; tel: (401) 831-9327,* is an arts centre consisting of a café performance space and two studios showing works of present-day Rhode Island painters and sculptors.

During the second weekend in June, a **Festival of Historic Houses $** house and garden tour is sponsored by the **Providence Preservation Society** *21 Meeting St; tel: (401) 831-7440.*

Right
Rhode Island State House

Above
The Arcade of 1828, America's
first indoor shopping mall

Accommodation and food in Providence

The **PWCVB** *(tel: (800) 233-1636 or (401) 274-1636)* is a reliable source
of updated lodging listings in all price ranges, but making reservations
is your affair. For a central location downtown (which the locals call
Downcity), choose between two prominent high-rises: the slick
Westin Providence $$$ *1 West Exchange St; tel: (800) 228-3000 or
(401) 598-8000* or the older (1922) but wholly renovated **Omni**

Biltmore $$ *Kennedy Plaza; tel: (800) 843-6664 or (401) 421-0700*. For a homier alternative, the *circa*-1889 **State House Inn** $$ *43 Jewett St; tel: (401) 351-6111*, stands a few blocks from the state capitol building. Originally the rectory for St John's Church, the Italianate Victorian-style **Old Court Bed & Breakfast** $$ *144 Benefit St; tel: (401) 751-2002*, is advantageously situated on the 'Mile of History'.

Proportionate to its size, Providence has an impressively large number of very good restaurants where courageous young chefs habitually distance themselves from traditional New England cooking. Two dozen Italian–American trattorias and cafés draw visitors to the Federal Hill neighbourhood, bounded by Broadway and Atwells Ave.

Al Forno $$$ *577 S Main St; tel: (401) 273-9760*. The city's best-known restaurant, acclaimed for its eclectic menu and excellent wood-grilled food.

Café Nuovo $$ *1 Citizen's Plaza; tel: (401) 421-2525*. Indoor–outdoor seating overlooking the Riverwalk while dining on Caribbean, Asian and US Southwest meals.

Federal Reserve $$ *66 Dorrance St; tel: (401) 621-5700*. A recycled bank lobby, complete with a turn-of-the-century vault, sets the tone for contemporary New England dining.

Grill 262 $$ *262 S. Water St; tel: (401) 751-37001*. Recommended for grilled steaks and spit-roasted chicken.

Hemenway's $$ *1 Old Stone Sq; tel: (401) 351-8570*. International seafood galore in the restaurant, plus an oyster bar.

New Rivers $$ *7 Steeple St; tel: (401) 751-0350*. A classy bistro atmosphere for fusion cuisine with worldwide influences.

Pot Au Feu $$$ *44 Custom House St; tel: (401) 273-8953*. Providence's *haute-cuisine* French restaurant, with arguably the best wine list in town.

Trinity Brewhouse $ *186 Fountain St; tel: (401) 453-2337*, and **Union Station Brewery** $ *36 Exchange Terrace; tel: (401) 274-2739*, are brew-pubs serving inexpensive meals accompanied by their house brands of beer and ale.

Suggested tour

Total distance: 4–5 miles (additional 8 miles for the zoo)

Time: Half day or full day. Since streets leading from downtown to College Hill are quite steep, you might prefer driving up that way or relying upon public transport – and a car is needed to reach the zoo. So consider dividing your sightseeing into a downtown walking

ℹ Blackstone Valley Tourism Council
171 Main St, Pawtucket; tel: (800) 454-2882 or (401) 724-2200; www.tourblack stone.com

Bristol County Chamber of Commerce *654 Metacom Ave, PO Box 250, Warren; tel: (888) 278-9948 or (401) 245-0750; www.bristolcountychamber. org*

ℹ Roger Williams Park & Zoo $ *Rte 95 South, Exit 17; tel: (401) 785-9450 (park), (401) 785-3510 (zoo). Park open daily 0700–2100. Zoo open Nov–Mar daily 0900–1600; Apr–Oct Mon–Fri 0900–1700.*

Slater Mill Historic Site $ *67 Roosevelt Ave; tel: (401) 725-8638. Phone ahead for opening days, times depending upon the season.*

Blithewold Mansion & Gardens $ *101 Ferry Rd, Bristol; tel: (401) 253-2707. Grounds and arboretum open daily year-round, 1000–1700. Mansion open mid Apr–late Sept Tue–Sun 1000–1600.*

Herreshoff Marine Museum $ *7 Burnside St, Bristol; tel: (401) 253-5000. Open May, Sept–Oct Mon–Fri 1300–1600, Sat–Sun 1100–1600; June–Aug daily 1100–1600.*

ℹ The East Bay Bike Path extends 14.5 miles between East Providence and Bristol.

segment and a motoring segment for more distant touring. Major non-profit points of interest are on the city-centre **Banner Trail**, marked by colour-coded flags for easy orientation.

Begin at Kennedy Plaza, Downcity's hub. On the plaza's Dorrance St side, view **City Hall ❶**, dating from 1874, a Second Empire-style showpiece of civic architecture. From there, walk north, crossing Exchange Terrace and Memorial Blvd to **Waterplace Park ❷**, then uphill further north via Francis and Hayes Sts to visit the **RHODE ISLAND STATE HOUSE ❸**. Return downhill, crossing Exchange St's bridge to reach Westminster St downtown; stroll through the **ARCADE ❹**. Several of the city's other landmark buildings face Weybosset St – including the **Providence Performing Arts Center ❺** in a Beaux Arts movie palace from 1928, the 1857 **Custom House ❻**, the 1875 **Wilcox Building ❼** with its cast-iron façade, the 1856 Italian palazzo-style **Bank of North America ❽** and the early 19th-century **Beneficent Congregational Church ❾**. Parallel Westminster St also has notable examples of varied past-century motifs.

Cross one of the Riverwalk bridges to reach the East Side. **BENEFIT ST ❿** and its rows of historic houses and buildings is two blocks from any bridge. First, though, head north; turn right on Meeting St, then left onto Congdon St to reach **Prospect Terrace ⓫**, site of a statue of Rhode Island's 'founding father' Roger Williams and an ideal perch for panoramic views of Downcity. From Benefit St, go uphill via either Waterman or George Sts to the campus of **Brown University ⓬**, an Ivy League academic stalwart founded in 1764. Thayer St is the liveliest College Hill thoroughfare for bookstores, clothing shops and student-budget eateries. Going nine blocks south on that street (or the same direction on Benefit St) gets you to hip and trendy **Wickenden St ⓭** in Providence's Fox Point neighbourhood (George M Cohan, old-time vaudeville's song-and-dance trouper, was born here). The street's determined funkiness is evident on telephone poles, festooned with goofy sculptural concoctions.

Roger Williams Park & Zoo ⓮, covering 435 acres on the southern edge of Providence, is far enough away from downtown to be considered a special-interest side trip. The park comprises waterways and formal gardens, greenhouses, boathouse, Planetarium and Museum of Natural History. The US's third-oldest zoo (1872) is widely regarded as the best in New England.

Northern Detour: From downtown Providence, drive 4 miles north on the I-95 motorway to Exit 27 for **Pawtucket**. At that city's Main St/Roosevelt St intersection, you'll come upon the riverside **Slater Mill Historic Site✦✦**, where in 1793 Yankee tinker Samuel Slater designed and built the US's first reliably operative textile-manufacturing machinery, thereby launching the American Industrial Revolution. The adjacent park is a pleasant picnic spot.

Colt State Park/Coggleshell Farm Museum *Off Poppasquash Rd, Bristol; tel: (401) 253-9062. Park open daily year-round. Farm Museum open summer 1000–1800, winter 1000–1600 (closed Jan). Free.*

Green Animals Topiary Gardens $ *Cory's Lane, Portsmouth; tel: (401) 847-1000. Open May–Oct daily 1000–1700.*

Southern detour: Leaving Providence via the I-95 motorway, head south to the I-95/I-195 intersection; turn right on to Rte 114 for a 6-mile East Bay drive to **Warren✦✦**, worth a stop if you'd like to browse through that town's numerous antiques shops. Continue 4 miles to photogenic **Bristol**, where an attraction overlooking Narragansett Bay is **Blithewold Mansion & Gardens✦✦**, former summer estate of a Pennsylvania coal baron, well known for its arboretum including a Japanese water garden, exotic bamboo stands and the biggest Redwood tree east of the Rockies. Elsewhere in town, the **Herreshoff Marine Museum✦✦** focuses on the boat works where eight America's Cup defenders were built (1893–1934) and includes the America's Cup Hall of Fame. Also in Bristol is **Colt State Park✦✦** (spacious picnic grounds) and its **Coggleshell Farm Museum✦✦**, a working farmstead relying solely upon 18th-century agricultural methods, including seasonal sheep-shearing and maple sugaring.

Continuing southwards, drive 6 miles through bayside pastureland to **Portsmouth** via the Mt Hope Bridge (toll) if you'd like to tour **Green Animals Topiary Gardens✦✦**, a great-for-kids layout with sculpted animals and birds, plus rose arbours, formal flower beds, and geometric forms made from English boxwood as well as a Victorian toy museum.

The Southern Green Mountains

Ratings

Arts and Culture	●●●○○
History	●●●
Museums	●●●○○
Nature/scenery	●●●○○
Shopping	●●●
Food and drink	●●○○○
Beaches	●○○○○
Children	●○○○○

Some of Vermont's most idyllic towns lie nestled in the rolling Green Mountains and the valleys that separate them from the Taconics in neighbouring New York state. From stylish Manchester to tiny Weston, isolated in its mountain vale, these towns blend scenery with history and the great outdoors.

Miles of hiking and walking trails criss-cross the mountains, and towering forests are reflected in lakes and streams, the latter often spanned by covered bridges. The region is small but filled with the elements that personify Vermont: green-clad mountains, skiing, white churches, country stores, summer theatres, craft studios and historic homes.

This is one of Vermont's most popular corners, especially in autumn, when maple trees paint the mountainsides red. Expect the heaviest traffic on Rte 9, especially in Wilmington and around Manchester Center.

ARLINGTON✢✢

Battenkill Canoe, Ltd $$$ *Rte 7A, Arlington; tel: (802) 362-2800 or (800) 421-5268.* Rentals can include drop-off and pick-up.

Ethan Allen Days *Arlington; tel: (802) 375-6144.* Mid June with a re-enactment of Revolutionary War skirmishes.

Nearly 200 notable buildings line the streets of the Historic District, for many years the summer home of the artist Norman Rockwell, who used its residents as models for his popular magazine covers. Some of these works are shown in the **Norman Rockwell Exhibition✢**, on Rte 7A (*tel: (802) 375-6423*).

Just north of town are the **Fisher-Scott Memorial Pines✢✢**, on Red Mountain Rd, 0.2miles from Rte 7a, a rare stand of huge first-growth trees that were here when the first colonists settled. Nearly all New England's 'King's Pines' were cut as masts for the Royal Navy or in later lumbering, making this hillside a rare sight. Leave your car to see the Batten Kill Valley from the river itself, stopping at **Battenkill Canoe, Ltd✢✢** to rent a canoe. The narrow river offers easy paddling through farms and forests and under a covered bridge in West Arlington.

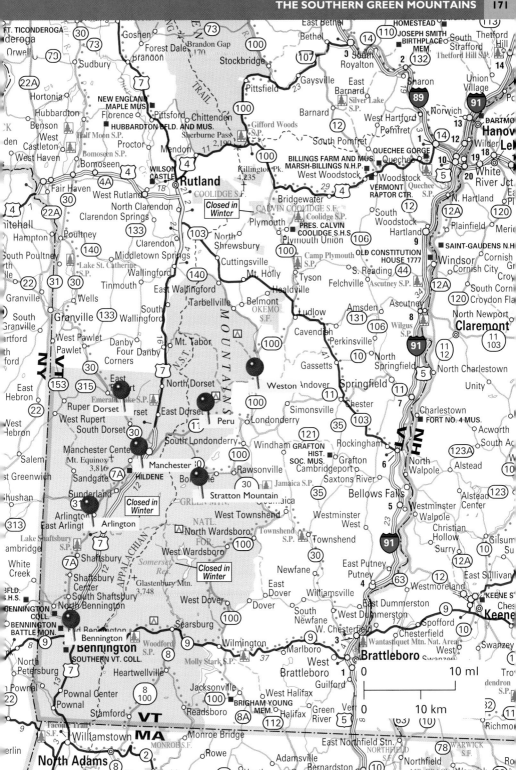

Bennington's Park-McCullough House, built in the second empire style

BENNINGTON❖❖

❶ **Bennington Chamber of Commerce** *Rte 7A; tel: (802) 447-3311.*

❶ **Bennington Battle Monument $** *Rte 9, Old Bennington; tel: (802) 447-0550. Open mid Apr–Oct daily 0900–1700.*

Bennington Museum $ *West Main St (Rte 9), Bennington; tel: (802) 447-1571. Open Mar–Nov daily 0900–1700.*

Park-McCullough House and Gardens $ *Off Rte 67A, North Bennington; tel: (802) 442-5441. Open June–Oct Thur–Mon.*

❶ **The Potter's Yard** *324 County St, Bennington; tel: (802) 447-7531. Open daily.*

The 306-ft obelisk you see from nearly any point in town is the **Bennington Battle Monument**❖, in Old Bennington. The battle it commemorates is considered the turning point of the Revolution, causing General Burgoyne to rethink and abandon his northward thrust to divide the colonies in half. An elevator takes you to the top for views of three states.

Old Bennington❖ is worth seeing, even for those to whom the monument is less than a shrine, since it is filled with finely restored colonial-era homes surrounding an 1806 church where Robert Frost is buried. You will hear this poet quoted throughout New England in such phrases as 'but I have promises to keep, and miles to go before I sleep'.

On Rte 9 on the way to the monument is **The Bennington Museum**❖❖, known for its collections of early American glass, pottery, quilts and for the work of the primitive artist Grandma Moses. A poignant statue of President Lincoln stands in front.

The Potters Yard❖❖, in an old wooden factory building, is the outlet for seconds of high-priced Bennington Pottery, manufactured on site. Dinnerware, bakeware and accessories of first quality sell here at lower-than-gift-shop prices; blems are a real bargain.

In North Bennington is the Victorian **Park-McCullough House**❖❖, among America's earliest Second Empire homes. On the grounds are a carriage barn, striking flower gardens and a playhouse, a miniature version of the mansion.

Accommodation and food in Bennington

Alldays and Onions $ *519 E Main St, Bennington; tel: (802) 447-0043. Open Mon–Sat 0800–2100.* Healthy whole grains hold their sandwiches, but the pastries are positively sinful.

Blue Benn Diner $ *Rte 7, Bennington; tel: (802) 442-8977.* An old-fashioned diner atmosphere, but with a modern twist to the menu.

Greenwood Lodge $ *Rte 9, Bennington; tel: (802) 442-2547.* An American Youth Hostel high on a mountainside, close to hiking trails.

Molly Stark Inn $ *1067 E Main St, Bennington; tel: (802) 442-9631.* Homey country Victorian with handmade quilts.

DORSET❖❖

Dorset Summer Theater Festival *Rte 30; tel: (802) 867-2223.* A professional company performing since 1929, late June–early Sept.

The Dorset Historical Society *tel: (802) 867-4450. Open Sat 1000–1200 or by appointment.*

Emerald Lake State Park *Rte 7, East Dorset; tel: (802) 362-1655.*

In 1785, North America's first commercial marble quarries opened in Dorset, cutting over 15.5 million cubic ft of stone in the next 150 years, including the marble for the Jefferson Memorial in Washington, DC.

Note the odd stones bordering the J K Adams workshop, south of the village. These are leftovers from cutting the columns for the New York Public Library. Shop here for cutting boards, salad bowls and other fine wooden ware sold at factory prices.

Borrow the excellent **Dorset Walking Tour**❖❖ tape and player from the **Historical Society Museum**, along with a book of photographs to help you spot each building. The museum displays local pottery, farm implements and old photographs of the quarries.

Stop to buy Vermont cheddar (but don't tell them Vermont didn't invent it!) from Peltier's Store (on Rte 30 in centre of village), which has been there for generations. Next door is the unique United Church, built entirely of marble, and decorated with beautiful stained glass windows of local landscapes, by Tiffany Studios.

On the opposite side of the 'marble mountain', in East Dorset, **Emerald Lake State Park**❖❖ surrounds a scenic lake with a swimming beach, picnic grounds, and campsite with tent pitches and caravan park. A free booklet describes the half-mile nature trail and a steeper trail climbs 1.6 miles to a natural bridge over a narrow gorge.

Accommodation and food in Dorset

Inn at West View Farm $–$$ *Rte 30, Dorset; tel: (802) 867-5715.* A rambling, comfortable country inn – and an outstanding dining room using locally-grown ingredients.

The Marble Inn West $–$$ *Dorset West Rd, Dorset; tel: (802) 867-4155 or (800) 453-7629.* In a fine old home with stencilling and antique features, but deliciously comfortable; reserve ahead for weekend dinner.

MANCHESTER✦✦✦

ℹ Manchester & the Mountains Chamber of Commerce 2 Main St, Manchester Center; tel: (802) 362-2100; www.manchestervermont. com

🏛 Robert Todd Lincoln's Hildene $ Rte 7A, Manchester Village; (802) 362-1788. Open mid May–Oct daily.

Mount Equinox Skyline Drive $$ Rte 7A, Manchester Center; tel: (802) 362-1113. Open May–Oct.

American Museum of Fly Fishing $ Rte 7A, Manchester Center; tel: (802) 362-3300. Open June–Oct Mon–Fri 1300–1600.

Vermont State Craft Center Rte 7A, Manchester Village; tel: (802) 362-3321.

Gleneagles Golf Course $$$ Rte 7a; tel: (802) 362-3223.

Southern Vermont Craft Fair $ Hildene Meadows, Manchester Village; tel: (802) 362-2100. Late July, with 250 juried craftsmen.

Don't confuse Manchester Village with Manchester Center. The former, to the south, is a genteel village with marble sidewalks and impeccable large homes surrounding the elegant pillared facade of The Equinox, Vermont's only vintage grand hotel. In the rarefied atmosphere of 'the village', wealthy New Yorkers once spent idyllic summers, and you'll still see their mansions here.

The best known is **Robert Todd Lincoln's Hildene**✦✦✦, built in 1902 by Abraham Lincoln's eldest son. Along with the family rooms, the servants' quarters and the surprisingly small kitchen are open to view. Carefully restored gardens overlook the valley, and are at their height in June and July.

Vermont State Craft Center✦✦ is among the Equinox Shops, facing the hotel. Displayed and sold here are works by the state's top craftsmen in all media, from pottery and wood to weaving and fine art prints. Behind the craft centre, the **Gleneagles Golf Course**✦ flows down the hillside, surrounded by mountain views. It's a championship course, beautifully designed, not surprisingly, since both it and the hotel are owned by Guinness.

Behind the hotel rises Mount Equinox, and it can be yours without any exertion at all, via the 5-mile **Mount Equinox Skyline Drive**✦✦, a toll road to the top. Below, the **American Museum of Fly Fishing**✦ covers the sport through history, with mementoes of fishing greats and examples of fine hand-crafted gear.

Just north is Manchester Center, a succession of up-market **factory outlet malls**✦✦ selling off-price goods (some seconds, most simply last season's over-stock). Most of the outlets sell designer and brand-name clothing and home decorations.

Accommodation and food in Manchester

The Equinox $$–$$$ Rte 7A, Manchester Village; tel: (802) 362-4700 or (800) 362-4747. Golf course, spa and outdoor activities for guests; fine dining in the formal dining room or Scottish-themed restaurant.

The Inn at Ormsby Hill $$ Rte 7A, 1842 Main St, Manchester; (802) 362-1163; www.ormsbyhill.com. Antique-furnished mansion built by Lincoln's law partner, now a classy inn with double whirlpool baths, fireplaces and a full-course breakfast served in a magnificent dining room.

STRATTON MOUNTAIN*

Stratton Mountain
Bondville; tel: (802) 277-2200 or (800) STRATTON.

Sun Bowl Ranch
Stratton Mountain; tel: (802) 297-9210 or (800) STRATTON. Trail rides mid June–mid Oct 0900–1700.

Not just a ski area, Stratton Mountain presents a year-round sports and activities schedule, as well as a *faux*-Alpine village filled with shops, cafés and restaurants. The **Stratton Gondola**** operates in good weather year-round to take visitors to the top of southern Vermont's tallest mountain. Golf, tennis, mountain biking and hiking are all within easy reach of this self-contained resort.

Sun Bowl Ranch* offers trail rides on horseback, along with rides in their farm wagon drawn by two big Belgian draft horses. Sleighs replace the wagons on winter weekends.

WESTON**

The Vermont Country Store *tel: (802) 824-3184. Open Mon–Sat 0900–1700.*

Below
The Vermont Country Store

The remote location in a mountain valley doesn't keep visitors from finding this lovely little town that clusters around its village green and bandstand. The main draw is **The Vermont Country Store*****, not a replica or a restoration, but a real original, complete with high button shoes, pot-bellied stove, and rows of penny candy jars. But it's more than a museum, with carefully chosen natural fibre clothing, quality housewares, foods and necessities of gracious country living.

The **Farrar-Mansur House*** is a colonial tavern, which combines

Farrar-Mansur House and Mill Museum $ *On the Green, Weston; no tel. Open June–mid Oct Sat–Sun 1330–1630; July–Aug Wed–Fri 1330–1630.*

Weston Bowl Mill *Main St, Weston; tel (802) 824-4215. Open Mon–Sat 0900–1500 and Sun 1000–1500.*

Weston Playhouse *on the Green; tel: (802) 824-5288 presents Broadway musicals late June–early Sept, with pre-theatre dinner and cabaret après.*

with an adjacent water-mill to form the town's historical museum. Displays include antique furnishings, clothing, utensils and firearms.

Elsewhere in town are craft studios and shops selling quilts, braided rugs, pottery and needlework. The **Weston Bowl Mill** has made wooden ware since 1902 and you can choose from seconds or first-quality salad bowls, chopping boards and wooden toys. If it's small and made of wood, you'll probably find it, from ladles to quilt racks.

Accommodation and food in Weston

Colonial House Inn and Motel $ *Rte 100, Weston; tel: (802) 824-6286.* A homey B&B-cum-motel, with home-cooked meals and a bakery famed for peach pie.

Village Sandwich Shop $ *Weston; tel: (802) 824-5477. Open daily 1000–1730.* Sandwiches, light meals and pastries.

Ethan Allen and the Green Mountain boys

Colonial Royal Governors of New Hampshire and New York each had a defensible claim under their patents from the King, to what is now Vermont. New Hampshire granted over 100 towns to settlers who carved farms out of the forests.

When New York sheriffs began driving these farmers from their homes and giving their farms to New Yorkers, brothers Ira and Ethan Allen, a feisty pair of New Hampshire grant-holders, rallied a band of rowdy riflemen who sent 'Yorkers' packing. The Allens had their eye on a separate province. These 'Green Mountain Boys' maintained a stand-off until the two sides temporarily joined forces during the American Revolution.

After the Green Mountain Boys captured Fort Ticonderoga, they were hailed as heroes of the Revolution. But this was just a skirmish in their larger battle, which they won with the formation of an independent Republic of Vermont and finally, in 1791, acceptance of Vermont as the 14th state.

Suggested tour

Total distance: 130 miles; 144 miles with detour

Time: 3 hours' driving. Allow a day for the main route, with or without detour, more if you will stop to tour attractions. The route can be broken into two loops, each beginning in Manchester. Those with limited time should concentrate on Bennington or Manchester.

Links: To reach the Berkshires Route, follow Rte 7 south from Bennington to Williamstown, Massachusetts.

Above
Fall colour at Wardsboro, near Stratton Mountain

To join the Upper Connecticut Valley Route, take Rte 9 from Bennington over the Green Mountains and scenic Hogback Mountain to Brattleboro. This is a winding, but good road that literally goes over the tops of two mountain ranges; the best views are from Hogback. To the Lake Champlain and Northern Green Mountains Route, follow Rte 7 or the more scenic Rte 30 north from Manchester to Middlebury.

Route: From downtown **BENNINGTON** ❶ follow Rte 7A to Rte 67A into North Bennington to the Park-McCullough House. Rte 67 connects to Rte 7A, which travels north to **ARLINGTON** ❷ and **MANCHESTER** ❸ From Manchester Center, follow Rte 30 to **DORSET** ❹ continuing through East Rupert to Pawlet.

Detour: At East Rupert, turn left (west) onto Rte 315, which leads to the **Merck Forest** ❺ and **Farmland Center**✣ ❻ (*tel: (802) 394-7836*). This working organic farm has miles of walking trails, including a labelled nature trail, along with farm animals, a maple sugar house and frequent special family programmes on farming and the environment.

Take Rte 153 north to **West Pawlet**✣ ❼. Almost the whole town was built in the 1890s to house stone-workers for the newly-opened quarries. These gabled American Queen Anne homes have decorated porches and trims. Each has a slate roof, and you'll see why, when you pass right through the slate quarry at the north end of the village.

When Rte 153 meets Rte 30, turn right (south). The **Valley of Vermont** ❽, through which you've been driving, is enclosed by the Taconics on the west and the Green Mountains on the east. Here the valley widens into fertile farmlands, and several large farms with

Mach's General Store *Pawlet; tel (802) 325-3405. Open Mon–Sat 0700–1830, Sun 0800–1230.*

Marion Waldo McChesney Potter *Pawlet; tel (802) 325-3100.*

Bromley Mountain *Manchester Center; tel (802) 824-5522.*

Danby Village Restaurant $$ *Main St, Danby; tel (802) 293-6003. Open Thur–Tue 1130–1430 and 1800–2100 (winter Thur–Sun). On the not-your-usual-menu Greek influences blend with New American.*

Adams Farm *15 Higley Hill, Wilmington; tel: (802) 464-3762. Visit the farm if you have children, to see the baby animals and learn how a Vermont farm works. Pony and hay rides can be arranged there.*

P *Parking in Wilmington is available, off Rte 100, just south of the Rte 9 crossing.*

barns and silos dotting the landscape, still a vital part of Vermont's rural heritage.

Rte 30 intersects Rte 133 in the centre of Pawlet, where the **pottery studio** ❾ of Marion Waldo McChesney is in the ground floor of the brick house opposite **Mach's General Store** ❿. The store itself is worth a visit to see the cabinet in the back, whose glass top looks straight down into the chasm cut by the benign-looking **Flower Brook** ⓫.

From Pawlet take Rte 133 until you reach a right fork signposted 'Danby'. Follow this unnumbered road through Danby Four Corners, and over the hill.

You literally drop into **Danby**＊⓬ once home of the author Pearl Buck, who wrote *The Good Earth*. She worked tirelessly to keep the little town alive as the marble industry declined, and is largely responsible for saving its 19th-century buildings. There's not much to do here, except browse through the many rooms of **the Danby Antiques Center** ⓭ on Main St, next to the restaurant, to see an eclectic range of Americana.

Go south on Rte 7, past **Emerald Lake State Park** ⓮ to MANCHESTER CENTER ⓯ where you take Rte 11 to Peru. **Bromley Mountain** ⓰ 6 miles west of Manchester Center, was one of the earliest ski slopes, built in the 1930s. A family-friendly area, it has trails for all skills and minimal ski lift-queues. You can get your thrills on the mountain even in the summer, by riding the two-third-mile **Alpine Slide**＊⓱ the longest alpine ride in the country.

In Peru, follow signs to **Hapgood Pond State Park**＊⓲ *(tel: (802) 362-2307)*, where you will find a swimming beach, tent pitches and walking trails. From here you will enjoy a real Vermont experience: travelling on an unpaved road to **WESTON** ⓳, If you shun gravel roads, return to Rte 11 and go north to Weston on Rte 100.

Leave Weston on Rte 100 south to Rawsonville, then take Rte 30 west to Bondville, and the entrance road to **STRATTON MOUNTAIN** ⓴ Returning to Manchester Center on Rte 30, you can reach your starting point in Bennington via fast, limited-access Rte 7.

Also worth exploring

Instead of returning to Manchester on Rte 30, continue down the winding, scenic Rte 100, 'The Skier's Highway' to **Wardsboro**, **West Dover** and **Wilmington**. At West Dover you will pass **Mount Snow Ski Area**, with its attendant businesses and lodgings. In Wilmington, at the crossroads of Rte 100 and Rte 9, are dozens of giftshops catering to tourists, in addition to some of the worst weekend traffic you are likely to see in the state. Rte 9 west takes you back to Bennington, through the **Green Mountain National Forest**.

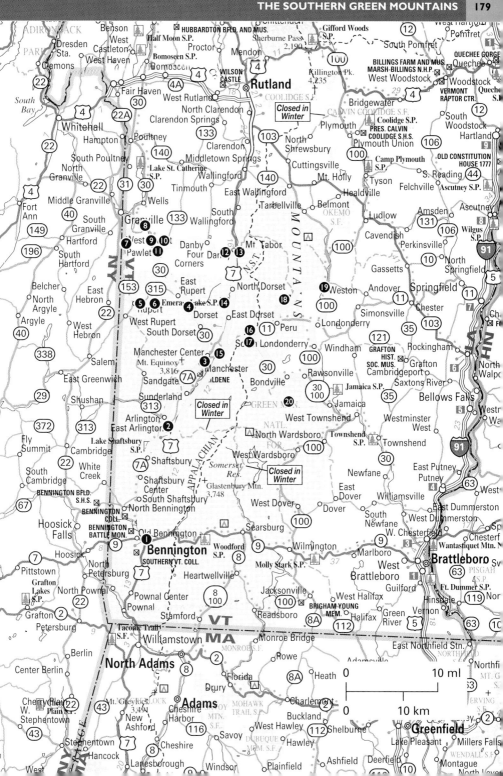

Lake Champlain to the Northern Green Mountains

Ratings

Nature and scenery	●●●●○
Art and culture	●●●○○
Food and drink	●●●○○
Shopping	●●●○○
Beaches and watersports	●●○○○
History	●●○○○
Museums	●●○○○
Children	●○○○○

Caught between the Green Mountains and the broadest part of huge Lake Champlain, Burlington rises from its marina to the University of Vermont's stately hilltop buildings. In between is downtown, centred in lively Church St, with shops, entertainment and abundant restaurants. From sailing on the lake to skiing in the Mountains, Burlington has it.

Nearby Shelburne Village is an assemblage of historic buildings (even a steamboat that once plied the lake) filled with collections of Early Americana.

Expect steep, narrow, winding roads if you travel over the passes at Smugglers Notch or Appalachian Gap, but otherwise only gentle hills as you explore these routes.

BURLINGTON✦✦✦

ⓘ Lake Champlain Regional Chamber of Commerce, 60 Main St; tel: (802) 863-3489.

ⓠ Champlain Valley Weekender $$ College St; tel: (802) 463-3069 or (800) 707-3530.

Northern Spy $$ Perkins Pier, Burlington; tel: (802) 343-3645; daily in good weather.

The lake is a part of downtown Burlington, bordered by a greensward of parks and a cycling/foot path leading to beaches, marinas and playgrounds. **Church St Marketplace✦✦✦** is alive with activity, especially in good weather, when the pedestrian-only street is filled with sidewalk cafés, vendors, music, and people. At any time of year shops, restaurants and entertainments keep things busy, and a free shuttle connects the area to the college and waterfront.

Departing from the waterfront, the restored 1930s passenger cars of **Champlain Valley Weekender✦✦** makes two round trips daily to **Middlebury**, stopping in **Vergennes** and **Shelburne**. Nearby, the 42-ft schooner **Northern Spy✦✦** takes passengers for 2-hour sails around the lake in a traditional wooden craft. Take the helm, help with the five sails or just enjoy the views. For a more conventional excursion, board

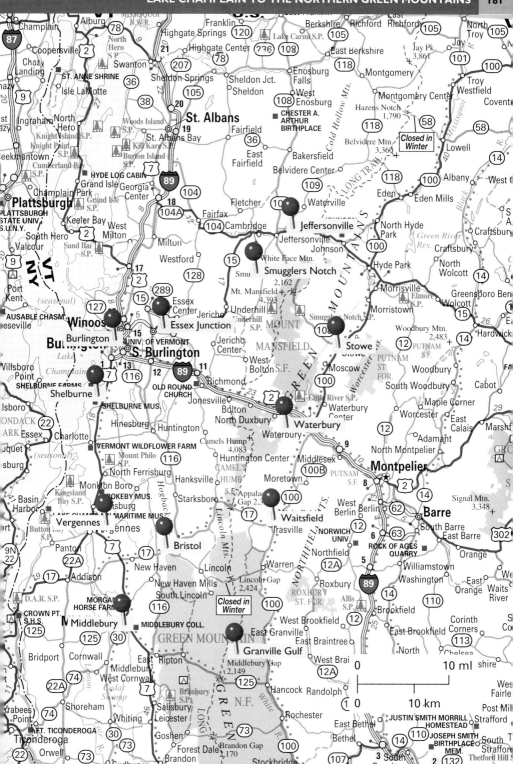

Spirit of Ethan Allen II $ *Spirit Landing, Burlington Boathouse, College St; tel: (802) 862-8300.*

Lake Champlain Basin Science Center $ *beside Boathouse, 1 College St; tel: (802) 864-1848. Open mid June–Aug daily, weekends year-round, 1230–1600 or 1700.*

Ethan Allen Farmstead $ *signposted from North Ave and Rte 127; tel: (802) 865-4556.*

the *Spirit of Ethan Allen II*** for a narrated dinner or sunset cruise.

Children will learn about the lake and the critters that live there – and have fun in the process – through interactive exhibits at the **Lake Champlain Basin Science Center***.

Two centuries away from busy downtown is the **Ethan Allen Farmstead****, where visitors learn about this cheeky Vermonter and his exploits in the Revolution. Along with the farmhouse, you can tour interpretive trails in the Wetlands Nature Center, identifying the abundant bird and plant life with a self-guiding brochure.

The Ethan Allen Farmstead

Accommodation and food in Burlington

Burlington Redstone B&B $ *497 S Willard St (Rte 7); tel: (802) 862-0508.* Historic home within easy walk of downtown.

Butler's $$ *70 Essex Way, Essex Junction; tel: (802) 878-1100.* Many cuisines blend creatively at the hands of New England Culinary Institute students.

Five Spice Café $–$$ *175 Church St; tel: (802) 864-4045.* Asian eclectic with New England touches.

The Inn at Essex $$ *70 Essex Way, Essex Junction; tel: (802) 878-1100.* Stylish new hotel run by New England Culinary Institute.

Trattoria Delia $–$$ *152 St Paul St (City Hall Park); tel: (802) 864-5253.* Unforgettable Mediterranean dining with wild game specialities.

MIDDLEBURY**

ⓘ Chamber of Commerce 2 Court St; tel: (802) 388-7951; www.midvermont.com

🏛 The Sheldon Museum 1 Park St; tel: (802) 388-2117. Open late May–mid Oct Mon–Sat, 1000–1700, weekends all year.

UVM Morgan Horse Farm $ 2.5 miles from downtown Middlebury, at 74 Battell Drive (Rte 23), Weybridge; tel: (802) 388-2011.

◯ Vermont State Craft Center Frog Hollow, 1 Mill St; tel: (802) 388-3177. Open year-round Mon–Sat, Sun June–Dec.

⚙ Middlebury Snow Bowl Rte 125, Ripton; tel: (802) 388-4356. Ski Lift $$$

◯ Summer Festival on the Green tel: (802) 388-0216, a mid-July week of performing arts.

College campus and town flow together seamlessly, each with its share of historic architecture. Marble is so plentiful in Vermont that you'll see entire buildings of it, such as **The Sheldon Museum****, an 1829 merchant's home and the oldest community museum in the United States. Ten rooms show furniture, art and daily life of early Vermont. To see (and buy) fine contemporary craftwork, visit the **Vermont State Craft Center****, with styles from smart to homey.

University of Vermont Morgan Horse Farm* offers films on this remarkable breed and a chance to meet some horses in person during the tour.

Middlebury Snow Bowl* is a unique, uncrowded place to ski, without the glitz, queues or price of its Vermont neighbours. Trails for Nordic skiers begin near the **Robert Frost Wayside Trail***, which leads to the cabin where the poet wrote for 22 summers.

Accommodation and food in Middlebury

Brookside Meadows Country B&B $$ *Quarry Rd; tel: (802) 388-6429 or (800) 442-9887; www.brooksmeadow.com.* A newly built, hospitable and elegantly appointed lodging with beautiful gardens.

Chipman Inn $–$$ *Rte 125, Ripton; tel: (802) 388-2390 or (800) 890-2390.* Payment for rooms in this historic home includes hearty breakfasts; dinner $$ can be reserved.

Judith's Garden B&B $ *Forest Rd # 32 (between Goshen and Ripton), Goshen; tel: (802) 247-4707.* Guests get personal attention in a remote location amid gardens overlooking the Adirondack Mountains.

Woody's $–$$ *5 Bakery Lane; tel: (802) 388-4182 or (800) 346-3603.* Seafood reigns here at lunch and dinner.

SHELBURNE***

🏛 Shelburne Museum $$ Rte 7; tel: (802) 985-3346. Open late May–mid Oct daily 1000–1700, shorter winter hours.

Shelburne Farms $ Harbor Rd; tel: (802) 985-8686. Tours June–mid Oct daily 0930–1330.

Ten miles south of Burlington, Shelburne is best known for the **Shelburne Museum*****. Early New England quilts, painted tin and woodenware, roundabout horses, furniture, horse-drawn sleighs, carriages and entire buildings, even a covered bridge, lighthouse and the steamship *SS Ticonderoga* are among the 80,000 artefacts.

Baronial estates are not common in New England, which makes the grand barns and turreted farmyard at **Shelburne Farms**** even more unexpected. On this 1400-acre working 'gentleman's farm' are gardens, historic barns, a children's farmyard where you can try milking a cow, and a dairy where cheese is made.

SMUGGLERS NOTCH✦✦✦

Smugglers' Notch Resort $–$$ *Rte 108, Smugglers Notch; tel: (802) 644-8851 or (800) 451-8752; www.smuggs.com.* Hotel or modern slope-side condos with full kitchens, fireplaces and whirlpool tubs.

Boyden Valley Winery *Rtes 15 and 104; tel: (802) 644-815. Tours year-round Tue–Sun.*

Smugglers Notch Area Winter Carnival *Smugglers' Notch; tel: (802) 644-8851;* early Feb. Nordic races, snow sculptures, food, snowshoe hikes and social events.

Quilts for sale in Shelburne village

The road over Smugglers Notch is like no other in New England, so narrow that caravans are not allowed over it; they would be unable to manoeuvre the sharp turns between giant boulders that line its sides. Park between them and climb a short distance for sweeping views of Vermont, New York and Canada. Snow ploughs can't navigate the road, so it closes for the winter. Then you can ski over the top, Alpine-style, from **Smugglers' Notch Ski Resort✦✦✦** to the slopes of Mount Mansfield at Stowe (note that for some reason, the resort has s' whereas the area doesn't). Smugglers' Notch is a self-contained resort with year-round sports facilities, including horse-riding, kayaking, tennis, swimming and climbing. In winter, the skiing is superb. It is perfect for families, with many year-round programmes for children.

At nearby **Boyden Valley Winery✦**, set on a dairy farm, they combine their own grapes, local berries and apples with maple syrup to make wines and cordials, along with hard cider.

STOWE✦✦✦

ⓘ Stowe Area Association *Main St;*
tel: (800) 24-STOWE;
www.stoweinfo.com.

♫ Meadow Concerts
$$ Trapp Family Lodge;
tel (800) 24-STOWE. Late
June–Aug; Vermont
Mozart Festival late July.

Apart from skiing, Stowe is also popular year-round for its shopping, and restaurants. Crafts and handwork dominate in the up-market shops along Stowe's Main St, where the pace is relaxed and friendly.

Rent bicycles at Stowe Hardware Store *(tel: (802) 253-7205)* on Main St to bike the paved 5.3-mile **Stowe Recreation Path**✦✦ along the river, leading past lodging, dining, gardens and mountain vistas. Walkers, skaters and runners all enjoy the path.

In May–Oct Sundays 1100–1500, it leads past the **Stowe Farmers Market**✦, on Mountain Rd *(tel: (800) 24-STOWE).* Shop here for locally produced picnic ingredients: fresh baked breads and goat's cheese, country sausage and fruits.

On Rte 108, near the ski area, is the short trail to **Bingham Falls**✦✦, one of the state's most beautiful. Above the falls look for potholes carved by swirling waters. For your own safety, and to protect fragile banks from further erosion, descend well away from the gorge's sides to view the falls from below.

If the urge for comfort food is overwhelming, sidetrack to **Sage Sheep Farm**✦ for a proper tea with sweets or savouries, served on a veranda overlooking gardens. The shop has wool and herb crafts.

A **Gondola Skyride**✦✦ **$** *(tel: (802) 253-3000)* travels to the top of Mount Mansfield, Vermont's highest, for sweeping views and access to hiking trails, or you can drive to the summit on the 4.5-mile Auto Road **$$**.

The **Trapp Family Lodge**✦✦✦, overlooking rolling meadows and mountains, is as much a part of Stowe as skiing itself. The hills are alive with the sound of music, all summer long, when the von Trapps host **Meadow Concerts**✦✦ and the **Vermont Mozart Festival**✦✦. Bring a picnic and watch the sunset to music.

The flower-decked lodge is the centre for activities, with many open to the public. Excellent cross-country skiing, snowshoeing, sleigh rides and maple-sugaring keep winter guests busy; summer programmes for families include fishing, bird-watching, hiking and llama treks.

The Underground Railway

From the first days of its statehood, Vermont prohibited slavery in its Constitution. Abolitionist sentiment ran strong before the Civil War, and the state was a major conduit in the underground railroad. Several of the secret routes that carried escaped slaves to freedom in Canada followed Vermont rivers and mountain roads, over which slaves were transported, hidden under hay loads or in barrels labelled as everything from pork to molasses. Despite Federal law that required courts to return slaves to their owners, many Vermont judges refused.

Accommodation and food in Stowe

Gracie's $ *Main St; tel: (802) 253-8741.* Big burgers, sandwiches, generous dinners until 2400 daily.

Green Mountain Inn $–$$ *Main St; tel: (802) 253-7301 or (800) 253-7302; www.genghis.com.* Canopy beds, whirlpool baths, terry robes, electric fireplaces, afternoon cider and fresh-baked cookies in the lobby.

Sage Sheep Farm $ *West Hill Rd; tel: (802) 253-8532. Open mid June–mid Oct Wed–Sun 1200–1730.*

The Gables $–$$ *1457 Mountain Rd; tel: (802) 253-7730 or (800) GABLES-1; www.stoweinfo. com/saa/gables.* Warm and unpretentious family-owned inn with fireplaces, whirlpool tubs and mega-breakfasts. Restaurant $–$$ open to the public.

Trapp Family Lodge $$ *Trapp Hill Rd; tel: (802) 253-8511 or (800) 826-7000; www.trappfamily.com.* Dining room $$–$$$ (included in room rate for guests) is Austrian-Continental, with live harp music.

Stowe landscape, looking to Mount Mansfield

VERGENNES✧✧

🛈 **Lake Champlain Maritime Museum**
$$ *Basin Harbor Rd; tel: (802) 475-202. Open early May–mid Oct daily 1000–1700.*

Rokeby Homestead $
Rte 7, Ferrisburg; tel: (802) 877-3406. Open mid May–mid Oct Thur–Sun, tours 1100 and 1400.

Halfway between Burlington and Middlebury, Vergennes is one of the oldest towns in Vermont, and the smallest. Barely more than a mile square, it packs in an **Historic District**✧✧ of 80 noteworthy buildings. In the basin below **Otter Creek Falls** the ships that prevailed at the Battle of Plattsburgh in 1814 were constructed.

    This and other historical detail is provided at the **Lake Champlain Maritime Museum**✧✧✧, spread along the shore and into its waters. Many of the boats there were recovered from the lake's floor. Blacksmiths and ship builders demonstrate and exhibits tell tales of the many shipwrecks and naval action during the War of 1812 with

Rokeby Homestead $ *Rte 7, Ferrisburg; tel: (802) 877-3406. Open mid May–mid Oct Thur–Sun, tours 1100 and 1400.*

England. Sailboats, rowboats, canoes and kayaks are available for rent. **Rokeby Homestead**✢✢ is one of the few places in Vermont (or anywhere) with a well-documented history as a station in the Underground Railroad. Written records of this clandestine network's activities were rarely kept, for fear of discovery and prosecution. Writer Rowland Robinson did keep records, and his home is now a museum chronicling this and other events in two centuries of a remarkable family.

Accommodation and food in Vergennes

Emersons' B&B $ *82 Main St; tel: (802) 877-3293.* Comfortable Victorian home in downtown setting.

Roland's Place $–$$ *Rte 7 South, New Haven; tel: (802) 453-6309.* Simply put, it's tops, with a French chef who values fresh local produce and farmed game. Lunch and dinner daily, early dinners $ 1700–1800.

Strong House Inn $–$$ *82 West Main St; tel: (802) 877-3337; www.flinet.com~bargieleer/ shi_inn.htm.* Beautifully restored Federal mansion overlooking the Adrirondack Mountains from amid gardens in summer and backyard skiing, skating and sledding in the winter.

WATERBURY✢✢

Ben and Jerry's Ice-Cream Factory $ *Rte 100; tel: (802) 244-5641. Open daily year-round.*

Cold Hollow Cider Mill *Rte 100, Waterbury Center; tel: (802) 244-8771 or (800) 327-7537. Open daily July–Oct 0800–1900, Nov–June 0800–1800.*

Green Mountain Coffee Roasters *off Main St; tel: (800) 223-6768. Open Mon–Fri 0630–1700, Sat 0800–1300.*

Free Thursday Concerts *Rusty Parker Memorial Park; tel: (802) 244-7352; summer only, 1830.*

Most people come to Waterbury looking for the home of Vermont's favourite ice-creams, at **Ben and Jerry's Ice-Cream Factory**✢✢. If you haven't tried it, here's your chance not only to sample the stuff everyone raves about, but to see how it is made. Tours include samples.

At **Cold Hollow Cider Mill**✢✢ you can watch the cider being pressed year-round, with free samples. Various apple products, including apple butter and cider jelly, as well as maple and other speciality foods are sold, along with Vermont crafts, in the shop and bakery.

Waterbury has some fine Victorian buildings and a **Historical Society Museum**✢ in the library building. It's a typical mix of local treasures, with a good collection of Berlin work, beading and handmade lace. Also downtown, **Green Mountain Coffee Roasters**, Vermont's coffee-of-choice, has a factory outlet store, with full-bean coffee and off-price accessories.

Accommodation and food in Waterbury

1836 Cabins $–$$ *Rte 100; tel: (802) 244-8533.* Modern, self-catering cabins, in pine woods.

Also worth exploring

The **Champlain Islands**❖❖, north of Burlington, stretch all the way to the Canadian Border. North of Colchester, take Rte 2 toward South Hero, via a long bridge near **Sandbar State Park**❖. The landscape across the bridge is low, gentle farmland echoing the slower island pace. Rte 2 passes **Grand Isle State Park**❖ and **Knight Point State Park**❖, both with lakeshore beaches, and **Hyde Log Cabin**❖❖. Rte 129 leads to **St Anne's Shrine**❖, at the site of the first European settlement in Vermont, on **Isle La Motte**❖❖.

Grunberg Haus $–$$ *Rte 100, Duxbury; tel: (802) 244-7726 or (800) 800-7760.* Rooms in an inviting Alpine chalet or cosy hillside cottages, all including sumptuous breakfast with piano accompaniment.

Tanglewoods $–$$ *Guptil Rd, off Rte 100 North; tel: (802) 244-7855.* New American menu with a southwest accent.

The Old Stagecoach Inn $–$$ *18 Main St (Rte 2); tel: (802) 244-5056 or (800) 262-2206.* Historic coaching stop with well-furnished rooms, genial hosts and fresh home-baked croissants. Occasional weekend fixed-price dinner $.

Villa Tragara $–$$ *Rte 100 North; tel: (802) 244-5288.* Italian doesn't get any better, even in Italy. Fresh local ingredients and sunset views.

Suggested tour

Total distance: 140 miles; 158 miles with detours

Time: 4 hours' driving. Allow 2 days for the main route, 2½ days with detours. Those with limited time should concentrate on Shelburne, Burlington, Smugglers Notch and Stowe.

Links: Follow Rte 7 south to Danby and the Southern Green Mountains Route, or I-89 from Waterbury to Barre to join the Northeast Kingdom Route.

Route: From **MIDDLEBURY** ❶ follow Rte 7 to **VERGENNES** ❷ and Ferrisburg ❸ with a detour to **Charlotte** ❹ to ride the ferry to Essex, New York and back.

Rte 7 continues through **SHELBURNE** ❺ to **BURLINGTON** ❻, with views east towards the **Green Mountains** ❼ and west over the lake to the **Adirondacks** ❽. From Burlington, follow Rte 15 through Essex Junction to Cambridge and to **Boyden Valley Winery** ❾. Follow Rte 15 alongside the **Lamoille River** ❿ to **Jeffersonville** ⓫. You can float through the scenic valley in a canoe, exploring the river environment during a Wetlands and Wildlife Tour with Green River Canoe. Guided tours include instruction for beginners. In Jeffersonville, Rte 108 leaves on its steep, winding route south over **SMUGGLERS NOTCH** ⓬ to STOWE ⓭

Detour: In winter, or to avoid the notch in bad weather, continue on Rte 15 through **Johnson** ⓮ and **Hyde Park** ⓯ turning south on Rte 100 in Morrisville. Before the turn are acres of themed gardens at **Cady's Falls Nursery** ⓰. Rte 100 leads to STOWE ⓭.

Continue on Rte 100 to **WATERBURY** ⓱ and **Waitsfield**❖❖ ⓲ home of a rare round barn at Round Barn Farm. In Irasville, Rte 17 heads over **Appalachian Gap**❖❖ ⓳ 2300ft high at its dramatic summit on the spine of the Green Mountains. As you enter **Bristol** ❂ ❷⓿ notice the Lord's Prayer carved on a boulder beside the road.

Bristol is an attractive small town where, near the intersection of Rte 116 with Rte 17, you'll find **Bristol Memorial Forest Park** ❂ ❷❶ with picnic sites overlooking a gorge and waterfalls. From Bristol, follow Rte 116 South to Rte 125 in East Middlebury, which leads back to the starting point in Middlebury.

Detour Instead of climbing Appalachian Gap, continue on Rte 100 from Irasville through the wild cleft of **Granville Gulf** ❷❷, past **Moss Glen Falls** ❂❂ ❷❸, to Hancock. Follow Rte 125 past **Texas Falls** ❂❂ ❷❹ and over the Green Mountains at Middlebury Gap, passing **Middlebury Snow Bowl** ❷❺.

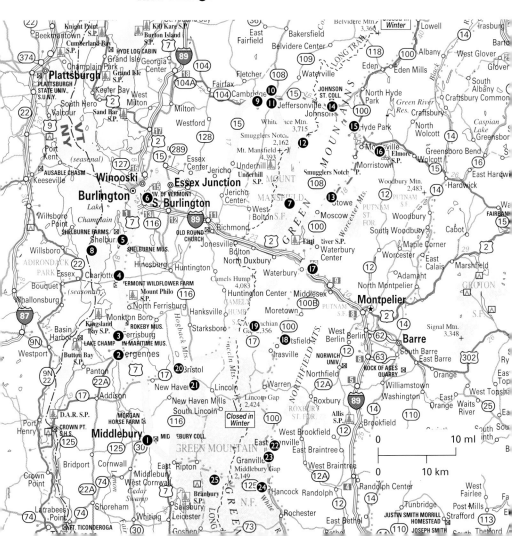

The Northeast Kingdom

Ratings

Nature/scenery	●●●●
Arts and culture	●●
Beaches/watersports	●●
Children	●●
Museums	●●
Food and drink	●
History	●
Shopping	●

This remote corner of Vermont is rarely visited by tourists, so remains quiet and uncrowded. Covered bridges cross streams that have cut long narrow valleys through the hills, and in some areas moose outnumber people.

St Johnsbury is home to an entire hilltop of fine Victorian churches, homes and public buildings, which include a charmingly old-fashioned natural history museum. The subject is appropriate, since nature has blessed this region so abundantly, from the rich fine-grade granite of its bedrock to the wildlife that roams its woods and flies through its clean, clear air.

BARRE❖❖

Barre Opera House
City Hall; tel: (802) 476-8188; a restored Victorian opera house with year-round theatre, opera and classical music performances.

Rock of Ages $
Websterville; tel: (802) 476-3119. Open June–mid Oct Mon–Fri 0915–1500, free self-guided tour and video Mon–Sat 0830–1500, Sun 1200–1700.

Granite built Barre, literally and figuratively, and you can tour the world's largest granite quarry, the 450-ft deep **Rock of Ages❖❖**. Even the giant hills of tailings that surround its approach don't prepare visitors for the size of this man-made hole. Ride the shuttle to a working quarry; stone cutting demonstrations complete the tour.

Barre's fine grade of granite is ideal for carving into monuments, and especially in the **Downtown Historic District❖** you will see public statuary, architectural ornamentation and even business signs of granite. But nowhere will you see a finer collection that at **Hope Cemetery❖❖❖**, on Merchant St (Rte 14). Here the most skilled Italian stone carvers created monuments to their loved ones – and themselves. These range from lifelike figures and art deco designs to granite representations of everything from an airplane to a soccer ball.

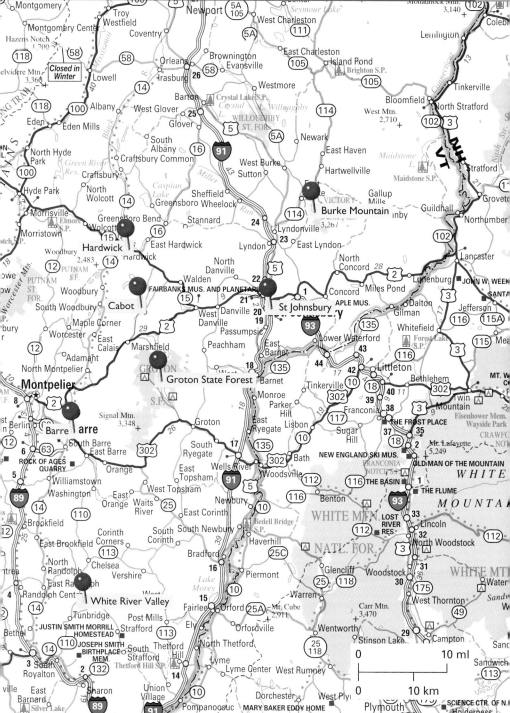

BURKE MOUNTAIN✧✧

Trout River Brewing Company
Rte 114, East Burke; tel: (802) 626-3984. Open Mon–Thur 1200–1900, Fri–Sat 1200–2000, Sun 1300–1700.

Burke Mountain
Mountain Rd, East Burke; tel: (802) 626-3305 or (800) 922-BURK.

The Snack Shack $
Rte 14; tel: (802) 479-5508. Hamburgers, grilled hotdogs, sausage and handcut chips.

Oktoberfest *Burke Mountain Ski Area; tel: (802) 626-5230. Mid Sept. German food, beer and Alpine music.*

Northeast Kingdom Sled Dog Races
Wildflower Inn; tel: (802) 626-8310; in mid Jan.

Residents at the family-friendly Wildflower Inn

Bailey's Country Store *(Rte 114, East Burke; tel: (802) 626-3666)* is a combination local general store and giftshop for tourists. Look here for Vermont crafts, picnic makings, the mosquito repellent you'll need if you are hiking. Sample menus from local restaurants fill a basket in the back corner. Behind Bailey's is **Trout River Brewing Company✧**, whose six different ales you can sample on a free tour.

Overlooking town, **Burke Mountain✧** is a family ski area with a novice trail from the top of the mountain. It becomes **Burke Mountain Auto Road✧✧** when the snow melts, so you can enjoy the view any time of year. Cross-country ski trails traverse 50 miles of forest and meadows. Volkswalks are sponsored by the Kingdom Kickers, the area's very active Volkssporting group, which also sponsors an **Oktoberfest✧✧** at Burke Mountain.

Wildflower Inn✧✧✧ spreads across a ridge with views over the mountains framed by perennial gardens. A barnful of baby animals, sleds for the sledding hill, a lighted skating rink, and sleigh- and hayrides are features of this small family-run resort/B&B. The outstanding dining-room is open to the public.

The entire ridge was part of an 8000-acre farm. Drive farther along Darling Hill Rd to see the mansion and several huge barns.

Accommodation and food in Burke Mountain

The Wildflower Inn $–$$ *Darling Hill Rd, Lyndonville; tel: (802) 626-8310 or (800) 627-8310; www.vtnek.com*. Dining-room $$ reservations suggested.

Burke Mountain Northern Star $ *East Burke; (802) 626-8903 or (800) 541-5480*. Self-catering condos with woodburning stoves or fireplaces, at the ski area.

River Garden Café $–$$ *East Burke; tel: (802) 626-3514*. Open year-round for lunch and dinner Tue–Sun, with an eclectic menu.

CABOT/HARDWICK❖❖

Lamoille Valley Railroad $ *tel: (802) 888-7183; operating July–mid Oct.*

Cabot Creamery $ *Main St (Rte 215), Cabot; tel: (802) 563-2231. Open June–Oct daily 0900–1700, shorter winter hours.*

Perennial Pleasures *Brick House Rd, East Hardwick; tel: (802) 472-5512. Open late May–Sept Tue–Sat.*

Old Time Fiddlers Contest $ *Hardwick; tel: (802) 472-5501.* More than 60 contestants in New England's biggest fiddling event.

Perennial Pleasures❖❖ is the loving work of a professional restorer of almost-lost gardens. Painstaking research and searches for historically accurate plants led to the opening of a nursery to help others in similar quests.

Lamoille Valley Railroad❖❖, which once served the quarries of Hardwick, now offers excursions along the scenic Lamoille River, passing through **Fisher Covered Railroad Bridge**❖, the only covered railroad bridge still in use in the United States. Picnic tables are on the riverbank near the bridge.

The modern **Cabot Creamery**❖❖ makes Vermont cheddar and other cheeses. After watching the process through glass windows on a tour, you can sample all their cheeses in the shop (you can also sample and buy without the tour).

Accommodation and food in Hardwick/Cabot

Brick House Guests $ *2 Brick House Rd, East Hardwick; tel: (802) 472-5512*. With featherbeds and antiques – and 'real' tea.

GROTON STATE FOREST❖❖

Groton State Forest Headquarters *Marshfield, Rte 232; tel: (802) 584-3820.* Excellent booklets are available on the natural and human history of the area.

Geological and natural sights and plenty of trees fill the 25,000 acres of Groton State Forest. Three campsites (one with caravan facilities), a swimming beach and miles of hiking trails are spread along the 14-mile stretch of Rte 232 north of Groton. A good place to get an overview of the park's natural history is at the **Nature Center**❖, a museum with displays of local plants and animals. Diagrams illustrate the region's geology, from its origins at the bottom of a sea to scouring by glaciers. A **Nature Trail**❖ begins here, described in a booklet available at the museum.

Hawks often circle above **Owls Head**❖❖, a 10-minute walk from the upper parking area, or a stiff climb from the bottom. This granite knob

Bob's $ *Rte 302, Groton; tel: (802) 584-3225.* Take-away or dine there on hearty portions.

was scraped clean by glaciers, exposing stripes of different-coloured rock formed during earlier volcanic action.

ST JOHNSBURY**

Northeast Kingdom Chamber of Commerce *30 Western Ave; tel: (802) 748-3678 or (800) 639-6379.*

Fairbanks Museum and Planetarium $ *Main St; tel: (802) 748-2372. Open Mon–Sat 1000–1600, Sun 1300–1700. Planetarium shows Sat–Sun 1330, daily July–Aug.*

St Johnsbury Athenaeum and Art Gallery *Main St; tel: (802) 748-8291. Open daily, varying hours.*

Main St, uphill from the business district (everything here is up- or downhill), is an avenue of fine **Victorian buildings**** clustered around the Romanesque-style red sandstone **Fairbanks Museum** and the perpendicular gothic **Congregational Church**. This outstanding ensemble is described in a walking-tour brochure available at the museum.

Inside the **Fairbanks Museum and Planetarium****, collections centre on natural history, ethnology and history, plus just plain 'curiosities' once the private collections of the town's benefactor. The interior is also of architectural note, with an oak barrel-vaulted ceiling and arcade of cherrywood display cases along the upper gallery. Don't miss the bizarre Victorian 'bug art' portrait of George Washington.

Just down the street is the **St Johnsbury Athenaeum and Art Gallery***, with Albert Bierstadt's monumental painting *The Domes of Yosemite* on display. The street clock in front of the Athenaeum is from the old Grand Central Station in New York.

Maple Grove Maple Museum and Factory** is the world's oldest and largest maple candy factory, begun in the kitchen of a family farm in 1915. The museum shows old methods of gathering sap and making syrup, and a tour takes visitors through the candy-making process – with samples, of course.

Maple Grove Maple Museum and Factory $ *167 Portland St; tel: (802) 748-5141. Open Mon–Fri 0800–1600.*

Accommodation and food in St Johnsbury

Echo Ledge Farm Inn $ *Rte 2, East St; tel: (802) 748-4750.* An old farmhouse with homey atmosphere and warm hospitality.

The Northern Lights Bookshop Café $ *79 Railroad St; tel: (802) 748-4463.* Open daily for breakfast and lunch; bistro menu Thu–Sat dinner.

WHITE RIVER VALLEY❖❖

Porter Music Box Museum $ *Rte 66, Randolph; tel: (800) 811-7987. Open May–Dec Mon–Sat 0930–1700; Jan–Apr Mon–Fri 0900–1600.*

Foggy Bottom Farm B&B $ *Randolph; tel: (802) 728-9201.* An 1840 farmhouse with afternoon tea served by the fireplace.

Tunbridge World's Fair $ *Rte 110; tel: (802) 889-5555. Mid Sept;* traffic clogs the single road to this tiny town's famous agricultural fair.

Four almost parallel branches of the White River flow southwards to join the main river within 10 miles of each other. Each has a scenic road beside it. Two of these roads, Rtes 110 and 14, are bordered by a succession of **covered bridges❖❖**. On Rte 110, in 8 miles between South Royalton and Chelsea, are six bridges, five of them within easy sight of the road, crossing the First Branch.

The 1883 Mill Covered Bridge and an 1820 brick sawmill form the centre-piece of **Tunbridge Village Historic District❖**, a well-preserved agricultural settlement of about a hundred pre-1850 buildings. **Randolph Center Historic District❖**, on the Second Branch, has a number of outstanding buildings arranged on a 19th-century plan.

In Randolph, which sits on Third Branch, **Porter Music Box Company❖**, the world's only manufacturer of large-disc music boxes, has a museum and gift shop, with a collection of historic music boxes and a unique reproducing piano.

Brookfield Floating Bridge❖❖ spans a 320-ft pond, and is suspended on the surface of the water by nearly 400 wooden barrels. As you cross (the bridge is still in daily use, except in winter), the roadway undulates and water creeps between the floorboards.

Suggested tour

Total distance: 233 miles; 272 miles with detours

Time: 6 hours' driving. Allow 2 days for the main route, with or without detours. Those with limited time should concentrate on Barre or St Johnsbury and the White River Valley.

Links: I-89 connects Barre with Waterbury and Burlington (Lake Champlain Route) and with White River Junction (Upper Connecticut Valley Route).

Route: From downtown **BARRE** ❶ follow Rte 14 north to Rte 2. Follow Rte 2 north to Marshfield, then Rte 215 through **CABOT** ❷ to Rte 15, which leads to **HARDWICK** ❸. From there, follow Rte 14 north, leaving it just past **Lake Eligo** ❹ to take the scenic road through **Craftsbury** ❺.

The WilloughVale Inn $–$$
Rte 5A, Westmore; tel: (802) 525-4123, www.willowvale. com. Overlooking Lake Willoughby from inn rooms or lakefront cottages, dine in the Taproom or dining-room.

Lakefront Motel $ Cross St, Island Pond; tel: (802) 723-6507. Just as it says, right on the lake.

Jennifer's Restaurant $ Cross St, Island Pond; tel: (802) 723-6135. Three meals daily with generous portions.

Miss Lyndonville Diner $ Rte 5, Lyndonville; tel: (802) 626-9890. A diner with a loyal following.

P&H Truck Stop $ Rte 302, Wells River; tel: (802) 429-2141. Reliable and informal, with terrific pies.

South Strafford Café $ Main St, South Strafford; tel: (802) 765-4671. Open year-round for lunch or tea.

Main Street Grill and Bar $–$$ tel: (802) 223-3188 and **Chef's Table $$** tel: (802) 229-9202, both at 118 Main St, South Strafford have student chefs.

La Brioche Bakery and Café $ 89 Main St, South Strafford; (802) 229-0443. Modern café with excellent pastries and sandwiches.

The Inn at Montpelier $$ 147 Main St, South Strafford; tel: (802) 223-2727. In two restored early-1800s homes, a block from the centre of town.

In Irasburg, take Rte 58 to Orleans, then head south on Rte 5 to Barton. Follow Rte 16 to Westmore and the loch-like **Lake Willoughby ❻**, following Rte 5A along its cliff-lined shore to West Burke, where a short unnumbered road is signposted to **East Burke ❼**.

Detour: Rte 5A heads north from **Westmore** to an intersection with Rte 105, which leads to the outpost town of **Island Pond ❽**. A two-storey brick and granite **Railroad Station❋ ❾**, now a local museum, hints of the town's history as an important rail junction (13 different lines once converged here). Behind it rises a neighbourhood of **Victorian houses❋ ❿** and the Gothic Revival Christ Church.

Lady of the Lake❋❋ ⓫ (*$; tel: (802) 723-6649*), a stable pontoon excursion boat, takes passengers on narrated tours around the lake. Board at the Senior Center or the Lakefront Motel dock. To explore the lake on your own, hire a canoe at the Lakefront Motel, which also has a sailboat and a fishing boat for hire.

On the opposite side of the lake, **Brighton State Park❋❋ ⓬** has hiking trails, tent pitches, lean-to shelters, a beach and nature programmes, but few frills, making it a favourite of those who love the quiet boreal forest and the cry of loons on the lake. Native animals seen there include deer, moose, black bear, bobcat, racoon and squirrels. The woods, meadows and bogs around Island Pond offer some of the best bird-watching in the state.

From Island Pond, follow Rte 114 to **East Burke ❼**. Rte 114 leads south into **Lyndonville ⓭**, where it joins Rte 5 to St Johnsbury. Rte 5 continues down the **Connecticut River Valley❋❋ ⓮**, though several historic river towns, to **Wells River**.

Detour: From St Johnsbury, follow Rte 2 west through Danville to Rte 232, which leads through the centre of **GROTON STATE FOREST ⓯**. This road ends at Rte 302, by which you can return Wells River.

When you reach Ely, take Rte 244 west along the shores of Lake Fairlee to Rte 113 in Post Mills. Follow this south to Thetford Center, keeping a sharp look-out for an unnumbered road across a covered bridge, signposted to South Strafford. When you reach Rte 132, turn west (right) into **South Strafford**.

Two miles north in **Strafford**, the **Justin Smith Morrill Homestead❋❋ ⓰** is a 17-room Gothic Revival mansion, unchanged and complete with original furnishings, gardens and outbuildings. It is worth visiting just to see the hand-painted window in the library ceiling.

Rte 132 leads to Sharon, where you turn right on to Rte 14, heading west along the **WHITE RIVER VALLEY ⓱**. In 5 miles, Rte 110 heads north to Tunbridge, along the White River's First Branch. Past the village take the well-signposted route to East Randolph.

Rte 66 leads to Randolph, where you meet Rte 12. Follow it north

Brighton State Park *Rte 5, Island Pond; tel: (802) 723-4360. Open mid May–mid Oct.*

Justin Smith Morrill Homestead $ *Strafford; tel: (802) 765-4484. Open June–mid Oct Wed–Sun 1100–1700.*

through the Brookfield Gulf to Rte 65, which leads into Brookfield, crossing over the unusual **Floating Bridge**. From Brookfield, Rte 14 returns to the starting point in Barre.

Also worth exploring

Montpelier is America's smallest state capital. Next to the Capitol Building is the **Vermont Historical Society Museum** (tel: (802) 828-2291). Home of New England Culinary Institute, Montpelier is known for its **abundant restaurants**, several of which are operated by students. **Morse Farm Sugar House and Museum** (tel: (802) 223-2740) shows the maple production process and has a gift-shop.

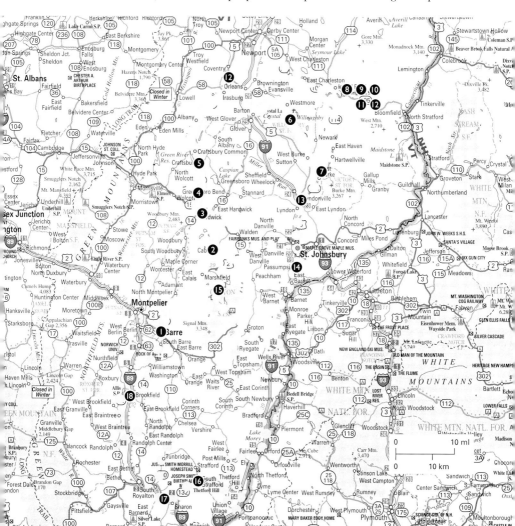

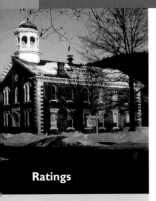

The Upper Connecticut Valley

Ratings

Arts and culture	●●●●
Nature/ scenery	●●●●
Food and drink	●●●
History	●●●
Museums	●●●
Shopping	●●●
Beaches/ watersports	●
Children	●

The Connecticut River divides not just two states, but the ancient rocks of two continents. The eastern, New Hampshire side of the river is a bit of Africa left from the collision of continental plates, which accounts for the different landscapes and geology.

Interstate Highway 91 follows the valley, providing fine views across the winding river to New Hampshire. Near by some of Vermont's most picture-perfect villages lie between the hills – Grafton, Chester and Newfane.

Roads here may wind through the countryside, but are relatively level, with no mountains to climb in the beautiful Valley of the Connecticut River.

BRATTLEBORO✦✦

ℹ Brattleboro Chamber of Commerce On the Common, Putney Rd or 182 Main St; tel: (802) 254-4565.

Brattleboro Farmers Market Rte 9, West. Open May–Oct Sat 0900–1400, Main St Wed 1000–1400, craft fair first Sat Dec, Main St.

This small riverbank city has the relaxed air of people who have migrated back to the land. The New Age is alive and well here, and Main St shops reflect local interest in ethnic clothing, handicrafts, music, books and natural foods. One entire shop is filled with beads, another with fabrics from all over the world. You'll also find five used-book shops, two breweries and one of New England's best sporting goods, camping and sportswear stores at Sam's (tel: (802) 254-2933).

No place is the 'Brattleboro Spirit' better experienced than at the **Brattleboro Farmers Market✦✦**. Small homestead farmers join craftsmen and makers of preserves, fresh-baked breads, maple syrup and organic honey. Many people go just to enjoy lunch at the international food stands and live music on the shaded lawn.

Brattleboro Museum and Art Center $ *Bridge St; tel: (802) 257-0124. Open mid May–Oct Tue–Sun 1200–1800.*

Connecticut River Safari $$$ *Putney Rd; tel: (802) 257-5008. Open May–Oct. Kayak and canoe rentals*

The Arts Council of Windham County *69 Main St; tel: (802) 257-1881. Seasonal schedule of cultural events.*

Art and music are happening everywhere, with a busy schedule of concerts by local musicians and **Gallery Walks**◆ the first Friday evening of each month, when 15 art galleries serve up refreshments and live music.

Estey organs were manufactured in Brattleboro and you can see examples, as well as changing exhibitions of art and antiquities at the **Brattleboro Museum and Art Center**◆. Three group shops, Le Tagge Sale (*tel: (802) 254-9224*) on *Putney Rd* (Rte 5 N), Twice Upon a Time (*tel: (802) 254-2261*) on Main St, and Black Mountain Antique Center (*tel: (802) 254-3848*) on Rte 30, each fill vast floorspace with antiques and collectables.

The **Belle of Brattleboro**◆◆ (*tel: (802) 254-1263*), a canopied excursion boat, takes passengers on sunset, dinner and moonlight cruises from its dock where the West River flows into the Connecticut. Near by, **Connecticut River Safari**◆◆ rents kayaks and canoes. Blue herons, egrets, beavers and even eagles are seen along the low banks of the West River.

Accommodation and food in Brattleboro

40 Putney Rd Bed & Breakfast $$ *Rte 5; tel: (802) 254-6268 or (800) 941-2413.* An antique-filled French château near downtown.

T.J. Buckley's $$ *132 Elliot St; tel: (802) 257-4922.* Tiny, eclectic and impeccable.

CHESTER◆◆◆

Chester Area Chamber of Commerce *On the Green; tel: (802) 875-2939.*

The Green Mountain Flyer $$ *tel: (802) 463-3069. Operates late June–early Sept Tue–Sun; and Sept–mid Oct Sat–Sun. Reservations advised.*

The Rose Arbour Tea Room $ *School St; tel: (802) 875-4767. Open Tue–Sat 1000–1700, Sun 1200–1700. Serves teas and ploughman's lunches; giftshop and attractive B&B rooms.*

Well-kept Victorian buildings in the **Chester Village Historic District**◆◆◆ surround the Green, described in a Walking Tour brochure from the TIC kiosk. Spanning the century from 1820 to 1920, they show how architecture evolved in streets lined with distinguished houses and perhaps Vermont's finest **Federal-style church**◆◆, topped by a five-layer spire reminiscent of Charles Bulfinch (Boston architect).

The brick Academy is now the **Chester Historical Society Museum**◆ and **Chester Art Guild**◆, displaying local art, furniture, textiles and farm implements.

Chester has three separate villages, the second surrounding the imposing Town Hall and the **Victorian Railway Station**◆◆. The **Green Mountain Flyer**◆◆◆, a sightseeing train, travels 26 miles between Chester and Bellows Falls, with fully restored wooden coaches from 1913 and 1891. The train passes two covered bridges, and pauses suspended above the void of Brockaway Gorge.

The third, **Stone Village**◆◆, is built of granite quarried from the hill above. You will not see a finer ensemble of stone buildings than the school, church and nearly 30 houses facing each other across Rte 103.

ℹ️ Chester Historical Society and Chester Art Guild *On the Green; tel: (802) 875-3767. Open June–Oct Tue–Sun 1400–1700.*

During the summer **Victorian Ghosts and Gossamer Weekend**✦✦, locals and visitors dress in turn-of-the-century costumes to take part in lawn croquet, an Edwardian fashion show, and musical events against the backdrop of Victorian architecture.

GRAFTON✦✦✦

ℹ️ Information Center *next to the Old Tavern; tel: (802) 843-2255. Open May–Mar daily 1000–1800.*

🏠 Grafton Village Cheese Company *Townsend Rd; tel: (802) 843-2221 or (800) GRAFTON. Open Mon–Fri 0800–1600, Sat–Sun 1000–1600.*

Grafton Historical Society Museum *Main St; tel: (802) 843-1010. Open June–mid Sept Sat–Sun, mid Sept–mid Oct daily 1330–1600.*

Grafton Museum of Natural History *Main St; tel: (802) 843-2111. Open June–mid Sept Sat–Sun, mid Sept–mid Oct daily 1330–1600.*

Grafton Blacksmith Shop *School St. Open June–Oct Thur–Mon 1000–1500, demonstrations 1100–1200 and 1300–1400.*

🍴 The Old Tavern at Grafton $$ *Main St; tel: (802) 843-2231 or (800) 843-1801. Historic, welcoming and fine dining-room.*

Many Vermonters claim that Grafton is not a town at all, but a carefully created museum. They may be right. The whole town is owned by the Windham Foundation, whose purpose is to keep it exactly as it is. That makes Grafton a pleasant place to visit, with its air of a 19th-century farming village – albeit a tidier and more 'kept up' version than the original. **Grafton Village Cheese Company**✦✦ makes cheddar : you can watch the process and sample the results. **Grafton Historical Society Museum**✦✦ creates new exhibitions yearly, illustrating local life in past centuries. **Grafton Museum of Natural History**✦✦ explains the surrounding natural world with live and interactive exhibits that allow visitors to watch bees make honey or learn why some minerals glow in the dark. At the **Grafton Blacksmith Shop**✦ you can see the tools of this ancient trade and watch a blacksmith work. Walking trails (which metamorphose into cross-country ski trails) lead past an exhibition on sheep-raising and to the never-crowded **Grafton Swimming Pond**✦✦.

Up-market galleries and shops emphasise the handmade and the antique; the Grafton Village Store (*tel: (802) 843-2348*) is a grocery and deli, but with fine wines, quilts and hand-knitted Guernseys.

Plummer's Sugar House (*tel: (802) 843-2207*), outside the 'pale' is a real farm, tapping trees and making maple syrup Feb–Mar; syrup and stencilled sap buckets are sold year-round.

HANOVER✦✦✦

Hood Museum of Art *Wheelock St; tel: (603) 646-2808. Open Tue–Sat 1000–1700, Wed until 2100, Sun 1200–1700.*

Baker Library Special Collections Room *Dartmouth College. Open Mon–Fri 0800–1630.*

The Hanover Inn *$$–$$$ on the Dartmouth Green; tel: (603) 643-4300 or (800) 443-7024. Beautiful rooms, top location and excellent dining.*

Peter Christian's Tavern *$ 39 South Main St; tel: (603) 643-2345. Open daily; sandwiches, generous entrées.*

Dartmouth Winter Carnival *Dartmouth College; tel: (603) 795-2143. Mid Feb. Featuring snow sculptures, sports events.*

From its beginnings as a school to educate Native Americans, Dartmouth College has been at the centre of life in Hanover, providing the town's intellectual and cultural focus. The college's **Hood Museum of Art**✦✦✦ has extensive collections ranging from 9th-century BC Assyrian reliefs to the entire suite of Picasso's Vollard etchings.

Less known are the treasures in **Baker Memorial Library**✦✦, with fresco murals by the Mexican artist Jose Clemente Orozco (described in a free brochure). The Hickmott Shakespeare Collection, a folio first edition of Audubon's *Birds of America*, 150 works printed before 1501, and 200 volumes illustrating the art of fine book binding are on display.

The library faces a wide green, decorated in midwinter by the giant snow sculpture of **Dartmouth Winter Carnival**✦✦. Opposite is the **Hopkins Center for the Performing Arts**✦✦✦ (*tel: (603) 646-2422*), with a diverse year-round concert, ballet, opera, jazz and theatre schedule.

PUTNEY✦✦

Yellow Barn Music Festival *tel: (802) 387-6637. Tue, Fri and Sat evenings, late June–early Aug. Chamber music showcasing both known and rising artists.*

Above right
Dartmouth Winter Carnival

Putney transports you back into its world of the 1960s, when it was a haven for back-to-the-land homesteaders. The communes have gone, but Putney is still an enclave of artists' and craftsmen's studios. In the village centre are Putney Bound, with beautiful papers and hand-bound books, and Putney Clayschool, a riot of whimsical sculptures and practical pottery dinnerware. Green Mountain Spinnery on Depot Rd (*tel: (802) 387-4528*), the smallest in the United States, produces knitting wool and patterns, and sells clothing knitted by local craftsmen. The Putney Woodshed offers hand-crafted boxes, kaleidoscopes, toys, miniatures and more.

Putney Bound
*Putney Tavern; tel:
(802) 387-4204. Open
Wed–Sat 1000–1700, Sun
1100–1700.*

Putney Clayschool
*Kimball Hill; tel: (802) 387-
4395. Open Wed–Mon
1000–1700.*

Basketville *Main St; tel:
(802) 387-5509. Open daily
1000–1730.*

Putney General Store *(tel: (802) 387-5842)* is not all tarted up for tourists; it's the real thing, providing essentials to the town since 1843. Sandwiches and daily hot specials ($) are served from a marble lunch counter. Or watch the town go by from the front porch of Putney Hearth Bakery and Coffee House, across the street. The rambling world of Basketville has more baskets than you've ever dreamed possible, from picnic hampers to beds for Rover.

Accommodation and food in Putney

The Putney Inn $–$$ *Depot Rd (at Exit 4 of I-91); tel: (802) 387-5517.* Well-maintained old inn with adjacent motel rooms and well-known dining-room.

Putney Hearth Bakery and Coffee House $ *Putney Tavern; tel: (802) 387-2100. Open Mon–Sat 0700–1700, Sun 0800–1500.*

Casa del Sol $ *Rte 5; tel: (802) 387-5318. Open Apr–Jan.* Authentic Mexican food.

WINDSOR AND CORNISH

**American Precision
Museum $** *196 Main
St; tel: (802) 674-5781.
Open late May–Oct daily
1000–1700.*

**Old Constitution
House** *North Main St; tel:
(802) 672-3773. Open
June–mid Oct, daily
1000–1700.*

**Vermont State Craft
Center** *Windsor House,
Main St; (802) 674-6729.
Open daily.*

**Catamount Brewing
Co $** *Rte 5; tel: (800) 540-
2248. Open Mon–Fri
0900–1700, Sat
1100–1600.*

**Saint-Gaudens National
Historic Site $** *Rte 12A,
Cornish, NH; tel: (603) 675-
2175. Open June–Oct daily
0900–1630.*

These twin towns are joined by the **longest covered bridge**❖❖ in the United States, built in 1886. **Windsor Village Historic District**❖ is lined by brick buildings from the 1800s, when the town led in founding the precision tool industry. The first interchangeable machine parts were designed and built here, as were the famed Enfield Rifles that won the Crimean War. This chapter in the Industrial Revolution is told at the **American Precision Museum**❖❖.

Old Constitution House❖❖, the tavern where Vermont was born, is an historical museum and the 1840 Windsor House contains the **Vermont State Craft Center**❖❖, featuring Vermont-made work; ask for the self-guided Architectural Tour brochure.

See (and taste) how beer is made at **Catamount Brewing Co**❖, and in the same complex watch molten glass become useful and ornamental tableware at **Simon Pearce Glass**❖❖.

A century ago, Cornish was a summer colony of artists and writers, including the noted sculptor, Augustus Saint-Gaudens. His home is preserved as **Saint-Gaudens National Historic Site**❖❖❖, and many of his works are shown in the studio and throughout the lovely gardens.

The Connecticut River flows wide and calm between Windsor and Cornish, and the best way to enjoy it is by canoe. **North Star Canoe Livery**❖❖ (**$$$**; *tel: (603) 542-5802*), south of the bridge, rents them and provides a shuttle service, as well as raft trips and guided river explorations.

WOODSTOCK✦✦✦

❶ Woodstock Chamber of Commerce *18 Central St;* tel: *(802) 457-3555.*

❸ Dana House Museum **$** *26 Elm St;* tel: *(802) 457-1822. Open mid May–late Oct Mon–Sat 1000–1700, Sun 1400–1700, occasionally in winter.*

Billings Farm and Museum **$** *River Rd; tel: (802) 457-2355. Open May–Oct daily 0900–1700; Nov–Dec weekends.*

Warning: Woodstock police impose fines on motorists who even slightly exceed the low speed limit.

The money that has always infused Woodstock is apparent from the well-kept homes and gardens and the stylish shops that line its streets. Around its **Village Green**✦✦ are several historic buildings, and a covered bridge crosses a river only a block away.

Woodstock is the only town in America with five bells made by the patriot Paul Revere. The oldest is on the porch of the Congregational Church; another is at the Woodstock Inn and others in churches and the Masonic Temple.

Dana House Museum✦✦, a Federal-style 1807 merchant's home, recalls local history with collections of furniture, art, toys, costumes, textiles, kitchenware and farm equipment.

Still an active farm, **Billings Farm and Museum**✦✦✦ mingles working barns and shops with exhibit areas and the home of the farm's manager. In the creamery downstairs is all the equipment used to make butter and cheese; special events highlight farm seasons.

In December the town is aglow with holiday decorations, and a **Wassail Parade**✦✦ (*tel: (802) 457-1509*) the second weekend in December features horse-drawn carriages and wagons. This is horse country, and you can join an escorted trail ride, or a surrey, wagon or sleigh ride at **Kedron Valley Stables**✦ in South Woodstock (**$$$**; *tel: (802) 457-1480*).

Josiah Bellows House Bed and Breakfast $ *North Main St, Walpole; tel: (603) 756-4250 or (800) 358-6302.* Antique-furnished rooms and fresh-baked breakfasts and afternoon tea.

Burdick's Chocolates $ *Main St, Walpole; tel: (603) 756-3701. Open Mon–Fri 0900–1800, Sat–Sun 0900–1700.*

The Fort at No 4 $$ *Rte 11, Charlestown; tel: (603) 826-5700. Open June–mid Oct Wed–Mon 1000–1600.*

Juniper Hill Inn $–$$ *Juniper Hill Rd, Windsor VT; tel: (802) 674-5273 or (800) 359-2541.* A gracious 1901 mansion overlooking the valley. Dinner $$ by reservation in the candle-lit dining room.

Windsor Station Restaurant $$ *tel: (802) 674-2052. Open Tue–Sun 1730–2100.*

Accommodation and food in Woodstock

Canterbury House $–$$ *43 Pleasant St; tel: (802) 457-3077 or (800) 390-3077.* Sumptuous breakfasts and downtown location.

Lincoln Inn $ *Rte 4, West Woodstock; tel: (802) 457-3312.* Homey rooms and world-class dining $–$$ next to a covered bridge.

Suggested tour

Total distance: 172 miles; 231 miles with detours

Time: 4.5 hours' driving. Allow 2 days for the main route, with or without detours. Those with limited time should concentrate on Hanover, Woodstock and Chester.

Links: From Brattleboro, I-91 leads south to Northfield, Massachusetts and the Pioneer Valley Route; Rte 9 goes west to Bennington and the Southern Green Mountain Route.

Route: Leave **BRATTLEBORO ❶** on Rte 5 North through a gauntlet of shopping plazas to Rte 9, on which you will cross the river into New Hampshire. Stop at **Chesterfield Gorge⁺⁺⁺ ❷** to walk the wooded half-mile path into the chasm carved into solid rock, or picnic under the pines. Retrace Rte 9 to Rte 63 and follow it north through historic Park Hill, a settlement of exceptionally fine homes dating from the 1700s and one of New Hampshire's earliest (and best) meeting houses, built in 1762. The road winds through rich valley farms before reaching Rte 12.

Turn left (north) and continue to **Walpole ❸**, making the short sidetrack into the hillside village to see its classic green surrounded by 18th- and 19th-century houses. Stop for a pick-me-up at **Burdick's Chocolates ❹**, where, along with the fine chocolates made here, they serve hot chocolate, tea or espresso with sinfully good pastries.

Cross the river into Vermont, heading north a short way to I-91. Follow it north, enjoying sweeping river views, to Springfield, and cross back into New Hampshire on Rte 11. On the river bank is **The Fort at No 4⁺⁺⁺ ❺**, New England's only living history museum of the French and Indian Wars period. Costumed interpreters tend daily chores of 1740, when Queen Anne reigned and this was the northernmost frontier of her New England colonies.

Return to I-91, exit at Ascutney (Exit 8) and continue north on Rte 5 to **WINDSOR ❻**. Cross the covered bridge to **CORNISH ❼** and follow Rte 12A north to Lebanon.

Detour: From Lebanon, take Rte 4A along Mascoma Lake, where you can't miss the six-storey granite **Great Stone Dwelling⁺⁺⁺ ❽** dating

Above left
Woodstock's covered bridge

MV *Mount Sunapee II* $$ Sunapee Harbor
(off Rte 11); tel: (603) 763-4030. Cruising mid May–mid June Sat–Sun 1430; mid June–Aug daily 1000 and 1430; Sept–mid Oct Sat–Sun 1430.

Enfield Shaker Museum $ Rte 4A, Enfield; tel: (603) 632-4346. Open July–Aug Mon–Fri 1000–1600, Sat 1000–1600; June–mid Oct also Sun 1300–1600.

The Shaker Inn $–$$ Rte 4A, Enfield NH; tel: (603) 632-7810. Rates include breakfast.

Calvin Coolidge Historic Site $ Tel: (802) 228-5050. Open late May–mid Oct daily.

Quechee Recreation Area Rte 4; tel: (802) 295-2990. Tent pitches, picnic grounds and walking trails.

Echo Lake Inn $–$$ Rte 100, Tyson; tel: (802) 228-8602 or (800) 356-6844. Attractive rooms and excellent dining.

from 1841, the largest structure ever built by the Shakers. This religious sect built an entire village here, and their creamery is now **Enfield Shaker Museum** ✱✱ **❾**, with authentically restored gardens. Frequent events interpret the Shaker way of life and the shop sells baskets and Shaker crafts. The Stone Dwelling has been meticulously restored as The Shaker Inn, with authentic Shaker furnishings and original built-in cabinetry.

Continue on Rte 4A, turning right on Rte 11 and right again on to Rte 114 through the college town of New London. **New London Barn Playhouse** ✱✱✱ **❿** (*tel: (603) 526-4631 or (800) 633-2276*) has been operating since 1934, presenting summer performances of lively Broadway musicals in the renovated barn.

Rte 114 rejoins Rte 11 to skirt Lake Sunapee, leading to the town of Sunapee Harbor, where the excursion boat **MV *Mount Sunapee II*** ✱✱✱ **⓫** is docked. During the 1.5-hour trip the Captain's narration is laced with local lore. Rte 103B leads to **Mount Sunapee State Beach** ✱✱ **⓬**. Follow Rte 103 north to Newport, then Rte 10, which joins with I-89 to return to Lebanon.

From Lebanon, take Rte 10 to **HANOVER ⓭**, crossing the river into Norwich, Vermont. Follow Rte 5 south to White River Junction and Rte 14 west to Rte 4, which crosses the 162-ft-deep **Quechee Gorge** ✱✱✱ **⓮**. In Quechee, shops overlook a covered bridge, and the modern Quechee Gorge Village (*tel: (802) 295-1550*) has an Antique Center with over 450 dealers, and an Arts & Crafts Center representing 220 artisans.

Continue on to **WOODSTOCK ⓯**, then follow Rte 106 to North Springfield, and Rte 10 to Rte 103, which leads south into **CHESTER ⓰**. Rte 35 takes you to **GRAFTON ⓱** and on to Townsend, with its attractive village green and meeting house.

Rte 30 heads south to **Newfane** ✱✱ **⓲**, one of New England's 'postcard' towns, with fine buildings and the Sunday Newfane Flea Market. South of Newfane, cross the covered bridge over the West River, on an unnumbered road through Dummerston Center to Rte 5. Two miles north on Rte 5 is **PUTNEY ⓳**. I-91 brings you back into **Brattleboro ❶**.

Also worth exploring

West of Woodstock, Rte 4 follows the Ottaquechee River through Bridgewater to Rte 100A, which leads through Plymouth Notch and **President Calvin Coolidge Historic Site** ✱✱✱. His family farm, where he took the oath of office, is a museum complex showing Vermont rural life. Rte 4A joins Rte 100, which leads to Ludlow, where Rte 103 leads back to the main route in Chester.

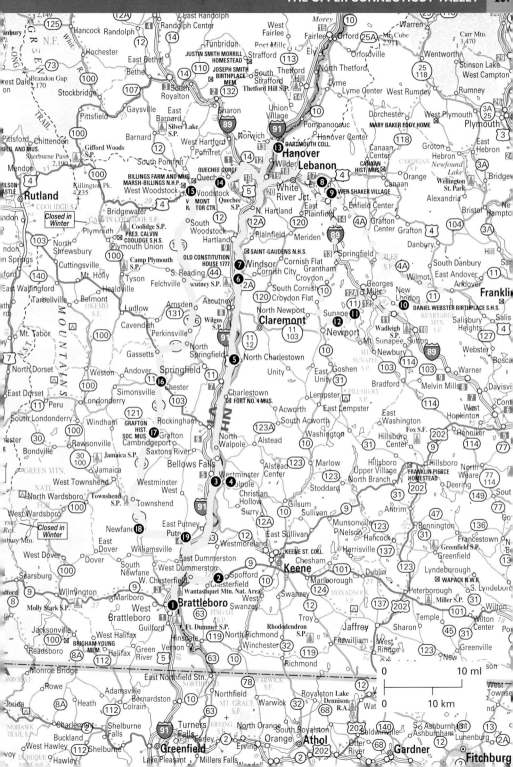

The New Hampshire Lakes

Ratings

Beaches and watersports	●●●●○
Children	●●●●○
Shopping	●●●●○
Nature/ scenery	●●●○○
Food and drink	●●○○○
Museums	●●○○○
Arts and culture	●○○○○
History	●○○○○

The blue of Lake Winnipesaukee splashes unevenly across the centre of New Hampshire's map, making it the state's most popular region for sailing and water sports. The shores are dotted with resorts and camps, along with the diversions that such a concentration of holiday-makers inevitably brings. Recreation complexes, shops, craft and antique centres and big resorts congregate on Winnipesaukee's western shore, creating weekend traffic snarls. The eastern shore and nearby Squam Lake are quieter.

Surrounding the lakes are the mountains, one of them providing the state's best-known view: Mount Chocorua reflected in the lake at its feet.

Chocorua❖❖

ⓘ Greater Ossipee Chamber of Commerce *Rtes 16 and 25W, West Ossipee; tel: (603) 539-6201 or (800) 516-5324.*

ⓘ White Lake State Park $ *Rte 16, Tamworth; tel: (603) 323-7350. Open late May–mid Oct.*

Mount Chocorua (pronounced 'chok-OR-oo-ah') is New Hampshire's signature mountain, shown on calendars and postcards in one of two poses: framed in white birch trees from a hilltop or rising from the deep blue foreground of Chocorua Lake. You can see both from Rte 16: the hilltop is just north of Chocorua Village, which lies clustered around its old stone dam. Below the hill is the lake, with benches along its scenic shore.

White Lake State Park❖❖ is an idyllic campground and picnic grove under tall pine trees, beside a clear lake with a sandy beach and another fine view of Mount Chocorua.

Practise casting with catch-and-release at **Sumner Brook Fish Farm❖** or keep your trout, paying by the inch. Children enjoy watching baby fish in growing pools.

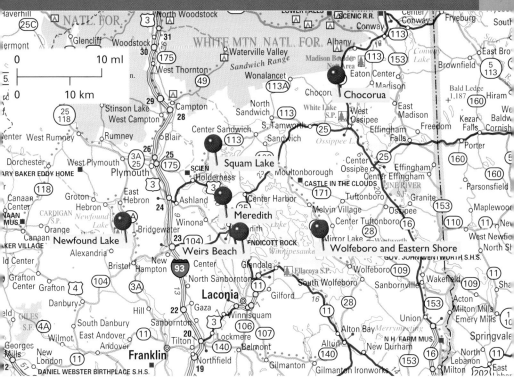

Sumner Brook Fish Farm $ *Rte 16, Ossipee; tel: (603) 539-7232. Open May and Sept Sat–Sun; June–Aug daily.*

Accommodation and food in Chocorua

Tamworth Gardens Dining Room $$ *Main St, Tamworth Village; tel: (603) 323-7721. Open Tue–Sat for dinner, nightly mid Sept–mid Oct.*

The Tamworth Inn $$ *Main St, Tamworth Village; tel: (603) 323-7721 or (800) 642-7352.* An 1833 inn, opposite Barnstormers Summer Theater.

The Yankee Smokehouse $ *Rtes 16 and 25, West Ossipee; tel: (603) 539-7427. Open May–mid Nov, mid Dec–Mar daily.* Succulent pork, chicken and beef are barbecued over wood fires.

MEREDITH❖❖

Information Center *tel: (603) 279-6121. Open May–Oct daily.*

The lively town borders a dock-lined lakefront with hotels, shops and eateries. At its centre, Mills Falls Marketplace (*tel: (603) 279-7006*) is a multi-storey complex of 18 shops, selling everything from local books to ice-cream and fashionwear.

Annalee Doll Museum❖❖ shows 35 years-worth of these flexible felt dolls prized by collectors. Posed and outfitted for favourite sports, including fishing and golf, or dressed for the holidays, each doll has a

🏛 **Annalee Doll Museum** *44 Reservoir Rd; tel: (603) 279-6542. Open June–Oct daily 0900–1700.*

◒ **Burlwood Antique Center** *Rte 3; tel: (603) 279-6387. Open May–Oct daily 1000–1700.*

happy expression on its hand-painted face. **Burlwood Antique Center** has 170 dealers selling antiques and collectables.

Winnipesaukee Scenic Railroad✢✢ **$$** *(tel: (603) 745-2135, May–Oct)* runs passenger cars along the shore between the stations in Meredith and Weirs Beach for one- and two-hour scenic rides. An ice-cream parlour car is popular or you can reserve a box lunch or turkey dinner.

Accommodation and food in Meredith

The Inn at Bay Point $–$$$ *Meredith; tel: (603) 279-7006 or (800) 622-6455.* Modern rooms all have views of Lake Winnipesaukee, as does its excellent **Boathouse Grille $$–$$$**, open daily lunch and dinner.

NEWFOUND LAKE✢✢

🏛 **Wellington State Park $** *Rte 3A, Bristol; tel: (603) 744-2197.*

Polar Caves $$ *Rte 25, Plymouth; tel: (603) 536-1888 or (800)273-1886. Open mid May–mid Oct daily 0900–1700.*

Groton's sculpted rocks

A lovely lake close to I-93, but largely untrammelled, Newfound's shores are lined by trees and bird-filled marshlands instead of cottages. At its northern end are protected lands of **Paradise Point Nature Center**✢✢ *(tel: (603) 744-3516)*, where you can walk the trails helped by a descriptive pamphlet from the small museum, in which interactive exhibitions examine loons and other local wildlife.

Sculptured Rocks✢✢, farther along North Shore Rd in Groton, show the force of running water when it's given enough time. The tumbling river has worn giant pot-holes in solid granite, some 10ft in diameter. Picnic tables overlook the gorge.

At **Wellington State Park**✢✢, on the lake's southern rim, a half-mile beach of fine white sand is ringed by tall pine trees. Never crowded, it is a good choice for swimming.

Polar Caves✢✢ are not the true caves that form in limestone, but glacially-constructed chambers and passages, through which children love to squirm. Deep in these cool rocky recesses you may find ice in the summer. Visit the Maple Sugar Museum and Mineral Display.

Accommodation and food in Newfound Lake

Crabapple Inn B&B $–$$ *Rte 25, Plymouth; tel: (603) 536-4476.* Federal-style home with four-poster beds, handmade quilts.

The Italian Farmhouse $–$$ *Rte 3 South, Plymouth; tel: (536) 4536. Open Mon–Sat 1700–2100, Sun 1100–1400 and 1700–2030.* Country Italian menu and rustic setting.

SQUAM LAKE✦✦

ℹ Squam Lake Association *Rte 3, Holderness; tel: (603) 968-7336.*

📞 Golden Pond Boat Tours $ *Rte 3, Holderness; tel: (603) 279-4405. Departures June–Sept daily 1030, 1330.*

Riverside Cycles *Rte 3, Ashland; tel: (603) 968-9676. Bicycle rentals.*

🏛 Science Center of New Hampshire *$–$$ Rtes 3 and 113, Holderness; tel: (603) 968-7194. Open May–Oct daily 0930–1630.*

Nature Cruises $$ *July–Oct varying times from 0600–1900.*

A beautiful lake with little visible development to disturb its nesting loons or mar its quiet wooded shores, Squam is where *On Golden Pond*, starring Katherine Hepburn, was filmed. **Golden Pond Boat Tours**✦✦ operate two-hour guided cruises, and a map of bike and hiking trails is free from local shops.

At the **Science Center of New Hampshire**✦✦, a wildlife sanctuary for rescued animals, meet black bear, bobcat, river otter and a bald eagle as you walk the exhibit trail, or examine frogs up close from a boardwalk. A mile-long loop trail climbs Mount Fayal for views of Squam Lake. **Nature Cruises**✦✦ explore the habitat of resident loons with a trained naturalist.

Red Hill Inn✦✦✦ is a small resort in the summer estate of the inventor of the soda fountain. Its casual elegance is ideal for quiet escapes, and walking trails become a cross-country ski centre in winter. The excellent dining-room is open to the public.

Accommodation and food in Squam Lake

Little Holland Court $–$$, *Rte 3, Ashland; tel: (603) 968-4434.* Self-catering cottages set on Little Squam Lake, in addition offering boat rentals.

Red Hill Inn $$ *Rte 25B, Center Harbor; tel: (603) 279-7001 or (800) 573-3445; info@redhillinn.com.* Full country breakfast included, open for dinner daily.

The Inn On Golden Pond $$ *Rte 3, Holderness; tel: (603) 968-7269.* Beautiful B&B accommodation in an 1879 lakeside farmhouse.

The Mary Chase B&B $ *Rte 3, Holderness; tel: (603) 968-9454.* Charming rooms, great breakfasts, overlooking Squam Lake from a hilltop.

The Pressed Petals Inn $$ *Shepard Hill Rd, Holderness; tel: (603) 968-4417.* Elegant country Victorian-style inn with breakfast and afternoon tea.

WEIRS BEACH✧✧

MV Sophie C $
Lakeside Ave, Weirs Beach; tel: (603) 366-5531. Operates May–early June and Sept–mid Oct Sat–Sun; mid June–Aug daily.

MS Mount Washington Cruises $$ *tel: (603) 366-BOAT. Departs Weirs Beach May–Oct daily 1000 and 1230, July–Aug 1500.*

MV *Sophie C*✧✧✧ explores Winnipesaukee, sailing among its 365 islands and into secluded coves, all in a day's work for a genuine working mailboat. Day or sunset cruises are 2–3 hours. To tour via a larger boat, choose the venerable **MS Mount Washington**✧✧✧, departing Weirs Beach for Wolfeboro, Center Harbor and Alton Bay. Evening cruises include dinner and dancing to live music.

If you like getting wet, **Weirs Beach Water Slide and Surf Coaster** have several water-soaked activities, including a wave tank, water slides, rafting and a spray ground for small fry. **FunSpot** brings miniature golf, bowling, kiddy rides and a game arcade together.

WOLFEBORO AND EASTERN SHORE✧✧

Wolfeboro Chamber of Commerce *32 Central Ave; tel: (603) 569-2200 or (800) 516-5324.*

Wright Museum $ *77 Center St; tel: (603) 569-1212. Open Nov and Feb–Apr Sat–Sun; May–mid Oct daily 1000–1600.*

Libby Museum $ *Main St (Rte 109), Wolfeboro (no tel). Open June–Sept Tue–Sun 1000–1600.*

Wentworth State Park $ *Rte 109; tel: (603) 569-3699. Open May–June Sat–Sun; July–Aug daily.*

Still in progress, showing life on the homefront and in the field during World War II, the **Wright Museum**✧✧ has themed exhibits and an entire building of military hardware, including tanks and half-tracks. Stop to watch the video on women Air Corps pilots. The **Libby Museum**✧✧ focuses on the area's natural history with exhibitions on native birds and animals and a collection of local Indian artefacts.

Board the 65-ft **MV *Judge Sewall*✧✧✧** *(tel: (603) 569-3016)* at the Town Dock, for a narrated cruise (**$–$$**). You will pass a loon refuge, old boatyards and several of Winnipesaukee's many islands. **Wentworth State Park**✧✧ has a small, beach on Lake Wentworth, separated from Lake Winnipesaukee by a narrow strip of land at Wolfeboro.

Drive uphill to **Castle in the Clouds**✧ **$** *(tel: (603) 476-2352)*, the stone mansion of a former summer estate, for house tours, lake views, a tram ride to the source of a spring, and giftshop.

Accommodation and food in Wolfeboro and Eastern Shore

Bittersweet $$ *Rte 28, Wolfeboro; tel: (603) 569-3636. Open May–Dec Mon–Sat for dinner, Sat–Sun 1100–1400.* European and American dishes, always well prepared.

PJ's Dockside $ *Main St, Wolfeboro; tel: (603) 569-6747.* Sandwiches, salads, lobster rolls and seafood dinners on the dock.

Pop's Doughnuts $ *45 Center St, Wolfeboro; tel: (603) 569-9513. Open daily 24 hours.* Fresh doughnuts and coffee served 'to go' or at a tiny counter.

The Woodshed $$ *Lee's Mill Rd (off Rte 109), Moultonborough; tel: (603) 476-2311. Open Tue–Sun* for dinner, prime rib and more, served in an old farmhouse and rustic barn.

Castle in the Clouds

Tuc-Me-Inn B&B $ *118 North Main St, Wolfeboro; tel: (603) 569-5702.* Comfortable and unpretentious, and downtown.

The Shakers

Originally known as 'Shaking Quakers', Shakers came to the United States in 1774 from Manchester, England, led by the illiterate textile worker Anne Lee. Mother Anne's tiny group flourished despite early persecution, and by the 1840s had more than 6000 members living in farm-centred communities in New England, New York and the midwest. They led a celibate communal life stressing simplicity, work ethic and fine craftsmanship. Among the first to package and sell garden seeds, they also led in packaging medicinal and culinary herbs. Their practical inventions include home improvements such as the flat broom and the clothespeg. Shaker craftsmen were known for the strength and beauty of their furniture, and their styles have profoundly influenced American design ever since.

Suggested tour

Total distance: 120 miles; 183 miles with detours

Time: 3 hours' driving. Allow 2 days for the main route, 3 days with detours or boat rides. Those with limited time should concentrate on Squam Lake, Wolfeboro and a boat tour.

Winnipesaukee Kayak Company 17 Bay St, Wolfeboro; tel: (603) 569-9926. Kayak rentals and instruction.

Pepi Herrmann Crystal off Lily Pond Rd near the airport, Gilford; tel: (603) 528-1020 or (800) HANDCUT. Open year-round, tours Tue–Sat 1000 and 1400.

Elisha Marston House Maple St, Center Sandwich; tel: (603) 284-6269. Open June–Sept Tue–Sat 1100–1700.

Lin-Joy Cabins $ Robert's Cove Rd, Alton; tel (603) 569-4973. Rustic self-catering cabins with a swimming pool.

Lakehurst Housekeeping Cottages $ Rte 11-D, Alton Bay; tel: (603) 875-2492. May–June nightly, July–Sept weekly only. Well-kept lakefront cottages.

Victorian House $$ Rte 11, Gilford; tel: (603) 293-8155. Open daily 1700–2100. A restored 1821 stagecoach inn with an outstanding, innovative menu.

Sandwich Home Industries Main St (Rte 109), Center Sandwich; tel: (603) 284-6831. Open mid May–mid Oct Mon–Sat 1000–1700, Sun 1200–1700.

Country Braid House Clark Rd, Tilton; tel: (603) 286-4511. Open Mon–Sat 0900–1600.

Links: I-93 connects this route to the White Mountains and to Lowell, Massachusetts (West of Boston Route).

Route: From Exit 23 of I-93, follow Rte 104 east to **MEREDITH ❶**. Go south on Rte 3 to **WEIRS BEACH ❷** and follow the lake shore on Rte 11B to Gilford. Here **Pepi Herrmann Crystal❖ ❸** creates hand-cut glassware, which you can watch being made during a studio tour.

Continue along the shore on Rte 11 to Alton Bay.

Follow signs to Rte 28A, hugging the opposite shore and leading to Rte 28, which climbs rolling hills and drops into **WOLFEBORO ❹**.

Rte 109 follows the shore to Moultonborough, from which you follow Rte 25 to West Ossipee. Turn north on Rte 16, past White Lake to **CHOCORUA ❺**.

After seeing **Mount Chocorua ❻**, just north on Rte 16, return to the village and take Rte 113 through Tamworth to Rte 25. Go west on 25, through Moultonborough, to Center Harbor, where Rte 25B climbs over the hill to Rte 3. Follow Rte 3 north along the quiet shore of **SQUAM LAKE ❼** to Holderness.

Detour: In Tamworth, instead of Rte 113, follow winding Rte 113A past the tall pines and trails of Hemenway State Forest to the remote village of Wonalancet, and on to **Center Sandwich❖❖❽**. One of the state's prettiest villages, it is home to several craftsmen whose studios you can visit.

Sandwich Home Industries❖❖ ❾ displays and sells a wide selection of fine New Hampshire handcrafts, from hand-woven clothing and wooden ware to stuffed toys and pottery. Sandwich Historical Society's **Elisha Marston House❖❖ ❿** preserves the life and times of a village shoemaker in the 1850s. Rte 113 continues along the scenic northern shore of **Squam Lake ❼**, rejoining the main route in Holderness.

Rte 3 leads to Ashland, crossing I-93 and heading north into Plymouth. Follow Rte 25 to Rumney Depot, then an unnumbered road south (left) signposted to Groton, where signs lead to **Sculptured Rocks ⓫**. Continue to Hebron, on **NEWFOUND LAKE ⓬**, and along its western shore, bearing left along the lake to Rte 3A in Bristol. Rte 104 leads returns to New Hampton.

Detour: Instead of returning to New Hampton, stay on Rte 3A to Franklin, following Rte 3 into Tilton. Shop for hand-braided rugs or learn how they are made in a studio tour of **Country Braid House❖❖ ⓭**. Complete kits teach this traditional craft.

Lakes Region Factory Stores is a huge outlet complex featuring overstocks and seconds of big labels like Reebok, Levi, Izod and more than 50 others, at low, tax-free prices (New Hampshire has no sales tax).

Lakes Region Factory Stores *off I-93 at exit 20, Tilton; tel: (603) 286-7880 or (888)-SHOP333. Open Mon–Sat 1000–2100, Sun 1000–1800.*

Canterbury Shaker Village $$ *Exit 18 off I-95, Canterbury; tel: (603) 783-9511. Open May–Oct daily 1000–1700; Apr, Nov–Dec Fri–Sun 1000–1700.*

The Creamery Restaurant $ *Canterbury Shaker Village; tel: (603) 783-9511. Open daily for lunch May–Oct, Fri–Sun Apr, Nov–Dec; Fri–Sat 1845 candlelight dinner $$$ by reservation only.*

Rte 132 'shun-pikes' I-93 to Canterbury Center (at Exit 18), where you follow brown signs east (left) to **Canterbury Shaker Village**✦✦✦ ⓮ , a perfectly preserved set of 24 housing, farm and workshop buildings, now a museum perpetuating the art and ideals of the community. Tours not only show the buildings, but explain Shaker philosophy and daily life. The restaurant re-creates authentic Shaker meals and the Summer Kitchen sells snacks.

Follow the road past the Shaker Village to Belmont, where a left turn on to Rte 140 brings you to I-93 at exit 20, two exits south of your starting-point in New Hampton.

Also worth exploring

From Chocorua, Rte 113 leads east to Madison, where you can see the gigantic **Madison Boulder**✦✦, perhaps the world's largest glacial erratic. Tiny **Crystal Lake**✦✦ reflects picture-perfect **Eaton**, and Rte 153 leads along (and over) the Maine border, passing more lakes on its way to the beautiful **Wakefield Historic District**✦✦. Rte 109 leads back to Wolfeboro.

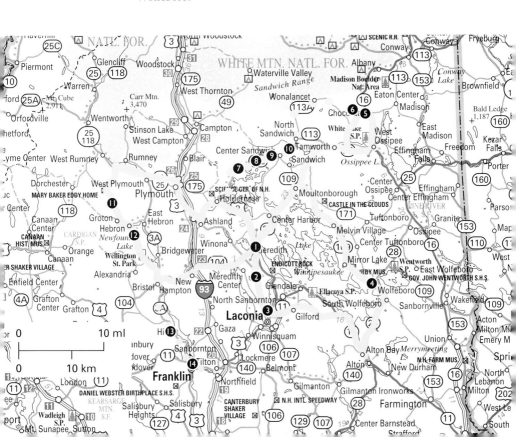

The White Mountains

Ratings

Nature/scenery	●●●●●
Children	●●●●○
Shopping	●●●●
Food and drink	●●●○○
History	●●●○○
Museums	●●●○○
Arts and culture	●●○○○
Beaches/watersports	●○○○○

The White Mountains crown New England with its highest elevations. Almost since their first exploration, they have been a playground for hikers, climbers, skiers, fishermen and those who simply appreciate looking at the views and breathing the fresh, cool mountain air.

Views are everywhere, and some of the best spread before you as you drive: row upon row of mountains, tiny villages clustered around a white church and a covered bridge, crystal rivers rushing over rocky beds, even waterfalls dropping beside the road.

Expect some steep winding roads, and heavy traffic on summer weekends, especially around the shopping mecca of North Conway. Travelling in the evening or night, be wary of moose, which have no fear of cars. In a head-on confrontation, the moose will win, so drive more slowly then and scan the roadsides.

BRETTON WOODS

Mount Washington Cog Railway $$$ *Off Rte 302, Bretton Woods; tel: (603) 846-5406 or (800) 922-8825. Operates Sat–Sun in May, daily June–late Oct. Reservations suggested.*

The **Mount Washington Hotel**◆◆◆ is far more than a place to stay; more even than a resort. It is a last reminder of an opulent era, gleaming in meticulous restoration. Its owners are keen to share it, offering free daily tours, and showing the conference table where the Bretton Woods Monetary Agreement to set a world monetary standard after World War II was signed. Frequent tours also visit the historic print shop and the Stickney Chapel, with Tiffany-signed windows.

The **Mount Washington Cog Railway**◆◆◆, first of its kind in the world, has puffed and steamed its way up the steep mountainside to the summit since the 1860s. The three-hour return trip allows time to explore New England's highest peak. On a clear day the views from the summit of **Mt Washington**◆◆◆ seem endless. You can depend on wind; in April of 1934, the highest wind gust ever recorded blew past

White Mountain National Forest charges $$ per vehicle for a one-week pass, currently available only in Lincoln, Conway or Pinkham Notch (*tel: (603) 528-8721*)

the Mt Washington Observatory at 231 miles per hour. You can learn about the observatory and about the alpine habitat in a small museum at the top.

To ascend under your own steam, wait for good weather, begin early, and take layers of warm clothing. Perhaps the most scenic, the **Ammonoosuc Ravine Trail**✦ begins at the Cog Railway's base station, passing a waterfall and breaking through the tree line to skirt Lake of the Clouds before the final climb to the summit. Expect at the top to diminish the rewards offered by lesser, lonelier peaks.

A shorter, far easier climb with a view all its own, **Mt Willard**✦✦ sits at the head of **Crawford Notch**✦✦✦. Its well-surfaced trail was a bridle-path for guests at the Mount Washington and other grand hotels lining the valley. The summit overlooks the grand sweep of the notch, with its steep walls.

Below
The Mount Washington Hotel, Bretton Woods

Accommodation and food in Bretton Woods

The Mount Washington Hotel $$–$$$ *Rte 302; tel: (603) 278-1000 or (800) 258-0330.* Dinners are included in the rates.

Top o' Quad Restaurant $–$$ *Bretton Woods Ski Area; tel: (603) 278-5000 or (800) 232-2972.* Ride the chairlift or their van to dine overlooking the valley.

DIXVILLE NOTCH

The Balsams Grand Resort Hotel $$–$$$ *tel: (800) 255-0800 in NH, (800) 255-0600 elsewhere.* The only 'American Plan' hotel remaining, with all meals (and what meals they are!) and activities included in the room rate. The outstanding dining room $$ is open to the public by reservation.

Dixville Notch is wild, a narrow cut though often jagged rocks, through which climbs a winding road. Around it is wilderness; wild animals, including moose, are common sights. So common, in fact, that at the eastern end of the notch a special platform has been built along Rte 26, overlooking a boggy area where moose munch in the evening.

Few resorts anywhere have so spectacular a setting as The Balsams, under the crest of Dixville Notch. This classic turn-of-the-century grand hotel nestles under steep walls, mountain views from every window, with its own lake, golf course and ski area. Visitors are welcome to stroll the gardens and stop at the Spring House; guests have a full plate of activities taking advantage of the natural setting, with nature walks, fishing trips, and climbs to the overlook at **Table Rock****, where the hotel looks like a toy far below.

FRANCONIA NOTCH

The Flume $$ *tel: (603) 745-8391. Open mid May–late Oct daily 0900–1700.*

Old Man of the Mountain Museum *tel: (603) 823-5563. Open June–mid Oct daily 1000–1730.*

Aerial Tramway $$ *tel: (603) 823-5563. Open mid May–Oct daily.*

Interstate Highway 93 briefly becomes the Franconia Notch Parkway, narrower, but still a dual carriageway. The first exit leads to **The Flume****, a natural chasm with vertical walls. A boardwalk runs through it close to river level.

The Basin** is a 20-ft natural pot-hole at the base of a small waterfall, where melting glaciers wore away the granite with their swirling force. A short walk beyond are the sloping ledges of **Kinsman Falls****, a lovely series of cascades.

High above Profile Lake is New Hampshire's symbol, the 40-ft group of granite ledges forming the **Old Man of the Mountain*****. A layby alongside the northbound lane offers clear views, or you can park at the base of the Aerial Tramway and walk down to the lake, stopping at the **Old Man of the Mountain Museum****. It explains the geology of the profile and its preservation, and shows collections of souvenirs picturing the 'Old Man'.

The **Aerial Tramway***** begins here, carrying passengers to the 4200-ft summit of Cannon Mountain. Views extend to Canada on clear days, and trails circle the summit. In the winter the tramway carries skiers.

Accommodation and food in Franconia Notch

Lafayette Campground $ *Rte 3; tel: (603) 823-9513.* Well-spaced tent pitches and a campers' store.

Hilltop Inn $–$$ *Main St, Sugar Hill; tel: (603) 823-5695.* B&B with well-decorated, very comfortable rooms and a lively atmosphere.

Polly's Pancake Parlor $ *Rte 117, Sugar Hill; tel: (603) 823-5575. Open Mon–Fri 0700–1500. Sat–Sun 1700–1900* serving fresh-made pancakes with real maple syrup.

JACKSON/GLEN

Wentworth Resort Golf Club *Rte 16B, Jackson; tel: (603) 383-9641.*

Heritage New Hampshire $$ *Rte 16, Glen; tel: (603) 383-4186. Open mid May–mid Oct daily 0900–1700.*

The small village of **Jackson**✦✦, accessed through a red covered bridge, has always been a centre for summer resorts, a tradition carried on at the venerable Wentworth Hotel, whose beautifully restored Victorian buildings form the town's centre-piece. Behind the hotel stretches the green expanse of **Wentworth Resort Golf Club**, where golfers have enjoyed the greens and the mountain views since 1895. **Jackson Falls**✦✦ cascades over a series of stair-stepped ledges beside Carter Notch Rd, providing a natural picnic sites along the way.

Explore history at **Heritage New Hampshire**✦✦✦, beginning on the realistic pitching ship that brought the first settlers. Although it is designed for children, adults will enjoy the engineering of interactive

Right
Wentworth Resort, Jackson

Storyland $$$ (all inclusive) *Rte 16, Glen; tel: (603) 383-4186. Open early June–Aug daily; Sept–mid Oct Sat–Sun.*

Attitash Bear Peak $$ *Rte 302, Bartlett; tel: (603) 374-2368. Open mid June–mid Sept daily (to mid Oct Sat–Sun) 1000–1800.*

displays detailing 'King's Pines', royal grants and Native Americans. **Storyland**✦✦✦ is straight out of a fairy-tale book, where you can literally sail off in a wooden shoe as favourite nursery rhymes and tales spring to life.

Attitash Bear Peak✦✦ is a multi-activity resort park with a ski area, an Alpine slide, water slides, mountain bike trails, horseback riding and a chairlift to the top for 360-degree views.

Accommodation and food in Jackson/Glen

Wentworth Resort Hotel $$–$$$ *Rte16A, Jackson Village; tel: (603) 383-9700 or (800) 637-0013.* Fine old resort with year-round sports and an outstanding dining-room.

Carter Notch Inn $–$$ *Carter Notch Rd, Jackson; tel: (603) 383-9630 or (800) 794-9434.* Well-decorated rooms with character; great breakfasts.

The Prince Place $$ *Rte 302, Glen; tel: (603) 383-9131.* Alpine Europe provides inspiration; local farms the ingredients.

KANCAMAGUS HIGHWAY (AND LINCOLN/WOODSTOCK)

White Mountain Attractions Association $$$ *Rte 112 at Exit 32 off I-93, North Woodstock; tel: (603) 645-9889 or (800) 346-3687.*

Loon Mountain Park *Rte 112, Lincoln; tel: (603) 745-6281.* **Archery Range $** *ext 5569. Open late June–Aug daily 0900–1900.* **Wildlife Theater $** *ext 5562.* **Equestrian Center** *ext 5450. Open daily late May–mid Oct.*

Clark's Trading Post $$ *Rte 3, Lincoln; tel: (603) 745-8913. Open late May–June Sept–mid Oct Sat–Sun, July–Aug daily 1000–1800.*

Whale's Tale Water Park $$$ *Rte 3, Lincoln; tel: (603) 745-8810. Open mid June–Sept daily 1000–1800.*

The **Kancamagus Highway**✦✦✦ stretches 35 miles from Conway on the east to Lincoln on the west. The steep and winding, but good road has a number of laybys, which you should take advantage of, since many fine vistas cannot be seen from the road itself. On the Conway end are **Rocky Gorge and Lower Falls**✦✦, on the Swift River, popular for swimming and picnics. Shortly after a covered bridge is the trail to **Sabbaday Falls**✦✦, where the stream flows through a gorge with 40-ft walls. Wooden railings make it possible to look straight down at the waterfall and pot-holes.

At the western end of the highway, **Loon Mountain Wildlife Theater**✦✦ teaches about native animals and birds in shows so lively that kids will never notice they're educational. Pat a live snake and watch owls or a baby mountain lion.

Loon Mountain Park✦✦ is best known for skiing, but its Equestrian Center offers trail rides for every skill level and the Archery Range has lessons and equipment. Mountain biking trails lead to waterfalls, and a shuttle is provided if you want to take the cycle path through Franconia Notch.

Clark's Trading Post✦✦✦ is a wholesome, spotless theme park whose main theme is fun. Children love the steam train ride through the woods, parents the Victorian Main St, and everyone likes the antics of the trained bears. **Whale's Tale Water Park**✦ is a good place to take kids on a hot summer day, with speed slides, a wave pool and two huge water slides.

Accommodation and food around Kancamagus Highway

Mountain Club at Loon $–$$ *Rte 112, Lincoln; tel: (603) 745-3441 or (800) 229-STAY*. Modern hotel with balconies, pools.

Woodstock Station $–$$ *80 Main St, North Woodstock; tel: (603) 745-3951*. Serves three meals a day; adjacent brew-pub.

Right
Conway Scenic Railway

NORTH CONWAY

🛈 **Mt Washington Valley Chamber of Commerce** *Rte 16; tel: (603) 356-3171 or (800) 367-3364.*

🚃 **Conway Scenic Railway** $$ *Main St; tel: (603) 356-5251. Operates mid Apr–mid May and Nov–mid Dec Sat–Sun, mid May–late Oct daily, Notch train late June–Aug Tue–Sun, Sept–mid Oct daily.*

North Conway has one of the largest concentrations of outlet shops in the entire northeast, grouped into malls that line Rte 16. Settler's Green and Tanger Outlet Center are the foremost, but many other independent outlets lie all the way from Conway to North Conway. Seconds and overstocks are often drastically reduced, but not everything is a bargain. New Hampshire has no sales tax.

There's more to North Conway than outlets and the traffic congestion they create. Across the wide valley, Cathedral Ledge rises from **Echo Lake State Park**✧✧ (*tel: (603) 356-2672*). Rock climbers scale the cliffs in good weather, and a road leads to the top for views of the valley. The lake has a fine – although often crowded – swimming beach and picnic area.

Conway Scenic Railway✧✧✧ travels along the wide valley floor amid mountain views, or climbs through the narrow defile of Crawford Notch. At the Victorian North Conway Station, where trips begin, is a museum and vintage trains.

Accommodation and food in North Conway

Fox Ridge $–$$ *Rte 16; tel: (603) 356-3151 or (800) 343-1804*. Well-decorated motel with balconies and sports facilities.

Green Granite Resort $$ *Rte 16; tel: (603) 356-6901 or (800) 468-3666*. Family-friendly modern hotel with pools, sauna.

New England Inn $$ *Rte 16A; tel: (603) 356-5541*. Traditional New England foods in an 1806 inn.

The Ledges $–$$ *White Mountain Hotel, West Side Rd; tel: (603) 356-7100*. Three varied meals daily.

PINKHAM NOTCH

ⓘ Pinkham Notch Visitors Center *Rte 16; tel: (603) 466-2727. For an event schedule, write to AMC, PO Box 298, Gorham, 03581.*

🏠 Mt Washington Auto Road $$$ *Rte 16; tel: (603) 466-3988. Open mid May–late Oct daily 0730–1800 (shorter hours spring and autumn).*

🏠 Appalachian Mountain Club $ *Rte 16, Gorham; tel: (603) 466-2727. Rustic lodging and three daily meals.*

Dana Place Inn $–$$ *Rte 16; tel: (603) 383-6822 or (800) 537-9276. Charming rooms; fine dining in riverbank setting.*

Everything in Pinkham Notch is along Rte 16, which climbs from the village of Jackson. Although not the most dramatic of New Hampshire's notches, it offer fine views of Mt Washington, which forms its western slopes.

Your first stop should be at **Glen Ellis Falls✦✦✦**, a short walk from the road. Here a mountain stream rushes over cascades before dropping 65ft through a granite cleft. Native stone safety walls blend with the natural setting.

The **Pinkham Notch Visitors Center✦✦** is headquarters of the Appalachian Mountain Club, with a good selection of books, maps and other information about trails, wildlife and nature, and a giant relief map of Mount Washington. Year-round programmes and classes include nature hikes, mountaineering, botany, photography and travelogues. Some programmes are free, classes require advance registration; some include lodging.

At the head of Pinkham Notch is the entrance to the **Mt Washington Auto Road✦✦✦**, 8 miles of 12 per cent climb with breathtaking views at every turn. Drive it or ride in a van with a guide pointing out historic sites and unusual geologic formations along the way. If you drive, stop at the **Alpine Gardens✦**, where wild plants common to much higher elevations flourish on a windy heath; bloom is best in June.

Opposite the Auto Road at the **Glen House Carriage Barns✦✦**, all that's left of one of the grand hotels, see vehicles that have carried passengers up the mountain: the first coach, wagons, a Pierce Arrow and others.

Great Glen Trails✦✦ ($–$$$ *tel: (603) 466-2333*) is an outdoor sports and trail centre for cross-country skiing, snowshoeing, ice skating, bicycling, guided nature walks, archery, concerts, barbecues and kite-flying. Rental bikes, skis, snowshoes and Scandinavian-design kick sleds are available.

⟨ Black Bear Lodge $$ Tel: (603) 236-8383 or (800) GO-VALLEY. Self-catering family suites, with pool.

The Valley Inn $–$$ Tel: (603) 236-8336 or (800) GO-VALLEY. Hotel with the warmth of an inn; good dining-room.

⟨ The William Tell $–$$ Rte 49, Thornton; tel: (603) 726-3618. Open Dec–Mar daily, Apr–Nov Thur–Tue. Swiss and continental menu, with cosy atmosphere.

Accommodation and food in Pinkham Notch

Appalachian Mountain Club $ Rte 16, Gorham; tel: (603) 466-2727. Rustic lodging and three daily meals.

Dana Place Inn $–$$ Rte 16; tel: (603) 383-6822 or (800) 537-9276. Charming rooms; fine dining in riverbank setting.

The grand hotels

In the 19th century, wealthy society families, fleeing the sweltering cities to seek cool mountain air, made the White Mountains their watering-hole-of-choice. Grand hotels adorned the most scenic settings, featuring opulent ballrooms, full orchestras, grand salons, wide porches for promenading in the evening, and gala activities to amuse the wives and offspring of the rich.

They had their portraits painted, rode the cog railway to the top of Mt Washington and horseback to the look-out atop Mt Willard. Attending them was an army of nannies, personal maids and attendants who kept their ballgowns pressed and their collars starched.

This Golden Era died with World War I, and the hotels fell one by one until only a handful remain today. Three – The Balsams, The Mount Washington and The Wentworth – are restored to their original grandeur to carry on the Golden Age traditions.

Suggested tour

Total distance: 143 miles; 413 miles with detours

Time: 4 hours' driving, 9 with detours. Allow 2–3 days for the main route, 4 days with detours. Those with limited time should concentrate on Franconia Notch and Bretton Woods.

Links: I-93 leads north to St Johnsbury, Vermont and the Northeast Kingdom Route, or south to New Hampton and the Lakes Route. Maine's North Woods Route can be reached via Rte 2 east from Gorham.

Route: Begin at Plymouth, at I-93 Exit 25, and travel north on Rte 175 through Campton, which has three covered bridges.

Detour: From Campton, follow Rte 49 until it ends in a cul-de-sac in **Waterville Valley**✦✦✦ ❶ (tel: (603) 236-8311 or (800) 349-2327), a mountain-surrounded resort, with golf, tennis, bicycling, hiking, swimming, a skateboard park, year-round ice-skating rink, mountain biking and winter sports that centre around the ski area. Most activities are free for resort guests, but also open to the public. If

Far right
The Old Man of the Mountain looks out from Franconia Notch

Lost River $$ (garden free) *Rte 112, Kinsman Notch; tel: (603) 745-8031.* Open mid May–late Oct daily 0900–1700, July–Aug daily 0900–1800.

The Grand Victorian Cottage $ *Berkley St, Bethlehem; tel: (603) 869-5755.* Elegant summer mansion, decorated in antiques.

Six Gun City $$$ *Rte 2, Jefferson; tel: (603) 586-4592.* Open May–mid June Sat–Sun, mid June–Aug daily, 0900–1800. Admission price includes all rides and activities.

Rosa Flamingo's $ *Main St, Bethlehem; tel: (603) 869-3111.* Favourite dishes; upbeat setting.

Barbara's Little Restaurant $ *Rte 116, Whitefield; tel: (603) 837-3161.* Three generous home-style meals daily.

Lost Nation Natural Foods *Main St, Lancaster; tel: (603) 788-4141.* Good source of picnic foods.

Midtown Restaurant $ *Rte 3, Pittsburgh; tel: (603) 538-6679*

The Spalding Inn $$ *Mountain View Rd, Whitefield; tel: (603) 837-2572 or (800) 368-8439.* Gracious inn with excellent dinners daily. Lawn croquet on a real court.

The Glen $$ *Rte 3, Pittsburgh; tel: (603) 538-6500 or (800) 445-GLEN.* A classic wilderness lodge and surrounding log cabins on a lake.

unpaved roads don't scare you, return to Rte 175 on wooded Tripoli (pronounced 'triple-eye') Rd, or backtrack on Rte 49 to Campton.

Continue north on Rte 175, joining Rte 3 through Woodstock and into **NORTH WOODSTOCK** ❷. **LINCOLN** ❸ lies a mile east on Rte 112. **Agaziz Basin**•• ❹ is a gorge with a waterfall, right beside Rte 112, at Gavoni's Restaurant just west of North Woodstock. A bridge over the falls makes viewing safe. **Lost River**••• ❺ disappears under a tumble of glacial boulders, reappearing occasionally to plummet in waterfalls on its way down the steep ravine. You can explore all the rock caves and wriggle through tunnels or bypass them on boardwalks and stairs. The 'lemon squeezer' is one tight passage that the claustrophobic should avoid. At the top is a garden of woodland wild flowers, many rare.

Route 3 melds with I-93 through **FRANCONIA NOTCH** ❻, beyond which Rte 18 leads into the valley village of Franconia, with the lovely **Sugar Hill**•• ❼ just above it on Rte 117. Views from **Sunset Hill Rd**•• ❽ are among the best in the mountains. Rte 142 leads from Franconia over a steep hill to **Bethlehem**•• ❾. Nine antiques shops tempt travellers along Bethlehem's short Main St, Rte 302, which you follow to Twin Mountain.

Detour: From Bethlehem, take Rte 116 to Whitefield, rejoining Rte 3 to Lancaster. In Whitefield is one of the most scenic golf courses in the state, **Mountain View Golf and Country Club** ❿ (*tel: (603) 837-3885*), opposite the derelict and ghostly Mountain View Hotel.

Route 3 leads through Lancaster and Groveton to Colebrook, following the Connecticut River, which marks the border between New Hampshire and Vermont. Route 3 continues through Pittsburgh to the Canadian border, past Lake Francis and the Connecticut Lakes, along a stretch known locally as **Moose Alley**•• ⓫, for the number of moose seen by its roadside. After exploring this road, backtrack to Pittsburgh and take Rte 145 south (crossing a covered bridge) along a scenic ridge. Just before reaching Colebrook, you will pass **Beaver Brook Falls**•• ⓬ on your left, a picnic park at its base.

From Colebrook, Rte 26 leads east over **DIXVILLE NOTCH** ⓭, passing The Balsams just before reaching its craggy height. The road follows Clear Stream to Errol, where Rte 16 leads south along the scenic Androscoggin River to Berlin. Climb steep Mount Forist St to see the gold-domed Russian Church before continuing on to Rte 2 at Gorham. Follow Rte 2 west to Rte 115A, with fine views of the Presidential Range to the south. In the early summer the fields near Jefferson are blue with lupine.

Six Gun City•• ⓮ isn't just for kids, although they love its rootin'-tootin' fun. Adults marvel at New England's best collection of horse-drawn vehicles, all beautifully maintained. Rides and a water slide provide a day's entertainment for youngsters.

Wilfred's Turkey Dinners $ *Main St, Gorham; tel: (603) 466-2380.* Turkey and other homey dishes.

Gorham House B&B $ *55 Main St; tel: (603) 466-2271.* Victorian inside and out.

Notchland Inn $$–$$$ (including breakfast and dinner) *Rte 302 Bartlett, Harts Location; tel: (603) 374-6131.* Elegant rooms and five-course dinners with hiking trails from the door.

Bungay Jar $–$$ *Easton Valley Rd, Franconia; tel: (603) 823-7775.* B&B with gardens, sauna, fireplaces.

Rte 115A joins Rte 115 south to Rte 3, which ends the detour by rejoining the main route with a left turn on to Rte 302 in Twin Mountain. This leads to east to **BRETTON WOODS** ⓯ and through the beautiful **Crawford Notch**✦✦✦ ⓰ to **GLEN** ⓱ .

Detour: From Glen, Rte 16 leads north to **JACKSON** ⓲ , accessed by a short loop on Rte 16B, and on through **PINKHAM NOTCH** ⓳ . Backtrack for a whole new set of views as you head south through the notch, rejoining Rte 302 in Glen.

Rte 16 blends with Rte 302 south through **NORTH CONWAY** ⓴ , where they separate south of town and Rte 16 continues to Conway. South of Conway's centre, take Rte 112 west (to the right), known as the **KANCAMAGUS HIGHWAY** ㉑ . This scenic road crosses the spine of the mountain, passing Loon Mountain, and returns to Rte 3 and I-93 in Lincoln/North Woodstock. Follow I-93 back to Plymouth.

Also worth exploring:

From Sugar Hill, north of Franconia Notch, follow signs to Easton, a town high in the mountains, where you can follow Rte 116 through the wild and lonely Kinsman Notch. Rte 116 continues over mountainous terrain until it reaches the stately old town of North Haverhill, overlooking the Connecticut River. A short distance south on Rte 10 is elegant Orford, with its Bullfinch-designed homes along the common. Route 25A returns east over the mountains to Wentworth, which is west of Plymouth on Rte 25.

Previous page
Kinsman Notch – the Lost River

Right
Mount Washington Cog Railway

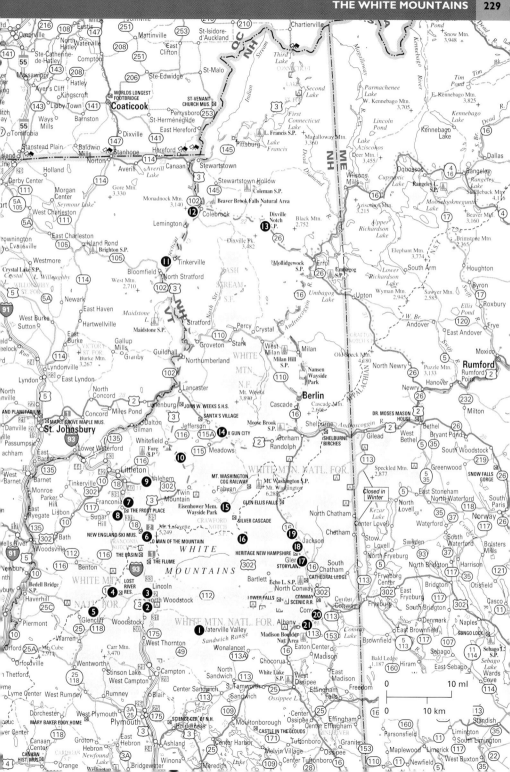

Maine's North Woods

Ratings

Nature/ scenery	●●●●●
Food and drink	●●○○○
Arts and culture	●○○○○
Beaches	●○○○○
Children	●○○○○
History	●○○○○
Shopping	●○○○○
Museums	●○○○○

New England has many outdoor recreation areas, but only Maine's north woods have remained a true wilderness. For the most part, towns in this part of New England are outposts – places to sleep, eat and get supplies – and indoor attractions are few. The untamed landscape alternates between forested mountainsides, rolling spruce bogs and broad lakes and rivers. Moose and deer are so plentiful as to constitute a driving hazard. Travel in the north woods tends to be slow, often on poorly maintained roads or by canoe rather than car. But for the hiker, canoeist, fly-fisher or wildlife photographer, no other part of New England can match Maine's north woods.

ALLAGASH WILDERNESS WATERWAY❖❖❖

Allagash Canoe Trips Greenville $$$ tel: (207) 695-3668 is a knowledgeable and reliable operator running wilderness expeditions on the Allagash. The Moosehead Lake Region Chamber of Commerce (see page 233) can supply a list of other recommended outfitters.

Strictly controlled as wilderness (no permanent habitation, no development), this 92-mile ribbon of lakes, ponds, rivers and streams pierces the deep woods of northern Maine from just west of **Baxter State Park** to within a few miles of the northern border with Canada. The only way to travel the length of the wilderness is as the Abenaki tribe did: by canoe. The trip generally takes 7 to 10 days. Rapids are few, but some large lakes pose wind hazards and canoeing is best undertaken with a group.

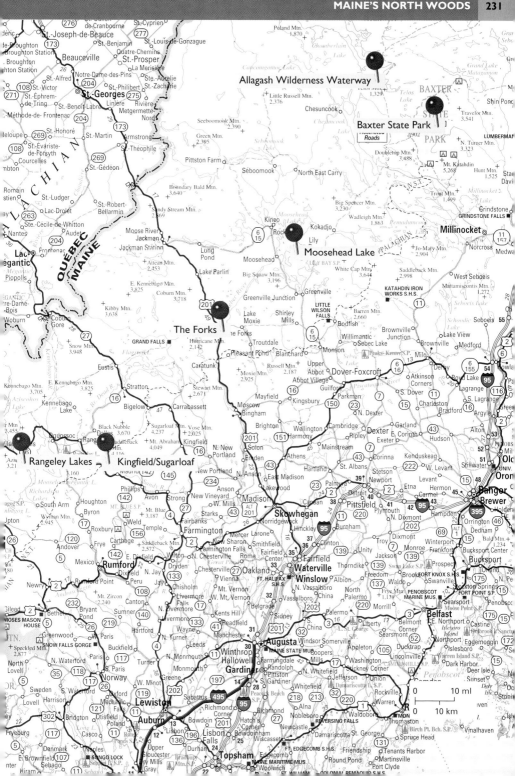

Baxter State Park❖❖❖

Entry is through Togue Pond Gate off Millinocket Rd, an extension of Golden Rd downstream from Ripogenus Dam.

Baxter State Park Headquarters *64 Balsam Dr, Millinocket; tel: (207) 723-5140.*

Campgrounds $ Ten facilities offer a range of accommodation including lean-tos, cabins, bunkhouses and tent pitches. Advance registration required and accepted after 1 January. Contact reservations clerk at Baxter State Park Headquarters address (above).

Professional rafting operators include **Magic Falls Rafting** *tel: (800) 207-7238*, **Moxie Outdoor Adventures** *tel: (800) 866-6943 or (207) 663-2231*, **Northern Outdoors** *tel: (800) 765-7238 or (207) 663-4466*, and **Professional River Runners** *tel: (800) 325-3911 or (207) 663-2229.*

This 201,018-acre wilderness park is named after the former governor who used his own money to purchase the land because short-sighted legislators would not create a state park. If Allagash is for canoeists, Baxter is for hikers, with 175 miles of trails for all abilities. The park contains 46 mountain peaks and ridges, including 18 higher than 3000ft. The chief attraction is **Mount Katahdin**❖❖❖, the tallest mountain in New England and the first place the sun rises on the US. The summit is 5267ft and the slopes support rare alpine plants surviving from the last ice age.

Maine Woods sunrise

The Forks❖❖❖

The Dead River comes in from the west and the Kennebec from the east to create 'the Forks', a fast spill of white water famous for exhilarating rafting and kayaking ($$$). The season begins with spring run-off trips on both rivers and continues on the dam-controlled Kennebec until October. River rafting doesn't get any better than running the Kennebec Gorge, a 12-mile stretch of class II and III rapids with tall cliffs on either side.

KINGFIELD✧

Sugarloaf/USA
$$–$$$ *Carrabassett Valley; tel: (800) 843-5623. Accommodation ranges from chalets to motel rooms.*

The resort of **Sugarloaf/USA**✧✧✧ powers the economy along the Carrabassett River valley, including the farming community of Kingfield. At 4237ft, Sugarloaf Mountain provides dynamic skiing, the longest season in New England and a vertical drop second only to Killington, Vt. Summer activities include hiking, mountain biking, and golf on a Robert Trent Jones course.

MOOSEHEAD LAKE✧✧✧

Moosehead Lake Region Chamber of Commerce *Rtes 6 and 15, Greenville; tel: (207) 695-2702.*

It's easier and more interesting to search for moose in the company of an experienced naturalist. **Main Street Station $$$** *Main St, Greenville; tel: (207) 695-2375* and **Moose River Store $$$** *Rte 15, Rockwood; tel: (207) 534-7352* arrange moose-sighting safaris and cruises.

Forty miles long and 20 miles wide at its extremities, Moosehead Lake is an inland sea trapped in the last ice age. The 350-mile shoreline is densely forested, and the lake itself is a legendary fishing ground. It's well named, since the shores (and often the waters) are full of moose. Two towns are gateways to the lake. **Greenville**✧✧, on the southeastern tip, began as a timber town and developed in the mid-19th century as a destination for adventurous (and wealthy) 'sports'. Until the current road system was built in the 1930s, steamboats were the chief transportation. The sole survivor, the 1914 **SS *Katahdin*✧✧** now makes scenic cruises. Greenville is a primary base for wilderness outfitters and fishing guides and boasts the largest float plane fleet in New England. Hunting for moose (with cameras) ranks as the chief tourism activity, with options for various fitness levels, including van trips, canoe trips and even 'bellyboats' (Camouflaged flotationdevices). The Chamber of Commerce updates its map of moose sightings daily. The other access to Moosehead is **Rockwood**✧, on the western shore at the narrowest and most dramatic point of the lake, with the best hunting and fly-fishing. Among the popular outings from Rockwood are trips across the water to 760-ft **Mt Kineo**✧✧, a near-island peninsula that has been a popular hiking destination since the days of Henry David Thoreau.

Accommodation and food around Moosehead Lake

Greenville Inn $$ *Norris St, PO Box 1194, Greenville; tel: (888) 695-6000 or (207) 695-2206.* Rooms in the historic country inn often share baths. The dining-room ($$$) is an oasis of gourmet eating in an area rarely known for gastronomic finesse.

Lodge at Moosehead $$–$$$ *Lily Bay Rd, PO Box 1167, Greenville; tel: (207) 695-4400.* All rooms have whirlpool baths and fireplaces as well as extraordinary hand-carved furniture. This luxurious outpost on the lake also boasts stunning sunset views.

RANGELEY LAKES✧✧

❶ Rangeley Lakes Chamber of Commerce *Public Landing, Rangeley; tel: (800) 685-2537.*

⑩ Dockside Sports Center $$$ *Town Cove, Rangeley; tel: (207) 864-2424 rents canoes and powerboats in the summer and snowmobiles in the winter.*

Rangeley Region Sport Shop *85 Main St, Rangeley; tel: (207) 864-5615 sells fishing gear, rents canoes and can recommend fishing guides.*

The Rangeley Lakes are legendary for **fly-fishing**✧✧✧ for land-locked salmon and native brook trout in a dramatic landscape where tall mountains surround deep glacial lakes. The chain of lakes includes Rangeley, Mooselookmeguntic (the largest at 2 miles wide and 11 miles long) and about ten others in an area of about 450 square miles. The town of Rangeley serves as the base for all outdoor activities in the region. It is also a winter snowmobiling centre, connecting to 140 miles of trails. Many fishermen camp at the 691-acre **Rangeley Lake State Park**✧✧, central to more than 40 trout and salmon ponds and lakes.

Suggested tour

Total distance: 509 miles

Time: 14 hours' driving. Allow 4 days minimum.

Route: Few areas so exemplify the punchline of an old Maine joke, 'You can't get there from here'. Vast tracts of forest and rugged mountains divide road systems, which follow the north–south lines etched by the retreat of glacial ice. While the **RANGELEY LAKES ❶** and **KINGFIELD ❷** are best approached from the west via Rte 16 from the White Mountains (*see page 216*), the most direct route to **BAXTER STATE PARK ❸**, the **ALLAGASH ❹** and **MOOSEHEAD LAKE ❺** begins in **Millinocket✧ ❻**, a timber-company town southeast of Baxter. From Portland, follow I-95 north 193 miles to exit 56, and turn west on Rtes 157 and 11 for 10 miles. Once you leave Millinocket you will be driving through rugged, wooded country on roads that are, for the most part, unpaved. Watch for park signs west of town, make a right on to Golden Rd and continue 18 miles to the **Baxter State Park's ❸** Perimeter Rd at Togue Pond Gate. Golden Rd continues west through a timber-company gate (road-use fee $$$) for 24 miles to Ripogenus Dam and the Telos Rd turnoff. Although the beginning of the **ALLAGASH WILDERNESS WATERWAY ❼** is only 22 miles north on Telos Rd, the road is often deeply rutted and the drive can take up to two hours. Backtrack to Golden Rd and continue west. The road turns left and becomes more rutted as it becomes Greenville Rd, leading 35 slow miles through spruce bogs. The slowness of the road is an asset, as moose abound here, feeding in the roadside ponds and bogs. The slower you drive, the better the chance to photograph them, or at least to

Moose on the loose

The moose (*Alces alces*) is the world's largest member of the deer family, with the bulls weighing up to 1400lbs and cows reaching 900lbs. The population has grown rapidly in recent years and moose are expanding from the northern wilds into urbanised areas. They are usually shy and gentle except during the October rutting season. Moose can be seen along northern roadsides in the spring, licking up salt residue from winter de-icing efforts. They are also frequently spotted while feeding knee-deep in bogs and other swampy areas.

Rangeley Inn $–$$
Main St, PO Box 398,
Rangeley; tel (800) 666-3687
or (207) 864-3341. The
main inn dates from 1877
and features the most
atmosphere, but some
rooms in the newer motel
have wood stove fireplaces.
The dining-room ($–$$)
serves good traditional
New England food.

avoid hitting one as it ambles across the road. When pavement commences, Greenville is close. After the backwoods, it will seem like a metropolis. Greenville functions as the chief point of access to **Moosehead Lake** ❺, with Rockwood, another 20 miles west on Rtes 6 and 15, serving as the other. To take the scenic route back to I-95, continue west for 31 miles to **Jackman*** ❽, another wilderness outfitting town and turn south on Rte 201 to descend 26 miles to **THE FORKS** ❾. Views of the Kennebec River are extraordinary for the next 32 miles south to Solon, where Rte 201 turns inland, crosses through Skowhegan in 15 miles and then follows the Kennebec River for another 14 miles to exit 36 of I-95, just 78 miles north of Portland.

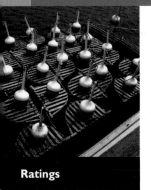

New Hampshire and the Southern Maine Coast

Ratings

Beaches	●●●●○
Nature/ scenery	●●●●○
Children	●●●○○
History	●●●○○
Museums	●●●○○
Shopping	●●●○○
Arts and culture	●●○○○
Food and drink	●●○○○

Old seafaring towns, raucous beach communities and up-market summer resorts are interwoven along this stretch of coastal New Hampshire and southern Maine. Sudden spits of rock interrupt long sandy strands and the roadways skirt the ocean's edge along a coastal plain where bird-filled marshlands creep down to the sea. The beaches and associated attractions make this an excellent holiday area for families with children, while Portsmouth, the Yorks and the Kennebunks also offer many historical attractions and Ogunquit has a lively art scene. Traffic is heavy and slow during July and August, so travellers should maintain patience and a sense of humour.

HAMPTON BEACH❖

🅿 Although metered parking is available on **Ocean Blvd**, all spaces are claimed early in July–Aug. There are numerous pay lots on streets leading toward the beach from Rte 101.

ℹ *180 Ocean Blvd.; tel: (603) 926-8717 Open daily mid June–Labor Day (first Mon in Sept), Sat–Sun only Apr–mid June and early Sept–Oct.*

The mile-long strand of Hampton Beach offers superb swimming, with soft sand, rolling waves and water on the warm side of brutal. Very popular with Quebecers on holiday (it is the closest ocean beach to Montreal), Hampton is jammed with tanned bodies during July and August, yet tranquil and scenic in May and September.

Hampton Beach State RV Park $ *(Rte 1A; tel: (603) 926-8990)* is a prime recreational vehicle park south of the main beach with only 20 spots. It's open mid May–mid Oct, but begins accepting reservations in January *(tel: (603) 271-3628)*.

KENNEBUNK VILLAGES✦✦

ℹ Kennebunk Lower Village *Port Rd; tel: (207) 967-0857. Open Mon–Fri 0900–1700 (also 0900–1700 on weekends late May–mid Oct).*

Kennebunk lies directly on Rte 1, while the other villages are strung along the waterfront on Rte 9. **Intown Trolley $** *tel: (207) 967-3686. Tour relates Kennebunkport history during drive past beaches, Blowing Cave, Spouting Rock and Bush estate. Reboarding allowed all day.*

🏛 Brick Store Museum $ *Rtes 1 & 35; tel: (207) 985-4802. Open mid Apr–mid Dec Tue–Sat 1000–1630 (closed Sat rest of year). Museum also offers architectural walking tour of historic district mid June–Sept on Wed at 1000 and on Fri at 1300.*

🚋 Seashore Trolley Museum $$ *195 Log Cabin Road; tel: (207) 967-2800. Open mid June–Sept 0930–1800 (museum), 1030–1600 (trolley rides). Call for spring and autumn hours.*

Former president George Bush exemplifies the wealthy, politically conservative class that summers in the villages of Kennebunk (Kennebunk, Kennebunkport, Kennebunk Beach and Cape Porpoise). The town grew wealthy from 19th-century shipbuilding, resulting in the trophy Colonial, Federal, Greek Revival and Victorian homes of the **Kennebunk National Historic District**✦ (Main and Summer Sts and part of Rte 1). The **Brick Store Museum**✦✦ occupies an 1825 store and three adjacent buildings in the district. Its exhibitions focus on local maritime history and on fine and decorative arts.

Kennebunkport is the liveliest of the villages; its heart is **Dock Square**✦, the former shipping centre now given to boutiques, restaurants and art galleries. The **Seashore Trolley Museum**✦ features 50 refurbished trolley cars from around the world. Although the least prettified part of the Kennebunks, the working harbour of **Cape Porpoise**✦, marked at its entrance by Goat Island lighthouse, is perhaps the most scenic, with lobster fishermen and yachtsmen sharing the same anchorages.

Right
"Wedding-cake house",
Kennebunk

Accommodation and food in the Kennebunks

Fontenay Terrace Motel $–$$ *128 Ocean Ave, Kennebunkport; tel: (207) 967-3556.* Small motel on tidal inlet is good spot to enjoy natural beauty of the harbour.

Grissini Trattoria $$ *27 Western Ave, Kennebunk; tel: (207) 967-2211.* Northern Italian trattoria standards plus large pasta selection.

Historic Inns of Kennebunkport *tel: (800) 950-2117* is a consortium of six excellent B&Bs in historic homes with a strong emphasis on luxury and romance. One of the more relaxed members is **The Maine Stay $$** *34 Maine St, Kennebunkport; tel: (800) 950-2117 or (207) 967-2117.*

Port Lobster $ *Ocean Ave, Kennebunkport; tel: (207) 967-5411.* Seafood market also sells superb take-away lobster rolls.

White Barn Inn $$–$$$ *Beach St (POB 560), Kennebunkport; tel: 207 967-2321.* Luxurious retreat also has Maine's best white-linen gourmet dining.

OGUNQUIT⁑

❶ Ogunquit Chamber of Commerce *Rte 1 S (POB 2289), Ogunquit; tel: (207) 646-2939.*

❷ Ogunquit Trolley $ *circles from town to beach to Perkins Cove. Operates mid May–mid Oct.*

❸ Ogunquit Museum of American Art $ *Shore Rd; tel: (207) 646-4909. Open July–Sept Mon–Sat 1030–1700, Sun 1400–1700.*

❹ Ogunquit Playhouse $$$ *Rte 1 S; tel: (207) 646- 2402 or (207) 646-5511.* Presents three musicals and two plays by touring companies mid June–Aug.

Maine's most gay- and lesbian-friendly resort, Ogunquit has **superb sand beaches⁑** (entrances at Beach St and 2 miles north of town via 'the footbridge'). Clusters of art galleries and boutiques are found both in the town centre and in **Perkins Cove**, a former fishing harbour that's now part art colony, part tourist emporium. **Marginal Way⁑**, a 1.2-mile footpath on cliffs above the ocean, connects the cove with the beaches. Thickets of beach roses line the route and many benches are available to enjoy the view. Ogunquit's art colony began around 1900 but came into its own in the decades between the world wars. That heyday is well represented at the **Ogunquit Museum of American Art⁂**, which overlooks Perkins Cove, worth visiting for the Marsden Hartley paintings alone.

Accommodation and food in Ogunquit

Arrows $$$ *Berwick Rd; tel: (207) 361-1100.* Stunning gardens surround country restaurant dedicated to gourmet excess. *Open May–late Nov.*

Beachmere Inn $–$$ *12 Beachmere Pl; tel: (800) 336-3983 or (207) 646-2021.* Modernised Victorian inn and classic motel with grand views and gate on to Marginal Way. All rooms have cooking facilities.

Norseman Motor Inn $–$$ *41 Beach St; tel: (800) 822-7024 or (207) 646-7024.* Sprawling motel at beach car-park provides great beach access but limited peace and quiet.

Riverside Motel $–$$ *Shore Rd (POB 2244); tel: (207) 646-2741.* Excellent motel complex connects to Perkins Cove over pedestrian drawbridge.

Village Food Market $ *Ogunquit Sq; tel: (207) 646-2122.* Full-service grocer's deli counter, also makes excellent take-away sandwiches.

OLD ORCHARD BEACH❖❖

❶ Old Orchard Beach Chamber of Commerce *First St; tel: (800) 365-9386 or (207) 934-2500. Open June–Aug daily 0900–1700, Sept–May Mon–Fri.*

Seven miles of sandy swimming beaches made Old Orchard one of New England's first summer resorts. A family destination, Old Orchard's giddy scene cranks up when school ends and halts abruptly on the first weekend in September. The 1898 **Ocean Pier❖** at the centre of the town concentrates game arcades, souvenir stands and food vendors. Nearby amusement arcades feature old-fashioned games of 'skill' along with modern electronics. **Palace Playland❖❖** features mechanical rides, roller-coaster and Ferris wheel. Least crowded beaches are north of the town centre along Rte 9.

Accommodation and food in Old Orchard Beach

Grand Ave is lined with dozens of modest motels, all steps from the beach. Eating here is more a continuous than a periodic activity, as stalls selling pizza, hot dogs and ice-cream far outnumber actual restaurants.

Atlantic Birches Inn $$ *20 Portland Ave; tel: (888) 934-5295 or (207) 934-5295.* Ten rooms in two buildings in quiet location away from the beach.

The Edgewater $$ *57 W Grand Ave; tel: (800) 203-2034 or (207) 934-2221.* Lovingly maintained classic two-level motel situated right on the shore.

Joseph's $$ *55 W Grand Ave; tel: (207) 934-5044.* When cotton candy and clam rolls no longer suffice, Joseph's serves traditional American meals.

PORTSMOUTH❖❖❖

❶ Strawbery Banke Museum $$ *Marcy St; tel: (603) 433-1100. Open mid Apr–Oct daily 1000–1700.*

Portsmouth's fervour for historic preservation saved its colonial and Federal architecture, launching this small city's revival as a destination. Crafts shops, boutiques and restaurants fill the 18th-century chandleries and warehouses of the **Old Harbor❖❖** (Bow and Ceres Sts), and the 10-acre **Strawbery Banke Museum❖❖** preserves 300 years of Portsmouth domestic life in 40 buildings. Walking to the six historic mansions scattered around the city on the **Portsmouth Harbor Trail❖❖** gives a better sense of the intersection of history and

ℹ **Greater Portsmouth Chamber of Commerce** *500 Market St, Portsmouth; tel: (603) 436-1118.* Information kiosk in Market Sq provides Harbor Trail map. *Open daily May–Oct, weekends Apr and Nov–Dec.*

modern life. Among them, they chronicle Portsmouth's merchant and privateer class from 1716 to 1807.

Accommodation and food in Portsmouth

Bow Street Inn $$ *121 Bow St; tel: (603) 431-7760.* Nine pleasant rooms near the harbour in a building that also houses a professional theatre company.

Café Mediterraneo $–$$ *152 Fleet St; tel: (603) 427-5563.* Pizza, calzones and contemporary Italian seafood.

Inn at Strawbery Banke $$ *314 Court St; tel: (800) 428-3933 or (603) 436-7242.* Large 19th-century inn with striking wraparound porch near Strawbery Banke Museum.

Lindbergh's Crossing $$ *29 Ceres St; tel: (603) 431-0887.* New American bistro shows panache and innovation.

Oar House $$ *55 Ceres St; tel: (603) 436-4025.* Old-style seafood restaurant with outdoor deck overlooking harbour.

The Oracle House Inn $$ *38 Marcy St; tel: (603) 433-8827.* Former printshop of the town's first newspaper, the *Oracle*, this 18th-century building has three superb rooms, each with a fireplace.

SCARBOROUGH***

Scarborough Marsh Nature Center *Pine Point Rd; tel: (207) 883-5100 or (207) 781-2330. Open mid June–early Sept daily 0930–1730. Walking tours $, canoe tours $$.*

Scarborough possesses a rough beauty rarely equalled along the New England coast. More than 3000 acres of tidal and freshwater marsh, salt creeks and uplands are protected in the **Scarborough Marsh Nature Center***, where a boardwalk nature trail is dotted with observation blinds to observe shy waterfowl. The exclusive summer community of **Prout's Neck*** occupies a striking rocky knob where the artist Winslow Homer painted many of his best seascapes round the turn of the century.

Accommodation and food in Scarborough

Bailey's Pine Point $ *Rte 9, Scarborough; tel: (207) 883-6043.* Large wooded pitches; shuttle bus to beaches.

Black Point Inn Resort $$$ *Prout's Neck, Scarborough; tel: (800) 258-0003 or (207) 883-4126.* This historic beachfront resort consists of the main inn plus several cottages; the amenities include a yacht club and a golf course.

WELLS**

Wells Auto Museum $ *Rte 1; tel: (207) 646-9064. Open late May–mid Oct daily 1000–1700.*

Wells National Estuarine Reserve $ *342 Laudholm Farm Rd; tel: (207) 646-1555. Trails open daily 0800–1700, visitor centre open Mon–Sat 1000–1600, Sun 1200–1600. Free guided tour.*

Lighthouse Depot *Rte 1N; tel: (207) 646-0608* may not be in a real lighthouse but the selection of lighthouse-theme gifts and souvenirs is mind-boggling.

Adjacent Ogunquit caters to adult couples, but Wells embraces families. The 7-mile-long strand of **Wells Beach** fronts on shallow waters and the town of souvenir shops has a naïve appeal. An attraction for all ages is the **Wells Auto Museum**, which displays a collection of nickelodeons and other Americana along with more than 80 antique and classic automobiles. Less than 2 miles from the hubbub of the beach and highway strip are a couple of striking wetlands preserves. The **Wells National Estuarine Reserve** at Laudholm Farm preserves 1600 acres of field, forest, wetlands and beaches criss-crossed by 7 miles of nature trails.

The **Rachel Carson National Wildlife Refuge*** protects 4800 acres of wetland habitat critical to several migratory bird species. A mile-long interpretive nature trail departs from the headquarters car-park, allowing you to explore on foot.

Accommodation and food in Wells

Maine Diner $–$$ *Rte 1; tel: (207) 646-4441.* Traditional diner makes good use of its vegetable garden out back.

Pinederosa Camping Area $ *128 N Village Rd; tel: (207) 646-2492.* Mix of wooded and open field sites only 2 miles from Wells Beach.

THE YORKS**

ⓘ Chamber of Commerce *Rte 1 at I-95 connector; tel: (207) 363-4422 Open daily 0900–1700 with extended summer hours.*

ⓘ Old York Historical Society $$ *Jefferds Tavern Visitor Center on Lindsay Rd; tel: (207) 363-4974. Open mid June–Sept Tue–Sat 1000–1700, Sun 1300–1700 (also weekends in Oct).* Each building can also be toured for small individual charge.

York is very proud to have been the first permanent English settlement in the region. The **Old York Historical Society**** preserves six 17th- and 18th-century buildings as a museum with more than 30 galleries and period rooms. The most interesting and least visited of the bunch is the **Elizabeth Perkins House***. Its 20th-century owners had an idiosyncratic vision of colonial life and strongly influenced New England's Colonial Revival movement.

Three other villages lie within York's boundaries. **York Harbor*** and **Cape Neddick***, both lovely to stroll, boast rich summer homes and yacht slips. Just off the tip of Cape Neddick is the oft-photographed **Nubble Light***. Brassy **York Beach**** is the very public junction of two superb swimming beaches.

Accommodation and food in the Yorks

Camp Eaton $ *Rte 1A, York Harbor; tel: (207) 363-3424.* RV hook-ups and wooded tent pitches near Long Sands Beach.

Goldenrod Restaurant $ *Railroad Rd and Ocean Ave, York Beach; tel: (207) 363-2621.* Meals are simple 'home cooking' but the main appeal is an old-fashioned soda fountain and the salt water taffy made on the premises.

York Harbor Inn $$–$$$ *Rte 1A, York Harbor; tel: (800) 343-3869 or (207) 363-5119.* A 19th-century inn with 35 rooms overlooking the harbour near Nubble Light. Formal dining-room with grand ocean view serves traditional New England cuisine **$$$**. The Wine Cellar pub is more casual in menu and attire **$$**.

Suggested tour

Total distance: 110 miles with detours

Time: 4–5 hours of often slow driving. Allow 2–3 days.

Links: The southern end of this route connects to the Massachusetts North Shore Route (*see page 66*), while the northern end runs into Portland (*see page 246*).

Route: From the New Hampshire Turnpike, take Exit 2 to **HAMPTON BEACH ❶**. At Ocean Ave turn north on to Rte 1A, which follows the ocean through Rye Beach, with fine swimming at **Wallis Sands State Park ❷** and gentle hiking and bird-watching at **Odiorne Point State Park ❸**, where a children's science museum highlights marine ecology.

Wallis Sands State Park $ *Rte 1A, Rye. Open daily late May–Oct. Beach accessible all year.*

Odiorne Point State Park $ *Rte 1A, Rye. Park open daily May–Oct.*

Seacoast Science Center $ *tel: (603) 436-8043. Open May–Oct daily 1000–1700.*

Kittery Outlet Malls *tel: (888) 548-8379.*

Kittery Trading Post *Rte 1, Kittery; tel: (207) 439-2700 has been equipping travellers for camping, backpacking, fishing and other outdoor activities since 1938.*

The Line House $ *Rte 1, Kittery–York; tel: (207) 439-3401. Tiny restaurant a 3-minute drive north of outlet malls serves filling and frugal home-style meals.*

Arundel Antiques *Rte 1, Kennebunk; tel: (207) 985-7965, about 3 miles north of Kennebunk, is the best multi-dealer group antiques shop along the Maine coast.*

Route 1A rejoins Rte 1 as it enters **PORTSMOUTH ④** past about 2 miles of handsome Greek Revival houses, continuing into the Old Harbour district, and over the Piscataqua River on Memorial Bridge into **Kittery** to a traffic roundabout. Just north of the roundabout, 120 factory outlet stores in a mile-long thicket of Rte 1 constitute one of the largest concentrations in the US.

Shopping-induced congestion suddenly eases as Rte 1 continues 5 miles to Rte 1A, which threads along the shoreline through the **YORKS ⑤** for another 5 miles before rejoining Rte 1 for the leafy 3-mile drive into **OGUNQUIT ⑥**. Route 1 continues another 4 miles north past strip malls to the Mile Rd turnout to **WELLS BEACH ⑦**, then another 3 miles to the junction of Rte 9. Three miles north of the junction on Rte 1 is **KENNEBUNK ⑧**; Rte 9 goes 4 miles northeast into **KENNEBUNKPORT ⑨** (the two villages are joined by Rte 9A).

Route 1 is more direct, but the shoreline scenic route follows Rte 9 north for 16 miles into the towns of Biddeford and Saco, then down the north side of the Saco River to its mouth and north along the shore to **Ocean Park⁕ ⑩**, a summer cottage community with camp meeting origins, and then through **OLD ORCHARD BEACH ⑪**. At the Pier, Rte 9 becomes E Grand Ave and continues north 8 miles past uncrowded swimming and surfing beaches before turning inland at Pine Point to pass the Scarborough Marshes. Route 9 joins Rte 1 to continue north to **SCARBOROUGH ⑫** for 4 miles to Rte 207, Black Point Rd, which leads to Prout's Neck. Alternately, Rte 1 continues into Portland.

Also worth exploring

Isle of Shoals⁕⁕

These nine small islands continue to spark the imagination of New Englanders and legends persist of pirates' gold and rum-runners' fortunes buried in their mere 200 acres. One islands was the site of the infamous (and unsolved) 1873 murders on which Anita Shreve's novel, *The Weight of Water* is based. Privately owned for the most part, two islands are accessible for exploration. **Star Island⁕** has a variety of self-guided nature walks. Poet Celia Thaxter planted flowers on **Appledore Island⁕**, where she wrote her classic *An Island Garden*, illustrated by painter Childe Hassam. The 1894 book provided plans to restore the gardens in 1977. Tours are offered Wed afternoons mid June–Aug. Appledore is accessible on request from the **Shoals Marine Laboratory** *Cornell University Ithaca NY 14853; tel: (607) 255-3717.* **Isles of Shoals Steamship Company** $$$ *Barker Wharf, 315 Market St; tel: (800) 441-4620 or (603) 431-5500* offers service from Portsmouth to the islands.

Greater Portland

Ratings

Food and drink	●●●●○
Arts and culture	●●●○○
Shopping	●●●○○
Beaches	●●○○○
Children	●●○○○
History	●●○○○
Nature/ scenery	●●○○○
Museums	●●○○○

As the cultural and business centre of New England's north coast, the small city of Portland has more shopping, dining, arts and entertainment than communities three times its population of 65,000. Situated on a peninsula in the focal point of sheltered Casco Bay, it is central to superb beaches on the south and Maine's woodlands only a few miles inland. Portland is often treated as a convenient departure point for winter skiing in Maine's rugged mountains or summer sightseeing through coastal villages, but the city itself is lively and engaging. Farsighted city planning salvaged the architectural shell of Portland's 19th-century heyday as a shipping and shipbuilding centre, and an influx of young professionals to the software and banking industries has created a bustling cultural and entertainment scene.

Sights

ⓘ Convention and Visitors Bureau of Greater Portland *305 Commercial St; tel: (207) 772-4994.*

Ⓟ Public parking meters (2-hour maximum) are cheap. Off-street car-parks charge slightly more, but most shops give validation stamps good for one hour of free parking at municipal lots and garages.

Arts district✦✦✦

In recent years Portland's commercial district along Congress St, between Mercy Hospital and the handsome beaux arts City Hall, has been spruced up and promoted to its own citizens as the 'Arts District'. Two museums give credence to the claim. The **Children's Museum of Maine**✦✦ intentionally appeals to the under-14 set with many general science exhibits common to such institutions as well as some decidedly local exhibits, such as a lobster boat. The top-floor camera obscura that surveys Portland's skyline is an optical delight for all ages. The **Portland Museum of Art**✦✦ occupies a strikingly modern building designed by the I M Pei firm and erected in 1983 – a welcome relief from the expanse of Victorian red brick around it. The museum has an outstanding collection of paintings and graphic art by late 19th- and early 20th-century artists who worked in Maine, including

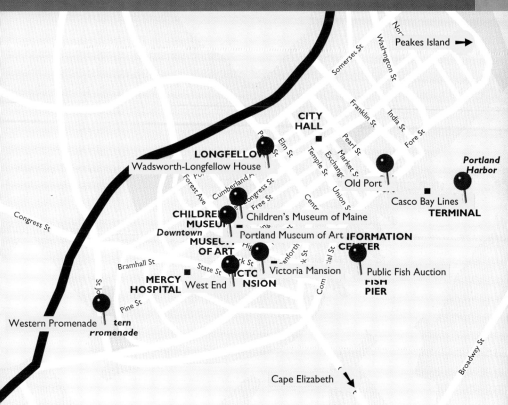

Peakes Island ➡

CITY
HALL

Portland
Harbor

LONGFELLOW
Wadsworth-Longfellow House

Old Port

Casco Bay Lines

TERMINAL

CHILDRE
MUSEU   Children's Museum of Maine

Downtown   Portland Museum of Art   IFORMATION
MUSEU..   CE TER
OF ART

Victoria Mansion   Public Fish Auction

MERCY   State St   CTC   NSION   FISH
HOSPITAL West End   PIER

Western Promenade   tern
rromenade

Bramhall St

Congress St

Cape Elizabeth

Children's Museum of Maine $ *142 Free St; tel: (207) 828-1234. Open Mon–Sat 1000–1700, Sun 1200–1700 (closed Mon–Tue June–early Sept).*

Portland Museum of Art $ *7 Congress Sq; tel: (207) 775-6148. Open Tue–Sat 1000–1700 (Thur until 2100), Sun 1200–1700.*

Wadsworth-Longfellow House $ *485–489 Congress St; tel: (207) 879-0427. Open June–Oct 1000–1600*

Andrew and N C Wyeth, Edward Hopper and Rockwell Kent. Its Winslow Homer oil paintings and watercolours, many of which were painted at nearby Prout's Neck, rank among the artist's finest.

Portland has a claim in the literary arts as well. Poet and translator Henry Wadsworth Longfellow was born in Portland and grew up in the **Wadsworth-Longfellow House**✣, a brick home now in the centre of town but far on the outskirts when Longfellow's grandfather, General Peleg Wadsworth, built it in 1786. Far more restrained than the mansions that Portlanders would build a century later, it reveals Longfellow's modest upbringing.

Calendar Islands✣

The Casco Bay archipelago across the mouth of Portland harbour is known as the Calendar Islands because legend has it that there are 365 of them (the actual number is closer to 200, and many of those are little more than ledges exposed at low tide). Similar exaggerations exist about the history of the islands, often involving unscrupulous characters who lured ships on to the rocks in storms to salvage them when the weather cleared. The larger islands are now pleasant

Casco Bay Ferry
$–$$ *Commercial and Franklin Sts; tel: (207) 774-7871* offers year-round ferry service and summer sightseeing cruises to the Calendar Islands.

Eagle Tours $$–$$$
Long Wharf; tel: (207) 774-6498 offers cruises to Portland Head Light and has a variety of sightseeing and seal-watching cruises.

Fort Williams Park
1000 Shore Rd. Free admission to grounds.
Lighthouse museum $
tel: (207) 799-2661. Open June–Oct daily 1000–1600, Apr–May and Nov–Dec Sat–Sun 1000–1600.

residential neighbourhoods. **Peaks Island**✦, just offshore, has a fine waterfront park and beach ideal for a picnic. It enjoys a frequent ferry service on the **Casco Bay Lines** commuter boats. Cliff, Chebeague, Long, Little Diamond and Great Diamond islands are also accessible by ferry, but with limited service.

Cape Elizabeth✦✦

Although less than 2 miles south of downtown Portland, Cape Elizabeth boasts a radically different geography. Ancient geological forces pushed the sea-bed to the surface here, creating a buffer-zone of rocky promontories between sandy barrier beaches on the south and Casco Bay on the north. The contrast of landforms has haunted painters since the early 19th century. **Crescent Beach State Park**✦✦ off Rte 77 offers excellent swimming on a south-facing beach that trails from sand on the east to stones on the west. Less than half a mile away is **Two Lights State Park**✦, where a steep and rocky shoreline overlooks the Atlantic Ocean. The park is named for the two 19th-century lighthouses that still signal this southern opening of Casco Bay. Painter Edward Hopper so admired their stark desolation that he painted them from several views in 1927 and 1929. In general, Maine lighthouses warn sailors of rocks and ledges (as opposed to merely shallow water) and are therefore sited on prominent elevations that offer spectacular views. That is certainly true 3 miles north at **Fort Williams**✦✦, constructed in 1791 to defend Portland harbour from anticipated British attacks. Now a city park much favoured by kite fliers, the fortifications have crumbled but **Portland Head Light**✦✦ remains intact. One of the most photographed lighthouses in Maine, Portland Head offers striking views down into swirling currents around ledges and islets. There is a small lighthouse museum inside the base.

Whales of New England

The most frequently spotted New England whales are the 5-ft harbour porpoises, which sometimes even visit Boston's busy harbour. The offshore whales are larger, more striking baleen whales that feed on shrimp-like krill and plankton in the shallows from Cape Cod into the Gulf of Maine. Pilot whales, black and about 20ft long, are common in large pods spring and fall. The streamlined minke whale, blue-grey on top and about 25ft long, is common in all but the coldest months. The 70-ft finback also feeds off the New England coast in large numbers from March through November. The showman of the whales, the 40-ft humpback whale, is famous for its great leaps, or 'breaches'. Although infrequently seen by commercial whale watches, almost the entire 300-individual population of the endangered northern right whale also swims in New England waters.

⊙ Greater Portland Transit District $
tel: (207) 774-0351).
Although many attractions are clustered near each other, using the city bus system cuts walking time, especially on Portland's steep hills.

⊙ Free Casco Bay Weekly and Go (a Thur supplement to the Portland Press Herald) provide complete listings of theatre, concerts, club performances, art galleries, dance, film and performing arts.

Aucocisco tel: (207) 772-6828. A 9-day festival in April celebrates Portland's connection to the sea.

Portland Pirates Cumberland County Civic Ctr Spring St; tel: (207) 828-4665. This minor-league hockey team plays Oct–Apr.

Portland Stage Company Portland Performing Arts Center 25A Forest Ave; tel: (207) 774-0465. The largest professional theatre company in northern New England produces contemporary and classic dramas and musicals Oct–May.

Portland Symphony Orchestra 30 Myrtle St; tel: (207) 773-8191 performs classical, pops and chamber concerts in City Hall Auditorium.

Right
Portland Head Light

Victoria Mansion $
*109 Danforth St; tel:
(207) 772-4841. Open
May–Oct Tue–Sat
1000–1600, Sun
1300–1700.*

**Aucocisco Cross
Jewelers** *570
Congress St; tel: (207) 773-
3107* has an excellent
selection of jewellery
featuring the pink and
green tourmalines mined
in Maine. *Open weekdays
only.*

Maine Potters Market
*376 Fore St; tel: (207) 774-
1633* provides one-stop
shopping for work by
many of Maine's best
ceramic artists.

Nancy Margolis Gallery
*367 Fore St; tel: (207) 775-
3822* carries superb crafts
in all media with a good
representation of Maine
artists.

Old Port✦✦✦

Many travellers spend their entire time in Portland in the Old Port
district bounded by Commercial, Franklin, Congress and Union Sts.
Portland's port and mercantile exchange area was completely rebuilt
in red brick after the Great Fire of 1866, making it a later and more
robust architecture than that found on most New England
waterfronts. After World War II, most of Portland's sea traffic shifted
to the deeper waters of South Portland and the waterfront fell into
decay. Revived in the 1970s, the Old Port Exchange, as it is sometimes
called, has boomed as a shopping, drinking and dining district,
complete with cobblestone streets, pedestrian-only ways and artfully
enhanced quaintness at every turn. Micro-breweries and pubs have
flourished and much of Portland's casual nightlife is found in the Old
Port.

The wharves still constitute a working port, with sightseeing vessels
berthed next to scallop draggers, lobster boats and offshore purse
seiners. In fact, a substantial portion of Maine's catch is offloaded at
Portland Fish Pier, where there's a **public fish auction**✦ several
afternoons each week.

West End✦✦

As in many port towns, the wealthy merchants built their homes on
the highest point of land. As a result, Portland's West End managed to
escape the flames of the 1866 conflagration, and it has survived the
economic vicissitudes of much of the 20th century. Now the
showpiece homes of one of the best-preserved Victorian residential
districts in the US sparkle with fresh paint. The West End's
neighbourhood park is the **Western Promenade**✦✦, a landscaped
public walkway along the edge of a west-facing cliff some 175ft above
sea-level, an altitude sufficient that the White Mountains of New
Hampshire are visible in the distance on a clear day. The houses are
the real marvels, and none is more marvellous than **Victoria
Mansion**✦✦, an 1858 Italianate villa of inordinate flamboyance for a
city where extravagance is always suspect. The original owner engaged
an operatic set designer to create the interiors.

Accommodation and food in Portland

Many moderate chain motels line Rtes 1 and 9 south of Portland in
Scarborough and South Portland.

Andrews Lodging $$ *417 Auburn St, Rte 26, Portland; tel: (207) 797-
9157.* Shared cooking and limited laundry facilities help compensate
for distance from city centre in residential area.

Fore Street $$$ *288 Fore St; tel: (207) 775-2717.* Locals favour this
restaurant for its roasted and wood-grilled entrées.

Gilbert's Chowder House $ *92 Commercial St; tel: (207) 871-5636.* This casual spot near the docks is a good bet for chowder and baked fish.

Gritty McDuff's $ *396 Fore St; tel: (207) 772-2739.* Portland's first brew-pub serves English-inspired pub food.

Inn by the Sea $$$ *40 Bowery Beach, Cape Elizabeth; tel: (207) 799-3134.* Striking resort-style complex of one- and two-bedroom condos and two-bedroom suites on Crescent Beach, a short drive from downtown Portland.

Pomegranate Inn $$ *49 Neal St, Portland; tel: (800) 356-0408 or (207) 772-1006.* This 1884 Italianate home and carriage house near the Western Promenade has eight guest rooms.

Portland Regency $$$ *20 Milk St, Portland; tel: (800) 727-3436 or (207) 774-4200.* Posh hotel in an historic armoury sitting in the centre of the Old Port.

Radisson Eastland $$ *157 High St, Portland; tel: (207) 775-5411.* Landmark hotel in Arts District at Congress Sq has 204 rooms on 13 levels.

Street & Company $$$ *33 Wharf St; tel: (207) 775-0887.* This restaurant is known for its innovative fish preparations.

Two Lights Lobster Shack $$ *Two Lights Rd, Cape Elizabeth; tel: (207) 799-1677.* Oceanside picnic tables have a great ocean view.

Wassamki Springs $ *855 Saco St, Westbrook; tel: (207) 839-4276.* Convenient for Portland, this campground for tents, trailers and recreational vehicles (RVs) is sited on a private 30-acre lake.

Suggested walk

Total distance: 3.5 miles

Time: All day. Portland is a safe and compact city where walking is usually easier than driving. This walking tour concentrates on attractions in the Old Port, Arts District and West End.

Route: Begin at the corner of Commercial and Center Sts on the waterfront at the Information Centre, where architecture buffs may wish to purchase inexpensive brochures for four historic walking tours at. Directly across Commercial St is **Fish Pier ❶**, site of the weekday fish auction. Walk three blocks along Commercial St past the working wharves to High St, turn right and walk two blocks to Danforth St, making a half-block detour to **Victoria Mansion ❷**. Continue four blocks up High St to Congress Sq to the **Portland Museum of Art ❸**. The **Children's Museum of Maine ❹** is practically next door on Free St, one block above the Civic Center Auditorium, the city's chief venue for concerts and expositions.

From the front of the Museum of Art, turn left on Congress St, passing through 'Portland's Downtown District' (as the merchants call the Arts District) with several interesting shops and the galleries associated with the Portland School of Art. Congress St meets State St at **Longfellow Sq ❺**, which honours Portland's most famous native son, Henry Wadsworth Longfellow.

Pine St leads off Congress Sq to the left, entering the **WEST END ❻** district of historic homes dating mostly from between 1865 and 1900, Portland's economic high point. Walking the streets perpendicular to Pine (Neal, Vaughn and Chadwick) for their modest four-block length is a pleasant way to tour the neighbourhood. At the end of this cross-hatch lies **Western Promenade ❼**, where stately mansions on one side contrast with long scenic vistas on the other.

Follow Western Promenade to its conclusion. Turn right on Bramhall

Freeport Outlet Malls *tel: (207) 865-1212.*

L L Bean *Main and Bow Sts; tel: (207) 865-4761 is open 24 hours a day.*

Harraseeket Inn $$ *162 Main St; tel: (800) 342-6423 or (207) 865-9377.* Elegant country inn with modern expansions; also boasts exceptional gourmet dining ($$$).

Harraseeket Lunch & Lobster $$ *On the docks; tel: (207) 865-4888.* A good place for dockside dining away from the outlet shopping.

St and right again on Congress St to return to the centre of town. Approximately 1 mile down Congress on the left is **the Wadsworth-Longfellow House ❽**. Continue three blocks down Congress and turn right on to Exchange St, which enters the 'Old Port Exchange', the former centre of shipping offices and warehouses. Portland's main boutique and restaurant district begins two blocks downhill towards the harbour. The warren of small streets and pedestrian walkways eventually leads to Commercial St and the waterfront.

Also worth exploring

Freeport✦✦✦ was once a sleepy town 18 miles north of Portland on either I-95 or Rte 1. Now it is one of the busiest sites in northern New England, thanks to the presence of more than 110 **factory outlet stores✦✦**. The legendary outdoors outfitter, **L L Bean✦✦✦**, opened here long before the outlets (1905) and continues to hold its own with every imaginable item for a walk in the park or an expedition into the back woods.

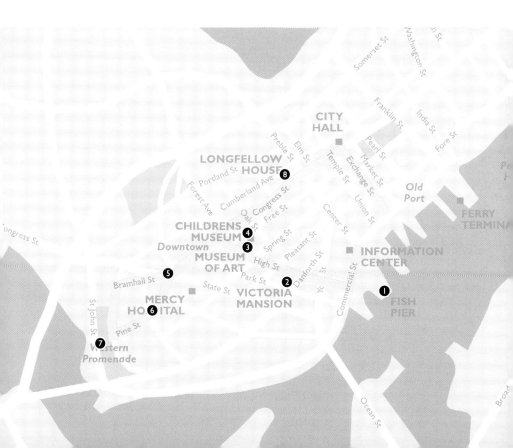

Midcoast Maine

Ratings

Nature/scenery	●●●●●
Arts and culture	●●○○○
Beaches	●●○○○
Food and drink	●●○○○
History	●●○○○
Shopping	●●○○○
Children	●○○○○
Museums	●○○○○

Between Casco Bay and Penobscot Bay, the Maine coast fragments into hundreds of miles of long, narrow peninsulas that dangle off the mainland like a hank of crooked parsnips. With a stony and barren beauty, each peninsula harbours tiny villages where lobstering, clam digging and scallop-dragging remain a dominant way of life. Route 1 joins the larger towns and villages at the mouths of rivers that once flowed with huge timber booms, and most travellers stay on this route towards Acadia National Park farther north. But the midcoast is most rewarding to those who like to wander, to follow a twisting road down to the tip of a granite peninsula for the sheer exhilaration of watching the waves crash angrily on long grey ledges. Attractions, per se, are sparse. The look and feel of the place is everything.

BATH✧✧

ⓘ Bath-Brunswick Region Chamber of Commerce Tourist Information Center *Rte 1 N; tel: (207) 443-9751* provides information about Bath and neighbouring Brunswick.

ⓗ Maine Maritime Museum $$ *243 Washington St; tel: (207) 443-1316. Open daily 0930–1700.*

In an area of fishermen and sailors, Bath is a sprawling industrial town of riveters and steel workers. It began as a port for shipping mast timbers for the King's Navy, and at one point more than 200 Bath shipyards built nearly half of America's wooden ships. The **Maine Maritime Museum✧✧** deals in depth with this history. Its late 19th-century shipyard buildings trace the process of creating a wooden ship from preliminary designs to launch, and several historic boats can be toured at anchor. Now Bath makes destroyers for the US Navy. Excursion boat tours offered by the museum travel upriver to **Bath Iron Works✧**, where it's not unusual to see several large naval warships in for renovation.

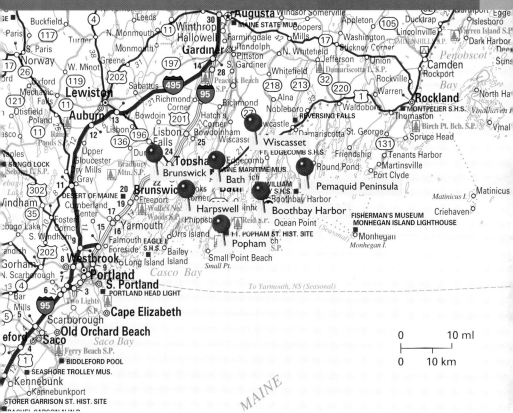

BOOTHBAY HARBOR✧✧

ⓘ Boothbay Region Chamber of Commerce Rte 27; tel: (207) 633-2353.

ⓒ Balmy Days Cruises $$–$$$ Pier 8; tel: (207) 633-2284. Offers harbour tours and supper cruises aboard motor launch or 1.5-hour sails on 31-ft sloop.

The self-styled yachting capital of **Boothbay Harbor✧✧** has been a summer resort community since 1870, and its popularity has earned it the best access highway of any town at the end of a midcoast peninsula. Souvenir shops and boutiques sit cheek-by-jowl in the harbourfront town, but some of the most scenic areas require drives (or bicycle rides) southwest to Southport Island, ringed with lighthouses, or east to Linekin Neck, where the single road overlooks favourite basking ledges of harbour and grey seals.

Boothbay Harbor's protected waters are a fine yachting anchorage and fishing-boat captains at the docks offer deep-sea fishing excursions when the tuna are running. The waters surrounding Boothbay peninsula are best appreciated from a boat, and Boothbay Harbor has no shortage of sightseeing cruises, ranging from half-day sails aboard the 64-ft schooner *Appledore✧✧* (*Fisherman's Wharf; tel: (207) 633-6598*) to naturalist trips aboard the boats of **Cap'n Fish's Whale Watch and Scenic Nature Cruises✧✧** (*Pier 1; tel: (207) 633-3244*).

Accommodation and food in Boothbay

1830 Admiral's Quarters Inn Bed & Breakfast $–$$ *71 Commercial St, Boothbay Harbor; tel: (207) 633-2474.* The six guest rooms in a renovated sea captain's home have decks overlooking the harbour.

Ebb Tide $–$$ *67 Commercial St; tel: (207) 633-5692.* This diner serves breakfast all day and also offers good chowder and home-made pies.

Linekin Bay Resort $$ *92 Wall Point Rd, East Boothbay; tel: (207) 633-2494.* This coastal resort has five lodges and thirty cabins. Rates include use of sailboats and three meals a day.

Spruce Point Inn $$$ *Grandview Ave, Boothbay Harbor; tel: (800) 553-0289 or (207) 633-4152.* There is a broad variety of lodging choices in this turn-of-the-century inn with tennis courts, spa and pools. Rates include breakfast and dinner. With a fabulous ocean view and an elegant New American menu, the dining-room ($$–$$$) ranks among Maine's best.

BRUNSWICK✣✣

Bowdoin College Museum of Art
Walker Art Bldg, Main St; tel: (207) 725-3275. Free admission. *Open Tue–Sat 1000–1700, Sun 1400–1700.*

Peary-MacMillan Arctic Museum *Hubbard Hall, Main St; tel: (207) 725-3000.* Free admission. *Open Tue–Sat 1000–1700, Sun 1400–1700.*

Miss Brunswick Diner $ *101 Pleasant St; tel: (207) 729-5948.* Heavily remodelled diner remains a good place for simple food and rather surprising Tex-Mex specialities.

Maine Festival of the Arts *tel: (207) 772-9012.* Four-day event in early Aug celebrates the variety of Maine creativity – from dance and theatre to comedy, visual arts to folk arts, literary arts to storytelling.

This handsome town of sea captains' mansions is dominated by the park-like campus of Bowdoin College, Maine's first college of genteel education and alma mater of Nathaniel Hawthorne, Henry Wadsworth Longfellow and Arctic explorers Robert Peary and Donald MacMillan. The **Bowdoin College Museum of Art**✣✣ is noted for Winslow Homer, Andrew Wyeth and late 19th- and early 20th-century American paintings. The **Peary-MacMillan Arctic Museum**✣✣ pays tribute to the adventurers with a variety of artefacts, including the instruments with which Peary made the controversial 1909 observations to claim he had reached the North Pole.

Pemaquid Peninsula's uplifted shales

HARPSWELL*

Harpswell Inn $–$$
*141 Lookout Point Rd;
tel: (207) 833-5509.* This
1761 inn offers relative
sophistication in a
decidedly unsophisticated
region.

Lying due south from Brunswick on Rte 123, the town of Harpswell gathers seven villages and forty-five islands under a single place name. Except for the odd painter or poet, most residents earn their living from trapping lobsters and catching fish with hand lines from small boats. **Harpswell Neck***✴ is a narrow granite peninsula where Rte 123 connects the four largest villages. A bridge from North Harpswell joins the peninsula to the scenic island villages of **Great, Orr's and Bailey islands**✴.

Food in Harpswell

Cook's Lobster House $$ *Garrison Cove Rd; tel: (207) 833-6641* and **Estes Lobster House $$** *Rte 123; tel: (207) 833-6340* are both large seafood houses supplied by local fishermen. Cook's has the better view, but Estes is famous for their triple lobster plate.

PEMAQUID PENINSULA✴✴✴

**Pemaquid
Fishermen's
Museum $** *Pemaquid Pt
Lighthouse; no tel. Open late
May–early Sept 1000–1700.*

The Pemaquid peninsula is perhaps the most scenic and low-key of all the well-travelled parts of Maine's midcoast. **Damariscotta**✴, at the head of the peninsula, is bypassed by Rte 1, leaving intact a charming village renowned for 2000 years for its exquisite oysters – the Abenaki tribe left behind 20 centuries of shell middens. Some of the shells were as large as plates.

A dozen miles south at **Pemaquid Point**✴✴✴, interlaced streaks of granite and black lava produce some of the coast's most dramatic shoreline. Atop the promontory is Pemaquid Point Light, so quintessential an image that it frequently adorns tourism literature. The base of the 1827 lighthouse holds the **Pemaquid Fishermen's Museum**✴.

Accommodation and food on Pemaquid Peninsula

Newcastle Inn $$ *60 River Rd, Newcastle; tel: (800) 832-8669 or (207) 563-5685.* Federal-style inn on the Damariscotta River has 15 guest rooms, some with fireplaces. The creative French-influenced dining-room (**$$$**) excels at preparing local fish.

Sea Gull Shop $–$$ *Pemaquid Pt; tel: (207) 677-2374.* This combination restaurant and souvenir shop makes good casual use of local provender in blueberry French toast, crisp fried clams and meaty crab rolls.

Shaw's Fish and Lobster Wharf Restaurant $$ *New Harbor; tel: (207) 677-2200.* A fishlover's nirvana, Shaw's is the best among hundreds of Maine's 'in the rough' seafood restaurants serving local lobster, crab and finfish at picnic tables next to the boats that caught dinner.

POPHAM❖

Fort Popham State Historic Site *Rte 209; tel: (207) 389-1335. Free admission. Open late May–Sept 0900–dusk.*

Popham Beach State Park $ *Rte 209; no tel. Open late May–Sept 0900–dusk.*

Popham was the site of the first English colony in New England (1606) as well as the spot where colonists built the first ocean-going vessel (1607) so they could rush home after the first brutal Maine winter. Archaeological excavations of the Popham Colony are nearly complete, and a small exhibit inside **Fort Popham**❖ tells the tale of these '120 knights, gentlemen, merchants, and other adventurers'. The fortress's circular staircases rise to towers with sweeping views, including the white beaches of nearby **Popham Beach State Park**❖❖, one of the few places in Maine with soft beaches and large waves for surfing.

WISCASSET❖❖

Nickels-Sortwell House $ *Main and Federal Sts; tel: (207) 882-6218. Tours given June–Sept Wed–Sun 1300–1600.*

Musical Wonder House $$ *18 High St; tel: (800) 336-3725. Tours given late May–Oct daily at 1100, 1300 and 1500.*

Known among frequent drivers of Maine coastal roads as 'the prettiest little bottleneck on Rte 1', Wiscasset is a veritable architectural museum of late 18th- and early 19th-century architecture and its downtown is lined with antiques shops, cafés and art potters. The **Nickels-Sortwell House**❖ reflects the fortunes of Wiscasset's sea-trade days, which came to a crashing halt with the Embargo Act of 1807, the year the house was built. Tours include impressive period gardens. The **Musical Wonder House**❖❖ is less historic, but endlessly entertaining, with player pianos and music boxes from around the world.

Accommodation and food in Wiscasset

Edgecomb Inn $–$$ *306 Eddy Rd, Edgecomb; tel: (207) 882-9586.* Technically across the Sheepscot River in Edgecomb, this combination of motel rooms, cottages and self-catering units has striking views of Wiscasset harbour.

Red's Eats $ *foot of Main and Water Sts; no tel.* Classic tiny food stand serves outstanding lobster and crab rolls.

Sea Basket $–$$ *Rte 1; tel: (207) 882-6581.* Unpretentious diner known for its lobster stew.

Above
Cooking up a classic lobster
'bake' of steamed lobster and
corn in wet seaweed

Lobsters

Once so plentiful that they could be picked up off the beaches, the Maine lobster (*Homarus americanus*) was considered fit food only for prisons, poorhouses, orphanages and servants. Not until the 1940s did lobster begin to evolve as a 'gourmet' seafood in New England. The crustacean now fetches a high price because almost all of Maine's 20-million-lb annual catch (more than half the US haul) is harvested by small-boat fishermen tending heavy wooden or wire traps.

Lobsters are at their sweetest in June, before shedding their shells in early July. Most New England lobsters are relative youngsters, weighing 1.25–1.75lbs, a size of maximum flavour. Traditionally, lobster is boiled or steamed and served with corn on the cob, boiled potatoes and copious quantities of drawn butter.

Suggested tour

Friendship Museum
$ Rte 220; no
telephone. Open July–early
Sept 1300–1600.

Moody's Diner $
Rte 1, Waldoboro; tel:
(207) 832-7468. Every
trucker stops at Moody's
for good road food at
reasonable prices.

Edgecomb Potters
Rte 27, Edgecomb, tel:
(207) 882-6802 create
high-fire porcelain with
rich glazes and display
high-quality work by other
Maine artists working in
craft media.

Total distance: 117 miles; 196 miles with detours

Time: 4–5 hours' driving. Allow 2–3 days.

Links: Connects via Rte 1 to Portland Route on southern end, via Rte 1 to Penobscot Bay Route on northern end.

Route: The route barely begins before there are a couple of good reasons to depart from it. Begin at Pleasant St (Rte 1) in **BRUNSWICK** ❶, 6 miles north of Freeport (I-95, exit 22). Main St intersects in 1 mile, with Bowdoin College and fine Federal homes south of Rte 1.

Detour: Main St turns into Rte 123, Harpswell Rd, for a drive 13 miles through the rural fishing villages on the **HARPSWELL** ❷ peninsula. To reach **Orr's and Bailey's islands** ❸, backtrack 7 miles to the Ewin Narrows Rd bridge, explore the islands on Rte 24S, then return 15 miles north to Rte 1 via Rte 24.

Route 1 continues 5 miles into the centre of the active shipbuilding town of **BATH** ❹.

Detour: Rte 209 leads south from Bath for 15 scenic miles to **POPHAM** ❺ to visit the site of the first English colony in New England, or to swim or surf the high waves at **Popham Beach State Park** ❻, one of the few sandy beaches on the midcoast.

Back on Rte 1, cross the drawbridge from Bath to Woolrich and continue 10 miles to **WISCASSET** ❼. Two miles north, turn right on Rte 27. Two miles south on Rte 27 is the excellent art pottery, **Edgecomb Potters**✹✹ ❽. **BOOTHBAY HARBOR** ❾ lies another 9 miles south on Rte 27. To see the peninsula's more rural side, return north 4 miles on Rte 27 and turn right on to River Rd, continuing north along the scenic banks of the Damariscotta River to join Rte 1B in Newcastle. Cross the old bridge in the village of Damariscotta, and turn right to drive south on the **PEMAQUID PENINSULA** ❿ for 3 miles on Bristol Rd (Rtes 129 and 130). At the fork, veer left on Rte 130 and continue 13.5 miles to Pemaquid Point. Double back via Rte 130 for 3.5 miles, then turn right on to Rte 32. This road passes through a string of small fishing villages separated by meadows and woodlands along the Muscongus Bay as it winds along the coast for 20 miles to rejoin Rte 1 in **Waldoboro** ⓫✹, another erstwhile shipbuilding centre now known for its antiques dealers, landmark diner and strict enforcement of the speed limit. At the bottom of the hill in Waldoboro, Rte 220 heads south for 10 miles into the village of **Friendship**✹ ⓬, a fishing community noted for its boatbuilding since the 1750s. The Friendship sloop, an unusually responsive vessel created for the difficult conditions of Maine's peninsular waters, originated here and a 'homecoming' race of the sloops is held each July. The 1851 one-room schoolhouse holds the quirky **Friendship Museum** ✲ **⑰**, with extensive boat construction and local history exhibits. Route 220 circles back northward and rejoins Rte 1 at South Warren, 1 mile west of Thomaston and the beginning of the Penobscot Bay.

Also worth exploring

The Maine coast is dotted with literally thousands of islands, but few have the allure of **Monhegan Island**✲✲✲, which has been a 15th- and 16th-century base for Basque fishermen, a 17th-century French–English battleground, an 18th-century pirate's lair, and one of New England's most successful fishing communities for the last 250 years. Beginning around 1905, it also became a seasonal retreat for many of America's most distinguished artists. Monhegan closes its commercial fishing in the summer and folks with easels and brushes take over. Many species of birds alight here and whales favour Monhegan's coastal waters. Only 12 miles offshore, Monhegan can be reached by passenger boat year-round from Port Clyde, and in the summer from Boothbay Harbor and New Harbor.

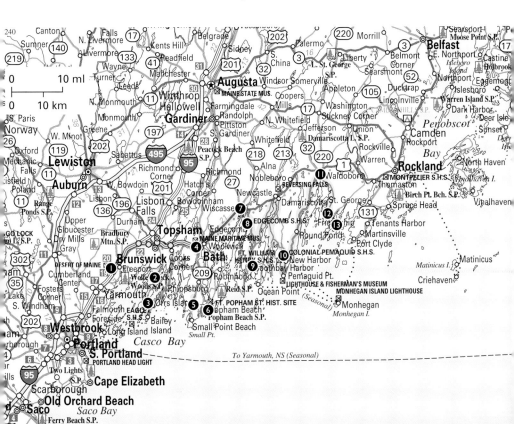

Penobscot Bay

Ratings

Nature/scenery	●●●●●
Arts and culture	●●●●○
History	●●●●○
Museums	●●●○○
Children	●●○○○
Shopping	●●○○○
Beaches	●○○○○
Food and drink	●○○○○

The deep cleft of Penobscot Bay divides the Maine coast in two. The march of hills from inland Maine suddenly snaps off into deep harbours on the western shore, where the little towns demonstrate that good things come in small packages. From the hard-working commercial port of Rockland, with its fleet of cruising schooners, to Searsport, the last shipmasters' capital of the age of sail, the high road on the western shore offers nearly uninterrupted vistas of the bay's spruce-tufted islands. Striking Federal, Greek Revival and Italianate homes in every town attest to the 19th-century wealth of these communities. Most travellers overlook the eastern shore, formed by Cape Rosier, Deer Isle and the Blue Hill peninsula. But its labyrinth of twisting rural roads leading past long hay fields and blueberry barrens delivers the patient traveller into picturesque yachting and lobstering harbours.

BELFAST*

ℹ Belfast Area Chamber of Commerce $$$ *31 Front St; tel: (207) 338-5900.*

ⓢ Belfast and Moosehead Lake Railroad $$$ *Public Landing, Belfast; 1 Depot Sq, Unity; tel: (800) 392-5500 or (207) 948-5500.*

Belfast has reclaimed its genteel elegance of a century ago, when the small city was inhabited by retired sea captains who sat in their Federal and Greek Revival manses surrounded by Oriental porcelains and counted their money. Favoured as a residence by writers, artists and craftspeople, Belfast is one of the less expensive and less crowded bases for touring the Penobscot Bay region. Not all of Belfast tries to be chic. **The Belfast and Moosehead Lake Railroad*** runs hugely popular steam train excursions (often with staged train robberies) through the Waldo County countryside to Unity. Special foliage runs are offered in late September.

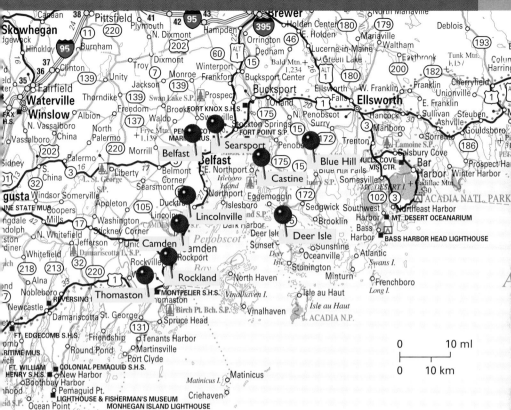

Accommodation and food in Belfast

Harbor View House of 1807 $–$$ *139 High St; tel: (207) 338-2244.* Restored Federal house with antiques shop on the premises has great views of Penobscot Bay.

Jeweled Turret Inn $$ *16 Pearl St; tel: (207) 338-2304.* Unique architectural features and craftsmanship set this B&B apart.

Young's Lobster Pound $–$$ *Mitchell Ave, off Rte 1; tel: (207) 338-1160.* Lobster fresh off the boat or cooked to order for take-away.

BLUE HILL**

So many New Yorkers spend the summer in Blue Hill that the *New York Times* outsells the local daily paper and the spiffy little country village has an air of Central Park West. Blue Hill is well known for its art galleries and art potters, of which **Rackcliffe Pottery** and **Rowantree Pottery** welcome visitors. For a good take on the Blue Hill

Rowantree Pottery *Union St (Rte 177); tel: (207) 374-5535* has been making functional tableware with local clays and minerals since the 1930s. **Rackcliffe Pottery** *Ellsworth Rd (Rte 172); tel: (207) 374-2297* continues the tradition with more contemporary design.

Blue Hill Fair *tel: (207) 374-3701.* Highlights of this traditional country fair include agricultural and livestock exhibits, a blueberry pie eating contest and the pig scramble.

(counter-) culture, tune in to WERU at 88.9FM, a homespun radio station promulgating 'dangerous' ideas and local singer-songwriter music.

Accommodation and food in Blue Hill

Blue Hill Inn $$–$$$ *Union St (Rte 177), Blue Hill; tel: (207) 374-2844.* This inn dates from 1840, Blue Hill's shipping heyday, and, while beautifully maintained, shows its age with creaky floors and walls out of plumb. Rates include full board. The dining-room (**$$$**) serves an exquisite three- or five-course fixed French menu.

Left Bank Bakery and Café $ *Ellsworth Rd (Rte 172); tel: (207) 374-2201.* Acoustic musicians perform several nights a week, while diners enjoy fresh breads, soups and salads.

CAMDEN****

🛈 **Rockport-Camden-Lincolnville Chamber of Commerce** *Public Landing; tel: (800) 223-5459 or (207) 236-4404* provides information for all three towns.

🎟 **Lively Lady Too $$$** *Bayview Landing; tel: (207) 236-6672.* Motor yacht makes 3- and 6-hour cruises of Penobscot Bay.

🏛 **Camden Hills State Park $** *Rte 1; tel: (207) 236-3109.* Mount Battie Auto Road *open May–Oct.*

🎨 **Camden Art Show** *tel: (207) 236-4404.* Juried outdoor exhibition of local painters is held in the third weekend of July.

Wedged between the tall Camden Hills and a stunning, bowl-like harbour, Camden is almost too pretty to be believed – when it can be seen through the crowds. One of the most popular destinations on the Maine coast, Camden has a bustling shopping district of boutiques, old-fashioned shops, art galleries, art supply stores and outdoors gear shops. A few excursion schooners still operate from Camden, but the harbour is usually so thick with private motor yachts that one could walk from one shore to another on their decks. Two miles north of the village on Rte 1, **Camden Hills State Park**✷ has 30 miles of hiking trails. Both hiking trails and a toll road ascend Mount Battie, a peak with sweeping views of Penobscot Bay all the way to the mountains of Mount Desert Island.

Accommodation and food in Camden

Blackberry Inn $$ *82 Elm St; tel: (800) 388-6000 or (207) 236-6060.* This colourful Victorian home with ten guest rooms is within walking distance of downtown Camden and the harbour.

High Tide Inn $–$$ *Rte 1; tel: (800) 778-7068 or (207) 236-3724.* Lodging choices include motel units and lodge rooms at this 7-acre property with a private beach.

Lobster Stu's $–$$ *Sharp's Wharf; tel: (207) 236-8763.* The place to go for a simple lobster dinner.

Mama & Leenie's $ *27 Elm St; tel: (207) 236-6300.* Bakery-café has good soups and salads and great cookies.

Swan House $–$$ *49 Mountain St; tel: (207) 236-8275.* Six-room Victorian B&B sitting at the foot of Mount Battie.

CASTINE✷

🏛 **Maine Maritime Academy** *tel: (207) 326-4311.* Call for schedule of tours of *State of Maine* when it is in port.

Walking the sleepy, elm-arched streets of Castine, it's hard to believe that so many regional and world powers have fought over it since the 1600s: Castine's been under French, English, Dutch, Canadian and American flags. During the American Revolution, British sloops-of-war handed the American Navy a humiliating defeat and occupied the town from 1779 until 1783. Following the peace treaty, British loyalists floated their homes on barges to St-Andrews-by-the-Sea, New Brunswick. As a result, most of Castine's finest houses date from the 19th century. The main action in town focuses on the **Maine Maritime Academy**, which trains merchant marine officers. Cadets conduct tours of the 499-ft training vessel ***State of Maine***✷✷.

Accommodation and food in Castine

Castine Inn $$ *Main St; tel: (207) 326-4365.* Some of the 20 rooms in this old inn have harbour views. The dining-room (**$$**) features regional American cuisine, such as a smoky lobster stew and roast venison.

Dennett's Wharf $–$$ *Sea St; tel: (207) 326-9045.* Seafood dinners are the speciality of this bar and restaurant right on the docks.

DEER ISLE❖❖

🔁 **Isle-au-Haut Boat Company $$$**
Seabreeze Ave, Stonington; tel: (207) 367-5193. Offers year-round ferry service to the island.

⬆ **Isle-au-Haut Turtle Gallery** *Deer Isle village; tel: (207) 348-9977.* Excellent fine art in crafts media.

Terrell S. Lester Photography Gallery *Deer Isle village; tel: (207) 348-2676.* Fine-arts photography by Lester and other artists.

In just a 5-mile stretch, Deer Isle epitomises the cultural dichotomy of this region. The village of **Deer Isle**❖❖ is chock-a-block full of art galleries, not surprising since the famed **Haystack Mountain School of Crafts** is just outside town. At the southern end of the island in **Stonington**❖❖, lobster fishermen in gum-boots rule the roost. Deer Isle is tranquil and idyllic, Stonington gritty and authentic – it's the home of the Maine Lobstermen's Association. Stonington is also the departure point for boats to the scenic **Isle au Haut**❖, part of Acadia National Park and a superb spot for sighting pelagic birds.

Accommodation and food on Deer Isle

Bay View Restaurant $–$$ *Seabreeze Ave, Stonington; tel: (207) 367-2274.* Quintessential Maine coastal fare, from grilled cheese sandwiches on spongy white bread to transporting lobster stews.

Eaton's Lobster Pool $–$$ *Blastow Cove, Little Deer Isle; tel: (207) 348-2383.* Shore dinners are available to eat at picnic tables or take-away.

Inn on the Harbor $$ *Main St, Stonington; tel: (207) 367-2420.* This casual lodging, where rooms share an excellent deck, actually juts out into Stonington harbour amid the lobster boats and scallop draggers.

LINCOLNVILLE❖

🔁 **Maine State Ferry $** *Lincolnville Beach; tel: (207) 789-5611.* Year-round passenger and auto service to Islesboro.

Right
King Neptune and the Maine Lobster Queen at the annual Maine Lobster Festival

Lincolnville is effectively two communities, one an inland farming village near beautiful lakes, the other a wide spot on Rte 1 where Ducktrap River flows into Penobscot Bay. **Kelmscott Farm**❖❖ is dedicated to preserving heirloom livestock breeds such as Cotswold sheep and Gloucester Old Spot pigs. **Lincolnville Beach**❖ on Rte 1 is a surprisingly good if tiny ocean swimming beach. Ferry service to **Islesboro**❖ departs at its south end. Just 1.5 miles offshore, Islesboro has a year-round fishing village and a summer village of huge 'cottages' handed down in wealthy families. The island is fun to

Kelmscott Farm $ Van Cycle Rd (off Rte 52); tel: (207) 763-4088. Open Tue–Sun 1000–1700 in summer, to 1500 in winter.

Maine Lobster Festival tel: (207) 596-0376. The 4-day event in early August is a New England classic, featuring a parade, boat rides, the crowning of the Lobster Queen and lobster dinners.

explore by bicycle. The rocky town 'beach' at Pendleton Point is often a good place to watch grey seals catching mackerel close to shore.

Accommodation and food in Lincolnville

The Mount Battie $–$$ *Rte 1, Lincolnville; tel: (800) 224-3870 or (207) 236-3870.* The decks of this 21-unit motel have great views of Penobscot Bay.

Lobster Pound Restaurant $$ *Lincolnville Beach; tel: (207) 789-5550.* Crack open a lobster and watch families play on the beach while ferries shuttle to Islesboro.

Ducktrap River Fish Farm $ *57 Little River Dr; tel: (207) 338-6280* sell their own smoked fish and seafood pâtés for take-away.

ROCKLAND***

ⓘ Rockland-Thomaston Area Chamber of Commerce Harbor Park; tel: (800) 562-2529 or (207) 596-0376. Chamber provides listings of windjammer cruise operators.

ⓣ Farnsworth Art Museum and Wyeth Center $$ 352 Main St; tel: (207) 596-6457. Open late May–mid Oct daily 0900–1700, remainder of year Tue–Sat 1000–1700, Sun 1300–1700.

Shore Village Museum $ 104 Limerock St; tel: (207) 594-0311. Open June–mid Oct daily 1000–1600.

While not as pretty as neighbouring Camden, Rockland has more substance. Its working harbour is spiked with the masts of 'windjammer' excursion schooners and dotted with squat trawlers and lobster boats. Moreover, it has one of the finest small art museums in New England. The **Farnsworth Art Museum and Wyeth Center***** emphasises Maine's place in American art with works by Fitz Hugh Lane, Winslow Homer, Edward Hopper, Milton Avery, Childe Hassam, Rockwell Kent and Louise Nevelson. The Center for the Wyeth Family opened in 1998 to hold the personal art collection of painter Andrew and his wife Betsy. The Farnsworth also opens the Olson House (where Wyeth studied and painted for more than three decades) to tours late May–mid Oct. Rockland's local history centre, the **Shore Village Museum***, displays a huge collection of lighthouse artefacts, including foghorns, bells and lenses as big as 6ft across. The giftshop sells more than 400 lighthouse postcards. Windjammer cruises must be booked 6 months or more in advance, but boats can be viewed at the public landing Sat evenings and Sun mornings.

Accommodation and food in Rockland

Café Miranda $–$$ 15 Oak St; tel: (207) 594-2034. Casual dining with Mediterranean flair.

Old Granite Inn $–$$ 546 Main St; tel: (800) 386-9036 or (207) 594-9036. Smoke-free lodging with 11 guest rooms near downtown and adjacent to ferry dock.

Windjammer cruises

The excursion boats sailing from Rockland, Camden and Rockport known generically as 'windjammers' are typically old three-masted coasting schooners built for the unglamorous trade of hauling stone and timber along the Atlantic seaboard. Because their cargoes were not time-sensitive and the boats were cheap to run, these old schooners stayed afloat when larger sailing ships were cut down to serve as barges. Accommodation on the windjammers varies, especially between the historic boats and some of the newly constructed ones. Few offer many luxuries; most have very tight sleeping quarters and rather crude toilet facilities. But they make up in romance what they lack in comfort, and most week-long sails are fully booked six to eight months in advance. Non-sailors can glimpse the beauty of the windjammers when several of them converge in Castine harbour or gather together to spend the night in the lee of Sears Island, visible south of Searsport from Rte 1.

SEARSPORT✧✧✧

ⓘ **Searsport &
Stockton Springs
Chamber of
Commerce** *Main St; tel:
(207) 548-6510.*

ⓜ **Penobscot Marine
Museum $** *Church St
and Rte 1; tel: (207) 548-
2529. Open late May–mid
Oct Mon–Sat 1000–1700,
Sun 1200–1700.*

ⓢ **Searsport Antique
Mall** *Rte 1; tel: (207)
548-2640.* The best group
shop in a town that used
to call itself the 'antiques
capital' of Maine. Many
other individual and group
shops are also found along
Rte 1.

Between its antiques dealers and its maritime memories, Searsport dwells almost entirely in the past. During the last third of the 19th century, nearly one American deepwater sea captain in ten called Searsport home, and its behemoth 'Downeasters', the largest wooden sailing vessels ever built, dominated transoceanic trade. The bold adventure of that last great Age of Sail reverberates at the **Penobscot Marine Museum✧✧✧**. Nine historic buildings display paintings, photographs, ship models (and even some small craft), along with China Trade art and artefacts. One wall features portraits of nearly 300 Searsport overseas trading captains. Many of the captains' capacious mansions now serve as B&Bs, making it a handsome town to tour.

Accommodation and food in Searsport

Captain A V Nickels Inn $–$$ *Rte 1; tel: (800) 343-5001 or (207) 548-6691.* Grand former sea captain's home with alluring front porch and ocean frontage on Penobscot Bay.

Colonial Gables $ *Rte 1; tel: (207) 338-4000.* Motel and self-catering cottages from 1940s with private beach overlook Penobscot Bay between Searsport and Belfast.

Jordan's $ *Main St; tel: (207) 548-2555.* Where locals head for fried fish and other home-style cooking.

Nickerson Tavern $$ *Rte 1; tel: (207) 548-2220.* Contemporary American cuisine using fresh local fish and produce.

Searsport Shores $ *216 W Main St, Searsport; tel: (207) 548-6059.* Campground with private beach organises daytrips and other activities for guests.

THOMASTON*

Maine Watercraft Museum $ *Knox St Landing; tel: (207) 354-0444. Open late May–Sept, Wed–Sun 1000–1700.*

Waterman's Beach Lobster $–$$ *Waterman's Beach Rd; tel: (207) 594-2489.* Eat lobster at a picnic table on a planked deck at the ocean's edge: a classic local pleasure.

First founded in 1630 and re-established in 1736, Thomaston is the oldest community for many miles around. Its era of vast wealth (*circa* 1800) is long gone, and the town has returned to its roots as a fishing and boatbuilding centre. Thomaston is easily bypassed, but is worth driving through to view some of the stateliest Colonial homes north of Newburyport. The **Maine Watercraft Museum***, on the site of many famous Thomaston shipyards, displays more than 100 antique and classic small craft built in Maine prior to 1960.

Suggested tour

Total distance: 135 miles, 155 miles with detours

Time: 4 hours' driving. Allow 2–3 days.

Links: Connects via Rte 1 to Midcoast Maine Route on southern end, via Rtes 72 and 3 to Mount Desert Island Route on northern end.

Route: Begin on Rte 1 in **THOMASTON** ❶, where the bluffs on the east side of town mark the southwest opening of Penobscot Bay. A 46-mile drive of striking beauty begins 4 miles north in **ROCKLAND** ❷. The high hills on one side of Rte 1 and the long meadows reaching to the sea on the other make even the worst summer traffic bearable. From Rockland continue 6 miles to duck into the one-cove village of **Rockport*** ❸, an artists' town with a good gallery and pretty harbour, then 2 miles into the solid wall of excited humanity on the streets of **CAMDEN** ❹. Rte 1 rises and turns to the right as it leaves Camden, passing handsome 19th-century inns and a stone castle before reaching open country with long views in the 6 miles to **LINCOLNVILLE** ❺ Beach.

Detour: The 15-minute ferry crossing to Islesboro is a scenic (if short) trip, well rewarded by the views from points all around the island. Route 1 climbs a long hill past modest homes as it leaves Lincolnville

Beach and rises to a high ridge above the sea that continues 13 miles north to **BELFAST** ❻. After crossing the Passagassawaukeag River (the view of Belfast harbour from the bridge is spectacular), Rte 1 continues north 7 miles to **SEARSPORT** ❼ with views of ledges and cliffs along the way. The landscape begins to change further north as it approaches the **Penobscot River gorge**✦✦ ❽. Just before the bridge, pull into the scenic turnout to view this deep gorge where eagles and ospreys are often seen fishing and where the Royal Navy upstart Americans in 1779. Cross into Bucksport and drive 2 miles to a right turn on to Rte 175. When 175 splits left in 7.8 miles, continue straight on Rte 166 into **CASTINE** ❾. Leave Castine by Rte 166N, turning right on Rte 199, then right again on Rte 175S, which is shortly joined by Rte 15S after a total of 17 miles. The high point of the road reveals a classic panorama: a foreground of blueberry barrens, a mid-ground of Penobscot Bay and its islands, and a background of the Camden Hills. In 8 miles, Rte 15 leads across the Eggemoggin Reach to **DEER ISLE** ❿. After crossing back to the mainland, turn right on to Rte 175 (Reach Rd) and follow it generally north and east approximately 25 miles to **BLUE HILL** ⓫. Route 172 from the centre of the village extends 10 miles northeast to Rts 1 and 3 at Ellsworth.

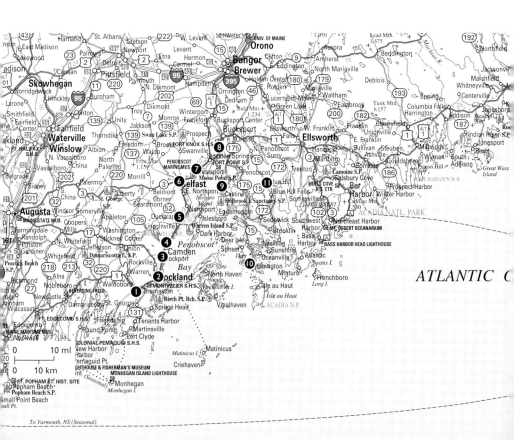

Mount Desert Island

Ratings

Nature/scenery	●●●●●
Children	●●●●
Food and drink	●●●●
Beaches	●●●
Shopping	●●●
History	●●
Museums	●●
Arts and culture	●

At 108 square miles, Mount Desert (pronounced 'dessert' by the locals) is the third largest island on the US Atlantic coast and the most dramatic. Its landscape consists of deep glacial valleys and over 15 rocky-topped granite mountains rising straight up from the sea. Nearly half the island is devoted to Acadia National Park, which draws 2.5 million visitors a year to this part of New England. Shaped like a lobster claw with its pincers divided by the fiord of Somes Sound, Mount Desert's awe-inspiring rough beauty is punctuated with small pockets of intense human activity. Bar Harbor functions as the principal shopping, lodging and dining town, its human bustle a counterpoint to the park's natural idylls. The boatbuilding centre of Southwest Harbor and the fishing village of Bass Harbor are less inundated with crowds but no less beautiful.

ACADIA NATIONAL PARK***

ⓘ Hulls Cove Visitor Center *off Rte 3 at Park Loop Rd; tel: (207) 288-3338. Open May–Oct.* **Acadia National Park Headquarters** *Rte 233 near Eagle Lake. PO Box 177, Bar Harbor; tel: (207) 288-3338. Open Nov–Apr. Day-use fee $ per person, $$ per automobile. Ranger-led activities are detailed in the Beaver Log, available June–Sept.*

Dedicated fans of the outdoors can (and do) spend entire seasons in Acadia without exhausting its attractions. More than 120 miles of hiking trails ascend every summit and traverse every valley, and the gladed woods are penetrated by nearly 56 miles of carriage roads ideally suited to walking, bicycling, horse-riding and cross-country skiing.

The easiest, and therefore the most travelled, way to sample the coast and the interior of Acadia is by driving the **Park Loop Rd***. In the course of its 27 hilly miles, the road passes virtually all the better-known highlights of the park. The entrance to the one-way circuit lies off Rte 3 at the **Hulls Cove Visitors Center**, an essential stop to learn about ranger-led mountain hikes, campfire talks and nature walks. Highlights include **Sieur de Monts Spring** where a nature centre and wildflower gardens offer a good orientation to some of Acadia's more obvious but diverse flora. Sharing the parking area, the

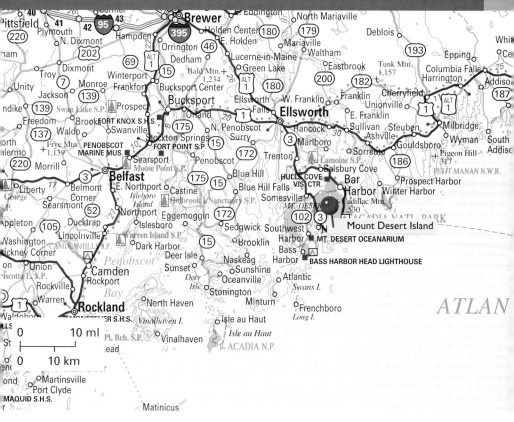

ATLAN

Tour buses $$
Several bus tour companies departing from Agarmont Park in Bar Harbor offer narrated tours of Acadia that last 2–3 hours. Stops are limited and sightseeing is rushed, but they save the frustrations of driving in park traffic.

Acadia Tape Tour $$
available for rent or purchase at Hulls Cove Visitor Center, provides detailed, narrated directions on cassette tape for a 56-mile driving tour through the park. The tape tour is extremely well researched and presented.

Abbe Museum⁕⁕ (Sieur de Monts Spring; tel: (207) 288-2179; open mid May, June, Sept, Oct daily 1000–1600, July, Aug daily 0900–1700). chronicles the Abenaki Indian culture and history of the region over the past 2000 years, with particularly strong coverage of the interactions of Native and European peoples since 1750.

Park Loop Rd passes **Champlain Mountain**⁕, where peregrine falcons nest from May to Aug, and quickly reaches seaside cliffs and **Sand Beach**⁕⁕, a broad bathing beach with coarse brown sand and waters that rarely rise above 12°C (54°F).

Although famous, **Thunder Hole**⁕ lives up to its name only when the three-quarter rising tide coincides with rough seas. Under those conditions, wave motion creates smashing thunderclaps inside hollow rocks at the shore. Nearby **Otter Cliff**⁕⁕, pounded by relentless surf, and **Otter Point**⁕⁕ are ultimately more interesting. Careful observers are rewarded by an astonishing variety of life forms in the low-tide pools of Otter Point.

Park Loop Rd turns inland and passes the entry to the **Jordan Pond House**⁕⁕⁕, a former farm converted to a tea house with beautiful gardens. Close by are the trails to **Jordan Pond**⁕⁕⁕ itself, a glacial kettle

Horse-drawn carriage tours $$$
Wildwood Stable; tel: (207) 276-3622 are the most luxurious way to see the park along the carriage roads built for John D Rockefeller, Jr.

pond with striking views of the twin monadnocks (steep-sided isolated hills) called the 'Bubbles'. One difficult ascent of the Bubbles departs from the pond's shore, but a trailhead that begins on the shoulders of the Bubbles can be accessed from the Loop Rd. Watch for the sign to 'Bubble Erratics', a reference to massive boulders deposited in precarious balance atop the mountains during the last glaciation.

The 3.5-mile winding road to the 1530-ft summit of **Cadillac Mountain**✦✦✦ begins near the end of Park Loop Rd. Very popular at sunrise and sunset, Cadillac's peak offers 360-degree views of all of Mount Desert Island, Frenchman Bay and its string of Porcupine Islands, and the Blue Hill peninsula. The most spectacular sunset views are not at the summit, but from the west-facing Blue Hill parking turnoff, at an elevation of about 1000ft.

Acadia's territories on the western lobe of the island are far less visited. The finest sandy swimming beach of the region is at **Echo Lake**✦✦, off Rte 102 south of Somesville village. Directly across the highway from the lake's car-park is the trailhead for the **Acadia**

Below
Acadia's granite ledges make for scenic hiking

Mountain Loop Hike❖❖, an easy hike up 2.5 miles of uncrowded trails to overlooks with broad views of Somes Sound and many small islands.

The portion of the park adjacent to Seawall campground south of Southwest Harbor includes three naturalist highlights. **Big Heath❖❖**, also known as Seawall Bog, abounds with carnivorous plants and native orchids and also functions as a nesting habitat for palm warblers and yellowthroats. The nature trails of **Wonderland❖** and **Ship Harbor❖❖** pass through woodlands inhabited by virtually all the warblers found in the northern US and emerge on a coast where harbour seals and porpoises gather and bald eagles are frequently observed plucking fish from the waters.

Accommodation and food in Acadia National Park

Blackwoods Campground $ *Rte 3; tel: (800) 365-2267.* Reservations are required mid June–mid Sept for 500 woodland tent pitches. Reservations may be requested after 1 Jan by writing to superintendent at the park headquarters (*see page 272*).

Seawall Campground $ *Rte 102A; no tel.* More than 200 tent pitches are available on a first-come, first-served basis. Many pitches require packing gear from a central car-park.

Jordan Pond House $–$$ *Park Loop Rd; tel: (207) 276-3316.* Although the restaurant also serves lunch and dinner, the classic experience of the Pond House is taking afternoon tea and popovers while seated at tables on the lawn.

BAR HARBOR❖❖❖

ℹ Bar Harbor Chamber of Commerce *93 Cottage St; tel: (207) 288-5103.*

◉ Downeast Transportation $ *tel: (207) 667-5796* provides shuttle bus service late June–early Sept from Agarmont Park to Sieur de Monts, Sand Beach and Blackwoods campground in Acadia National Park.

Bar Harbor is almost inescapable, as it contains the lion's share of lodging, dining and services for the entire island. Until a devastating fire scorched half of Mount Desert Island in 1947, Bar Harbor was a resort filled with the summer homes of wealthy New Yorkers. Some of the houses remain, mostly as B&Bs, but the town is more democratic these days, filled with travellers from around the world between June and October, then nearly deserted across the winter. Main and Mount Desert Sts function as the primary shopping district, with boutiques, food shops and galleries jammed one right next to another. A delightful 1-mile scenic walk, the **Shore Path❖❖**, stretches from Agarmont Park by the town landing past many oceanfront manses. During the four hours surrounding low tide, it is possible to walk across the sand bar (from which the town took its name) at the end of Bridge St to Bar Island. From the town pier, several companies operate sightseeing cruises with an emphasis on viewing wildlife.

Exploring Bar Harbor

P In-town parking is scarce June–Oct but free on most streets and at town pier. Recreational vehicle parking is permitted only in designated areas on the outskirts of town.

Accommodation and food in Bar Harbor

Route 3 north of Bar Harbor is lined with motel after motel, while the side-streets of town are filled with B&Bs. Even so, most establishments are booked solid in July–Aug. Reservations are essential. Although most visitors satisfy their hunger with hand-held food while walking about, Bar Harbor also has many good seafood and pasta restaurants as well as the inevitable resort taverns with bar food.

The Atlantic Eyrie $$–$$$ *Rte 3, Highbrook Rd; tel: (800) 422-2883 or (207) 288-9786.* Located north of town on a high hill, the aptly-

Acadia Bike & Coastal Kayaking 48 Cottage St; tel: (207) 288-9605 and **Bar Harbor Bicycle Shop** 141 Cottage St; tel: (207) 288-3886 rent mountain bikes for independent exploring.

Whale Watcher, Inc $$$ West and Main Sts (next to Town Pier); tel: (207) 288-3322. Motor cruises to observe marine mammals and birds and schooner sails to admire scenery.

Acadia Outfitters $ 45 Main St; tel: (207) 288-5592 offers a large selection of outdoors gear at good prices. This is the place to purchase hiking boots for scrambling up Acadia's peaks.

named Eyrie has stunning views of Frenchman Bay. Some suites are fully self-catering.

Barcadia Campground $ *Rte 198, RR1, Box 2165; tel: (207) 288-3520.* The 200 pitches, some oceanfront, some ocean view, share a private beach for fishing and boating. Barcadia operates shuttle a service to Bar Harbor.

Edenbrook Motel $–$$ *96 Eden St; tel: (800) 323-7819 or (207) 288-4975.* Bar Harbor's first motel, about a 15-minute walk from town, is lovingly maintained.

Holbrook House $$–$$$ *74 Mount Desert St; tel: (207) 288-4970.* One of the surviving late 19th-century 'cottages', Holbrook House has 12 guest rooms and a wide front porch where breakfast is sometimes served.

Jordan's $ *80 Cottage St; tel: (207) 288-3586.* Local hangout serving breakfast 0500–1400, but is closed for dinner. Local gossip passes up and down the counter in the early hours before most tourists rise for the day.

Porcupine Grill $$–$$$ *123 Cottage St; tel: (207) 288-3884.* Bar Harbor's leading gourmet restaurant takes a contemporary and innovative approach to great local seafood.

West Street Café $$ *West and Rodick Sts; tel: (207) 288-5242.* This old-fashioned restaurant offers the traditional Downeast meal of fish chowder, french fries (chips), steamed lobster and blueberry pie.

BASS HARBOR❖❖

Maine State Ferry Service $ *Bass Harbor dock; tel: (207) 244-3254.* Year-round service to Swan's Island and to Frenchboro on Long Island.

With its lobster boats and striking lighthouse, scenic little Bass Harbor is the most tranquil of Mount Desert's seaside villages. A good and inexpensive way to appreciate the coastal scenery is to take a return-trip on one of the state-run ferries from the town landing out to Frenchboro or Swan's Island.

Accommodation and food in Bass Harbor

Bass Harbor Campground $ *Rte 102A, PO Box 122; tel: (800) 327-5857 or (207) 244-5857.* Only a 10-minute walk from the ocean, this facility has separate areas for tents and RVs.

Bass Harbor Inn $ *Shore Rd; tel: (207) 244-5157.* This 1832 house turned B&B offers rooms with harbour or mountain views.

Keenan's $–$$ *Rte 102A; tel: (207) 244-3403.* A gutsy New American chef with Louisiana roots works wonders with seafood in this roadside restaurant.

NORTHEAST HARBOR*

Beal & Bunker $$
*Municipal Pier; tel:
(207) 244-3575* carries
mail year-round to the
Cranberry Isles with stops
at Great Cranberry, Little
Cranberry (Islesford) and
Sutton (summer only).

**Islesford Ferry
Company $$** *Town
Marina; tel: (207) 276-3717*
offers a scenic cruise
through the Cranberry
Islands with a lunch
stopover on Little
Cranberry.

**Sea Princess Cruises
$$$** *Town Marina; tel: (207)
276-5352.* Choices include
morning cruise of the
Great Harbor and Somes
Sound and a shorter, late-
afternoon cruise in Somes
Sound alone. All the trips
emphasise wildlife and
geology.

**Kimball Terrace
Inn and Main Sail
Restaurant $$** *Huntington
Rd.* Large motel
overlooking Municipal Pier,
literally steps from the
village centre. Casual
restaurant serves both
seafood and meat dishes.

This principally residential, up-market village is the preserve of such families as the Rockefellers and Pulitzers. The village centre contains an excellent cluster of boutiques as well as art and photo galleries, but most visitors come to gawk at the sleek craft moored at the yacht club or to board one of the excursion boats to the **Cranberry Isles** fishing communities located on Great Cranberry, Little Cranberry and Sutton islands south of Mount Desert Island. Islesford, on Little Cranberry, has developed as a summer retreat for many artists and craftspeople and is actually set up to receive visitors curious about island life. The National Park Service operates a small local history museum here during the summer.

Right
Quiet Northeast Harbor is a
pleasure-boat haven

SOUTHWEST HARBOR**

Cranberry Cove Boating $$ *Town dock; tel: (207) 244-5882 operates ferries to three of the Cranberry Islands, Great Cranberry, Little Cranberry (Islesford) and Sutton.*

Wendell Gilley Museum of Birdcarving $ *Main St and Herrick Rd; tel: (207) 244-7555. Open June–Oct Tue–Sun 1000–1600 (open until 1700 July–Aug), May, Nov, Dec Fri–Sun 1000–1600.*

Hinckley Company *Shore Rd, Manset (1 mile south of Southwest Harbor centre); tel: (207) 244-5531.*

Until about 1980, Southwest Harbor was a quiet fishing and boatbuilding village where tourists passed through to soak up a little local colour and moved on. Now several of its fine old houses have been transformed into B&Bs and the central village is chock-a-block with boutiques, souvenir shops and cafés. But craftsmanship is still a byword in Southwest Harbor. The **Wendell Gilley Museum of Birdcarving*** features the exquisite carved bird sculptures of Gilley as well as other wildlife art. The **Hinckley Company***, south of the village centre in Manset, is one of America's leading builders of luxury yachts. Visitors can walk the docks and the boatyard to admire these craft, but cannot board them. Across the street, the **Hinckley Ship Store**** is a nautical paradise of charts and boating paraphernalia.

Accommodation and food in Southwest Harbor

The Claremont $$–$$$ *Claremont Rd, PO Box 137; tel: (800) 244-5036 or (207) 244-5036.* The oldest summer resort hotel on Mount Desert Island affects a delightfully genteel air.

The Inn at Southwest $$ *371 Main St, PO Box 93; tel: (207) 244-3835.* Downtown Victorian home with wrap-around porch has nine guest rooms.

Smugglers Den Campground $ *Rte 102, PO Box 787; tel: (207) 244-3944.* This facility has oceanfront camping and a heated pool and is close to a freshwater swimming beach.

Beal's Lobster Pier $–$$ *Clark Point Rd; tel: (207) 244-3202.* No-frills lobster shore dinners in one of the region's principal lobster-fishing ports.

Preble Grill $$$ *14 Clark Point Rd; tel: (207) 244-3034.* Seafood gets a Mediterranean treatment in this elegant restaurant with high culinary aspirations.

Suggested tour

Total distance: 90 miles

Time: 3 hours' driving, but not recommended as a single-day tour. Stops will stretch tour to 3–4 days.

Links: Connects via Rte 3 to Penobscot Bay Route.

Route: Enter Mount Desert Island on Rte 3 from Ellsworth, following signs for 7 miles to Hulls Cove Visitors Center of **ACADIA NATIONAL PARK ❶**. Follow the 27-mile circuit of the Park Loop Rd, making the

Right
The North and South Bubble
Mountains viewed across Acadia
National Park's Jordan Pond

7-mile return-trip journey up Cadillac Mountain. On the last leg of
Park Loop Rd, watch for signs to **Eagle Lake*** ❷, reached 1 mile west
on Rte 233. Boats can be rented at the lake, which also offers good
fishing. Continue 3.5 miles west to the junction with Rte 198, bearing
right toward Somesville, the small village at the head of Somes Sound.
Turn left and follow Rtes 102 and 198 south for 1 mile, then turn right
on to well-named Pretty Marsh Rd, the northwest piece of Rte 102's
loop around the western lobe of Mount Desert. **Long Pond**✦✦ ❸ ,
which appears on the left in 1 mile, is the main body of water in this
marshy countryside, and canoes and kayaks can be rented here to
explore the marshland ecosystem. Route 102 passes through marshes
favoured by herons and grebes for the next 2 miles before turning

National Park Canoe $$ *Long Pond's End; tel: (207) 244-5854* rents canoes and sea kayaks and provides free instruction.

inland through boreal forest to emerge in 1 miles at scenic **Seal Cove** ❹ on the coast. The road alternates between coastal views and forest as it winds 5 miles to Tremont, where a right turn on to Rte 102A leads 1 mile into **BASS HARBOR** ❺. Rte 102A continues around the southernmost tip of Mount Desert as Seawall Rd, re-entering Acadia National Park. Along Seawall Rd are **Ship Harbor** ❻, **Wonderland** ❼ and **Great Heath** nature trails ❽. In 6 miles the road enters Manset, the boatbuilding village on a cove of **SOUTHWEST HARBOR** ❾, and rejoins Rte 102 just south of the Southwest Harbor village. Follow Rte 102 north for 3 miles to Echo Lake and the Acadia Mountain Loop Trail, then another 3 miles to Somesville. Turn right on to Rte 198, retracing old ground and bearing right down the eastern shore of Somes Sound (where Rtes 198 and Rte 3 share the roadway), following signs for 8 miles to **NORTHEAST HARBOR** ❿. Retrace Rte 198 for 1 mile north to rejoin Rte 3 and bear right, following the coastline with relentlessly scenic ocean views for 3 miles to the tiny village of **Seal Harbor*** ⓫, then 7 miles through hilly woodlands into **BAR HARBOR** ⓬.

Also worth exploring

Schoodic Peninsula** is part of Acadia National Park, but lies on the mainland across Frenchman Bay from Bar Harbor. Although only an hour's drive from Bar Harbor (passing through the village of Winter Harbor), the peninsula is rarely crowded. A park road off Rte 186 circles the perimeter. The 400-ft-high granite outcrop of **Schoodic Point**** is pounded by the sea, and the surrounding forests of spruce and jack pine are deep and wild.

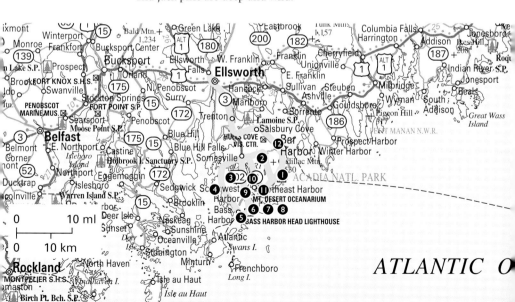

Language

How to talk New England:
Bubbler: Boston-speak for a water fountain
Buffalo Wings: Chicken Wings, usually fried and served with a spicy sauce as an appetiser, or as bar food
Chili dog or chili burger: Hot dog or hamburger disguised with chili, onions and cheese
Chips: Crisps
Clam roll: Fried clams, usually served on a hot-dog roll
Clam strips: Thin pieces of clams without the 'bellies'; a cheaper form of fried clams
Down East: Originally applied to Maine's coastal winds; now it's a place — either Maine or a part of its coast — and an attitude
Downtown: City or town centre
Frappé: Boston-speak for a milk shake, ie milk blended with ice cream and flavouring
Fries or french fries: Chips
Holiday: A public holiday, such as Labor Day, not a private holiday, which is a vacation
Ivy League: A group of eight prestigious universities in the northeastern US, including Harvard, Yale, Dartmouth and Brown in New England, where members of the US 'establishment' are educated
Microbrewery or brew-pub: A tavern that brews its own beer
Nor'easter: A coastal storm or gale blowing from the northeast (ie off the ocean), usually bringing heavy rain or snow
Outlet stores: Large stores specialising in factory overruns at reduced prices. Often, they are simply discount stores
Prep School: Preparatory school, a private High School for affluent adolescents heading for college (university)
Preppie: A student who attends prep school or who dresses like one who does
Quahog: An edible clam with a hard round shell (pronounced 'kwo-hog' or 'ko-hog' from the Narragansett *poqua'hock*)
Resort: A fancy hotel that specialises in leisure activities, such as golf, tennis and swimming
Road kill: Literally, animals killed by passing cars, but usually used to describe bad food
Soda: A soft drink, such as cola, anywhere but Boston
Tonic: A cola or other soft drink, but only around Boston, where it's pronounced TAW-nick; anywhere else, tonic (pronounced normally) is carbonated water.
Yankee: An old-fashioned New Englander, usually of WASP (White Anglo-Saxon Protestant) heritage, marked by a taciturn expression, frugal ways and stern character.

Some New England driving terms:
Big rig or 18-wheeler: A large lorry, usually a tractor pulling one or more trailers
Boston stop: Slowing at a stop sign, but not stopping
Bumper-to-bumper: Slow-moving, heavy traffic with little space between cars
Connector: A minor road connecting two highways
Divided highway: Dual carriageway
DUI or DWI: Driving Under the Influence (of alcohol or drugs), or Driving While Intoxicated, aka Drunken Driving; the blood alcohol limit in New England states varies from 0.08% to 0.10% and is very strictly enforced
Fender: Bumper
Garage or parking garage: Car park
Gas(oline): Petrol
Grade: Gradient, hill
Highway: Motorway
Hit-and-run: Illegally leaving the scene after being involved in a collision
Motor home: Motor caravan
Ramp: Slip road
Rubbeneck(er): Slowing down to peer while driving past the scene of an accident
RV: Motor caravan
Shoulder: Verge
Sidewalk: Pavement
Speed bump: A road hump intended to make motorists slow down
(Stick)shift: Gear lever
Yield: Give way

Index

A
Acadia National Park 272–275
Accidents 24
Accommodation 9, 14–15
Adirondack Mountains
Airports 15, 30
Allagash Wilderness Waterway 230
Allen, Ethan 176
American Revolution 35
Amherst 102
Amtrak 30–31
Architecture 36–37
Arlington, MA 64
Arlington, VT 170

B
Bar Harbor 275–277
Barre 190
Bash Bish Falls 112
Bass Harbor 277
Bath, ME 254
Baxter State Park 232
Bed and breakfasts 14
Belfast 262–263
Bennington 172–173
Berkshires 104–113
Bethlehem 227
Bingham Falls 185
Block Island 158
Blue Hill 263–264
Boothbay Harbor 255–256
Borders 18
Boston 42–55
Boston subway 43
Boston Tea Party 50
Boyden Valley Winery 184, 188
Brattleboro 198–199
Breakdowns 24
Bretton Woods 216–219
Brighton State Park 196
Bristol 169, 189
Brunswick 256
Burke Mountain 192–193
Burlington 180–182
Buses 31

C
Cabot 193
Calendar Islands 247–248
Cambridge 56–58
Camden 265
Camden Hills State Park 265
Campers (RVs) 14, 24
Canterbury Shaker Village 215
Cape Cod 84–95
Cape Code Bay 84–86
Cape Cod National Seashore 86
Cape Elizabeth 248
Cape Neddick 243
Car hire 24–25
Caravans and campers 24
Castine 265–266
Castle in the Clouds 210
Center Sandwich 214
Champlain Islands 188

Chatham 87–88
Chester, CT 134–135
Chester, VT 200–201
Chesterfield Gorge 205
Children 14
Chocorua 208–209
Clark's Trading Post 221
Climate 15
Clothing 23
Cockaponset State Forest 133
Colt State Park 169
Conanicut Island 158
Concord, MA 59–60
Connecticut 114–149
Connecticut River Valley 196
Conway Scenic Railway 222
Cornish 230
Cornish-Windsor Covered Bridge
Craftsbury 195
Cranberry Isles 278
Crane Beach 75
Crawford Notch 218
Crescent Beach State Park 248
Currency 15
Customs regulations 17

D
Damariscotta 257
Deer Island 266
Dennis 84
Devil's Hopyard State Park 138
Disabilities, travellers with 23
Dixville Notch 219
Documents 27
Dorset 173
Drinking and driving 17–18, 27
Driving 24–29

E
Eagle Lake 280
East Haddam 134–135
Easton's Beach 157
Eating out 18
Echo Lake State Park 222
Electricity 21
Emerald Lake State Park 173, 178
Entry formalities 18
Essex, CT 135–136
Essex, MA 75

F
Fairhaven 82
Fall River 76–78
Falmouth 88
Fenwick 138
Festivals 18
Food 9, 17
Forks, The (Maine) 232
Fort Adams State Park 157
Fort Independence 83
Fort Phoenix 82
Fort Williams 248
Foxwoods Resort & Casino 141
Franconia Notch 219–200
Freeport 253

Friendship 260–261
Fuel 25

G
Geography 32–33
Glen 220–221
Gloucester 66–68
Grafton 201
Grand hotels 224
Great Barrington 104–106
Great Stone Dwelling 205–206
Green Mountain Boys 176
Green Mountains 170–189
Green Mountains National Wildlife Refuge 65
Greyhound buses 31
Groton 140–141
Groton State forest 193–194
Guilford 139

H
Halibut Point State Park 71
Hammonasett Beach State Park 139
Hampton Beach 236
Hancock Shaker Village 106
Hanover 202
Hardwick 193
Harpswell 257
Hartford 114–119
Health 19
History 32–36
Hoosac Tunnel 109
Hyannis 88

I
Information 19, 27
Inns 14
Insurance 19–20
Isle of Shoals 244
Itineraries 40–41

J
Jackman 235
Jacob's Pillow Dance Festival 107
Jackson 220–221
Jamestown 158
Jeffersonville 188

K
Kancamagus Highway 221
Kennebunk 238
Kennebunk Beach 238
Kennebunk Village 238–239
Kennebunkport 238
Kent 124–126
Kent Falls State Park 124
Kingfield 233
Kittery 244

L
Lake Champlain 180–189
Lake Winnipesaukee 208
Ledyard 141–142
Lenox 107–108
Lexington 64
Lincoln, NH 221–222
Lincolnville 266–267
Litchfield 127–128
Lobsters 259

Loon Mountain Park 221
Lowell 60–62

M
Madison 139
Madison Boulder 215
Maine 230–281
Manchester, VT 174
Maps 19
Marblehead 69
Marion 83
Martha's Vineyard 89–90
Mashpee 94
Massachusetts 42–113
Meredith 209
Middlebury 183
Middletown 136
Minuteman National Historic Park 62–63
Monhegan Island 261
Monhegan Sun 149
Montpelier 197
Monument Mountain 104
Mount Desert Island 272–281
Mount Equinox Skyline Drive 174
Mount Greylock State Reservation 109
Mount Katahdin 232
Mount Kineo 233
Mount Washington 216–218
Museums 21
Mystic 142–143

N
Nantucket Island 91
Nantucket Sound 92
Narragansett Pier 158
National Parks 21
New Bedford 79
New Hampshire 208–229
New Haven 119–121
New London 144
Newburyport 70–71
Newfane 206
Newfound Lake 210–211
Newport, RI 150–159
Niantic 145
Noank 145
Norfolk 129
North Adams 109
North Bridge 62–63
North Conway 222–223
North Fork Wine Country
Northfield 102
Northampton 98
Northeast Harbor 278
Norwich 146

O
Ocean Park 244
Odiorne Point 243
Ogunquit 240
Old Greenfield Village 102
Old Lyme 137–138
Old Man of the Mountains 219
Old Orchard Beach 239
Old Saybrook 137–138
Onset 83
Opening times 21
Outer Cape 92–93

25

P
Packing 21–22
Parking 27
Passports 18
Pawlet 178
Pawtucket 168
Pemaquid Peninsula 257–258
Penobscot Bay 262–271
Penwood State Park 122
Petrol 25
Pilgrims 80, 92
Pinkham Notch 223–224
Pioneer Valley 96–103
Pittsfield 109
Plimoth Plantation 80
Plum Island 70
Plymouth, MA 80–81
Plymouth Notch 206
Police 27
Popham 258
Popham Beach State Park 258
Portland 246–253
Portsmouth, NH 240–241
Portsmouth, RI 169
Postal services 22
Providence 160–167, 168
Provincetown 94
Public holidays 21
Public transport 22
Putney 202–203

R
Rangeley Lakes 234
Reading 22
Rhode Island 150–169
Road signs 27, 29
Rock of Ages 190
Rock Neck State Park 145
Rockland 268
Rockport, MA 71–72
Rockport, ME 270
Rockwood 233
Roger Williams Park and Zoo 168
Rokeby Homestead 187
Route map 10–11
RVs (recreational vehicles) 10–11

S
Safety and security 22
Salem 72–74
Sandwich 84, 94
Scarborough 242
Sconset 91
Sculptured Rocks 210, 214
Searsport 269–270
Seasons 38–39
Seatbelts 28
Shakers 213
Sheffield 112
Shelburne, VT 183
Shelburne Falls 99
Shelburne Museum 183
Shopping 23
Six Gun City 227
Sleeping Giant State Park 122
Sleepy Hollow Cemetery 64
Smugglers Notch 184
South Egremont 112

Southwest Harbor 279
Speed limits 28
Sport 23
Springfield, MA 100
Squam Lake 211
St Johnsbury 194–195
Stockbridge 110–111
Stonington, CT 147
Stonington, ME 266
Stowe 185–186
Stratton Mountain 175
Sturbridge 101
Sunapee Region 206

T
Telephones 23
Time 22
Toilets 17
Tolls 28
Torrington 128
Touring itineraries 40–41
Trains 30–31
Two Lights State Park 248

U
Underground Railway 185

V
Valley of Vermont 177–178
Vergennes 186–187
Vermont 170–207
Visas 18

W
Waitsfield 188
Wakefield 158
Walden Pond 59, 64
Waldoboro 260
Wallis Sands State Park 243
Warren 169
Washington, Mount 216–218
Weirs Beach 212
Wellington State Park 210
Wells 242
Wells Beach 242
West Cornwall 129
West Dover 178
West Pawlet 177
West Stockbridge 112
Westerly 149
Westport 82
Weston 175–176
Wethersfield 122
Whales 248
White Horse Beach 83
Williamstown, MA 111
Wilmington 178
Windjammer cruises 268
Windsor 203
Wicasset 258
Wolfeboro 212
Woodstock, NH 221–222
Woodstock, VT 204–205

Y
York, ME 243
York Harbor 243

Acknowledgements

Project management: Dial House Publishing Services (tel: 01285 771044)
Series design: Fox Design (tel: 01373 834271)
Front cover design and artwork: Fox Design
Layout and map work: Concept 5D (tel: 0181 607 9858)
Repro and image setting: Z2 Repro, Thetford, Norfolk, UK
Printed and bound in Italy by Rotolito Lombarda Spa

We would like to thank the following photographers and organisations for the photographs used in this book, to whom the copyright in the photograph belongs:

Front cover: Townsend church (Rogers Associates); Lobsters (David Lyon); Bannard Tavern, Historic Deerfield (Rogers Associates).

Tom Bross (pages 36, 42A, 51, 58, 59, 64, 78, 124, 126, 136, 137, 147, 150 160A, 160B, 165, 236, 238, 241, 246, 249 and 251).

Ethel Davies (pages 3 (=114), 6 (=28), 8, 12, 13, 20, 24, 27, 28, 44, 46, 47, 48, 52, 54, 66B, 68, 70, 72, 73, 82, 114, 116, 132B, 140, 143, 146, 148, 153, 154, 156, 166, 175, 204 and 213).

David Lyon (pages 17, 18, 21 (=230), 35, 56, 60, 61, 62, 63, 66A, 69, 76, 79, 81, 84, 86, 87, 89, 90, 91, 93, 94, 104, 106, 107, 108, 110, 230A, 230B, 232, 254, 256, 259, 262, 264, 267, 269, 272, 274, 276, 278 and 280).

Jim Mcelholm (page 162).

Rogers Associates (pages 14, 22, 25, 30, 31, 32, 39, 41, 42B, 96, 99, 100, 132A, 134, 170, 172, 174, 177, 180, 182, 184, 186, 190, 192, 194, 198, 201, 202, 208, 210, 216, 218, 220, 222, 225, 226 and 228).

Feedback form

If you enjoyed using this book, or even if you didn't, please help us improve future editions by taking part in our reader survey. Every returned form will be acknowledged, and to show our appreciation we will give you £1 off your next purchase of a Thomas Cook guidebook. Just take a few minutes to complete and return this form to us.

When did you buy this book? ....
....

Where did you buy it? (Please give town/city and, if possible, name of retailer)
....
....

When did you/do you intend to travel in New England ....
....

For how long (approx)? ....

How many people in your party? ....

Which cities, national parks and other locations did you/do you intend mainly to visit?
....
....
....
....

Did you/will you:
❏ Make all your travel arrangements independently?
❏ Travel on a fly-drive package?
Please give brief details: ....
....

Did you/do you intend to use this book:
❏ For planning your trip?   ❏ Both?
❏ During the trip itself?

Did you/do you intend also to purchase any of the following travel publications for your trip?
Thomas Cook Travellers: New England ....
A road map/atlas (please specify) ....
Other guidebooks (please specify) ....

Have you used any other Thomas Cook guidebooks in the past? If so, which?
....
....

Please rate the following features of Signpost New England for their value to you (Circle VU for 'very useful', U for 'useful', NU for 'little or no use'):

The Travel Facts section on pages 14–25	VU	U	NU
The Driver's Guide section on pages 26–31	VU	U	NU
The Highlights on pages 42–43	VU	U	NU
The recommended driving routes throughout the book	VU	U	NU
Information on towns and cities, National Parks, etc	VU	U	NU
The maps of towns and cities, parks, etc	VU	U	NU

Please use this space to tell us about any features that in your opinion could be changed, improved, or added in future editions of the book, or any other comments you would like to make concerning the book:

....

....

....

....

....

....

....

....

....

....

Your age category: ❑ 21-30   ❑ 31-40   ❑ 41-50   ❑ over 50

Your name: Mr/Mrs/Miss/Ms ....

(First name or initials) ....

(Last name) ....

Your full address: (Please include postal or zip code)

....

....

....

....

Your daytime telephone number: ....

Please detach this page and send it to: The Project Editor, Signpost Guides, Thomas Cook Publishing, PO Box 227, Peterborough PE3 6PU, United Kingdom.

We will be pleased to send you details of how to claim your discount upon receipt of this questionnaire.